BITTERSWEET FREEDOM

Judith Bognar Bean

Copyright © 2019 Judith Bognar Bean

Hardcover ISBN: 978-1-7331793-0-0
Paperback IBSN: 978-1-7331793-1-7
Epub ISBN: 978-1-7331793-2-4
Mobi ISBN: 978-1-7331793-3-1

Library of Congress Control Number: 2017918771

All rights reserved. No part of this publication may be reproduced, stored in a retrieval system, or transmitted in any form or by any means, electronic, mechanical, recording or otherwise, without the prior written permission of the author.

Book cover designed by JD&J with stock imagery provided by Oleg Babich © 123RF.com
Moon photograph courtesy of Charlton A. Bean
Author's photograph and Butterfly photograph courtesy of Charles G. Bean Photography
All other photographs obtained from the author's personal archives

Published by Carpathian Valley Books, P.O. Box 249, Belews Creek, NC 27009
Website: www.carpathianvalleybooks.com
Email: judithbognarbean@gmail.com

Printed on acid-free paper.

Carpathian Valley Books
2019
Second Edition

DEDICATION

To my Beloved parents, without whose acts of selfless courage and sacrifice, I would not be alive today. You loved me with all your hearts, braving the unknown against insurmountable odds to bring me to America, the Land of Freedom. You fought valiantly against all those who looked to trample the joys of my childhood, instilled strong family values within my heart, taught me patriotism for America, and showed me that love is the strongest power on this earth. To your memory, I dedicate the words within these pages to a *Once Upon a Time* place: a balmy, starry, spring night when destiny and fate unlocked a magical portal in the vastness of infinity, hurtling two lost souls toward one another - a girl and a boy, destined to share an unbelievable journey, destined to Live the Grand Life of Forever Love.

To my soulmate, my champion, my loving and devoted Husband, Charles, thank you for your faithful fervor and fidelity in helping me in the care of my parents through their many years of trials, tribulations and tears, for encouraging me onward in the writing of this book, especially during the many days when my emotional strength was at its ebb. Thank you for loving my parents as you loved your own, for supporting me with your unconditional love, and showing me that with true love and faith, anything is possible.

To my loving, precious son, Charlton, thank you for your ardent support, for your encouraging ideas in the writing of this remembrance, for embracing your proud Hungarian heritage, for inspiring me with your passion for justice and freedom for all humankind, and most of all, for treasuring the memory of your *Nagymama* and *Nagypapa*.

To my sister, *Pilvia*, thank you for supporting me with your love through the dark days after the death of our father, for sharing in my hardship, adversity and heartache as I cared for our mother in her final days, for crying with me through all despondency and despair, and for loving our parents with all your heart.

To our family's steadfast friends in Florida, Lya and Carole, and Tommy and Laura, in Georgia, thank you for cherishing and loving my parents as you would your own family, for embracing them in your hearts throughout their living years, and beyond.

To Elizabeth Mae, thank you for your steadfast devotion in caring for my mother during the many days when I was unable to do so, for loving my family as you loved your own, and for giving me the joy of loving you as "my own little girl" throughout the years.

And finally, this dedication would not be complete without remembering the multitudes of Hungarians who gave the ultimate sacrifice in their fight against the ruthless Soviet Army during those fateful months of October 1956 and November 1956. Thousands died, thousands were tortured, and over two-hundred thousand of the country's citizens forced to take flight to other borders and lands.

The world's future generations *should* forever remember, *must* always remember, the 1956 Hungarian Freedom Fighter's heroic courage in their unquenchable quest for emancipation and truth, for in our remembering their valiant struggle against tyrannical forces bent on extinguishing their God-given right to freedom, and in our remembering *all* those on this earth who continue to fight for the inherent entitlement of freedom for all humankind, we will anchor future foundations of liberty and hope, knowing that such an iniquitous moment in time will never happen again.

Disclaimer

Works of nonfiction are scripted from memory, and all human memory is flawed. Memoirs and biographies are examples of such nonfiction. In many remembrances defined in this work, the author was only a small child and could not remember the exact words said by every individual mentioned in this reminiscence, or the exact details of events and circumstances, or the exact names of persons, and has depended on the stories and conversations held with her parents to fill in those gaps as best possible.

The descriptions of, and opinions of people, cities and towns, and the events surrounding those people, cities and towns, especially those taking place during the author's early childhood years, when she was not yet old enough to form intellectual opinions on any subject, are those expressed to the author by her parents and are *not* the opinions of the author.

The verbal exchanges within the pages of this story may not represent a play-by-play transcript of the actual words spoken, as the author may not yet have been born when such exchanges took place, or not physically present when those exchanges took place; therefore, the author, by recalling the stories told directly to her by her parents, has chosen to tell this narrative in a way that will arouse the feeling and emotion of how the words may have been expressed, but nonetheless, the interpretations of the narrative are authentically represented as relayed to the author by her mother and father.

This memoir and biography is a faithful saga about the life and times of the author's family, with embroidery included, when necessary, especially during the decades mentioned in this remembrance when it was obvious the author had not yet been born, or was too young to make her own intellectual assessment of situations regarding persons, circumstances, places or events, as her only information about the details of those times was as told to the author by her parents during their living years.

AND THEN THE DAY ARRIVED WHEN THE PERIL OF STAYING WAS MORE PERILOUS THAN THE PERIL OF LEAVING

FLASHBACK!

No, no, no! We will not end this way! As a last dogged attempt to save his family, Jozsef vaulted into the deranged actions of a madman, grabbing Erzsebet's arm, viciously tugging and pulling her and little Judit behind a thick stance of timber, a trembling finger placed upon his lips signaling them to be silent.

As she held her bawling baby daughter close to her petrified heart, quivering shudders of an inky-black, faceless, soulless doom clouded Erzsebet's terrified mind as it unwillingly flashed grotesque images of three, ravaged, bullet-riddled bodies sprawled about the forest floor, the last warm, oozing remains of their valorous, maroon-colored blood gathering thickly about them, as the viscera of the earth beneath them inhaled the crimson-colored juice of their trickling souls, the burgundy liquid seeking to nourish the buried seeds of the forest, perhaps to reincarnate into the veins of forest-green seedlings and saplings that would one day live again in the warmth of the sun - for no one would ever find them here, in this thick, muddy muck to give them a decent burial. No one.

Hardly able to take in even a shallow breath, Erzsebet dropped her knees into the slush of the cold, brown ooze, clasping Jozsef and her crying baby daughter close, whispering an anguished prayer of desperation towards the moon-filled sky, *"Please God, be merciful – take our souls swiftly and do not let my baby suffer!"*

Book Cover Description: The image on the book cover represents the family's former lives of oppression in communist Hungary and the new life awaiting them in the Freedom of the United States of America.

From left to right – The rider on the horse is Francis II Rakoczi, a Hungarian nobleman, and leader of the Hungarian uprising against the Habsburgs (1703-1711)) as the prince of the Estates Confederated for Liberty of the Kingdom of Hungary. He is considered a Hungarian Freedom Fighter and National Hero. As he rides his noble steed, the colors of the Hungarian Flag (red, white, and green) proudly wave, amidst the background of a gray, colorless sky, reflecting a world devoid of hope for the Hungarian people against the rule of Soviet oppression. The bridge represents the BRIDGE OF ANDEAU, a tiny wooden bridge that carried thousands of Hungarians to the free border of Andau, Austria, during the dark, mournful days of the 1956 Hungarian Revolution. The three shadowy figures represent the author, as a little girl with her parents, making their way toward the Icon of Hope before them, the flaming symbol of Freedom – The Statue of Liberty, proudly holding her bright torch of welcome for the little family crossing the bridge towards the shining light of a Free, New World. Trailing behind the family is the Hungarian Coat of Arms, symbolizing the family's old way of life being forever left behind

"Liberty and Love, these Two I must have. For my Love I will Sacrifice my Life. For Liberty I will sacrifice My Love."

— Sándor Petőfi – Beloved Hungarian Poet

A SUMMARY (DICTIONARY) OF HUNGARIAN WORDS, AND NAMES, TRANSLATED INTO THEIR ENGLISH FORM

In this tale of remembrance, character names undergo transformation over time, from their original Hungarian names to American names and nicknames.

For ease of reading, I have left out accent marks over some of the Hungarian words.

Below are the pronunciations and definitions of those names, as well as other Hungarian words in the text.

Anukam Edes (A-new-kahm Eh-desh) Mother dearest
Apukam Edes (A-poo-kahm Eh-desh) Father dearest
Bognar (Boag-nar)
Charles – Charlie – Author's husband
Charlton – Charl-ton – Author's son
Cigány (See-gun-yee) – Gypsy
Csimby (Chim-bee) – nickname for Judy (Judit)
Cimbalom (Sim-ba-lum) - A dulcimer (musical instrument)
Czárdás (Char-dosh) - a Hungarian dance
Draga (Draw-gaa) – Precious
Edes (Eh-desh) – Sweet
Erzsebet (Air-gee-bet) – [Judit's mother] Elizabeth – Liz - Mommy – Mama

Erzsebet Szabo – Judit's maternal grandmother
Gyorgy (Jor-gee) – Judit's paternal grandfather, also name of Judit's uncle (also called George)
Halasz (Hall-laas)
Hermina (Hair-meena) – Judit's paternal grandmother
Jozsef [Judit's father] (Yo-geff) – Joseph – Joe – Daddy – Papa
Jozsef [Judit's paternal grandfather] (Yo-geff) Professor Bognar – Mr. Bognar
Judit (U-deet) – Judy – Csimbike (Chim-bee-ka)
Kati (Caw-tee)
Kuki (Cookie), also "Pilvia" - Judit's sister
Nagypapa (Knudge-papa) - Grandfather
Nagymama (Knudge-mama) - Grandmother
Palinka (Pa-lin-ka) - Hungarian fruit brandy
Pillango (Pea-lon-go) - Butterfly
Sonny – Sunny – Judit's brother

Contents

REQUIEM FOR A FREEDOM FIGHTER 1
WHAT TO DO WITH MAMA 16
MAMA SHOWS ME THE WAY BACK HOME 31
HERMINA AND JOZSEF - 1933 37
YOUNG JOZSEF 56
ERZSEBET 64
WINDS OF WAR 77
THE LOVERS - 1950 97
MARRIAGE AND BIRTH 114
REVOLUTION! 129
ESCAPE! 151
FREE AIR 165
MASSACHUSETTS 178
FLORIDA 277
ATLANTA 404
THE BITTER END - Year 2003 441
THE DAYS OF MAMA AND ME 463
ELEGY FOR MY MAMA 498
MY PRIVATE THOUGHTS 509

REQUIEM FOR A FREEDOM FIGHTER

He was born the brightest star in the sky, a star twinkling with such brilliance that if I were to stare upon the pureness of his face for too long, I would have to avert my eyes – not because of my fear, but because of his pain – a long time ago pain, so deeply tucked away, it was barely discernable to the world.

But the pain was always there, living silently within his heart – a pain born out of the debauchery and depravity of a horrific world into which he had no choice to be born. But, *History* meant for him to be born into that place and that time, born to shake up, and take down, a regime of evil beliefs, to scourge the malignant force from his beloved country, and in doing so, he was molded into a man whose very character defied the definition of *bravery*, defied the definition of *righteousness*, and defied the definition of *Love*.

He was not born to be an ordinary man. He was not destined to lead an ordinary life, but destined to live the extraordinary life of an unsung hero of the 1956 Hungarian Revolution, destined to live through the monstrous atrocities inflicted upon the people of his country of Hungary by the Soviet Army, *destined to take lives to save lives*, and destined to be one of the most courageous men ever to be born – to be my father - Jozsef Frank Bognar – Freedom Fighter.

My parents and I made our exodus from Hungary in 1956, during the dark, mournful days of the Hungarian Revolution. We were but a small sum of thousands who had survived the treacherous passage to America, looking to escape the persecution of the nefarious Soviet Army whose corruption and malevolence had spread its iniquitous and repugnant shadow over our country.

But oppression can take different forms as our family was soon to discover during our early days in America, as we suffered through the insensible throes of ethnic persecution leading us to endure the tribulations and misery of discrimination, victimization, and financial ruin. But, however, disparaging the trials and afflictions of our early days in the Land of Freedom, in later years, we would look back on those infantile days in America as the happiest we had ever known, as the best years of our lives, for in those naïve, callow days, we were as newborn stars, having been given the opportunity to outshine the confines of our former galaxy, to radiate our luminous energy into the vast vacuum of our newfound freedom, living our lives with the innocent hearts of carefree, tender-footed children, rollicking in the sunshine of an unconquered world filled with possibilities.

But now, as I stood beside my father's lifeless form in *Death's Hall of Sadness*, my insides were bursting to tell the world, to tell everyone present, about the bravest, most loving, and kindest man I had ever known.

I had been with my father and mother from the beginning – and, I remembered…

My father died on Friday, July 25, 2008, after fifty-five years of a loving marriage, and sixty years of companionship with my mother. Mama wanted a simple funeral for her husband and chose for him to be cremated.

Gathered with me in the viewing room sat my mother, sister, my brother, his wife and their four children, my husband, my son, me, and my parent's next-door neighbors, Tommy and Laura, their dear friends for over twenty years.

Many years ago, my sister had sewn a beautiful shirt for my father with wide, billowy sleeves, narrowed at the wrist, embroidered with intricate flowers in the old Hungarian style, and we dressed our father in this sentimental garment for his last moments with us, as it represented her labor of love for him, and his love for his native land of Hungary. As my eyes swept over my father's form lying on a collapsible gurney with a blue blanket covering him from his chest to his toes, I couldn't help but grieve not only for my father's death, but for a funeral lacking a genuine reflection of the great man lying before me, for a funeral completely detached from displaying the deeds of my father's astonishing life. There was nothing here to commemorate my father's love of family, nothing here to celebrate his determination to succeed despite countless adversities, nothing here to show the depths of his courageous soul that had enabled him to survive atrocities that others would not have survived, and nothing here to show his love for America.

The quietness of the room was deafening, and the dull blandness of the surroundings blinding, for there was no strands of inspiring music drifting through the air and no colorful sprays of flowers to comfort the senses, except for a small bouquet of magnolia blossoms and vincas held in my hand, gathered from my parent's yard.

Years ago, my father expressed his idea, his wish, for a distinguished funeral, his perfect way "to go out of this world," stating, "I want to have a Viking-style funeral where I am placed on a raft set on fire and then pushed out to sea - then I would leave this world in an honorable blaze of glory!" How I wanted to carry out his request! Ironically, about a year prior, realizing my parents were "getting older," I contacted the proper entity for unusual burial requests and told such a funeral could not be performed. Per their explanation, "If the fire did not totally consume the body, and the remains of an unidentified person happened to wash up on shore, a police investigation would be launched for a possible homicide victim." It was not possible to honor my father's last request and I felt small, ashamed, and inadequate. I had failed him.

The drive from my home in North Carolina to my parent's home in Atlanta for my father's funeral had taken six hours. During that time, I had to make several painful decisions for my father's final ceremony: contacting the hospital for my father's transfer to the funeral home, arranging for my father's final clothes to be taken to the mortuary by Tommy and Laura; but the most important task of all was finding my father's wedding ring. The ring had been removed at the hospital when he was taken to the morgue, and for some reason, not sent with my father upon his transfer to the funeral home. Through Tommy's endeavors and persistence, he found the ring and returned it to my mother.

But, my most important accomplishment during that six-hour drive was held in my damp hand – a crumpled piece of paper on which I had written a Eulogy documenting the incredible life of my father.

No one had yet offered to say a prayer, because some family members believed my father did not portray himself as a religious man; however, if that was the case, he certainly lived his life as one.

My father was the epitome of Judeo-Christian values. He followed all Ten Commandments, not knowingly, but, followed them better than the most ardent churchgoer. For sixty years he had kept himself only to his wife, had never committed a crime, and was generous and kind to the less fortunate.

Such an example is when, a few years ago, my father was sitting in his car at a red light during the usual "People getting off work traffic jam." On the opposite side of the roadway were a variety of stores and cheap motels. Up ahead, standing on the concrete median of the road, was a Hispanic man and his wife who was heavy with child. They were approaching the stopped cars at the traffic light begging for money. They made their way to the driver's side of my father's car. "Please, please help us! The baby will be here soon. We have nothing! My wife needs good food to eat! We have lost our home!" They looked painfully wretched and desperate. The woman was in tears. My father asked, "Where are you living now?" The man pointed to a dingy motel across the way, "Over there, on the second level." Dad had only seconds to make up his mind before the light changed. He quickly dug his wallet out from his back pocket and pulled out five, twenty-dollar bills. He pushed the bills into the man's sweaty hand, "I wish I could give you more, but this is all I have right now. Use it wisely and take care of the baby!" The light changed, and my father forced to drive off, but not before he heard the man shout "Thank you Sir!"

Once home, Dad relayed to my mother how pitiful it all was, and how it reminded him of when they were expecting their first child (me). My parents were also "beyond poor" and had little food and comforts in the early days of marriage after World War II in Hungary. "I wish I could have given them more money," sighed my father, as he explained his most unusual encounter with the couple.

Later that same evening, not being able to remove the man's look of desperation from his mind, my father drove to the couple's alleged residence. He went to the motel manager's office and spoke with the owner, a small-framed, older, mellow man, also of Hispanic origin. My father told the manager the story of what happened on the highway and asked if the man and woman did live at his motel. The motel manager nodded, "Yes, they have been here for about a couple of weeks now. The man is looking for work, because he had lost his job, and they could no longer afford their prior living arrangement. I told him I would let them stay here for no more than a month, for free, until he can find a better way."

My father asked the manager if he would take him up to the couple's room because he wanted to "give them something." The manager called the room of the couple and announced he was coming up. The woman's husband opened the door. "Remember me?" asked my father. "Yes, yes, we are very grateful to you!" replied the very happy husband, "Look, see, my wife? She is eating grapes from your money!"

There on the bed, was the wife, her back resting against the bed's headboard, her swollen legs propped up on several pillows, balancing a huge bowl of yellow grapes on her rounded abdomen. She did not speak English, but my father understood every word she kept repeating to him, "Gracias! Gracias!" My father asked the husband to open his hand. The man did so hesitantly. My father firmly placed a gift into the astonished man's palm, "Please take this and I hope things get better for you soon!" It was another one hundred dollars.

How many people in this world would have done such a kind deed for total strangers in a traffic jam, and then worry so much about them as to follow up on them until almost midnight the same day?

It gave my father the greatest joy to help and give to those less fortunate. He taught us (his children) to always be grateful for what we had for there were millions of others in the world with a thousand times less. He reminded us that even when we felt "We didn't have as much as the other guy" the rest of the world was "ninety percent poorer than us."

My husband, Charles, had written a prayer. A few family members expressed that our father would have preferred no prayer. But Charles felt he must say something in remembrance of my father.

Charles' throat ached with grief, and with a taut voice, he prayed his prayer, trying desperately, but unsuccessfully, to hold back his tears. Charlie's words flowed softly and reverently, in deep respect for the man he had come to love as his own father.

"Our most gracious heavenly Father, we are here today to ask for your heavenly comfort and guidance in the loss of our dearly beloved father, husband, and friend, Joseph Bognar. We know Joseph is by your side looking down upon us with his wonderful smile. I ask you, our heavenly Father, to place your hand on Elizabeth and all of Joseph's children, and comfort them in this time of sorrow. We thank you Lord for all the time you let us have with Joseph while on this earth. Be with us Dear Lord throughout all our trials and tribulations and bring comfort to this family. We ask this in Jesus' name and for his sake. Amen."

My heart strained at its seams, my eyes expelling endless streams of tears at the sound of my husband's words. But no one else was offering to say anything to remember my father by! There was no minister present. We were not even having what I considered to be a "real funeral." Reflections of my father's memory cried out to me to raise my voice to the very heavens above, urging me to recount the crowning moments of my father's presence on this earth. Not caring to seek approval from the others, and feeling by right of being my father's firstborn, I inhaled deeply, and recited my words of remembrance for my father written while on the road to Atlanta.

Love, pure love – that is what my father was made of. It is how he lived his life. My father gave selflessly to his family- no matter the personal cost. He worked hard, sometimes with a great suffering pain to his body, to make sure his family never wanted for anything the way he had wanted as a child. The wealth of my father was great, but his wealth lay not in the monies of this world, but his wealth shone in how he was adored and loved by his wife, Elizabeth, his children, his grandchildren, and his friends. He was the perfection of what a father, husband, and friend should be: steadfast, true, loyal, dedicated, unselfish, brave, understanding, and loving.

My father was born a musical prodigy. The son of a music professor, he excelled at an early age playing and mastering his favorite instrument, the accordion, and it was on those ivory keys that his tiny fingers played with an inborn exhilarating grace and rhythm. Little did he know how important that instrument was to be for him later in life.

I remember many a warm summer's night in our small town of Greenfield, Massachusetts sitting by my father on the covered front porch of our home as he played his accordion; the sweet strains of his music fluttering through the neighborhood bringing inspiration to all who heard. I was only a little girl, but old enough to be appreciative of my father's talent and his ability to make others happy.

In Hungary, during World War II, my father was only a little boy, but war has no pity on anyone, not even children, and he was subjected to countless unspeakable, monstrous and ugly things that no small child should never have to endure: bombs, hunger, cold, and the abhorrent sights, smells, and sounds of death. During the miserable war years, he would stare at the glowing orbs in the night sky and wonder where God was? He pondered as to why God was allowing so many horrible things to happen to him and his entire world, why his tummy always rumbled, and why so many dead people were in the streets. The pain and anguish of his lost childhood was unbearable, and he was confused as to why God let children suffer. But he did not lose faith.

At age sixteen, my father met my mother at a school dance and at once fell in love with her, not knowing the beauty of their love would last for nearly six decades and would carry them across the sea on a whirlwind adventure to the shores of a new world.

And, then came the 1956 Hungarian Revolution, where my father, without care for his own safety, was willing to sacrifice his life to free his country from the tyranny of Soviet domination. Joining forces with thousands of other Freedom Fighters, my father climbed to the upper levels of buildings in downtown Budapest, ripping out the infamous hammer and sickle emblem from Hungary's flag - the sick symbol superimposed upon the brave colors of red, white and green by the *communist government; he dismantled the oppressive symbol of the Red Soviet star from the tops of Budapest's buildings, made Molotov cocktails, throwing countless scores of them at the scourge of Soviet tanks whose murderous guns thundered and plundered the city of Budapest, turning her streets red with the blood of the innocent. My father shot his way through the hellish frenzy of Soviet sacrilege by confiscating rifles from the fingers of dead Hungarian heroes and from the corpses of defiling Russian soldiers, determined to end the spawning savage reign of Russian dictatorship in his beloved Hungary.*

He saw the death of innocence, and the birth of corruption, as the Soviet regime crushed the Hungarian people, sentencing them to a life of indescribable misery and imprisonment within the walls of their own country.

I owe my life to my father, in every sense. After the Russians defeated the Freedom Fighters, we escaped from Hungary, and it was my father's loving arms that carried me and protected me from the onslaught of Soviet bullets flying around us, risking his life to bring me to the United States, so I could have a better childhood, a better life than his.

And through countless adversity, my parents did build a beautiful life for their children, working menial jobs in the early days of living in America, putting aside all pride, doing what had to be done to provide for their family, never taking a penny of assistance from the country that saved their lives; my father's brilliant mind eventually taking him to the top of the corporate ladder, where, even with the "handicap of being a foreigner," he accomplished more in his career than most people born in America.

Although my father did not "shout out his faith," God was always with him, sustaining him as a child; protecting him, my mother and me during our arduous escape from Hungary to the United States, guiding his steps on the long bridge of life called "Unknown," blessing him with three children to whom he gave his love and devotion, and granting him a long life to see his four grandchildren.

No, my father was not a man whom God had forgotten. God carried my father in his arms every day of his life, and in God's own time, he took my father's beautiful soul home, to reside in his own mansion of peace, where he will now do what he has loved to do since he was a small child: play his beloved accordion, and he can play anytime he desires, now and forever, for the inhabitants of the universe.

It is true - my father killed – he purged and extinguished the lives of satanic evil, but in so doing, he saved the lives of the valiantly pure. My heart is confident that God will find little to forgive my father for.

How I love you Daddy! How I will miss your honor, decency, integrity, and creative genius on this earth! I know that one wonderful day, we will meet again, and you will sing to me (the Frito Bandito song), just as your sweet smiling lips sang it to me many years ago while playing your accordion to the tune of Cielito Lindo (Mexican interpretation – "Lovely, Sweet One") - With all my love forever, your daughter Csimby.

After my speech everyone was silent, but I know my words had latched themselves about my mother's heart. She had been sitting in a wheelchair provided by the funeral home, being too careworn and too much in shock to stand, but now, in her eyes, I could see an inspired look of determination on her face as she pushed up from the chair, standing tall, filled with proud devotion for her husband as she made her way to his side. Her trembling, wrinkled hands gently stroked my father's wavy tendrils, who even at age seventy-five, still had the thickest head of nearly-black hair, except for a few small streaks of gray about his temples.

My mother's tottering form hovered over her husband's face, and then, her mouth tenderly rested upon his. The sadness of the moment washed over me as I realized this would be the last kiss of their sixty years together, the last time the velvety softness of their lips would meet in this world.

With slow, heavy movements, Mama draped her languished form over the chest of her husband, her arms embraced about his bloated girth (his body succumbing to the ravages of death, not being embalmed as he was to be cremated.)

My mother had not spoken nor made any other noise except for a few whimpers of grief since entering the viewing room; however, no longer able to control the overwhelming agony in her soul, she let burst a mournful, hoarse wail of release, the stinging words spoken in her native Hungarian resounding throughout the room, "A szerelmem, a lelkem, hogyan fogok élni nélkülem!" (My love, my soul, how will I ever live without you!) That was the end of Mama's strength. Her legs gave way as she fell into our arms.

It was nearing our time to leave this realm of remorse and nearing the time for our father to begin his last journey on this earth. As my family slowly exited to the outside lobby, I remained behind, for an unexplainable, silent force compelled me to return to my father's side, to be alone with him - just Daddy and me.

I enfolded my arms about my father's upper body, compressing his bones deeply into my flesh, taking in the "feel of him," remembering how as a little girl I would jump into his arms and he would clutch me tightly to his protective heart – it was the best place, the safest place, the most loving place I could ever hope to be. And on this day of blackness, I yearned for him to firmly hug me back, hoping that if we held each other closely enough, tightly enough, and if I prayed hard enough, my father would travel back to the world of the living from his abyss of darkness.

But Daddy was dead. All my desperate love and longing could not bring him back, nothing could bring him back, for such dreams only come true in fairy tales.

I whispered softly against my father's cool face, "I love you Daddy. Thank you for all you have done for me during my life, for loving me, for protecting me, for bringing me to America in your arms, for always being there for me. I will never forget everything you have done in your life. I will never forget all you taught me about the world, about my Hungarian roots, about how brave you have always been in building a life for your family. I will miss the beautiful music you created, and I will miss you every day of my life. I promise to take care of Mama. Watch over me Daddy, please … I will love you forever."

I kissed his pale cheek tasting the salt of my tears.

The next day, as I cared for my woe-beset mother, my husband returned to the funeral parlor to carry my father home to Mama, his cremated remains contained within a majestic piano wood vessel.

We children had to carry on. We had homes, jobs, and lives waiting for us. But first, we had to make the soul-wrenching decision as to which child would be the caregiver for our mother. Mama could not live alone. She had not cooked or driven a car for a long time, for my father had taken over those duties when her health dissolved over the last few years, being in a weakened condition for a long time, the result of a severe depression since moving to Atlanta from Florida.

Mom's depressive-state was not new; she had suffered periodic bouts of depression all her life, resulting from many egregious hardships and ordeals sustained as a young child and later in her life.

My parents were born in Hungary in the mid-1930's. When they were between the ages of seven and twelve the monstrous reign of Adolf Hitler cascaded its terror upon Europe. The United States was at war with Germany, and Germany wanted war with the world. The Nazi troops took over Hungary, killing, looting, raping, and plundering both for pleasure, hatred, and their twisted beliefs.

My then, "child parents," and thousands of other pure, innocent children, were caught up in a world with no pity for the young, old, or Jewish.

Mama's home was "bombed-out" and her family forced to find refuge in a deserted house whose owner was never to be seen again. Mama's "little girl brain" could not fathom the violence she saw against the people of her country, nor could she understand why anyone would render such terror upon little children.

Most of the time our mother was "normal" when things were going smoothly, and the way she liked them, but when stressed and unhappy she could be paranoid, stubborn and self-centered, but, nonetheless, always a loving mother, and we forgave and forgot any outbursts she may have exhibited for we understood the emotional and physical pain she had undergone in her early life.

In their later years, both my parents suffered from a severe depression, brought on by a series of surreal, unconscionable, unpardonable, and exorbitant late-life circumstances. Due to the emotional trauma caused by those stressors, Mama no longer slept well, and so, for years, my father indulged her in the use of his personal supply of antianxiety medications, with Mama taking five times the amount prescribed to be able to sleep, as well as taking my father's arthritic medication (written for his osteoarthritis). Poor Daddy! About the only way he could get any rest was to make sure Mama's pain and anxiety was under control. Most days, Mama slept until two in the afternoon. The time Mama spent sleeping was when Daddy would tend to his household routine, run his errands necessary for everyday living, and try to have some rest for himself.

Due to my mother's debilitated state in both her body and mind, my father's entire existence was one of enslaving himself to the needs of his wife - granting her every wish, whim and desire at the expense of his already failing heart, despite having suffered a heart attack at age forty-two, and then, subsequently, undergoing bypass surgery and several coronary stents in the 1990's. Nonetheless, he took care of Mama's personal hygiene, cooked, cleaned, shopped, did the bills, the lawn, and took her to doctor appointments.

After the funeral, we children sat downstairs in my parent's family room to discuss which child would take on the responsibility of a newly-widowed, deeply depressed, emotionally, and physically-debilitated mother.

My home had three bedrooms: me and my husband in one, our son in the other, and the third used as an office where I worked from home. We had a great room with a kitchen and dining room attached and two baths. We had no garage or basement. It was a small home, with no private place for Mama to call her own. My husband and I worked fulltime. My sister lived in a small apartment in Los Angeles where she also worked full-time.

My brother and his family lived in a nearly five-thousand square foot home in Virginia. His wife did not work. His daughters all lived at home and were home-schooled. All three children wanted to help, but we decided the best solution would be for Mama to live with my brother and his family. They had the space and plenty of helping hands.

On Sunday, July 27, 2008, my mother was placed in my father's green, 1995 Transport van, holding the vessel containing her husband's ashes in her lap. As my brother drove the van away, Mama's pinched, forlorn face stared out the window of the vehicle, her expression reminiscent of a confused, sad, distressed small child, as the world she and her husband had created disappeared from her view. Within forty-eight hours, the beautiful universe my mother and father shared since May of 1950, had come to a grinding, cruel end.

My husband, son, and I, stayed behind to do basic cleaning and picking up, but we could not stay for long. Our lives and jobs awaited us. We spent that night in my parent's house, resolving to return soon to finished what we had started.

The next morning, with the utmost respect and veneration, we locked the door to my parent's home, sealing in almost sixty years of their love and memories, and closing out the last chapter of the life they had conceived together.

But where would we all go from here?

WHAT TO DO WITH MAMA

It was a cool evening that October of 2008. My family and I were in an appliance store to buy a new microwave oven. My head ached from the glaring lights and the screeching sounds of the store's intercom as it blared out its in-store "specials." In the middle of all the noise my cell phone rang. It was Mama.

My mother's voice trembled with hoarse misery and exhaustion. "Judy, I cannot believe my Papa is gone. I miss him so much, he left me too soon. No one here understands what I am going through. They try, but they think I should go on with my life, but they do not understand, Papa *was* my life and now I have no life without him. Tonight, they gave me food, but I could not eat. I miss the food Papa made me!" Mama expelled her deep grief into the phone's receiver, leaving no space between her cries for me to interject. Then she blurted out the words I dreaded to hear, "I cannot take it here anymore. I miss my house! I want to go back to my own home in Atlanta!"

By the third week of October 2008, my Mama once again lived in her four-level house in Georgia. My brother had bought her some groceries and had helped her get settled in.

But how was Mama to care for herself! Weak in both her body and grief-stricken mind, she had not fended for herself in years. Daddy had done everything for her. Mommy could not even climb stairs without having to scoot up the stairs on her buttocks, one step at a time, and come down the same way. She had no strength to cook meals for herself or bathe.

My parents had created their will and estate planning, naming my brother as executor and trustee. As my sister and I had no control over Mama's finances we urged our brother to arrange for caregivers to visit Mama, care for her personal needs, pick up and help administer her medications, buy food, and cook meals for her, to which, he of course, agreed. My sister and I were relieved knowing Mama would have someone there with her every day to cook, clean, do her laundry, and take care of her personal hygiene.

I received a call from my mother shortly before Thanksgiving, but I was shocked and sickened by her words, "Judy, I am starving. There is hardly any food in the house. There are a few things to eat, but I have no strength to open the cans or cook." My throat constricted, "Mama what happened!"

Upon further probing, Mama explained the caregivers were not coming as scheduled, and were not preparing her meals. We were told by the homecare team that our mother would have daily meal preparation, or at least meals made ahead of time that she could heat up in the microwave. Mama continued in tears as my stomach dropped to my feet. "I am dirty. I have not had a bath or a shampoo since I got home. I am wearing stinky clothes and have not done any laundry since I came back home."

I *had* called my mother every single day since she went back to her home and she never once told me about her plight! I would ask if she was all right and if people were coming to help her and she had said, "Everything is fine." I was without a clue of Mama not having her very basic needs being met! I asked my mother why she had not told me the truth, to which she hesitantly replied, "Well…I knew you children had your own lives to live, and… I was very far away from you here in Atlanta. I did not want anyone to worry about me."

I fell into a dark ditch of morbid despair. Here I was, three hundred and sixty-five miles away, and my mother is on the phone telling me she is filthy and hungry, saying she had not eaten in over two days. At first, anger and rage built within me, upset with my mother for not telling me the truth, but then, as Mama began to cry over the phone, the reality of her suffering, her frailness and fragility overwhelmed me - Mama's mind was that of a scared little girl left alone in a big world all alone for the first time in six decades without her husband. I fortified myself, gathering my senses. My first gut instinct was to obtain food for my mother – and quickly!

"Mama, I will call you right back, I have to figure something out. I love you!" I hung up the phone and called the next-door-neighbors. They were always good and kind to my parents, but there was no answer. Their jobs required a lot of travel and they most likely were away for a few days. I then remembered a food store about three miles from Mama's house.

I called the food store and explained the appalling, but true facts to the store manager. I gave the manager my credit card information over the phone, stating I would "pay extra" to any employee who would drive to my mother's house with some hot food from the deli and stay with her to help her eat it. The manager was wonderful. Not only did she personally deliver the food, but she personally stayed with my mother until she finished the meal. She never charged me any extra for helping me and I was grateful beyond words that kind-hearted people still existed in the world.

Well, that solved today's problem, but what about all the tomorrows to come? It could not go on like this!

The next day I called my mother, and, after a long, restless, and thoughtful night, Mama told me that even though she did not want to go back to my brother's home, she *had* to go back there. The reality of her circumstances had "hit her hard," and she knew it was the only logical solution. I offered Mama to live in my home, regardless of the small space, but she declined.

The day before Thanksgiving Day, my husband and I drove from North Carolina to Atlanta, another one-way, six-hour drive. We pulled into the driveway of my parent's home. Amazingly, it looked the same as always, for Tommy, my parent's dearest neighbor, had taken care of the lawn and outside upkeep for Mama. It was good to see the house again. It felt warm and welcoming, and yet again, like a faraway, unexplored place.

We knocked on the door but there was no answer. I turned the knob and the door opened into the foyer. The energy of my parent's love emanated from the walls, the furniture - the very air – it was as if Daddy was still somewhere about. The house was too quiet! I did not see Mama downstairs. Fear struck at my core. Where was she? I darted up the stairs calling out, "Mama, where are you!" An almost inaudible, tiny, child-like voice responded, "I am here."

I found Mama sitting in her bedroom. Poised regally in her high-back, green velvet chair with side-arms, a chair resembling a throne (brought with her when they had moved to Atlanta from Florida). Mama sat straight, tall, and proud - like a queen surveying her kingdom. And she was a queen. She had been the Queen of this home, and Queen to her King, my father. Together they had "reigned" in love and glory within these walls.

I was stunned by how pretty Mommy looked! Somehow, despite her weakened condition, she had managed to shower, wash her hair, and dress in simple clothes. It must have taken her hours to get ready, for she appeared exhausted from the effort. "Oh Mama!" I cried, as I rushed over to kneel by her chair and hugged her by the knees. "I have been so worried about you!" Tears blurred my vision as I scanned her unhappy, pained face.

"My baby, I do not want to leave, but I have to. I cannot take care of myself. I have been sitting here for a very long time, looking at everything I know I will never see again. I miss Papa!"

Mama's shoulders trembled, and her face distorted as if she would lose control and have a good hard cry; however, she gathered her strength, sat up straight, and regained her composure. "Please bring me the fur coat with the mink collar Papa bought me when your sister was born." I found the coat in the upstairs hall closet. The garment looked the same as it had the first day Mama wore it during the winter of 1959. Mama stood up for me to help her with the coat, her legs nearly giving way from the strain of getting ready for my arrival on a nearly empty stomach. Charles held Mama as I bundled her up in the warmth of the faux fur, fastening the soft mink collar about her neck to keep out the unusually chilly air for this time of the year in Atlanta.

I assured Mama we would get her a delicious meal very soon. My husband aided me in helping her down two flights of stairs, supporting her between the two of us by her elbows. We then gathered Mama's most precious belonging – the beautiful piano wood box holding my father's ashes. After loading her clothing and other personal items, we were nearly ready to leave.

One more time, I found myself standing at the front door of my parent's home - my face centimeters away from the portal of their lost dreams. As I turned the key in the lock, I closed my eyes in silent reverie, "*Oh Daddy, please give me the strength to take care of Mommy. She is so lost without you. Give us hope for her to get well. I love you Daddy. Oh, Daddy, please watch over Mama!*"

As I sat in the backseat of the car with Mama holding her frigid hand, the vibrations of her painful oblivion slung their stinging arrows of depression deep within my heart. I braced myself for the long, six-hour trip back to North Carolina.

My brother arranged to meet us the same evening at my home to take Mama back with him that very night. Upon arriving at my home, I went through the motions of making dinner for everyone, and within three hours of setting foot in North Carolina, my exhausted, sad Mama was transported another four hours to my brother's house in Virginia, not arriving there until the early morning hours of the next day.

Christmas Eve was soon upon us. When growing up, our family had always opened our gifts on that holy night, as is the custom in many European countries. Prior to Christmas, I had offered many times to visit Mama at my brother's house, but she refused to let me come, saying, "It would be too hard on you."

I called my brother's home on Christmas Eve to speak with Mama, but there was no answer. I reasoned that with four children, my brother's family was more than likely caught up in their own traditional holiday festivities and did not hear the ringing of the phone.

I had especially wanted to converse with my mother on that special night, because it was on Christmas Eve of 1956, when we boarded an army ship, the USS General Haan, in Bremerhaven, Germany, the "miracle ship" that carried my father, mother and me to a new life of freedom and opportunity in America after escaping the Soviet regime's takeover of Hungary. We had to flee at a moment's notice as my father had received word that the Russian army was seeking out and killing all instigators of the 1956 Hungarian Revolution – one of whom was my father.

From that time on, Christmas Eve was always considered our own personal holiday, and each year we played the Hungarian National Anthem on our record player and listened to Hungarian Christmas songs. I did not want my mother to think I had forgotten the anniversary of that special day. Despite my many calls that evening, I did not get through to Mama. The ringing of the unanswered phone was a devastating letdown for me. But then, I wondered if Mama had even remembered.

I called again on Christmas Day and did speak with Mama. But I was speaking with only a hollow version of the woman she once was. Her voice was labored, spindly, and weak. And no wonder... in sixty years, this was her first Christmas without her husband.

For her sake, and to bolster my own downbeat feelings of lassitude about her situation, I tried my best to be cheerful and upbeat, asking what Christmas activities she had shared with the family and what gifts she received the prior evening. She mentioned the turkey dinner and the nice presents but was too sad and out of her element to enjoy any of it.

A few days later my world would be turned upside-down.

My brother called me on New Year's Day of 2009, his tone urgently upset and worried, "Please, you have to come and take Mama home with you! We don't know what to do with her anymore. Help me!" My heart turned over - something terrible must have happened!

According to my brother, the prior night, my mother had a panic attack. He had found her very frightened and confused, running up and down the upstairs hallway screaming, "The Russians are coming!" The stress of losing her husband had culminated into a type of post-traumatic stress disorder episode, reverting my mother's mind back to the days when the Soviet Army was invading Hungary. And, even more shocking, was Mama telling my brother that she was in "terrible pain," saying she had just given "birth to my father," and "when *he came out of her*, he grew up "really fast" in front of her eyes, and "he was back with her."

In my Mama's mind, she had helped her husband to be "reborn," bringing him back to life again. My brother said Mama had an "unearthly look about her" for she claimed to have seen my father. My brother said Mama's condition was very hard on his family, and since he knew Mama and I always had a tight emotional bond, he felt she might do better under my care.

Our poor, sweet Mama! She was battle-worn from the loss of her husband and from being "tossed back and forth" from her home in Atlanta, to my brother's home, back to her home, and then back to my brother's home again. I somehow would have to figure out a way to make a new existence for my mother. I could not blame my brother for feeling helpless in the care of our mother. Not everyone has the tenaciousness and resolve to assume the care of an emotionally traumatized person. Did I?

I contacted my sister, Pilvia, and the day after New Year's Day of 2009, my sister flew in from Los Angeles to my home in North Carolina. The next day, with my husband and sister, we drove to Virginia to carry Mama home with us.

When we were about one hour away from my brother's home. I called to let them know we would be there soon, to be sure they had Mama ready. I called several times with no answer.

After about thirty minutes of repeated calls, their oldest daughter finally answered the phone, telling me Mama was in the process of being taken to the hospital by my brother and his wife. Apparently, Mama had another panic-type attack and the family was planning to take her to the hospital. I begged them to please wait about thirty minutes until I got there since I had traveled a very long distance to take Mama home with me.

According to the daughter, Mama had not wanted to leave the house to go to the hospital, and, as she resisted being taken out of the house, Mama had tripped and fallen when walking down the front of the home's brick steps, suffering a cut to her right temple area. This injury now created a greater urgency to get Mama to medical treatment.

I obtained the name of the hospital from the daughter, plugged the information in my GPS, and we made a beeline to the facility.

After fighting lines of traffic, we finally arrived at the emergency holding area where my brother waited for us. I found him sitting in the corner of Mama's room, appearing extremely tired and emotionally devastated. My mother was lying in a hospital bed with closed eyes. She had aged so much - too much. Deep purple shadows encircled her eyes. I lightly stroked her soft gray hair, gently trying to awaken her, "I am here Mommy. It's Judy. I love you. Please wake up." I could see Mama fluttering her eyelids, struggling to keep her eyes open, and then finally, as recognition of me seeped into her tired mind, Mama whispered to me, "*Csimby*...please take me home with you!"

My brother felt Mama should not leave the hospital until a complete workup was done. He said the doctors had mentioned keeping her for a few days, but I did not have a few days! My sister had to get back to Los Angeles, my husband and I had to get back to work. My sister and I were not financially prepared to stay in town for several days. Besides, all the way to the hospital I had made up my mind to take Mama home with me - no matter what.

It was the longest day: the drive to Virginia, worrying about how I would get my mother out of the hospital, and now, it was well into the evening. After consulting with several doctors, my sister and I decided to let Mama finish out her tests that night. I did not want Mama to develop complications because I was in a rush to bring her home with me.

My mother's personal items were still at my brother's home. Charles and Pilvia made the one-hour drive to our brother's house to gather her belongings. It was decided my husband and I would drive back home that very night to rearrange our home for Mama's arrival. My sister ordered a rental car for the next morning and would drive Mama to our home the next day.

As my husband and sister journeyed to obtain Mama's things, torrential clouds of rain settled over the area, forcing Charles to not only fight his own exhaustion, but the darkness of a wet night with a deluge of water slapping against his windshield.

My sister and I explained to Mama we would have her at my home by the next evening, but by her bewildered expression, we were not sure if she understood. We assured Mama we were not abandoning her and explained how she would be leaving in the morning with my sister.

I told Mama she would no longer live with my brother, but with me. With welling eyes, Mama disbelievingly shook her head from side to side, "I love you *Csimby* .... goodbye *Csimby*."

"Oh Mommy, I promise, I will take you home with me!" I kissed her several times on her cheek and forehead, and with my heart still in hers, left her room to go to the bathroom for a good cry.

A few hours later, my husband called from his cell phone asking me to meet him at the front of the hospital for our drive back home. My sister would spend the night with our mother in her hospital room.

By now, my husband and I felt "sick." Our bodies and heads ached for want of food and rest. To make matters worse, the unrelenting rain made for a precarious drive. We left the hospital at approximately 10:30 p.m. and arrived home at 4 a.m.

At 7 a.m. the phone rang. It was my sister, hardly able to talk due to being severely upset, her voice catching in her throat as she tried to hold back tears of desperation, "The hospital refused to let me take Mama home! They told me Mama can't be released until our brother allows it, but they haven't been able to reach him to get the release. Why is this happening!"

Having worked in a hospital, I knew the only way a patient could be kept against their will is if they had undergone a thorough psychiatric assessment, and, it had been determined they were a danger to themselves or to others; or, if a patient had a designated power-of-attorney for healthcare *if* they could not speak for themselves. But Mama could speak for herself and had not been declared incompetent, had not been committed involuntarily, nor had she had any psychiatric assessment, and had no healthcare power-of-attorney.

Mama had announced repeatedly to the nursing staff and doctors of wanting to leave the hospital and wanting to live with me in North Carolina. Again, the staff told her they could not allow this without my brother's permission because he had checked her in. My sister barely slept the night before and was worn out, and at a total loss on what she was going to do. I comforted my sister, assuring her I would take care of things, "Don't worry Pilvia, I will get Mama out of there!"

My husband had a close friend, an attorney, whom he consulted about the situation. The attorney called the hospital charge nurse on my mother's floor. "At this point, your hospital can be charged with false imprisonment. You are confining the patient against her will and without legal authority. If you do not immediately release her from your facility, I will have no choice but to contact the authorities in your jurisdiction to press charges against your hospital for holding a patient without proper legal or psychiatric documentation."

That, and whatever else the lawyer may have said, resulted in my receiving another call from my sister saying the nurses had Mama dressed and ready to leave. The car rental company had delivered the vehicle to the hospital, and she and my mother would start the drive home within the hour. Mama was alert and aware of what she wanted and where she wanted to go, and again, had very clearly told the nursing staff of her wish to sign out against medical advice to go live with her daughter.

My brother was not aware of what had transpired at the hospital that morning. He had not yet called the hospital, or us, and it was nearing the noon hour! He had asked me to take Mama home, and so that is what my sister and I intended to do. I would talk to my brother later about everything. But, for now, we were all exhausted, Mama needed a place to live, and Pilvia was bringing her home!

My sister had a tedious, slow drive to North Carolina. Mommy needed several stops for restroom and stretching breaks due her deconditioned and debilitated state, resulting in my sister having to summon every ounce of strength to lift Mama in and out of the car several times. And, it was still raining.

Pilvia and Mama arrived at my home around six o'clock in the evening. The combined strength of me, my sister, and husband was needed to help Mama up the stairs of our deck into the house. We got her comfortable and made sure she had a good hot meal. Mama ate her food mechanically without desire, her face void of emotion, and her pained eyes staring into "nothingness."

After dinner, I sat with Mama on the couch, resolved to discover if she truly believed she had "given birth to her husband." I asked the question. She replied automatically, her lifeless eyes and blank face devoid of feeling, as she crossed both arms about her chest, rocking back and forth in a protective manner, "I did bring him back to life. It hurt bad to give birth to him, there was blood everywhere." Then unexpectedly, Mama changed the subject, "Please promise you will never take me back to that hospital again."

My dinner turned over in my gut. It was hard to fathom, to think, to believe, that my mother's mind was traumatized to this extent.

My thoughts were broken by Mama's voice speaking with a sudden clarity, "Judy, I am dirty. I need a shower. Please help me!" Pilvia and I propped Mama up under her armpits to my bedroom where we lay her down on the bed.

We undressed her in the manner of a newborn baby, manually lifting every limp limb, rolling her gently from side-to-side, as we manipulated the stretchy fleecy top and slacks off her thin, flaccid body. I had to physically get into the shower and hold Mama up as the soothing, warm spray sloshed over both of us, enabling my sister to soap Mama down. An hour later I helped my sister to bed due to her extreme fatigue.

Mama continued to actively hallucinate into the late evening, repeating over and over, "Judy, golden stars are falling from the sky all over you. See them fall? See them come out of the vents?" This could not be happening! Mama needed help! I had promised my mother not to take her back to the Virginia hospital; however, as midnight approached, I explained to Mama that I was worried for her health and would be taking her to my local hospital for examination. Mama did not refuse.

After a long night in the emergency department, relaying the very long story of my parent's childhood, the long story of the death of her husband, and the long story of events happening since then, including my concerns for her mental well-being, the doctors admitted Mommy to the Behavioral Health Unit for psychological examination and physical rehabilitation. During her exam in the emergency department, a tiny fracture of her pubic rami bone had been discovered, which the doctors felt was most likely caused by the fall Mama experienced at my brother's home.

There is only so much the human mind and spirit can endure. Certain individuals can handle one tragedy after another, can regroup, and come back stronger than before. Mommy was not one of those persons. She no longer had the resources to "make a comeback." She had reached her emotional and mental limit. I was fearful of my mother going insane. She had been through too much in her lifetime. Mama had always been my strength, and starting now, I had to be hers. I was determined to "bring her back." My love had to be strong enough and my life force powerful enough to handle the stressful long ordeal destined to be mine.

One week later, I wearily followed a hallway toward the Behavioral Health "lock-down unit" at the medical center, strolling the same familiar path since my mother's admission, my head and eyes aching from the harsh glare of fluorescent lighting. I approached the same cold, gray steel door, and next to it, on a gray wall, hung an in-house telephone. I picked up the receiver and waited for the nursing station to answer. I gave my name and "secret code number" and the door swung open, allowing me access to the high security psychiatric floor. The nursing station was straight ahead. The nurses appeared tired, almost "burnt out," yet they tried to be pleasant. "Please sign your name on the log sheet," a young, mousy-brown-haired nurse mechanically muttered. My hand moved through the motions of signing my name, but I couldn't feel it moving, feeling as if I were in another body moving without my permission or control. A second door opened leading to another nursing station. A kind-faced nurse, appearing to be in her early sixties says I can enter the patient's room across the hall from her desk.

I hesitantly approached the wide, gray door, beyond which was my worst nightmare, and, my biggest hope. I entered the room. A narrow hospital bed was on my left, and perched on its edge, was a pleasant older woman. A curtain divided her side of the room from the other. Another bed was placed against the opposite wall, above which, a window placed near the ceiling allowed streams of bright sunlight to permeate the small space.

I forced myself to walk the five feet towards the other bed. I did not want to be here! It made my body hurt all over to be in this place, but I had to be here!

Lying beneath thin, grayish-white hospital bedding was my mother. MY mother. My stomach tightened. My throat felt parched, but I had to keep myself "together" for her sake, and for mine. "Hello *Anukam Edes*," I said in our native language of Hungarian, meaning (Hello mother dearest.)

Mama slowly opened her hazel-green eyes and stared directly at me, her mind not grasping that it was really me standing in front of her. Her once happy eyes were glassy and dull, encased within dark-bluish circles from days of little to no sleep. She squinted them shut, and then opened them once more, the glazed crystals severing my soul as her painstakingly slow words stung my heart, "Judeeee… I do not feeeeeel good. Why deeeed Papa leeeev meeeee? I no longer have a home of my own anymooooore!" I tried to distract Mama by telling her about a hot baked potato I have snuck into the facility (wrapped in foil in my purse for her to eat as well as a nutritional drink as no outside food is allowed on the unit). Mama had not been eating well since being in the hospital, and I was determined she had to eat something! Mama seemed eager to dig into the potato as I searched my purse for the plastic cutlery to cut the potato in half. I pulled out a small, partially filled tub of butter from the bottom of my purse and put some on the potato, and began the slow process of feeding my mother, intermingled with sips of drink through a bendable straw.

After gulping a few bites, Mama sought my face for an answer, "When can I go home with you?" I wanted to tell Mama when she could leave, but I honestly did not know. "I'm not sure, Mama, maybe in a couple of weeks. You have a tiny fracture of your pubic rami bone."

But that was only a small part of why Mama could not go home yet. She was not only in shock from my father's death, but the mental trauma sustained by that shock, was pulling at her psyche, causing Mama to relive the tortuous events of her former life.

On my way home that day, I vowed to restore my mother's mental and emotional spirit. The gentle part of me felt guilty in placing Mama in the hospital, but the reasonable part of me knew she must be here to begin the catalyst of her healing.

It was time to begin a new era of our life together – the time of Mama and *Csimby*.

MAMA SHOWS ME THE WAY BACK HOME

I could not believe it was already January 27, 2009. A hard fall of ice and snow from the prior night's wintry storm would make this day of travel difficult and treacherous. Could things have been made any more strenuous on this day of all days, for Mama had been discharged from the hospital, and in a few hours, I would be admitting her to a physical rehabilitation center about seven miles from my house.

I had inspected the rehabilitation facility, noting it was not the fanciest place, but it was considerably cleaner than most of the other facilities. It had a kind staff and caring director; however, my major decision in choosing the facility was its nearness to my home. Mama had gained more emotional stability since being placed on antipsychotic medications, but she was far from being healed emotionally or physically.

After getting home from the hospital, I placed Mama in the shower of my master bedroom to help her "wash off the hospital," leaving the shower curtain open so I could securely hold Mama with one arm while I bathed her with the other.

I dried Mama off and assisted her to my bedroom and she immediately collapsed upon the bed. She said her legs could not hold her up anymore and I could see them trembling. I was already exhausted, and Mama was not even dressed yet! I helped Mama with her garments, lifting each leg as I pulled on her fleecy pink pants, lifting each arm into the armholes of her matching pink sweatshirt, and pulled on her thick socks and warm boots.

These movements had left me physically and emotionally threadbare, but more painful to me than my own physical deterioration, was the misery of witnessing the twisted tangle of emotions within my mother's heart. Mama was aware enough to realize, that once more, she was being shuffled to another foreign place filled with unfamiliar faces, and once more, would have to sleep in another strange bed far from her family.

I wanted to care for my mother at home, but her physical needs were beyond my physical abilities. My only consolation was that Mama would be close enough for me to see her every day, as she would most likely have to stay in physical rehabilitation for approximately three months, or more. An in-facility psychiatrist and medical doctor would visit Mama weekly to help with her emotional and physical well-being.

I explained to Mama exactly where we were going and why, and she did not oppose us, and with my son's help, we escorted my mother out the back door onto the crisp, clean, frozen snow. The crunching sound of ice resounded beneath our feet as we successfully crossed the treacherous slippery barrier to the safety of the car.

The drive to the skilled nursing facility was silent. Mama stared straight ahead without saying anything. I was also quiet. I shouldn't have been quiet. My heart was bursting with so much I wanted to say to my Mama. I wanted to tell my Mama how I never imagined her life would come to this. I wanted to tell my Mama how much I missed my father. I wanted to tell my Mama how much I wished she would not have to be going where I was taking her, how I wished I could "make it all better" by waving a magic wand, and I wished I could tell my Mama that I was just as afraid of the unknown future as she was.

But I did not have the luxury of being afraid. I could not appear weak or uncertain. I could not, and would not, give myself permission to embrace those feelings, because as much as I wanted to break down and cry about my mother's world coming to this sorrowful point in time, I knew Mama needed me, now more than ever, to be strong for her in every way possible. My head was so full of the worries of today for my mother, so full of worries for all our tomorrows, and so full of the beautiful memories of our family from the past, that I had no recollection of driving to the rehab facility, and then suddenly, I was there, and in response, my stomach curled in knots of dreadful anticipation as I thought about all the things that needed to be done in the next few hours.

A kind, elderly male volunteer, wearing a red coat, appeared at the passenger door, a wheelchair in hand, to help Mama inside.

The director was waiting for me and Mama in her office. We had a set appointment time with her, but we were an hour late, but she said nothing about it.

The director was a kind-faced, blonde-haired, thin lady, in her mid-forties. She introduced herself to me and my mother. Mama said she was tired. I asked Mama if she wanted to go to her room while I signed the admission papers, as Mama had made me her healthcare and legal power-of-attorney, via a notary, while she was in the hospital. She numbly nodded in agreement, and then Mama's wheeled conveyance took her down the hall to her new temporary residence. I seated myself at the director's desk to sign the documents.

I was dead tired. My head felt swollen. Every muscle in my body burned and ached. Why were there so many papers to sign? I felt guilty. Was I doing the right thing? Would bringing Mama here have a positive impact on her health? I had no choice. I could not continue to lift Mama and carry her the way I did today, every day.

I finally made my way to be with Mama in her room, shared with another female patient, a pleasantly demented, ninety-year old, thin lady. A curtain divided the room. On the other side of the curtain was Mama's bed, placed on the far side of the room next to a window, with a pleasant view of a snow-covered courtyard.

Mama said she was hungry. Numerous food trays, each with a different type of meal, were brought to her by a very understanding staff, but she pushed each away, saying she could not eat "the junk," and declared she was leaving. Her face was strained, and the whites of her eyes were red from tiredness. Mama adamantly announced, "I am going home to Atlanta – I hate it here!"

I know she hated it! I hated it! I loathed the whole idea! I detested doing this! This is not the way I envisioned my mother living. It is not the way Mama envisioned herself living, but deep down inside, Mama realized she must be here. Mama was very much aware of my inability to care for her, for every time I would help her to the bathroom, change her clothes, or bathe her, Mama's pitiful, sorrowful, but sweet voice would whisper softly to me, "I am so sorry, I am so sorry, my little *Csimby*, I am too heavy for you."

I had not slept well in a long time, and without rest, I was not good for anyone. Then, I heard Mama speak, clearly and lucidly, albeit through choked sobs. As if she had read my mind, she gently reached out and touched my arm, wearily giving me instructions, "I know you are tired. I am tired. Go home to your family. Your family needs you."

I sat on the edge of Mama's bed stroking her legs. Mommy said she was cold, but the room was warm - at least it was to me. I tucked the bedcovers firmly around her.

Again, the staff offered Mama food, but she only ate it if I fed her, as she had no strength to bring the spoonful of hot stew to her mouth.

After eating, I settled Mama into her bed. I placed a pink "spit tub" in her lap while I gingerly brushed her teeth. I helped her swish water around in her mouth and assisted her in expectorating the "toothpaste suds" into a pink tray. I washed her face and hands. I combed her hair. I tucked her in once more. I told Mama I would be here every day to see her, to bring food from home for lunch and dinner, and take her clothes home for washing.

Lightly, lovingly, and soothingly, I stroked Mama's soft, silver strands of hair, smoothing back the stray ones from her forehead. My eyes scanned her withered face, turning back the pages of her aging years, back to the days when Mama was young and beautiful, and so very much in love with my father. All Mama ever wanted, all she ever desired, was to bring, love, joy and comfort to her husband and children. All those things had now been taken from her. As I sat at my mother's bedside on her first gloomy night in this rehab center, Mama's agony of loss emanated into my heart with the weight of a one-hundred-pound nail, as my body, mind and soul absorbed the bereavement of her ruined world.

The only light in the room was provided by the faint illumination of a tiny night lamp. Mama's chest slowly rose and fell, her breathing, at last, becoming rhythmic and soft. Mama's strained, sad face finally relaxed, and the stressful dark lines seem to have faded away.

In the light of semi-darkness, my mind raced about, thinking back to my parent's beginnings, to the nightmarish memories they shared with me about their childhoods during the dark, desperate days of World War II, and the undoing of their lives as they suffered through the even darker days of the Hungarian Revolution of 1956. And how, by some miracle, out of all that depravity, they found each other, and promised to only love each other - forever.

My poor sweet Daddy! How inconsolable and anguished his spirit must be gazing down from his heavenly cloud upon his beautiful, forever love as she sleeps in her nursing home bed.

I felt the mournful sorrow of both my parents pressing hard against my chest and it was hard to breathe.

My remembrance was abruptly interrupted by Mama's moaning, the shock of her vocalization encouraging me to take in a much-needed breath. Was she dreaming of her sweetheart?

My dear Daddy was gone, and now, was my precious mother to lose her mind? If she did, what would I do? I pushed the thought from my brain as I lightly stroked my mother's legs under the blankets, her legs finally warm.

Since I was a little girl my parents had told me many stories of their prior lives in Hungary… "The old country," their birthplace, and mine, and in the twilight of Mama's little room, bits and pieces of memory called out to me as an unseen presence descended upon my heart, urgently imploring me to put my parent's story, our family's story into written form. Was the urging voice from beyond?

I promised the silent bidder to take on their pressing request: to chronicle the saga of my parent's lives from the very beginning, to document the beautiful and the bad, to recall the horrors and the joys, promising to recount their harrowing escape from Hungary as they fought their way to a world of freedom, promising to commemorate the life my parents built together in America, and most of all, promising never to forget the marvel of their love – a love that defied all odds and transcended decades.

Oh, Dear God! How did our family's once beautiful world end up in this pit of pain?

And with that final heart-wrenching thought, I sensed the lost ripples of time gently brushing their feathery softness within the passages of my mind…and now, at last, the story begins…

HERMINA AND JOZSEF - 1933

Hermina analyzed her reflection in the full-length mirror taking in her exquisite image from head to toe. She was, without a doubt, beautiful, and *knew* she was beautiful, blessed with the finely-refined features of her Hungarian-Italian heritage: a lustrous complexion, rosy high cheek bones, sparkling green eyes that tilted upwards at the corners, and dewy-soft lips of blushing pink. Her father, a well-to-do, Hungarian-Italian music professor, came from an illustrious musical family, having met Hermina's mother in Hungary on one of his many European business trips.

Her father's musical genius enabled him to provide a high standard of living for his family, enough so, to provide Hermina her own apartment in Budapest while she attended university. Hermina worshipped her father, adoring his emotional strength, his analytical mind, his musical genius. He made her feel safe and secure. Hermina desired the same in the man she chose for her husband.

Hermina estimated the baby would arrive in around seven months, or a little less. She was always slim, and even now, no one would ever suspect her shameful, unmarried "condition." Nonetheless, she was determined to further flatten the small, rounded bulge containing the new life growing within her.

On the nearby bed lay numerous long strips of cotton cloth. Hermina slowly wove each length of the thin fabric tightly about her abdomen, pulling snugly on the self-made girdle, successfully whittling her subtly advancing waistline to pre-pregnancy dimensions.

Many men wanted her, but she desired only one man, and now he would be hers. She continued wrapping the strips of cloth about her body, her mind wandering, remembering …

Hermina and Jozsef met in late May of 1933. A cascade of bright, morning sunlight streamed down upon Hermina as she relaxed in her chair at a sidewalk café, sipping her coffee, balancing a silken parasol over one shoulder, its shadow protecting her porcelain skin from the rays of a very warm sun. And then, he came walking by, unaware that the spring sun would be his undoing today, and unaware, that he would soon lose his heart to an enticing beauty hidden from his view.

Jozsef wove his way through the tightly knit café tables, seeking out a spot in the shade to indulge in his usual cup of expresso. An unexpected flash of yellow brightness blocked his view for only a moment, causing him to inadvertently stumble backwards into a precariously placed parasol knocking it to the ground. He quickly regained his footing, determined to make amends with his unsuspecting victim. Giving a formal bow, he spoke before even looking up into the face of his mishap, as he dejectedly handed her the object of his misfortune, "Miss, I beg your forgiveness for my most inappropriate action."

But then, it was too late for him to escape, for as his head rose to meet her emerald eyes, his piercing gaze beheld a set of half-parted, moist lips, curved slightly upwards at the edges, exposing a perfect dimple in her left cheek, leaving Jozsef instantly smitten and forever bewitched by the delicate beauty, charm, and snowy bosom of the fair lady before him. "May I, err … ah … would you, perhaps, accept a coffee as reparation for my error?"

Hermina was more than grateful to forgive this man, for she recognized him instantly, acutely aware of his eminence, prestige, and prominent standing in the musical community as one of the greatest musical conductors and professors in the country, having attended several of his concerts with her father.

And, she too, like the innumerable scores of other females who sought to gain his favor, was instantly captivated and mesmerized by his strikingly good looks, but although his fair countenance intrigued her, it was his notoriety and recognition throughout the region, his reputation of sweeping his audiences into outbursts of inspirational appreciation that sent an electrifying thrill of exhilaration through her heart. She enticingly cooed her reply, "Certainly, if you will keep me company for a while on this lovely day."

Well into the late afternoon, between sips of coffee and *Palinka*, Hermina listened attentively to Jozsef as he zestfully described the details of his admirable career, markedly honored to have such an enchanting woman engrossed in the details of his professional accomplishments.

Hermina found Jozsef to be the model embodiment of aristocratic dignity, his mannerism highly polished, but, yet again, not a man of vanity, yet he held a mysterious aura about him, something raw and unknown to her that she could not discern, but whatever that something was, she wanted to be part of it.

As the afternoon sun faded, Jozsef stood to leave, placing his calling card in Hermina's palm, "This will allow you access to my next concert. Please present it to the doorman and he will assure you a fine seat."

Jozsef was to conduct a concert the following week, where under his expertise, the finest musical prodigies were to perform for the city's elite. His students excelled in many varieties of musical instruments ranging from violin, cello, flute, saxophone, bassoon, trumpet, clarinet, to the accordion: all living proof of their master's genius.

The day of the concert could not come soon enough for the young suitor.

On the afternoon of the performance, Jozsef vigilantly scanned the audience from the wings of the stage, hoping beyond hope that Hermina had accepted his invitation. His eyes froze on the front-row center seat reserved especially for her. He was not disappointed: the object of his desire was seated a mere eight feet from his podium. The music professor's heart fluttered wildly, causing him to momentarily lose his breath, and his mind.

"Professor Bognar we are ready to begin," announced the stage manager.

But he heard nothing, his ears anesthetized to all sound, his mind drugged to all reason, his eyes magnetized upon the rise and fall of silken, ivory breasts straining to break free from the confines of a snug, lacy bodice. "Professor Bognar!" Once more, the tense voice of the stage manager demanded his attention, but the golden-haired angel had unnerved him to the core, clearing all thoughts from his mind to make room for her – only her.

"Professor Bognar it *is* time to take your place!" The unusually testy, short-tempered vocalizations of the stage manager broke Jozsef's spellbound state, slinging him back to reality. He stiffened his body for the recital at hand, determined to win Hermina's heart through his music. Her nearness twisted his nerves and disheveled his senses. He panicked. His mind had gone blank!

Jozsef's feet floated above the ground as his legs involuntarily made their way toward the stage, his eyes not daring to look upon the extension of his heart.

The professor bowed deeply to his audience. He then stepped onto his conductor's pedestal, raised his arms, and with the utmost of precision, urged the perfumed prose of his orchestra onward.

The melodious, sweet sounds of Jozsef's classical compositions and harmonious Hungarian rhapsodies flooded the music hall, pulling the helpless audience under the spell of its vibrations.

As much as Jozsef thrived upon the audience's thundering, admiring applause, he heard not one sound, for he was adrift in a private world of his own, floating on a celestial cloud of exquisite desire, lost in the enticing, enchanting glow of Hermina's smile.

After the concert Jozsef urgently pushed his way through the congested hall determined not to allow another suitor to interfere with his agenda. Would she have him? Could she love him? Did he deserve such an exquisite beauty?

He found Hermina admiring a spray of blood-red roses in the main foyer. Sensing his presence, she turned her full smile upon him as he approached. He reached for her hand, pressing his smooth lips to her velvety palm, exhilarated by the scent of her balmy skin.

"Yes, I would be most honored to see you again," he heard her tenderly reply. But he forgot he had asked the question. He summoned a taxi for her. She went home. His heart rode with her.

On her drive home Hermina rubbed her hand where it tingled from the brush of Jozsef's lips. Why was there an uneasy, yet thrilling sensation within her being? Why did her stomach tighten with anticipation when she thought of him? Hermina sloughed of her sentiments, reasoning to herself, "I am only feeling this way because such a dignified, handsome, and professional man is seeking my company. Of course, it does not hurt my cause that he is a man very much admired by the upper-crust of Hungarian gentility, and very much desired by other women, but they will not have him. He will be mine."

She knew Jozsef wanted *her*. Love was not a factor. Oh, it did help, but for Hermina, prestige and high society were a higher commodity than love. Love only clouded the mind. But Jozsef *was* the perfect candidate: a musical genius, debonair, cultured, intelligent, suave, financially secure and in a position of importance in the community. She liked him very much. And, her father would like him very much, for they were two of a kind. Yes, he would meet her needs quite nicely.

Having enamored many a male in the past, Hermina thrived on the game of conquest, and was determined to have control over this man who, was already, by all indications, her devoted servant. She found Jozsef's appearance disquietingly handsome, what one would call "aristocratically dignified," his striking persona cultivated by a natural air of sophistication, civility, and refinement. His wavy, dark hair complemented hazel eyes framed by gently arching brows. His fair complexion was smooth and clear, with just enough "age-lines" around his eyes and mouth to accentuate his professional aura. A bevy of Budapest's finest ladies had sought his attentions, but miraculously, he had eluded all attempts of entrapment.

Future security, prestige, and recognition were all within Hermina's greedy grasp and she prepared to set the stage for her performance.

In June, Jozsef asked Hermina to his Budapest apartment to gain her opinion of the latest musical repertoire for his next recital. Hermina sat sipping a cup of fruit tea as Jozsef played his accordion, serenading her with his latest renditions. Hermina genuinely applauded and smiled, "Oh Jozsef, you *are* so ingenious and clever! How are you able to create so many different melodies?" Looking deep into her glistening eyes, Jozsef replied, "With the right inspiration - it is easy."

The rest of the afternoon passed with sweet talk and wine. Hours disappeared, and when the shadows of evening grew long, and the golden sun dissolved behind the towers of the city, Jozsef pressed Hermina's soft bosom to his heart. Hermina's mind whirled in confusion. *Something was not right*! Hermina's "plan" was for *her* to seduce Jozsef as an end to her own unscrupulous means, but she had never expected, had never counted on her needful body betraying her with such a deep aching want of physical desire.

Hermina's icy, self-control melted away, until she was nothing more than a limp, defeated ragdoll, enlaced within the prison of Jozsef's arms. As Jozsef's grip about her became more demanding, Hermina gasped with the realization that she had fallen into her own trap, that it was too late for her to retreat, and willfully abandoned her selfless plot, her body commanding Jozsef to thirst only for her, to love and possess only her, to be hers - forever. *God help me! I do want him, I love him. I had not planned to love him but love him I do!*

Hermina had played a high stakes game – betting Jozsef to be a man of honor, wagering he would marry her should she become pregnant. A month later, much to Hermina's joy and shock, her winning number was announced early one morning as she violently vomited into the bowl of her china commode.

He *knew she was pure* the night the child was created - there had been no others before him, and he had repeatedly kissed her, and had thanked her for that precious gift. But, when she told him of the baby, would he "do the right thing?"

And, what would she do should he not wish to marry her? Was he only infatuated with her? Hermina *had* thought of an alternate plan. With so many men in the city begging for her attention, she would simply feign a romantic encounter with one of them, announce a pregnancy, and the poor love-smitten creature would believe the child to be his and marry her, saving her honor. The baby's early arrival would arouse little suspicion for such things happened. This would be a devastating end to an already haphazard plan because she loved Jozsef, and even more, loved his distinguished lifestyle.

The first week of July, after a romantic outing to Margaret Island, Hermina and Jozsef went to his apartment and remained cocooned within its walls for three days. Hermina *was* enchanted by this gentle, kind man, with the brilliant smile and loving heart, and it was to her detriment that she loved him, that she was madly in love with him. Hermina had certainly not gambled on *that*. She initially had sought only title and position, but her body had made other plans separate from those of her mind, and the deceit between the two entities had forced her heart to be lost forever to Jozsef, their two souls forever bound by the new life he had seeded within her womb. She announced her pregnancy during the first week of August. Jozsef was elated upon hearing the news - why would he not be the happiest man in the world, for he had found the woman who completed him, and not only wanted her, but desired her and loved her. The evening of her announcement, as they lay tightly woven together, Jozsef's words of love whispered into his Hermina's golden strands, "You are my Sun, my beautiful Hermina, and my life will forever orbit around you!"

And today… as she wound the cloth about her abdomen, he would keep his promise.

Hermina had spent too much time daydreaming. She glanced at the clock on her bureau, "I have only a few minutes remaining to dress!" She quickly finished tightening the strips of cloth about her waist, then took one final look in the mirror to study her coiffeur, admiring the way her haphazardly placed blonde locks swept upwards into a mass of golden curls and the way her silken bangs framed her emerald green eyes. She stepped into her floor-length silk slip and then reached for the wedding gown which hung on the back of the hotel room's closet door. Hermina had chosen her wedding dress with great care, selecting a metallic lame, floral pattern, ivory lace gown with flounce sleeves and V-neck back. She gently donned the garment, noting how it clung to her every curve, and, with her expert "wrapping," she appeared slender and lovely.

Jozsef had suggested they be married in a fashionable Budapest hotel as a matter of convenience. Hermina was relieved – she had experienced several fleeting moments of remorse for her premarital affair, and, in affiance with her feeling, she chose not to wear a wedding veil, viewing the veil as a symbol of purity, and being pure, she was not. Being raised in a strict Catholic household, her unmarried pregnant condition made her conscious get the better of her. A respectable civil ceremony soothed her nerves. There would be no priest and no religious verses to remind her of "sin."

What frightened Hermina more than God, was her father. She had worried about his reaction to her announcement of wanting to marry quickly, and of all sins, not to marry within the walls of the Catholic Church! Hermina's pregnancy was a secret from the world. Her mother may have understood. But her father would *not* understand. He idolized his daughter, idolized her rapturous beauty, and idolized her untouched, untainted, uncorrupted saintly status.

Her father had raised Hermina within the strict rules of the Catholic Church and would never suspect his daughter of "committing whorish acts." Hermina felt a slight twinge of self-reproach - well, perhaps more than *just* a twinge. Her father had always been good to her. Ever since she was little, he had showered her with attention, giving in to her every whim. She did not want her father to know of her dishonored state. *It would break his heart.*

Her father was very pleased when Jozsef came to ask permission for Hermina's hand in marriage, and it did greatly facilitate matters that he and Jozsef were like-minded in the musical arena. They both played the accordion and came from musical families. Her father's imagination took hold as he fantasized about "family concerts," with Jozsef and Hermina's two brothers, who were experts in wind instruments.

After receiving her father's blessing for the marriage, Jozsef left for home with a song in his heart. He was a fortunate man. Had someone told him a year ago he would be marrying such a lovely woman, and that he would soon be a father, he would have thought them insane. He had courted many women from the finest of families, but it was Hermina who made him whole, gave him purpose, made him feel alive. But his newfound happiness was intermingled with sadness, for Jozsef regretted his parents not being able to attend the ceremony, both having lost their lives to illness in the not too distant past. How they would have adored Hermina!

The evening after Jozsef asked for her hand, Hermina's father requested his daughter to come to his study. "Daughter, Jozsef is a highly esteemed citizen of the community. I truly admire his ambition and musical intellect. I have no qualms about granting permission for your marriage. I simply want to ask you one question. Is there anything you wish to let me know that may shed light on the swiftness of these nuptials?" Hermina's mind rushed to find the correct answer… something her father would believe. *I know he is trying to see if there is a reason to worry and charge into this marriage. I cannot let him know the truth, not ever. It would break his heart to know of my transgression.*

"Papa, the only reason Jozsef and I wish to marry now is our deep love for one another, and in so doing, to keep my honor until my wedding night." *There, that sounded just right. Just letting Papa know that if we do not get married, that in a moment of passion, we may not think clearly, and I would be bedded before wedding vows could be made.*

Her father looked deeply into the lovely green pools before him. His daughter was beautiful, vivacious, and charming, looking so much like his dear wife when he first met her, and in milliseconds, his mind floated back to the moment when he first set eyes on his beloved Ilona on the dance floor of the Budapest Opera Ball.

He had despised wearing his white tie and "tails," that evening, but his father, who was to conduct the orchestra for the event, had managed to obtain a special pass for his son to attend the high-society gathering, hoping his "boy," who was nearing the age of thirty, would at long last settle down should he find a favorite among the hundreds of lovely debutantes who were to be presented that evening.

It was easy for Hermina's father to understand why the young were always in a hurry to marry. He had wanted Ilona the moment she "was presented" in her virginal white gown. He had wanted her when her long silken mane of winter wheat flowed about her shoulders, spilling their silk over full, taunt, young breasts. He had wanted her, and did take her for himself, in the secrecy of a moonlight garden. He had asked her father for her hand and had received her unto his own. And until she died, had loved her with a grateful heart. Yes, once, long ago, he was young, and now, he was old, and very much aware of how easy it would be for his daughter and her young man to do something they may regret before marriage. He had not forgotten the thunderous beats of his heart when Ilona had merely touched his hand, or how their young bodies yearned and longed to be one with each other.

Sighing, he walked to his desk, sitting down in the comfort of his soft, broken-in leather chair. Hermina settled down on the floor near his feet, resting her head on his knee, so she could "feel her father thinking."

The old musician absentmindedly stroked his daughter's hair, the same way he had done countless times since she was a little girl. His mind drifting back to the days when little Hermina would burst through his office door, plant herself at his feet, and wrap her tiny arms about his legs to plead and beg her case for a new dress or toy. The long-engrained habit of running his hand through Hermina's golden tresses when she curled at his feet had not faded.

"Papa?"

"Umm," her father lazily replied, disturbed to be brought out of his youthful memories of Ilona. How his heart ached for his departed wife. Why did Spanish influenza steal her from his side? Hermina was only four years old when her mother died. He had strived to be good to his daughter, struggling to be both mother and father, and when away on business trips he had employed the finest of governesses to care for her.

He had assured Hermina received not only the finest academic education, but training in the social graces demanded of young women to assure a smooth transition into the upper echelons of society. But Hermina's favorite time was when her father allowed her to accompany him on his many business trips and musical concert tours throughout Hungary, exposing her to the culture of Europe's most beautiful cities, and the excitement of those trips never grew old for her.

Hermina gently pressed her father's forearm, "Papa, did you hear me?"

"Of course, yes, go on my dear." Still seated on the floor, holding onto one of her father's calves, Hermina turned her head upward seeking her place within her father's dream-filled eyes, "Papa, I do love Jozsef. He is good to me and kind. He reminds me very much of you." Stroking Hermina's cheek, her father agreed, "Yes my little one, I like him. He is a good man, actually a very brilliant man."

While her father was in a receptive mood, Hermina subtly added, "And Papa, the monies saved for an elaborate church wedding could be used perhaps toward a splendid party at the hotel after the wedding ceremony?"

Her father kissed the top of her head, his lips savoring the feel of the pale, glossy threads, "Yes, yes, my dear, it shall be as you wish."

He suddenly felt very tired. "Go on to bed now. We have much to do in a brief time. We are having a wedding!" Hermina stood up and hugged her father. She kissed his cheek, and with an excited "Oh thank you Papa!" rushed off to her bedroom to dream of her wedding day.

With moist eyes of happiness, an overwhelming surge of sudden weary nostalgia struck the old musician. He pulled his worn leather chair closer in toward his desk. He slowly removed his glasses, leaning his elbows onto the large walnut workspace. Holding his head of gray in aged hands, he exclaimed to the heavens above, "I am getting old and my daughter is to marry. Time and years have escaped me. How I will miss my precious girl! Oh, Ilona, I wish you were here!" He slumped his head down upon his forearm, his deep sobs muffled in the folds of his shirtsleeves.

A radiant Hermina, escorted by her father, made her way down the hotel's winding staircase, the elegant wedding room of the hotel draped in golden candlelight. More than one hundred admiring family, friends and guests had their eyes fixed on Hermina as she made her magnificent entrance. Hermina smiled in triumph as her sparkling eyes shone down upon Jozsef, who stood waiting for her at the bottom of the steps with the wedding officiate. Jozsef's heart flared with ravenous love and passion as he beheld the fairy angel who was to become his wife as she floated toward him in her gossamer gown. *My most precious treasure, my Hermina, my love, come to me!*

In their first weeks together, the attention and pleasures Jozsef lavished on Hermina fulfilled her every whim and need. He spoiled her, and in return, she spoiled him. Hermina found herself eagerly awaiting Jozsef's return home from his business outings for he never failed to show her how very much he had missed her.

And as the months of their marriage progressed, Hermina found their marriage to be fulfilling and exciting in ways she had not imagined. Jozsef gave his wife free rein to decorate their downtown Budapest apartment, which she did with fine taste and choice and provided her with a full purse to access the finest shops in town. Hermina had at last achieved her goal of marrying into the most prominent circles of Budapest society, enjoying every minute of her title, enjoying every moment in the sun, as *the wife* of one of Budapest's greatest music professors.

During the day, their large, seven-room apartment was full of activity with people coming and going with their offspring for tutoring, concert producers inquiring if Jozsef would care to use their facilities for a performance, and musical instrument salespersons bringing their instruments for Jozsef to inspect for possible purchase. And Hermina had her own entourage – the dressmakers.

Hermina was determined to keep her figure slim for as long as possible, employing the services of the city's most accomplished seamstresses to design dresses to bring out her best assets "during this inconvenient time," for how could she attend all the parties she was invited to as "Mrs. Music Professor" looking alluringly sensuous being pudgy with child? Therefore, Hermina continued flattening the rounding girth of her abdomen with homemade strips of wide, cotton cloth. When her husband questioned if the baby would be all right by her doing this, she nonchalantly replied, "Of course, all fashionable women do this until at least the sixth or seventh month of their pregnancy before they go into confinement." Jozsef, knowing little of the things woman did privately for themselves, believed her.

Thus, Hermina continued "binding herself" until her seventh month of pregnancy when it was useless to continue, for the growing child within her defied the confines of its bondage. *Why with all this binding did I not cause this child to miscarry?* The thought had crossed her mind every single day since her marriage. How stupid she was to put herself in this condition. *Had I held out, played hard to get, Jozsef would have most likely married me anyway. I should not have captured him in this manner. Had I waited till my wedding night to join with him I would have found a way to prevent a pregnancy!*

Hermina cursed the new life within her, determined to find ways to never again become pregnant without locking her bedroom door. Jozsef loved her; however, she knew he would not keep a marriage without intimacy, having legitimate grounds for divorce under those conditions, and, she *did* look forward to their tender times together. But there would be no more babies.

Jozsef Frank Bognar was born on March 21, 1934. It was just "one of those things," when their child was born early. Hermina had experienced a long labor. For fourteen hours the unrelenting, searing pains came and went, as Jozsef, along with several other prospective fathers, walked the waiting room floor of the hospital. When at last, the child came into the world, Hermina let out a conglomeration of curses rarely known to womanhood as the baby expelled itself from her body. Finally - it was over.

Jozsef's eyes beheld a beautiful baby boy with a mass of curly blonde hair and forest-green eyes. When the midwife placed Jozsef's newborn son into his arms, he happily exclaimed to Hermina, "He is a divine creation of our love! Thank you, my sweet, precious wife, for giving me a son. I love you with all my heart!" Hermina exhausted from her ordeal, gazed through half-lidded eyes upon her husband, barely glancing at the pink bundle in his arms, replying with what little strength remaining within her before falling into a deep sleep, "I am glad you are happy, as I did this only for you." Jozsef sat by his wife's bed holding their infant son, his heart filled with joyous gratitude to his wife, and instantaneous, unconditional love for his little son.

Little baby Jozsef, by the Grace of God, had been born physically perfect, untouched by the cruel bindings placed upon his innocent developing body (and the spiteful curses of a selfish mother).

Life now went on for the three. Jozsef continued to teach musical lessons in his apartment, in his student's homes, as well as performing his concerts.

Hermina continued her role as "queen of the musical social set," entertaining the privileged few of Hungarian society's affluent musical circles at home, about town, and mingling with the same at Jozsef's performances.

Hermina Bognar was impeccably dressed at all social functions, where she flirted graciously, where she was envied by women and admired by men, and whereby evening's end, she was always on Jozsef's arm giving him admiring kisses on the cheek as she waved goodbye to his devotees.

Little Jozsef never wanted for entertainment. Streams of students drifted in and out of his home every day, each bringing their own contribution of musical sounds and songs: the heavenly strains of the violin, the up-beat pitch of the clarinet, and the lilting, mellow tones of the accordion, the vibrations of all seeping into his very essence becoming one with his soul. Each day, the child was lost in a spectacular world of exploration as he touched, tasted, and toted about the diverse collection of musical instruments strewn about the apartment. And, when it was time for his little boy's bedtime, Professor Bognar, played his accordion, "rocking" his son to sleep with the lullabies of *Beethoven* and *Liszt*.

In his tortured, bound womb, music soothed and calmed the baby boy, and now, after birth, music cradled and comforted him in its loving embrace.

Little Jozsef needed all the warm love music could give, for he knew little of the loving hugs and kisses that mothers give their children.

It was a very rare instance for Hermina to kiss her little boy goodnight or hold him lovingly to her breast. The vain and selfish Hermina led an idealistic life.

Hermina was an exulted player in her high-society world. She was a dutiful and admiring wife to her husband, hanging on his arm while breathing pleasing small talk to his clients during their many soirées, and in the bedroom, she gave him no reason to want for more. Her efforts reaped the rewards she longed and yearned for, but the baby, well… the baby was just in her way.

Often, Hermina would think, "How nice my world would be if there was no baby to be concerned about!" Hermina wanted to have fun, to see the sights, and to be seen, but not with a child in tow!

To all those who knew her, appearances indicated Hermina was a caring and devoted mother. She performed the daily "chores" all mothers did for their children; however, her husband *did* notice his wife's diminished expression of affection for her child.

He did not understand why Hermina displayed such coolness toward her little boy. He surmised she was doing all she was "supposed to do." He knew Hermina had much love to give, for she had proved this to him countless times. *Perhaps, she feels this is just the way a mother should be with her child*, presuming her lack of demonstrable affection as trying to "raise the child with a loving, but firm hand."

He once observed his son crawling onto his mother's lap. Hermina firmly chided the child, saying "Little boys do not sit on lady's knees." Therefore, Professor Bognar resigned to make up where Hermina had left off. He indulged his little boy's whims and enjoyed every minute of being a doting father.

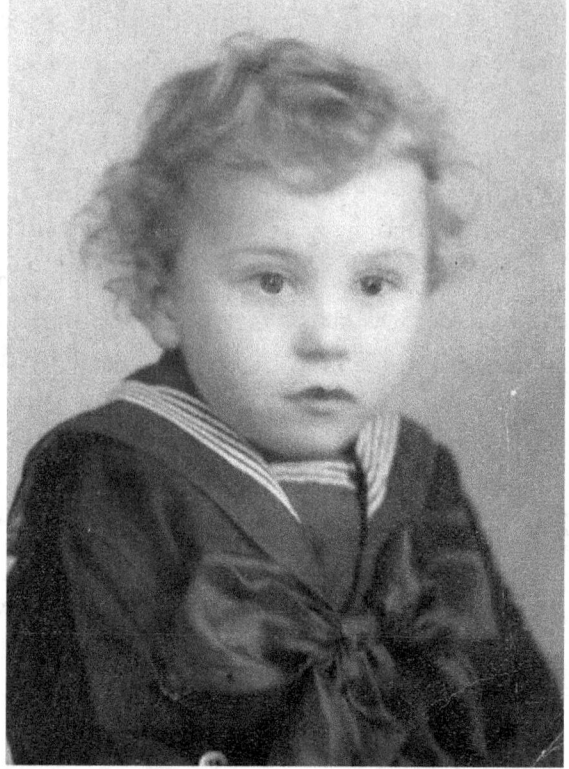

Little Jozsef - Age two

Unbeknownst to Hermina, while her baby boy had budded within the warmth of her womb, she had rendered upon him the only decent gift she would ever bequeath him – the music of life. All the symphonies, all the concerts, and all the musical arrangements drifting outside the confines of her baby's closed-off world had intoxicated the embryonic, sprouting neurons of her child's blossoming brain, each cell hungrily devouring the acoustical, melodious magic within every atom to its core, oscillating their enthralling frequencies into the nucleus of the child's spirit.

And then, at age three, her son's brain burst forth with the miraculous benefaction blindly granted him by his mother: the moment his arms gathered up a small, child-sized accordion.

His slight frame struggled with the weight of the bellowed instrument, as his stubby fingers clumsily, but then determinedly, moved smoothly along the accordion's ivory keys, plucking out make-believe tunes, and out of the making believe, something wonderfully real happened - Professor Bognar's ears beheld a splendid rendition of the first few stanzas of the musician's favorite melody – the *Blue Danube Waltz*.

Little Jozsef, whose innocent essence had been nurtured within the magnificent strains of the world's finest music since conception, had *become one with the music* – born with "Absolute or Perfect Pitch," the rare ability to produce a note in the absence of a reference note, the little boy was able to name and reproduce musical notes rapidly and effortlessly, on his own, without the benefit of even one music lesson.

YOUNG JOZSEF

Professor Bognar was ill. There was no official explanation given to little Jozsef regarding his father's sickness other than being told his father "did not feel well."

Little Jozsef was only seven years old that year of 1941, but he, too, along with thousands of Hungarians in his country, would soon come to suffer the same affliction affecting his father – an affliction named "fear," a foreboding fear of something monstrous and hideous spreading over Hungary, a dispiriting fear of something dreadful and beastly entering their lives that was beyond anyone's control.

Many evenings Little Jozsef was put to bed early. From his bedroom off the parlor he heard the voices of his parents and close acquaintances. He listened as the voices spoke about "Something terrible in the country." There was talk of war - something about Hungary, Germans, Russians, and Jews. The name "Hitler" was spoken of frequently. After each of these evening "talks," Little Jozsef noticed his father was always a bit "sicker."

The summer of 1941 had been one of disbelief for the Hungarian people, including Professor Bognar and his family. The majority of the family's musician friends and elite social circle were of Jewish descent. Hungary's Jewish population numbered well over eight hundred thousand, but now their population was rapidly dwindling. The professor *was* more than "sick." He was also disgusted, overwrought and appalled, for the world he had been educated for, had worked for, had planned for, was dissolving before his eyes. Hungary was "disappearing," and the everyday person was powerless to prevent their world from melting away - many of Professor Bognar's Jewish associates had been deported to German-occupied Ukraine, where it was said they had been executed by Nazi mobile killing units.

And out of all this demented chaos came financial struggle, for most of the professor's clients were Jewish. At first, the professor did not understand why his students had stopped showing up for lessons. He tried to contact them via post to inquire why their weekly lessons had stopped but had received no reply. Out of curiosity and worry, he visited their homes, only to be told by neighbors, "They no longer lived there," or, "Some men took them away in a truck," or, "They just disappeared overnight."

Hungary was slowly becoming entangled in World War II.

Mr. Bognar remembered learning about the Treaty of Trianon, created in 1920, to formally end World War I. The treaty allowed the territories of Hungary to be broken up, and in doing so, created new borders, causing the ethnicity of his nation to be cut into pieces. Because of the treaty, only about two-thirds of Hungarians remained within the original borders of Hungary. The others ended up living within the borders of Romania, Czechoslovakia, or Yugoslavia. It was easy to understand why the Hungarian people were in distress, for their country was being expurgated into extinction. The Professor had every right to be worried, for there was talk of the country to be further divided, to be absorbed into the belly of the other nations around them.

Many nights the Professor lay in bed with a queasy stomach and disquieting thoughts about his country's fate. *What will happen to our country, to us?* He urged Hermina to consider leaving Hungary "before the craziness knocked at their door," but she refused, feeling all would be set right, somehow, and so he stayed in Hungary, refusing to leave without her.

But, Jozsef's father had no idea how anything in the country could be normal again, not to mention their personal monetary crisis. There was little money to be made now-a-days from concerts or from teaching music, for most of the family's clients and friends had been taken away by Nazi forces to a place called "Auschwitz," and those who were taken there were never heard from again. The country was in a turmoil. Back in November of 1940, Pal Teleki, a staunch supporter of the Treaty of Trianon of 1920, was hoping to use Germany's strength to regain lands taken from Hungary due to the treaty. Teleki had backed Hitler when he had torn apart Czechoslovakia and Romania through pressured coercion and the giving up of territory in northern Transylvania. By 1940 Teleki had contracted a "Treaty of Eternal Friendship" with Yugoslavia. Not long after, a Yugoslavian revolt threatened Hitler's plan of invading the Soviet Union, during a campaign called "Operation Barbarossa." Hitler wanted the Hungarian people to support the Yugoslavian attack, and if they did so, promised the Hungarians he would return portions of Hungary's lands lost after the First World War.

And so, many nights as Little Jozsef slept, his father, mother and close friends gathered in the parlor of their apartment talking about how those in charge of Hungary's government wanted to overturn the Trianon treaty *even if they had to side with the Germans*, while attempting *not* to join forces with Germany in the war.

Little Jozsef was just a child, but an audacious, precocious child, whose gifted mind understood more about "the world" and "the sickness" than his parents could possibly perceive. Determined to help his father retrieve his lost income, little Jozsef launched his own perfect plan.

One evening before bedtime, little Jozsef asked his father to allow him to play his accordion in the many nightclubs and bars around town to supplement the family's finances. His father's heart immediately flinched at the very notion as his weathered hand rhythmically stroked the curly locks of his little boy's blonde hair, "You are but a child and should not even be seen in such places!" But his son was insistent, "I want to Papa. I really want to very much. I could just sit there and play my music all day and all night. I love my accordion!"

Truth be told, playing in smoky clubs was far better than staying home in the boring care of his mother, as she tended, most times, to leave Little Jozsef alone to seek his own amusements, preferring to entertain herself in a routine of daily frivolous pursuits; therefore, Little Jozsef found comfort in the arms of his dearly loved instrument - it was his best friend. He had only a few companions, mostly cousins, with whom his mother rarely allowed him to play, for the children loved tramping in muddy fields and soiling their clothes as boys usually do.

The last time Little Jozsef spent the day with his playmates he had come home with his best shoes encased in dried mud, forcing Hermina to scrub them clean, a task she considered too demeaning for a woman of her station. Once was enough. She would not muddy her hands with such things again.

Therefore, her son abandoned the adventures of the outdoors, and sought love and comfort within the bellows of his best friend.

While the Professor had trimmed his spending by foregoing his usual tobacco, shoe-shine, and weekly drinks with his friends, Hermina, willingly or unwillingly, spent freely, seeming oblivious to the state of their financial situation. Professor Bognar loved Hermina with all his heart and soul, but at times her denial of their monetary plight reluctantly grazed at his heart.

But Hermina's way of thinking was not all that difficult to discern. Since she had been a child living with her father, and now a married woman living with her husband, she had become accustomed to her elevated station, and was determined to keep living in the manner and style for which she had been groomed, even if it meant her little boy playing in bars and clubs.

Professor Bognar, and the many patrons of the town's bars, were good men caught up in the bad economic times of 1941, and it was for this reason that Little Jozsef's father decided to reconsider his son's heartfelt offer. *What joy my son could bring to those downtrodden souls seeking solace from the world in their sudsy brew.*

"Please Papa, say I can play in the clubs!" implored the young boy once more as he tugged his father's sleeve. What could the Professor say? His son was a miracle. The child was far more brilliant-minded than he ever was at his age, already surpassing and outshining him during their Sunday accordion duets. With both a proud and grievous heart, Mr. Bognar placed a hand on his son's slender shoulder, "You may go. Play to your heart's content, but your last song will be for me, always, *The Blue Danube*." Overjoyed, Little Jozsef hugged his father, and then ran off to his room to "practice."

No… the Professor, did not want his son to perform in those clubs, but the child had wanted to help him, and truthfully, he *needed* the help. He assured himself he had done the right thing. "It will make my son happy, and his happiness will give us a temporary reprieve until I can figure another way out of our situation."

And so, this is how Little Jozsef became planted on a chair amongst the odor of cigarette smoke and alcohol.

Sitting on his perch with closed eyes, his angelic face shone bright as his small, stubby fingers raced over his instrument's keys with incredible exactitude, dancing over the black and ivory boards with the precision of a person ten years his senior.

His accordion nearly equaled him in size, but his seven-year-old frame supported the bulk of the instrument with surprising ease.

His father accompanied his son to every performance, where the sweetness of his son's innocent offering, blended with the finesse of the boy's musical repertoire, brought tears to the music master's eyes and a deep ache within his paternal heart.

"Mama, why do you not hug and kiss me like Papa does?" Little Jozsef inquired one morning when the two were alone at breakfast. Hermina, busy with her pan of eggs, turned her head over her shoulder, "I hug and kiss you every night when you are sleeping so you will not become spoiled." Jozsef thought carefully about his mother's statement. *No .... Mama does not hug and kiss me at night in my bed. Often, when I cannot sleep, Mama has not come to check on me. She has not come to my room at night.*

Hermina *was* his mother. She should have been nurturing and attentive to her delicate child, taking love and pride in his brilliance, bragging on him to her friends; however, she remained distant and aloof, for her thoughts flowed only for her own selfish needs, with little consideration for the needs of her small boy.

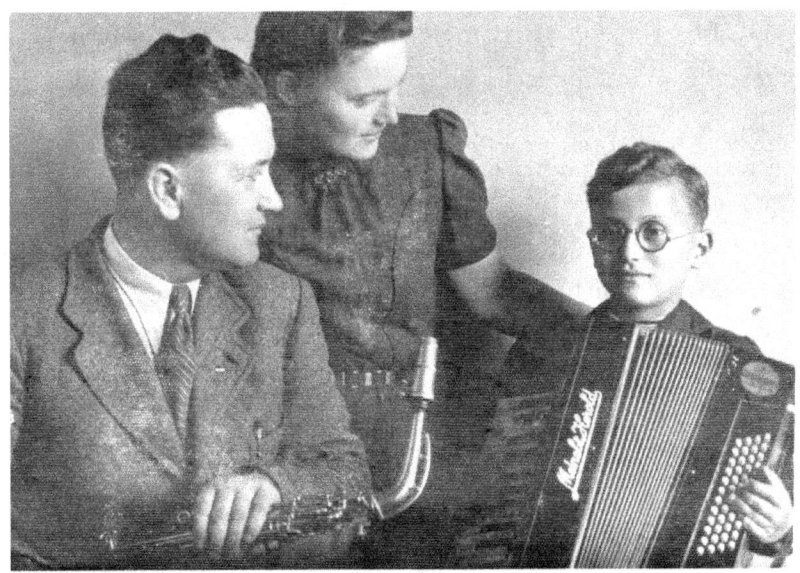

Little Jozsef, age eight, with his accordion, father and mother (circa mid-1940's)

Word of the ingenious child accordion player slowly spread throughout the city, enabling Little Jozsef to leave the wretched, dark ambiance of bars and nightclubs, thrusting him into the limelight. Despite the war, there were still good places in the city to go for entertainment if one had the financial means. It was in those grandly lit halls where Little Jozsef played his songs for the upper gentry, and for the country's vile occupiers.

That year, Little Jozsef visited Debrecen to spend time with his much-loved maternal grandfather. The sights and sounds of the city were enchanting. His grandfather adored the child and spoiled him. The boy's inquisitive nature mirrored his own and he allowed the boy to explore the city to his heart's content.

Debrecen was the marvelous and magnificent cultural hub and social center in Hungary, flowing with museums, churches, and the famous Reformed College, where rare books were housed and protected, and collections of fine embroidery and goldsmith craftwork displayed.

The exposure to the culture and music of the great city were golden days for Little Jozsef. The concerts he attended motivated him to scrutinize and analyze his own musical style, and even at such an early age, inspired him to strive for perfection. It was during this time when Little Jozsef decided to become a famous musician.

Upon returning home from Debrecen, Little Jozsef once again settled into his routine at the nightclubs. Most days were difficult and trying, for he still attended the local school, and had to awaken early. Nonetheless, he saw how his efforts were improving the quality of life for the family and noticed his father was not as "sick" as he used to be.

As per his word, Little Jozsef's father remained with his son during every performance. And, at the end of the evening, after the final notes of the *Blue Danube* drifted away, his father gave the little boy strong hugs and kisses, "I love you my Little Jozsef. You were perfect! Let us go home now, it is time for bed."

Some say there is a reason for the decisions we make, for those decisions lead us towards the things that will shape our lives. Though he was very young, Little Jozsef sensed an invisible force directing him towards an unseen place and an unseen goal, but where the force was to lead him, and what he was to accomplish once there, remained a mystery.

ERZSEBET

Erzsebet Halasz awoke to the happy chirping of a bluebird outside her bedroom window. Roosters crowed their announcement of the dawn. Narrow shafts of sunlight streamed in through threadbare, white cotton curtains illuminating the room with a soft, yellow glow. The coolness of the early morning air would soon give way to advancing warm spring breezes on this late day in May in the year 1938.

Little Erzsebet - age three

Erzsebet stretched out lazily in her small, slim bed, running both hands along the sides of her fine, chin-length, ebony hair, her dark bangs skimming the tops of her dark brows - a stark contrast to her skin of pale ivory and eyes of hazel.

The bedroom barely had space to hold her bed and dresser. The sheets were worn, but clean. Her quilted bedcovers were filled with goose feathers.

Flocks of geese had made the surrounding farmyard their home, allowing Erzsebet's mother to take advantage of their profitable leavings. Each week Erzsebet and her siblings gathered the snowy-white, downy plumes which Erzsebet's mother sewed into fine quilts, selling them to the city dwellers for extra income.

Soon everyone in the household would awaken to the aroma of home-made smoked ham and freshly gathered eggs. Erzsebet looked forward to her mother's breakfast creation containing sautéed bits of onion mixed with scrambled eggs and chunks of ham, with generous amounts of paprika sprinkled over the finished concoction to be eaten with fresh-baked bread and milk.

With thoughts of food aside, Erzsebet lay with both arms crossed behind her head enjoying the solitude of early morning, her young mind wandering back over the past two days when she had visited the farm of her grandfather, Gyorgy Halasz - her favorite place in the entire world. It was not a large piece of farmland but had enough acreage to produce a respectable sum of grapes used in Hungary's wine industry, and many livestock and poultry.

Every weekend she eagerly volunteered to help her grandfather with the animals and vineyard. The farmyard filled Erzsebet's senses with a myriad of sights, smells, and sounds: the sweet smell of fresh hay as the livestock stalls were cleaned and bedded, chickens cackling happily as they nipped the crisp dried corn at their feet, the mooing of cows begging to have their full udders milked, and the snorting of pigs greedily eating from their troughs. The farm produced a better than average living for her grandfather, and when times were lean, she knew her grandfather would always be there to supply her family with whatever was needed.

During Erzsebet's past visit she had tried to put water in the troughs for the animals. She struggled with the buckets of water, one in each hand, the thin metal handles digging crevices into the tender flesh of her hands, with more water sloshing out of the containers than was being kept in. Her *Nagypapa* (grandfather) Gyorgy observed her tiny, three-year-old frame buckling from the weight of her cargo. He quickly ran to aid her, taking the weighted pails from her, cradling her small pale hands within his, gingerly rubbing the reddened skin to relieve the pinched indentations in her palms.

"My little *Draga*, you work too hard!" Her grandfather held his granddaughter to his chest allowing Erzsebet to inhale the familiar scents of her Nagypapa: pipe tobacco, Barack brandy and worn leather. She buried her silky, black locks deep beneath the folds of her grandfather's somber-brown leather vest, clinging close to him as he embraced her, all the while listening to him whisper loving endearments into her little ears, to which she replied, "I love you too Nagypapa."

Her grandfather had "won" the farm in a card game at the age of thirty. Nagypapa Halasz had a few "vices," mainly his apricot liquor and gambling. One fateful night he was playing cards in a bar with an elderly, overzealous land owner, who had run out of money during the game. Young Halasz could hardly believe his ears when the wealthy property holder (who in an inebriated state) bet the deed to his property in lieu of cash.

It was one incredible moment of being in the right place at the right time. When the night was finished Halasz was hailed as the proud owner of a beautiful farm and grape orchard. There were too many witnesses to dispute the fact, and a bet was a bet, and a gentleman's promise, a promise - the defeated one honorably gave up what he had nonchalantly wagered away, and the victor was determined not to squander the gift he had miraculously achieved.

In his golden years Nagypapa Halasz had become more mellow and sentimental. Time had passed swiftly since the night he had won the farm. How he wished his lovely Ava could be here at this very moment. How proud she would have been of her little granddaughter.

Holding the child's hand, he led her between the rows of grape vines, "Did I ever tell you? It was at a grape harvesting festival where I met your grandmother! She was the prettiest girl I had ever seen. I saw her dancing with the young men to a lively *Czárdás*. She must have been wearing at least twenty petticoats under her dress, all different colors. When she swirled about to the rhythm of the music she looked like a butterfly in flight. I will always remember her pretty feet, how easily they moved to all the complicated dance steps! I remember … yes …the shoes were red, and, she had on blue stockings. I tell you, she looked like a butterfly! You have her hair - the beautiful ebony hair, and oh … her eyes – yes …you also have the shape of her lovely eyes." His rough, calloused hand stroked the little girl's hair slowly, as he remembered his wife's image of long ago. "She died not too long before you were born. She was very beautiful and full of life."

Her grandfather pointed to the neat rows of grape arbors, "Your grandmother worked hard to help me create all you see here, toiling in the grape fields, tenderly watering each little plant, helping me keep them warm during cool nights, even if it meant going without sleep. She never complained. She loved me, and she loved the land. But … I loved her more than life, more than the land… more than anything in the world. One morning she did not wake up. She was lying in her bed looking as lovely as the "Snow White princess" lying in her glass coffin. I tried all I could to revive her, but it was too late. I have no idea what she died from. I do not understand why the angels took her away from me at such a youthful age. I miss her every day. I am eternally grateful to her for giving me, my son, your father, *Gyorgy*. He is a lot like her - hard working and never complaining. Your father and I miss her all the time. I know she looks down upon you from Heaven and loves you as I love you."

Nagypapa Halasz squatted down, face level with his little granddaughter, "One day, when God feels it is the right time, he will take me to be with your grandmother. Then your Mama and Papa will inherit this fertile land. One day, when you marry, you may want to live here and be the hostess of your own wine festivals!" Erzsebet's eyes sparkled as her mind wove the future scene.

Her Nagypapa dreamt on, "My little one, I can envision you wearing an embroidered cap and a dress with many colorful petticoats as you dance the *Czárdás*. Can you not hear the gypsy bands playing the violins and the melody of the cimbalom? The clicking of the wine glasses filled with *Palinka*?" Letting out a chuckle, her Nagypapa held Erzsebet's tiny hand, "But my little one - do not be in too much of a hurry to grow up!" Erzsebet felt herself caught up into her Nagypapa's arms as he embraced her minute frame. With glistening eyes, he exclaimed, "I promise my *Edes* one, I promise to be here with you as long as I can! It is now time for us to eat!"

Erzsebet had two sisters and two brothers. Her mother, Erzsebet Szabo Halasz loved her children dearly, but none were planned, and life on the farm was hard. She had too many children to care for and too much work to do. Each evening as the veil of night settled in, overwhelming exhaustion left little sentimental emotion to offer her children. She felt guilty about not doing more for them, for she truly wanted to. Each evening as she lay her exhausted body down in bed, she promised, "Tomorrow, I will have more time to spend with my little ones." Days passed into weeks, weeks into months, and months into years, but there was never any more time.

Erzsebet Szabo was nineteen years old when she married Gyorgy Halasz, age twenty. The small farm upon which they lived was a section of land Grandfather Halasz had deeded them as a wedding gift. The young couple, determined to build a life for themselves out of the fertile ground, were immensely grateful for the land, resolute to build a successful farm of their own. It was a hard living filled with long days and short nights. Morning always came too soon. Life was demanding and difficult, but they loved one another and overcame each obstacle.

Erzsebet Szabo Halasz – my maternal grandmother

Erzsebet's father was kind, humorous, and affectionate. He loved his wife and adored his children. He was overly doting with his little ones, unconsciously making up for their mother's unintentional lack of affection.

Every summer day he faced the drudgery and sweat-filled conditions of working his farm, and each winter, he endured the freezing temperatures doing maintenance work about the property. Whatever the season, at the end of each day's work, as the sun shown its last amber rays on the horizon, he would appear in the doorway of his home with a smile for his family and hugs for all who dared to push past his dirt, grime and sweat. Erzsebet, being the smallest, was always able to manipulate herself between her siblings to plant a quick kiss on her father's cheek, and to make sure it was she who placed his bowl and mug on the kitchen table for the evening meal.

Gyorgy Halasz – my maternal grandfather

A typical dinner meal on the farm consisted of reliable themes: a pork dish, a chicken dish, rice or potatoes, seasonable vegetables, homemade breads and pies, and of course, the basic staple of every Hungarian household, goulash, consisting of chunks of beef sautéed with onions and lard, then mixed in with sweet paprika, bay leaves, potatoes and peppers, carefully stewed for two hours, and then served over dumplings.

On January eleventh of 1940, Erzsebet celebrated her fifth birthday. Her favorite gift from her Nagypapa was a beautifully illustrated book about little people, witches, and a lovely lost girl, trying to find her way home: "The Wizard of Oz."

That very spring, the movie was coming to the theatre! As a late birthday gift, her dear Nagypapa had given her the admission money to gain entrance to the "Magical Land of Oz."

Erzsebet's friend Kati came from a very well-to-do family. Kati told Erzsebet the film was only in town for a one-day showing on a Thursday. Kati wanted Erzsebet to see the movie with her and asked Erzsebet to meet her and her family at the front of the theatre an hour before the movie was to start as a large crowd was expected.

The day of the movie finally arrived. Erzsebet's heart skipped happily for she knew at two o'clock that afternoon she would be in a mystical place far beyond her dreams.

The only way to get to the theatre was to walk. Erzsebet put on her Sunday-best dress and reached into her closet for her black shoes. Despite the shoes being her "good pair" the soles were worn and slippery. She had to be careful not to fall, as the dilapidated soles slid much too easily across the floor. But where were her shoes? She looked under her bed and in the corners of her small room, but no shoes! She checked all about the small house, but they were not to be found. She cried hysterically for all the searching was causing her to fall behind schedule, and she had a one-mile walk to the theatre! She asked her mother if she had seen her black shoes. Her mother looked anxious. It *was* supposed to be a surprise, but now she had to tell Erzsebet about the shoes. "My sweet one, your father took your shoes to be re-soled. The soles were very shoddy, and he was worried about your walking in them. He had to wait until today to pick them up, because he had not been paid until late last evening for a carpentry job he had performed for extra money. The man was supposed to have paid him the day before, and your father could not bring the shoes home from the shoemaker without paying him first."

Her parents had done this with the best of intentions and love for their child, and now, even Erzsebet's mother's nerves were getting the best of her. Would her husband arrive home too late for Erzsebet to get to the movie in time? "Don't worry my little one," her mother said, as she anxiously looked out the kitchen window toward the road. "Your father will be home soon, I am sure." It was 1:15 in the afternoon.

The door abruptly burst open and her out-of-breath father raced to give Erzsebet a brown paper parcel holding her shoes. He quickly sat his daughter down on a chair and slid her feet into the shiny black flats with new soles. Gyorgy gave his wife an intensely worried look – he had a strange, uneasy cloudiness in his eyes that confused her; however, he quickly refocused on the task at hand. Urging his daughter on, he shouted, "You can make it my tiny one! Now run - run as fast as you can!"

With a quick, "Thank you, Papa!" Erzsebet bolted out of the house as fast as her little feet and legs could carry her. She had to stop to catch her breath several times, her sides ached, and sweat dripped from her forehead. *Why did Kati's parents not offer to come pick her up, they had more money than her family did, and they had a car! They could have drove her to the theatre? Why could her grandfather not have given her father the money for the shoes and let her father pay him back, so the shoes could have been picked up sooner?*

But it was too late to ponder those thoughts. Upon recovering her breath, she once again scrambled toward the movie house. There was no one in line! Maybe the crowd was not as huge as expected? Where was Kati? Why had they not waited for her? Maybe they were already seated inside? She hastily pushed open the theatre door and approached the cashier to purchase her ticket. "I am sorry," said the kind-faced, older woman, "All the seats are sold." Erzsebet felt as though she would faint. After all her struggle to make it this far, she was too late! Her heart nearly exploded in her chest, "Please!" she pleaded, trying to catch her breath, "There has to be room for me! Please make room! I am little. I will not take up any space at all … I will stand in the back of the theatre!" Tears welled in her eyes spilling over swollen banks onto her flushed cheeks.

The viewing room door suddenly sprang open as a woman usher came through to the front lobby.

Erzsebet stared at the door. She only had a split second to decide if she could run inside to hide in a corner to watch the movie. In a flash, she raced toward the closing door, and for one, brief, splendid moment, her color-starved eyes beheld a flash of beautiful iridescence– an image of a radiant Dorothy standing on a glowing yellow road. Oh, how pretty she was - far prettier than she could have ever imagined! Voices were telling Dorothy, "Follow the yellow brick road!" Those were the last sights and sounds Erzsebet heard before the door was slammed shut in her face by the disheveled woman usher.

Why would they not let her in? She could sit on the floor! Why could they not have compassion for a little girl? Erzsebet's tear-stung eyes stabbed into the icy depths of the slanted gray ones of the slovenly woman barring the theatre door. With a venomous roar, Erzsebet's little voice thundered at the iron guard, "You are a heartless witch just like the storybook says!"

Erzsebet's little shoulders slumped with grief as she walked home. Her nose was dripping from all her crying and she wiped the moisture on the sleeve of her dress. She was heartbroken. Of all days for her mother to worry about her shoes!

Shoes! The book said Dorothy had magical shoes that could transport her to any place she wished. Why could her new shoes not transport her to the front row of the theatre? *Oh Papa! Of all times to worry about my shoes!* She then thought of her father working an extra job to surprise her, and her young heart softened, but no matter, her dreams of escaping to that fairytale world were shattered. The "wicked witch" had banned little Erzsebet from the Land of Oz, forever condemning her to exist in a bleak, gray world, devoid of glorious color and mystical beauty.

Once home, Erzsebet cried herself out in her mother's arms. "Oh Mama, they could have let me in, but the mean woman did not care!" What could her mother say? There were so many more important things to think about. How could she tell her daughter the world was "going crazy?"

After Erzsebet had made her "run" to the theatre, Gyorgy told his wife the reason he was late in bringing the shoes home. He had met a friend at the shoe shop who had informed him, that little by little, all those of Jewish descent were being "collected." Kati and her family had never made it to the theatre. They had been taken far away, to place too ominous to think or speak about, never to return.

Erzsebet, a brokenhearted little girl, distressed over missing a movie, could not possible envision the evil forces cascading over her homeland. How could she possibly understand the approach of the voluminous, dark clouds of World War II enveloping Hungary.

Hungary belonged to the Axis powers consisting of Germany, Italy, Romania, and Bulgaria, fighting against the United States and its allies. Hitler, Germany's leader insisted the country of Hungary go with Germany's program of anti-Semitism against the Jews and for Hungarian men to join German's military to avoid future retaliation; therefore, Hungarian authorities assisted Nazi Germany in transporting thousands of Jewish people to multitudes of concentration camps to meet their deadly fate. In April of 1941, Hungary, along with Italy and Germany attacked Yugoslavia. In return, Hungary was given back the (Bácska) region, containing a large Hungarian population. An attempt to invade Croatia failed when Nazi Germany aligned with Romania against the Soviet Union. Hungarian officials urged participation in invading the Soviet Union in June of 1941.

It was not necessarily at Hitler's insistence for them to do this, but they hoped by doing so, Hitler would not favor Romania in the realignment of Transylvania's borders.

With its allies, Hungary declared war on the Soviet Union. Hungary was still afraid Germany would turn its support to Romania; therefore, to show good faith to Germany, Hungary sent armies to help the Germans during "Operation Barbarossa." This was a fatal error for Hungary, for in 1943 - almost all of Hungary's Second Army was killed in the Battle of Stalingrad.

Hungary realized her horrific error in siding with the Germans, and by 1944, was secretly attempting to switch over to the American and British sides. In return, Nazi Germany took its fury out on Hungary by invading the country in March of 1944. They ousted Prime Minister Miklos Kallay and replaced him with a devout follower of the Nazi German agenda, Dome Sztojay, assisted by Nazi Germany's Edmund Veesenmayer.

Realizing the devastating blow to their country by these political changes, the Hungarians again tried to become allies with the United States and Britain; and the Germans again retaliated by replacing Hungarian leader Horthy with another Hungarian, Ferenc Szalasi, a staunch Arrow Cross party supporter.

Under Szalasi's command, the Arrow Cross party's numbers grew and rained its horrors across Hungary. Their main target was the Jewish peoples, but anyone who got in their way, or showed defiance was killed. Their victim's bullet-riddled bodies lined the shores of the Danube River whose waters turned red with the blood of the innocent. Others were raped, maimed, or forced to walk on foot to death camps. The fortunate ones would die on the way, for they would not have to face the starvation, horrific medical experiments and torture awaiting them at those camps.

The ghastly and gruesome "Final Solution" decree was executed by Adolph Eichmann. All Jewish people were forced to sew a yellow "Star of David" on their clothing, visible to all. All Jewish activities were spied upon, their telephones and radios taken from them, including their businesses and any properties. Between May of 1944 and July of 1944, over four hundred thousand Hungarian Jews were taken away, most of them to Auschwitz. Upon arrival to the holding camps, husbands and wives, mothers and fathers, brothers and sisters were separated, stripped of their clothing, and sent naked to die in gas chambers. Others were sent to factories as forced slave labor to build machinery for the Nazi cause.

When the captives became too exhausted to carry on in the factories, they were immediately exterminated, and another unfortunate soul was sent in his or her place to work in the Nazi industrial plants.

In the years following the fateful day of the "movie tragedy," Erzsebet's young heart would come to experience the agonizing despair and heart-wrenching pain of an entire nation. There was nothing she or anyone could do to change the fate of her family, her people, or her country. Gloomy, futile circumstances were on the horizon. Malevolent forces were at work, ugly things that would forever alter not only Erzsebet's world, but the entire world of the *Magyar* people.

WINDS OF WAR

Erzsebet and Jozsef
The 1940's

In January of 1933, children such as Jozsef and Erzsebet were just figments of imagination, drifting souls waiting to be born. Unbeknownst to Jozsef's and Erzsebet's parents, their own fate, the fate of their unborn children, and the fate of Hungary along with other European nations, would rest in the hands and mind of a maniacal monster - Adolf Hitler.

Hitler, a lance corporal in the Bavarian Army in 1919, was discouraged by Germany's downfall in World War I, which had left the country fiscally defeated and legislatively dispirited.

Disillusioned with Germany's path, Hitler enlisted with a new up and rising establishment – the German Worker's Party, a group with a propaganda agenda hostile towards the Jewish people, but devout in its encouragement of allegiance to Germany.

Hitler proved to be an engaging voice in the civic arena, his magnetic personality attracted massive audiences who came from near and far to hear his vocalizations regarding how Jews, and those who admired Karl Marx (a German Jew), were responsible for the problems in the country.

Hitler mesmerized the crowds with his concept of keeping the Germanic race "pure," free of intermingling with Jews or other "inferior races."

By an overwhelming vote, in 1921, Hitler became the leader of the German Workers' Party, which later changed its name to the Nationalist Socialist German Workers' (*Nazi*) Party. Adolf Hitler was idolized by the Nazis and their supporters, who *believed in him*, not the constitution or the republic.

Adolf Hitler became the sworn leader of Germany in 1933, for the people believed Hitler would better the economy and rid the country of the politicians who cared nothing for the well-being of Germany.

Hitler claimed a belief in the system of free enterprise and bragged how he would destroy the Treaty of Versailles, and for these reasons, the people believed him to be the best choice for their future. The people felt he was "their savior," for their country was in a crisis with little work and little food.

The more conservative members of the ruling class of Germany wanted an end to the republic, wanting to install a government designed to take Germany back to function as it did in the days of Kaiser rule. Little did those individuals care if the country was ruined by Hitler. They reasoned, that later, they would simply un-install Hitler and place someone else in power. But, how would those who had initially placed Hitler in power, who had praised him, have any concept that he would soon become the *supreme* leader of Germany.

Never in their most far-fetched dreams could they have imagined their efforts to remove Hitler from command would be in vain, and his reign would cause a devastating second world war that would sweep in a holocaust of calculated slaughter, for Hitler would be responsible for the death of nearly fifty million human beings.

Hungary allied with Germany for political and economic gains, and in 1940, Hungary was forced to join the Axis powers because it depended very much on Germany for trade to support its economy; therefore, it had to support the Germans to ensure its survival.

On March 19, 1944, Germany invaded Hungary to install a Nazi-backed, military force-type government, as Germany was angered by Hungary's attempt to withdraw from the war. The Nazi troops made themselves at home in the streets and towns of Hungary. Demanding food, drink, and forcing favors from women. The great champion, who was to be Hungary's ally, became their greatest nightmare.

In April of 1944, as the war progressed, both American and British forces bombed Hungary to stop the German war apparatus. Hungary's land was rich in coal with major coalmining regions in Tatabanya and vast oil fields in the Lake Balaton region. Hungary's coal and oil reserves were necessary to support the life of the Nazi war machine; therefore, the American axis powers had no choice but to bomb Hungary to prevent Germany from feeding its monstrous contraption.

The temperatures remained cold that April. Erzsebet and her family had been "bombed out" of their farm home during the American aid-raids over German-occupied Hungary earlier in the month.

During the war, with an exodus of Hungary's citizens fleeing the country to find freedom, there was an unwritten "rule" amongst the war-stricken population. The "rule" was if you could find an abandoned house, you could stay in the house, repair it, and live there as if it was your own.

Such was the house Erzsebet's family lived in after their farm house had been bombed out. It was an ugly concrete house with no yard - only dirt about the home's perimeter.

The street was just a few feet from their front door. There was little space to grow vegetables or raise livestock, but there was a roof, a wood stove and fireplace to stave off the cold.

Erzsebet's father was skilled in carpentry and used his talent during this time of rebuilding from the war to earn money for food and other necessities.

Each day he left home to help restore the damaged stores, buildings, and homes. The money earned was used to buy the simplest staples such as bread, milk, and eggs, but the money bought little, for food prices were sky-high as the demand far exceeded the supply.

Erzsebet's older sister, Marie, who was now married, lived on the outskirts of town in a tiny apartment.

Much to the family's shock, Erzsebet's oldest sister, Magda, had made a daring underground escape from Hungary about a year earlier. They had no word of her whereabouts until a friend of theirs told the family she had settled in Sydney, Australia. How Magda got there and on what funds, was not explained.

Erzsebet's brother, George, was also married and lived in a Budapest apartment with his wife.

Erzsebet's oldest brother, Ferenc, in utter despair about the war, had become disillusioned with the socialist/communistic path of the New Hungary. As Magda, he too, had disappeared without a trace, until a letter arrived several months later announcing he had enlisted in the French Foreign Legion. There was no forwarding address.

That spring, the most pressing issue was food - they had so little. But the greatest heartache was the farm of Erzsebet's Nagypapa - the place where they could have gone to live and grow food, the place where Erzsebet had spent so many happy days, the land of her inheritance, the homestead where she planned to live one day – was gone. The land had been taken away.

The new communist government had created "land reform" by dividing the land amongst Hungary's poor. The communist ideology firmly believed in no man having more than another.

The great socialist agenda, its superior plan, was to take what a man had worked for, fought for, bled for, and died for, and simply give it away to those who did not understand what it took to create. Easily obtained goods, gained without the acknowledgement of physical or mental toil, can never be valued or appreciated.

Ironically, the portions of land received by the poor were hardly enough to sustain them agriculturally. Farming supplies and seeds of any kind were scanty, and when available, were minimally supplied to the new land owners.

Erzsebet's brother, Ferenc, in his "Foreign Legion" uniform

Without the materials and provisions to grow and work the land, the people continued to go hungry, and thus, the chances of the land, and people coming back to life, was doubtful.

Clothing was a luxury. Scavengers broke into abandoned homes, buildings, anywhere they might find something to wear. Underwear was nearly impossible to find.

Those who were once wealthy dressed as the poor, and the poor dressed as paupers. Necessities of daily living were paltry. The simplest creature comforts were not to be found. Erzsebet's family and thousands like them were simply fortunate to have their lives.

One not so fortunate to have his life, was Erzsebet's dear Nagypapa Halasz. The shock of losing his land to the communist government killed him.

The good news, if one could call it *good news*, was that at the time of her Nagypapa's death, the farm had not yet been occupied by its new tenants. On a Saturday, in mid-April of 1944, Erzsebet and the family discovered the *Elder Halasz* sitting in a rocking chair on his front porch near dusk, with the letter of "land reform" resting in his lap. He looked to be merely asleep, but he was dead, having died not too long prior to the family's arrival, as his body was still warm.

The scene before them was as if he had planned the time of his passing. He sat erect and proud in his favorite rocker, wearing his Sunday-best, brown leather vest, an open bottle of *Barack* grasped tightly in his hand. His last line of sight from the front porch would have been of the grape orchards. His positioning gave every sign that he died taking a last look at *his* land.

Little Erzsebet approached her deceased grandfather without fear, pressing her face against that of her Nagypapa's, her crystal tears coating his cheek.

"Papa, oh Papa, my sweet Nagypapa is gone!" Erzsebet tiny body shook with sobs.

Erzsebet's mother gently pulled her distraught daughter away from her grandfather and held her close, her usually sweet motherly voice hoarse and bitter, "The damn communists killed him without firing a shot upon his person! The communists killed his spirit, his zest for life and living!" Finally, her strength giving out, Erzsebet's mother's voice quavered, "This war took away the most important thing in the world to him – his land!" She covered her face within the folds of her woolen shawl, hiding the agony in her eyes and the grimacing pain distorting her face. Erzsebet observed her father place a trembling hand upon his father's shoulder as hot tears flowed down his face gathering their painful moistness in his thick mustache. Summoning strength in his grief-choked throat, the Halasz heir determinedly announced, "He *will* have his land! He *will* become one with it! Mama - find me a shovel and a sheet!"

That cool evening, by the light of oil lamps, the family found a patch of soft dirt by the grape arbors and buried the old patriarch in the beloved ground of his orchard in an unmarked grave.

The sounds of the shovel pelting brown earth upon the white sheet cradled about her grandfather's body hauntingly rang in Erzsebet's ears. It was the ugliest sound she had ever heard, because with each push of the shovel into the dark, moist soil, her loving grandfather disappeared further from the living world above. No one, not anyone, who would walk these orchards in future times, would know the story of the *true owner* of this land buried beneath their feet. After a brief prayer to send their loved one on his way, there was no more to be said or done.

The Halasz dream was over, for even if they had wanted to return to their destroyed farmhouse, they could not, as the land deeded to them by the *Older Halasz* was included in the "land reform deal."

Prior to leaving the farmstead, the family took one last despondent glance at their land, and one final look at the resting place of the man who had tried to give them a good life, the man who had loved them all unconditionally. Erzsebet's father pushed a small cart filled with the old man's last personal items, his daughter sitting in the cart amongst the "treasure," as he and his wife walked slowly home in the dark, their feet treading for the last time on Halasz soil, towards a life filled with hunger, fear, and uncertainty.

It was late April of 1944. The early morning air held a tinge of frost, very unusual for the time of year. Erzsebet's mother had asked her to walk to the corner store to buy bread for the next two day's rations. It was barely five o'clock, but if one did not rise early the food supplies were sure to run out. Mrs. Halasz would have gone marketing herself, but she was suffering from a sore throat and fever and did not have the energy to make the trek to the store. Erzsebet's father had already left home earlier that morning to begin looking for supplies and ways to earn extra money for his family. It was barely light outside, but Erzsebet would have to leave soon to get ahead of the crowds.

Mrs. Halasz surveyed the oversized coat she had placed on her little girl. *Well, at least it covered her down to her ankles.* It was a gray wool men's suit jacket, not really a winter coat, but it had to do. Erzsebet's mother was grateful for the wool jacket. They had found it in a closet of an abandoned house. All their own clothes were destroyed when their farm home was bombed and daily searches in abandoned homes for their clothing was the norm. She secured the coat at her daughter's waist with one of her husband's belts. She placed a scarf about her child's head. Erzsebet's shoes were thin and worn as were her socks. It was not that she had far to walk that worried Mrs. Halasz - it was the long food lines she worried about, concerned her little girl would be out in the cool, damp air for many hours. There was no doctor and no money for medicine. Nine-year-old Erzsebet could see the distress and signs of illness in her mother's face, "I will be all right Mama. Please do not worry."

Mrs. Halasz pushed money for the bread in the old coat's pocket. "Please be careful little one. Come home as soon as you can. I am sorry to send you. I am too sick and cannot go." Erzsebet gazed lovingly into her mother's tired, thin face, "Mama, I can do it. I will be home soon. Do you think we will have something to eat with the bread when I get home?" Mrs. Halasz looked upon the worried face of her daughter, uncertain of how to answer. She came up with a reply off the top of her head, smiling assuredly, "Of course! Your father will be home with something I am sure!" After kissing Erzsebet's cheek, she watched her daughter walk down the street with an empty stomach toward the store. How young and brave she was! What a horrible world for a child to be forced to live in! She remembered her own girlhood. Her parents were not rich. They lived a simple happy life. But that life seemed like a million years away. It was a kinder world filled with farm dances, innocent fun, and games. And the food… there was always so much food to eat! Now, her child had to do without. She felt worthless as a mother. A tight pain riveted within her chest. She closed the shabby wooden door of the hovel she called "home" and sat down at the kitchen table near the woodstove. Frustrated with life, she banged her fist on the homemade planks, tears streaming down her anguished face, "Why God? Why do you let my little child starve? Let me starve, but not my child. I can endure anything, but please, please, do not let my child go without food!"

Erzsebet made it to the market. She was the youngest in line. There were many people in front of her and behind her: elderly women bent over from the pains and ravages of old age, old senile men and old demented women, young women who looked old from being dirty and unkempt, young men unwashed and unshaven looking old and disheveled in tattered clothing, young and old people of both sexes crippled by the war, malnourished pregnant women with swollen ankles, and individuals impossible to distinguish as either men or women due to disarrayed clothing and lack of hygiene.

The counter curtain opened and a greasy-faced woman with a blotchy-red face and horribly yellowed teeth announced, "Two loaves per person, no more!" It was eerily silent, as one by one, each person took their turn at the counter. By the time it was Erzsebet's turn the bread counter curtains closed. The bread was sold out. The realization she had endured so much for nothing was incomprehensible. Erzsebet's head spun and she fainted from hunger and cold.

Upon reviving, Erzsebet found herself on the grimy floor, looking up into the pitifully strained and tired faces of a few women who had rushed to her aid. They reluctantly refreshed her with their rationed portions of bread, fearing to give her too much of their stash, for they had to bring food home for their own children. And so, with a stomach barely satisfied, Erzsebet walked home, her little legs barely able to move for lack of nourishment, exposure to the elements, and emotional and physical exhaustion. Upon entering her tiny, shabby dwelling, her nostrils were struck with the aroma of food! Erzsebet observed her mother hovering over the wood stove stirring something in a big iron pot with a long, homemade wooden spoon. In tears, Erzsebet explained what had happened at the bread market. Her mother saw the tired, hollow eyes of her little daughter. Dropping to her knees in front of her child, she clutched Erzsebet's thin body to her breast.

"Mama," Erzsebet managed between sobs, "What is in the pot?" Holding her daughter close, it took every ounce of strength for Mrs. Halasz not to cry over her child's plight, trying to reassure her exhausted little girl, "Your father and his friends found horses in the street that had died from malnutrition or other reasons. He and the others took advantage of the horse's misfortune to gain meat for our table." Her mother announced firmly. "We are having stew and you must eat!"

Erzsebet was famished. She sat down to the bowl placed before her on the table. She had never had horse meat before, but it did not smell too badly.

Unfortunately, her mother had no seasoning to use other than salt and a little paprika to make the brew more palatable.

As Erzsebet lifted the bowl to her dry lips to take a sip of broth, she immediately re-deposited the tiny bit of the soup in her mouth back into the bowl. "Mama!" Erzsebet whined, "This meat tastes horrid! I cannot eat anymore!" Her weary mother was exhausted from life - exhausted from everything…there was nothing else to eat and her child needed food to survive. She had prayed to God for food and God had sent the dead horse to feed her child. The horse meat may be the only thing they would have to eat for days. In drained desperation, Erzsebet's mother grabbed the knife she had used to carve the meat and pressed the blade of cold steel to her daughter's thin throat. As if a madwoman, she screeched her command, "You will eat all this meat, or I will kill you! I swear I will murder you myself before I watch you slowly starve to death!" Erzsebet was appalled! She had never seen her mother so wild-eyed, insane - so inhuman! Terrified of the shiny, silver blade pressing against her neck, she tried a small bite of the horse carcass. Erzsebet forced a tiny chunk into her stomach, but no sooner did it hit the emptiness below, she immediately vomited some of the rubbery concoction back up into her bowl. "I cannot eat it Mama!" howled Erzsebet, and she pushed the soup mixture far from her nostrils.

Erzsebet's mother announced victoriously, "You have one piece in your stomach – good - at least there is something in you!" With those words, Erzsebet ran to her tiny room, threw herself upon the narrow bed, and cried herself to sleep.

Later in the day, Erzsebet's mother crept quietly into her sleeping daughter's room and covered her with a thinly worn quilt. Guilt wrecked her soul for putting the knife to her child's throat. Had she become "mad?" But how were they to survive? What about tomorrow and the next day? What if there was nothing else to eat? She carefully lay herself down next to her little girl to avoid waking her. She could hear the constant growling and rumbling in her daughter's empty stomach demanding a reprieve she knew not how to fill.

Meanwhile in Budapest, Little Jozsef and his family also suffered. The city was low on food. The bombing seemed relentless.

Sleeping was nearly impossible, for as they lay in their beds at night, hungry and apprehensive, their only company was the whistling sounds of bombs falling from the air and the thunderous shaking of the earth as the unforgiving missiles found their targets.

The fear of being blown to bits every night was compounded by their empty gut. Bits of bread and weed soup was their fare and those tiny morsels went through them quickly.

The only way to fill the hollow gnawing of their stomachs was to drink heaps of water. With only anguish and gloom to look forward to each day, little Jozsef quietly prayed for the biggest bomb in the world to fall directly on them to end their incessant misery.

During one of the bombing raids, Little Jozsef's dear maternal grandfather, who had been so loving and good to him, was running from falling bombs trying to find a shelter, but his old heart, filled with fear, stress, and shock, could not keep up with the frailness of his later years, and he fell dead in the streets of Budapest. And, even if he had managed to make it to home that day, he would have only found a mound of burnt rubble as his home had also "died" that day, having succumbed to the falling capsules of fire.

Not too long after her father's death, Hermina discovered the financial inheritance her father had carefully preserved for her future had also disappeared, confiscated by the chaotic regime of the Iron Cross.

Little Jozsef's parents temporarily abandoned their Budapest apartment setting out for the safety of the countryside in the small coalmining town of Tatabanya, the home of his godmother.

Little Jozsef adored his godmother and she adored him. She doted on the child embellishing him with kisses and hugs. He was constantly being caught up in her arms, petted, and made over.

How wonderful it was to have such motherly affection and devotion poured on him! He and his godmother walked deep into the woods seeking vegetation to be used for soups.

It was an enchanted time for ten-year-old Jozsef. With her knowledge, he learned much about the forest's plant life. Treasure troves of edible wild mushrooms and dandelions were gathered up and boiled for a delicious "consommé." The soupy mix was not gourmet but tasted good and held vital nutrients. Besides, it was more than most folks in the city were eating and they were grateful for the feast. The woods also provided meats of squirrel and rabbit. Little Jozsef became adept in setting traps and was proud of his ability to provide sustenance for the dinner table.

In late summer Little Jozsef's family opted to return to the city to see if conditions were any better so they could return home – to check if their apartment had survived. They still had some money. They arrived hungry and tired.

They found a store they had patronized in the past: an old, small, grocer's shop, modeling a low, open ceiling with exposed rafters towering no more than one-half foot over his father's head, specializing in cheese, salami, sausage, and bread. At one time, there had been a small confectionary bakery in the back of the store, and Little Jozsef was excited to see if the bakery was still operational.

Little Jozsef's Godmother in Tatabanya

Four Nazi officers smartly decked out in their uniforms, clean-shaven, and smoking cigarettes entered the shop while the family was perusing for food. Little Jozsef had learned German in school and it was easy for him to decipher the officer's conversation about what items they were stocking for rations.

As his parents were making their selections, the soldiers walked up behind Little Jozsef and his parents. The parents, until this moment, were unaware of the soldier's presence; however, the strong odor of tobacco prompted them to turn around, only to find icy blue eyes, as cold and hard as steel piercing through them.

Little Jozsef pulled his shoulders back and stuck out his chest trying to appear staunch and unafraid, but his slight frame betrayed him. Indeed, he looked pitifully thin and exhausted from lack of a proper diet, his guise doing little to fool the faces of soulless evil.

At age three, Little Jozsef had been struck with Scarlet fever and the disease had left him with crossed-eyes forcing him to wear glasses. Uncontained tears of fear arose in his eyes, the salty moisture attaching itself to the inside of his spectacles, forcing him to remove the lenses to wipe away the wetness. As he did so, the malevolent ones grabbed Little Jozsef, causing him to drop his glasses to the ground. They quickly removed his pants belt, wrapped the belt around his wrists, and threw the remaining length of the belt over the rafters, pulling him up to the ceiling and tying him to the rafters with the leathery strip.

Little Jozsef painfully hung from the ceiling, crying, and pleading to be released, but his parents and the shop owner could only look on, terrified. The soldiers said nothing, but their squinting orbits relayed the message, *just try to get him down and you will see what will happen to all of you!* The soldiers had hoped for opposition, enjoying the dread they placed upon the innocent; however, they quickly tired of the game when their hopes for a clash evaporated. They mockingly laughed at the scene they had created, turned around, and walked out of the shop.

Little Jozsef's parents and the shop owner quickly scrambled to get the boy down, whose thin, bony wrists were already discolored from a lack of blood supply to the distressed joints, the belt having worn sharp indentations in his skin.

Little Jozsef tried to stop crying, but he could not, for he was positive that he and his parents were going to be killed. In pity for the family, the shop owner shoved a bundle of food in the arms of Jozsef's father and told them, "Leave town now!" Jozsef and his parents made a hasty return to Tatabanya.

Whatever force intervened that day had saved them all, blessed them with free food, and an unbroken set of glasses.

In Tatabanya, Little Jozsef, his family and other countrymen sought refuge and hope within the church. The Catholic religion was the dominant religion in Hungary and Protestant the secondary religion. Little Jozsef was raised as Catholic.

Little Jozsef went to the weekly church service every Sunday with his parents. One day, his father encouraged Little Jozsef to go to confession.

Little Jozsef felt he had nothing to confess. He was a good child. He had helped support his parents with his accordion playing and always did as he was told. But the one thing Little Jozsef could not understand was why God did not help them during the war, why God allowed him and his family to starve, and why God had let so many of his friends die from the bombs including his beloved grandfather.

Little Jozsef, age eight, with his mother and father

While in confessional Little Jozsef questioned the priest about those things, but he was not satisfied with the answer the priest had given him, "God allows us to suffer so we may seek him out and be closer to him." The young boy's mind did not understand why God would intentionally make anyone suffer, and replied with the most innocent of childish comments, "But Father, that is not very nice of God."

The priest became furious with Little Jozsef. He threw open the confessional curtain, grabbing the child by the collar of his shirt, dragging him to a corner where he grasped a wooden paddle and viciously beat it against the boy's small buttocks and frail back until Little Jozsef thought his bones would break. It was as if the priest was taking out all the pain and rage in his own heart about the war on the boy. Little Jozsef struggled with the deranged "Man of God," wrestling free from the relentless attack and ran home.

He kept the beating a secret from his parents, which was easy to do, since neither parent ever helped him bathe or dress. However, he refused to go to confessional again. Upon his parent's urging and much coaxing, he returned to church, but stayed close to his parents in the pews. His father sensed something was amiss in his son's behavior about going to church, thinking that his son had guilt about something he had confessed to the priest, but did not question his child.

As the war progressed many residents were forced to move from the town for one reason or another, and as a result, the congregation shrank, and the ungodly priest was transferred to another town where "he could do more good." The church closed. Maybe God was understanding after all.

Even more terrifying than the emotional and physical distress brought on by hunger, bombings, and fear of Nazi soldiers, was the dreaded nightly clamor and racket in the streets of Budapest and throughout Hungary of roaring truck engines, blaring horns, and the screams of men, women and children being forced to line up against buildings and shot for no reason other than being Jewish.

The Jewish population, the selected targets of the sick Nazi agenda, were forcefully dragged out of their homes, and those resisting were shot on the spot. Thousands of Jewish citizens across the country were loaded into large military vehicles, driven to railway stations, from where they were loaded into cattle cars for their final ride to various concentration camps including Auschwitz.

Just as horrifying and deadly, were the German raids in the Hungarian countryside upon outlying farmhouses, where, by force, the marauders helped themselves to whatever supplies they could carry, and as if it were not enough that the enemy left barren pantries behind for the farmers, the plunderer's barbaric minds played out their perverse, twisted amusements upon the helpless.

Erzsebet's family had friends who lived in one of those farmhouses. They had several children, all young boys, and one daughter, named Julia. Julia was nineteen years old. She was a very pretty girl with long, shining, flaxen hair, blue eyes and a smile filled with sunshine. Erzsebet and her family had gone to stay with Julia's family in the country for a brief respite from the drudgery of their disheveled shack. One afternoon they were sitting on the veranda outside the front room when they saw several German soldiers coming through the fields towards the cottage. Their friends quickly led them to a secret trapdoor of a root cellar where all could hide until the soldiers passed.

Unfortunately, by now, the Nazis had become quite knowledgeable about the peasant's "secret hiding places" from their many past raids. The family was found. The ravagers threw open the cellar door, barking staunch commands for everyone to remain still. Three soldiers made their way down into the dugout, glaring angrily and fiercely at the frightened families. Erzsebet could not breathe. Her lungs could not inhale, her body stiff from shock as she huddled against her mother for protection.

Then the nightmare began. The soldiers dragged Julia from her family. She violently kicked the intruder's legs and bit their hands, but to no avail. No one could help Julia. Several soldiers above the cellar had their rifles aimed downward to shoot anyone who dared to intervene. The only thing the cellar prisoners could do was to listen to the frightened cries of beautiful Julia fading away until there was only silence.

No one was sure as to exactly how much time had passed since Julia was taken, but finally, the families dared to venture out to the world above to discover the soft glow of sunset about them. They searched frantically for Julia, because soon, the last rays of the sun would take away any chance of finding her that evening. They searched the house, the adjoining fields and woods.

At last, the men shouted out - Julia had been found! By now lanterns had been lit, and the families gathered in the darkened woods where Julia lay face-down, her slight, lifeless body soiled by the muddy earth lay unmercifully conquered, coated by scores of viciously applied cuts and bruises. The damage inflicted upon her person was easily seen, for she was naked, her clothes having been stripped harshly away, her thighs and buttocks oozing a glistening red liquid – a testament to the invader's sacrilege upon her delicate innocence. Erzsebet's body shook with nauseating repulsion and shock. Her innocuous mind could not process the horrific vision before her. She did not know about sexual acts between men and women. She did not know why blood flowed from Julia's rectum and from between her legs. She only knew her dear friend Julia, who was so good to everyone, who was so sweet, gentle, and kind, had been "hurt by bad men." Erzsebet could not handle the gruesome sight before her. Her stomach lurched in revulsion, but her empty gut allowed her no relief.

At that moment, all Erzsebet wanted was to run far away to somewhere beautiful, where people had good food to eat, pretty clothes to wear, and where no one lived in fear of being killed or "made to bleed" by the soldiers.

Redemption appeared on December 26, 1944, when the Soviet Army entered Budapest, and by January of 1945, the Russians had freed approximately 80,000 Jews from numerous concentration camps.

On April 4, 1945, Hungary was liberated by the Russians, and the Soviet troops freed Hungary of the Nazis. The Hungarian Communist Party formed, holding majority in the new government's Provisional National Assembly. Immediately after the war ended, the government engaged in economic restoration. Hungary had been crippled and devastated during World War II. Nearly all of Hungary's industries had been demolished; however, reconstruction advanced quickly with the growth of mines and electric facilities.

The drastic restructuring of the land continued, with the government confiscating more large tracts of land, portioning the land out to the most indigent citizens. But what could a person do with the meager portions of land given them if not provided with the tools and seeds to cultivate the soil? To their detriment, despite the nutritious rich earth portioned out to them, the people remained hungry. In a brief lapse of time the colorful beauty, culture, and dignity of the Hungarian people had disappeared into a bleak mist of smoking bombs, painful screams, and rivers of burgundy-colored blood.

The only things relegated to Hungary's inhabitants was suffering, anguish, and a stark fear of the unknown, echoed in the desperate cries of millions of tortured souls ascending to the heavens, praying for the angels of deliverance, absolution, and emancipation, to free them from their insufferable bonds.

THE LOVERS - 1950

In the spring of 1950 Erzsebet and her family still lived in the "bombed out" house.

On a warm Saturday morning in late May, Erzsebet and her girlfriends were ecstatically waiting to attend a dance being held at their school that evening.

Erzsebet sat at the kitchen table where her mother was peeling potatoes. As she sipped a mug of warm milk, Erzsebet announced unexpectedly, that she would be attending the dance with her girlfriends. Not looking up from the potato in her hands, her mother calmly replied, "Erzsebet darling, you may go, but you must be chaperoned by your father." Her father? How could she have an enjoyable time with her father watching her? Her friends would think she was a baby! Frustrated, Erzsebet tried to reason with her mother, although, her idea of a good reason was not one her *mother* would consider a valid one. "But Mama the other girls are not going to have their fathers chaperoning them!" Her mother placed the potato on the table, dried her hands, reaching out to gently stroke her daughter's cheek, "My sweet one, you are not like the other girls. You are good, kind and very special to your father and me. You are only fifteen years old and your father would want to be sure you are safely escorted to the dance and back home. You are the only child left with us and we want you to be safe."

Tears welled in Erzsebet's hazel eyes. Her mother and father *were* good to her. Erzsebet was more than aware of how much her mother missed the other children: her brother and sister who had left the country and whose whereabouts were unknown, and the brother and sister living in the city trying to rebuild their own family's lives after the war.

Maybe it would not be so terrible if Papa came with me. He would like the music. Erzsebet's mind wandered. No, no! She must not give in to a chaperone! She did not really know if the other fathers would or would not be escorting their daughters to the dance, she just wanted to go alone to show she was *modern*. "Oh Mama!" were the only words Erzsebet could muster through choking tears as she ran to her room.

Fuming with irritation, Erzsebet lay on her bed with rebellious thoughts pouring into her head. *I do not need a chaperone! The world is changing! The war is over! Everything is different now.*

In 1949 the leaders of the "New Hungary" had created plans to transform Hungary into the *perfect socialist society*. They named Hungary the land of "Iron and Steel." The "New Hungary" had pledged to give all Hungarians equality, a peaceful state, and a rise above poverty. World War II had brought utter devastation to Hungary's large cities where most of the occupants had been killed or fled to other parts, but nonetheless, the people living in the country were now coming to the cities in droves to start new lives.

The perfect life promised by the new socialist government now meant Hungarians worked longer hours for less pay – a pay that barely sufficed for even a meager lifestyle. Any housing was hard to find, with up to three generations living in a two-room apartment (kitchen/living room/bedroom combination with a small bath).

Even though the government's promises had not been fulfilled to Hungary's citizens, Erzsebet and her family were thankful for their tiny "bombed out" house, thankful for living in such "good conditions," especially with the hundreds of people coming into the city seeking housing. Their father had worked hard to make the dilapidated dwelling livable. He built their furniture from scrap pieces of iron and wood found in the ruins after the war. He scavenged daily through the war-torn rubble for clothing and other materials to make his family's life more comfortable. And, her father's carpentry skills were very much in demand. Each day, Mr. Halasz found venues for his niche of skills in the rebuilding of the city. Someone always needed his services for something. He was fortunate in being able to scratch out enough of a living each week to help make ends meet. Her father's efforts aided the family in the purchase of flour, milk, eggs, and an occasional link of *kolbasz* or hoop cheese. Many times, Erzsebet's father was paid by barter, bringing home more luxurious food items such as rations of pork, beef, cherries, or potatoes.

Erzsebet and her friends learned about the outside world from listening to Radio-Free Europe, in determined defiance to the "new system" which frowned on anything "American." Thousands of young people were mutinously tuning in to broadcasts of the *real news* coming from America. *America -The place where dreams come true.* And then, there was the music! Jazz and the Big Band were the rage. The rhythm of the music invigorated the young people's dismal, war-weary world. Erzsebet had been practicing dance steps with her girlfriends. How she wanted to put those steps to good use!

It was mid-afternoon when Erzsebet heard a knock on her bedroom door, "Erzsebet dear, I am going to market. I am hoping to find some peppers for dinner tonight and for tomorrow. Are you going to the dance tonight with your Papa?" Erzsebet opened her bedroom door. Upon seeing her mother's tired, drawn face, Erzsebet's heart twanged with guilt for causing her mother distress. She hugged her mother's thin frame. "I am all right Mama. Do not worry. I am not going to the dance. It really does not mean that much to me. Do you want me to come with you?" She did not really want to go with her mother to the market, but the words sounded nice anyway. Her mother gave her a hug, happy to see her little girl not crying, and much to Erzsebet's relief, responded, "No, I will be fine, but if you will finish kneading the dough for tonight's bread it would help me a lot."

Erzsebet gazed into her mother's softly lined face. Her mother was still a pretty woman, despite enduring extreme hardships, as was the lot of most Hungarians since the First World War, and now, living in the aftermath of the second. "Of course, Mama," Erzsebet said softly, "I will finish the bread for you. I probably will go to bed early tonight. I will have some *kolbasz* and cheese later, so do not worry about my dinner. Is that all right?" Her mother kissed Erzsebet's cheek, "Of course it is. Sleep good and I will see you in the morning." Erzsebet hugged and kissed her mother goodbye and headed for the kitchen. In about an hour she had finished three balls of bread dough and covered them with towels to allow the dough to rise. "Well, I am certainly a mess with all this flour on me!"

She had tried to make a kind face to her mother as she walked out the door to do the marketing because she did not want to worry her. But it was useless to pretend she did not want to attend the dance. As Erzsebet made her way to the outside rain barrel to bring in buckets of water to heat on the wood stove to wash her floured hair and sponge bathe, her stomach tensed in despair about not going with her friends for the night's events. She felt like Cinderella. What was she thinking anyway? She had nothing lovely to wear and there was no fairy godmother to help her "get to the ball" in style. Of course, her friends were in her identical situation. Nonetheless, Erzsebet longed to be dressed in beautiful clothes, but with her family barely having money for food, having fine garments was a dream unto itself.

After allowing her silky hair to semi-air dry, Erzsebet began the task of rolling her hair up in pipe cleaners - a rag-tag way of hair curling. Real hair curlers were a luxury that could not be afforded by "everyday people."

After she twisted and secured her long ebony locks around the pipe cleaners she daydreamed about the dance. What would I wear if I were going? She walked to her bedroom closet and meticulously explored its sparse offerings. She had such few clothes, not to mention, anything new, fashionable, or glamorous enough for a dance. All her clothes were piecemeal, found here and there, by rummaging through the ruined lives of others.

For thirty minutes, she half-heartedly sorted through her small assortment of outfits, pairing this with that, attempting to find a decent combination. "Oh, there has to be something here I could wear!" She was about to give up when she spotted a yellow voile blouse sporting tiny black buttons and a curved black, laced collar. It was slightly worn-looking, but was dainty, and, if she left the two top buttons undone, it was respectably provocative. She joined it with her black sheath skirt, a wide black leather belt, and a pair of thin-soled, black, flat shoes to finish the effect. Erzsebet let out a long breath, "Well, at least I know what I may have worn had I gone to the dance tonight. I still wish I was going, but…" She lay down on her bed with thoughts of dancing drifting through her head.

Erzsebet was awakened by the smell of food coming from the kitchen. Her mother must have found peppers to cook. How long had she been asleep? She ambled out of bed and dejectedly walked toward the irregularly-shaped square window of the small room. The fading sun was low in the sky, its glowing shades of orange, azure, and pink melting into the oncoming firmament of evening. The dance would be starting at any time, but not for her. Too depressed about not going out that evening, Erzsebet chose not to face the family and stayed in her room, besides, she had told her mother she would go to bed early, so no one would be expecting her at the dinner table.

Erzsebet sat down in front of the small dresser made by her father. On the wall over the dresser hung a salvaged, long, oval-shaped mirror (with a crooked crack down the center). She began undoing the pipe cleaners from her hair, brushing, and arranging her ebony curls this way and that until she attained the desired effect. Erzsebet reflected upon the image of the girl in the mirror. *I am pretty! Too pretty to stay home and miss all the fun! I will not be gone for a long time - I just want to hear the music!*

Abandoning any thought of the potential consequences of her actions, Erzsebet quickly dressed in her preselected wardrobe and then scrutinized herself in the mirror.

Erzsebet had a petite figure, and the slightly worn, black leather belt encompassing her tiny waist emphasized the beauty of her form. *I wish I had lipstick to put on!* She had a bowl of cherries on her dresser to snack on (a very expensive treat her father brought home in lieu of payment for a job, at least he *said* it was from a "job"). She bit one in half, rubbing its red nectar on her lips to impart a rosy hue and applied the remaining juice to her cheeks. She placed a chair under her bedroom window, climbed onto it, and escaped through the opening. It was only about three feet to the ground below. Erzsebet left the window unlatched, assuring easy re-entry, and began the short walk to her school.

The dance floor was bustling with activity by the time Erzsebet arrived. The band, comprised mostly of the school's students, was playing not only traditional Hungarian music, but the *new sound* from America.

Her girlfriends stood in a corner across the way. Marika was wearing the same blue dress she wore to church on Sundays. Ilona wore a crisp, flower-embroidered, white cotton blouse and a full red skirt, which very much resembled traditional Hungarian dress, and Mitzi was dressed in a black dress with long sleeves, a mid-calf length skirt, and a high collar. Poor Mitzi looked miserable! Erzsebet could see why. Not only was her dress the kind one would wear to a funeral, but Mitzi's father *had* escorted her to the dance and was watching her every move! Observing Mitzi's miserable face, Erzsebet was proud of her daring escapade. *Look at them. I am glad I ran away to the dance without my father or I would be standing around in misery with Mitzi, while our fathers had a grand time talking the hours away! It is a good thing my girlfriend's fathers and my father do not know one another!*

Erzsebet made her way over to her companions who showered their friend with compliments on her choice of clothes. Erzsebet felt exhilarated, free, and happy. The realization of not being chaperoned and "alone on the town" fueled strong feelings of emancipation. She leaned against a wall, observing the musicians, her arms crossed in front, grasping her slight shoulders, her lithe body swaying to the exhilarating rhythm.

Unknown to Erzsebet, she was being fastidiously observed by a sixteen-year-old gentleman, determined to ask *her* to dance before she was discovered by the throngs of unattached males in attendance.

He too, had been leaning against a wall on the opposite side of the room, aloof from the other huddled groups of men. He was a stranger to this school, having been asked to play the accordion during the band's break time, but the break-time was a long way off, and he was bored. He had been passing time watching girls swirl around the dance floor in the arms of their escorts – or lovers. Who was to know? Such private encounters were kept secret, private, and no gentleman would dare brag of his liaisons with the opposite sex. It simply was not done, mainly out of respect for the lady, and out of centuries of engrained civil decorum.

As the young man surveyed the room, his eyes were drawn to the dark-haired girl across the way, obviously engrossed by the music, her sleek body keeping time to the melody. *What a lovely fairy of springtime! She looks different than the other girls. She has an air of dignity about her, holds herself with elegance, like a lovely Grecian statue.*

As if she could sense his stare, Erzsebet glanced across the room. The male eyes locked onto Erzsebet's hazel orbs and she could not look away. Erzsebet's heart pounded. *That man is devastatingly handsome. His hair is so thick and wavy. Oh, he has such wide shoulders. Is he walking toward me? No?... Yes?... I think he is.* Before she could continue her self-imposed argument, *he* was standing within arm's length of her. "Good evening, Miss. My name is Jozsef Bognar. I would be most honored if you would have the next dance with me." *He has the most beautiful green eyes, the color of ferns in the forest... He looks kind and honest. Why am I trembling?*

She did not remember replying "yes" to his request. Her surroundings became muted and the entire room suddenly became enveloped in a swirling mist blocking everyone else from view. One strong hand supported her about the waist while the other tenderly held the palm of her right hand. Erzsebet felt herself floating in Jozsef's arms. He pulled her close to him. She could feel the strength of him - the maleness of him. *How wonderful it is to be his arms. His touch feels warm and very familiar, as if we had been here before - in a dream.*

She gazed upward, her eyes meeting those of her admirer. Jozsef was mesmerized by her lovely face and shining eyes. Jozsef whispered against her cheek, "You are the most beautiful girl here. Tell me your name."

"My name is Erzsebet," she replied breathlessly.

"Erzsebet. It is a lovely name," murmured Jozsef.

Erzsebet's body was light, floating weightlessly upon invisible clouds of ecstasy, flying high beyond the confines of the earth. *How can I feel this way? This man ... I have just met him, yet every bit of my being and essence wants to stay with him, to be with him ... forever.* She placed her head on Jozsef's shoulder. Resting his chin upon her dark locks, Jozsef pulled her delicate softness closer to him while the band serenaded them to the tune of *Sentimental Journey*.

They danced through large open French doors into the quiet of the evening. Jozsef led Erzsebet to a bench nestled between two Acacia trees. They sat for a time, side by side, hand in hand, unable to remove their eyes from one another, until Jozsef broke the silence, "Do you believe in love at first sight? When I saw you tonight, I was compelled to be by your side, as if I had no choice, but to be with only you." Erzsebet glanced downwards, suddenly aware of strange feelings stirring within her, feelings disturbing and frightening, yet exciting and invigorating. She slowly turned her eyes up to meet those of the handsome young man beside her, "I feel the same, as if you were made to be my own. I have this strong yearning to be with you … for always. If this is a dream I do not want to wake up."

"Then we both shall not wake up," replied Jozsef as he tenderly stroked her wrist. I have never felt this way before. I know it is hard for you to understand, but in this brief moment of time, I know you are meant to be mine. I love you!" Erzsebet's heart fluttered in her chest, its confines unable to hold the gladness spreading within.

She stared deeply into Jozsef's face, into the man's eyes baring his soul to her. She placed her hand on his arm, feeling him, making sure he was real. How was this possible? Could one fall in love in an instant? She answered Jozsef the only way she could to rationalize her elated emotions, "Jozsef, I do not believe there are rules one can apply when it comes to the way a human heart feels or loves. But I do believe it is possible, that somehow, and that somewhere, in some other time, we have loved before?" Jozsef nodded in agreement, "I believe it is possible." He took hold both her hands, "Anything *is* possible when two people are destined to be together." His lips sought hers. He then kissed her, softly, slowly, savoring her sweetness. Erzsebet wanted the feeling of his tender lips upon hers to last forever. *I knew someday I would find him, my love, my life, the one I would be with till I am old.* Jozsef pulled Erzsebet tightly to his broad chest, caressing her small shoulders, running his trembling hands through the silkiness of her sweetly scented ebony hair, kissing the soft nape of her neck. *I have found her, my sweetheart, my angel, my world. I know this is right, that she is for me.*

Jozsef and Erzsebet - 1950- soon after they met

Wanting to discover more about each other, they talked about their families, how they grew up, and ... "The War." Erzsebet told about losing her grandfather's farm, the heartbreaking way he died, how the new government had taken his land from him. "We buried him with dignity, with his land. For that, I am happy. My father and mother worked a small farm given to them by my grandfather. It was such a lovely farm. We had geese, chickens, pigs, grapes, and other crops. We all worked hard to make the farm a success. But then, well, the war ... took the farm from us, destroyed our home, and we were forced to find an abandoned house... the one we live in now. Papa does his best to support us with carpentry work. He has fenced in the narrow backyard where my mother has managed to grow a few vegetables. My parents were going to inherit an incredibly beautiful grape orchard, but now – now their dreams are gone, as are the dreams of all Hungarians, except the ones who have become devout communists!" Somberly, Jozsef replied, "I truly feel sorry for your family, for all they have lost. You are right. Every Hungarian suffers except those who have sold their souls to the invaders of our country."

Jozsef told Erzsebet how he supported his family as a small child when his father was *sick* playing in the nightclubs. "I was very tired, Erzsebet, - out till such late hours to earn money for my family. I was just a little boy who should have been playing in the fields and getting dirty, but I wanted to do it, I wanted to help my parents. Somehow, word spread throughout the city about a brilliant child accordion player. That "word" pulled me out of the wretched, dark nightclubs, and opened doors for me to perform for a more dignified audience."

Trying to impress Erzsebet that he was engrained with a strong work ethic, Jozsef went on, "I earn my own money. I used much of my earnings in the early days to support my parents, until my father established new clients. I still help my parents financially when needed. My father is a professor of music. Despite all the hardship, I have managed to save money for myself."

Jozsef continued, "I was a child musical prodigy. At age twelve, I was allowed entrance into the Franz Liszt Music Academy. I studied trumpet, clarinet, and the accordion. I graduated top of my class. At age fourteen, I was invited to participate in the Hungarian National Opera Symphony. I currently perform on Hungarian National Radio playing Hungarian folk music, and at times, my father and I direct, and conduct, several small symphonies. Every now and then I also help my father in teaching students the accordion, trumpet, and clarinet. I have attended an academy dedicated to the repair and restoration of several types of musical instruments and recently graduated with honors as a *Master of Musical Instrument Making and Repair*. I am always working, I must, because one day, I want to obtain my own apartment. I do not want to live at home with my parents when I get married like other young people do. When I was little, my parents and I lived in a very upscale Budapest apartment, but then, the war came, there was no money, and our apartment was bombed. We now also live in an abandoned, small house on the outskirts of town. It is very different from the lifestyle we had before the war, but still, with what my father can earn and with my financial aid, we are doing better than most people. My father, at last, is doing better emotionally since the war. He has resentfully accepted the "New Hungary" we are living in; however, my mother is a bitter woman: bitter for she no longer has the privileged lifestyle she was accustomed to before the war, for now, she is just an "ordinary woman," according to *her*. She misses the high society life she had in the early years of marriage to my father."

With misted eyes, Jozsef's voice weakened, fading to barely a whisper, as his thoughts took him somewhere beyond their immediate realm, his mind traveling to a past time of unpleasant war memories.

With slumping shoulders, he let out a breath heavy with exhaustion, "Too much has happened to me, and to our world since I was six years old. Too much has happened to both of us since the war." His voice quavered, "How *did* we survive, Erzsebet?"

Erzsebet observed his young face suddenly appearing years older. Empathy for Jozsef's pain flooded through her. She held tight to both his hands, assuring him, "We were *supposed* to survive, Jozsef!" She exclaimed, her eyes shining with tears. "We were *made* to be together. We *had* to survive! You and I have suffered the same! We understand each other! We are one heart and mind!"

She found herself sinking into the unfathomable depths of Jozsef's tormented eyes – eyes that had seen too much. His eyes, like hers, had seen immeasurable misery and suffering, and in that second of recollection, Erzsebet knew she would spend the rest of her life with Jozsef. *I will let no one keep us apart. Destiny has made him mine. I love him. I do not understand how this can happen, but it has happened, and I will be his forever.*

They sat in silence, their hands as entwined as their hearts, each reflecting in the depths of the other's liquid pools, each swimming in the others pain, and suffering in the scars of the other's unhealed wounds, that could only be swam in, and suffered by, those who had endured such pain and had borne such scars.

Erzsebet then reached for Jozsef's arm, "I know we were brought together tonight by a miracle … *if* you believe in those things. We were meant to find each other, here, at this designated time and place by the stars above!" The gnarling grief of shared agony cocooned the couple in an embrace of bitter remembrance, each shedding tears for all that had been lost so early in their young lives.

What am I doing, crying in front of this lovely girl? I am acting frail and sickly. Jozsef stoically regained his composure and offered his handkerchief to Erzsebet to dry her tears. "I apologize for upsetting you. I do not know what came over me. I did not intend to ruin your lovely evening, reminiscing about the war is not a good thing to do."

Eager to ease his distress, Erzsebet assured Jozsef, "It is all right, despite what we went through - we are alive … wounded, but alive! We suffered hunger and saw terrible things little children must never see … but look!"

With her voice trapped in her throat, Erzsebet swallowed, and pointed to the evening sky, "See the stars, see the moon? This night is *ours*! It is full of life! *We* are full of life! We are young and beautiful! Let us push all the ugliness away and begin our lives anew, right now, tonight!" Jozsef smiled tenderly toward the lovely angel by his side. He stroked her cheek with trembling fingers, "I agree. Yes… everything *will* be new - beginning tonight."

After many apologies and tears were swept away, Erzsebet's curiosity urged her to ask Jozsef why he had come to the dance this evening. Holding the softness of her small hand, Jozsef explained, "I am here to play my accordion during the band's break time. I was asked to play some

American music." I can play any instrument. It just comes naturally to me. I have something called absolute hearing or absolute pitch. I can hear a song on the radio …like the one we were dancing to. I write the notes down to the song as I hear it. I also know the key the song is played in. It saves me a lot of money because I do not have to buy sheet music!"

Erzsebet sat transfixed by Jozsef. He was not only beautiful of face but had a brilliant mind.

An announcement on the loudspeaker by the band leader abruptly interrupted her thoughts. "Ladies and gentlemen, we are taking a break, but in the interim, for your entertainment, we would like to introduce that accordion virtuoso, the one and only, *Crazy Fingers*, Jozsef Bognar, who has graciously accepted our invitation to entertain you this evening!"

At the sound of his name, Jozsef jumped up, a surge of fresh energy wiping away all former fears. "It is time for my performance! Come with me!" Erzsebet quickly slipped her arm through Jozsef's as he swiftly escorted her to the foot of the stage. "Wait here for me, please, my *Edes*?" he implored, looking back at her as he mounted the band platform. Erzsebet stood at the base of the stage idolizing Jozsef's every move. Jozsef picked up his accordion, and in seconds, the silence was broken with wild renditions of American favorites including *Foggy Mountain Breakdown* and *Boogie Woogie Bugle Boy*. The crowd danced without abandon, with unbridled passion, to the untamed rhythm matching their unrestrained, free spirits.

When the numbers ended, the audience cheered Jozsef on, begging for more. And, there was more. Jozsef's eyes became lost in Erzsebet's smile. "And now … I would like to dedicate the following song to a lovely lady who has stolen my heart - *Some Enchanted Evening*."

"I *was enchanted* by your accordion playing tonight, thank you for dedicating your song to me," said an exuberant Erzsebet as she and Jozsef walked hand in hand toward her home. "I do believe everyone present was completely taken with your musical ability. I am very proud of you!"

Jozsef slowed his pace, and then stopped. He turned toward Erzsebet gently placing his hands along-side her pretty face, "Not as proud as I am of you. I feel like a king with you by my side. I do not want to leave you tonight, I never want to leave you." Erzsebet leaned her body into her sweetheart's strong shoulder for support, "Nor I."

They walked on, eventually stopping at a public park a few blocks from the school. It was a peaceful, quiet, balmy night. The only visible light was the soft glow cast by thousands of twinkling stars in the heavens and the golden light of a full moon.

Jozsef located a sweet-smelling Acacia tree in a secluded corner of the park, under whose white flowering branches he spread out his jacket for Erzsebet to sit upon.

With imploring eyes, Erzsebet asked, "Please, Jozsef, I cannot let my parents know about us – not now. They still look at me as a child and would not understand my deep feelings for you." Jozsef, lost in her sweet eyes, assured her, "Do not worry my *Draga*, no one will know. I will not tell my parents either. Not till the time is right. My father would understand, but my mother… well, my mother is another matter. We will have to figure out a means of communication to know when we can meet each other."

Under the Acacia tree was a sizeable rock. Jozsef hatched a plan, "Erzsebet, we will leave notes for each other under this rock. See? Here in this corner, where it lifts a bit from the soil? Place the note there. I will leave my note responding to yours in the same place!" Erzsebet's face glowed with excitement, "Yes, Jozsef, it is a wonderful idea – It will be our Love Rock!"

Jozsef - early 1950's

Jozsef's and Erzsebet's young lives had been colorless and dreary, without hope of seeing their country whole again. The early days of youth – days that should have been filled with innocent fun had been destroyed by the harbingers of evil, sentencing them to live out their childhood days in the dismal abyss gouged into their lives by the war.

For years, each had lived in the same morbid tomb of vacuous desolation, amidst the crumbled aftermath of war-tossed and bullet-scarred buildings.

There had been too many dreams remembering the horrors, too many memories of the anguish and torments of war, too much suffering trying to regain some sense of normalcy after the war, and too much of never having enough to eat - never having enough of anything.

Jozsef and Erzsebet – mid-1950

But on this night, a splendid breath of freshness had blown into their lives. Everything beautiful in the world was here for them in this one perfect moment of time. And, they were so fervently in love, starving to explore the myriad of feelings exploding within them.

And, on this evening of destiny, the despair and desolation of their former world dissolved into a blurred memory, for under the protective canopy of the Acacia tree, concealed by shadowy darkness, in the realm of their "love rock," the lovers sought the depths of each other's eyes, seeing in them the truth: the truth of knowing that even if they died this very moment, that their love was greater than, stronger than, more beautiful than any dream there was to ever dream, or had ever been dreamed by anyone in the world.

It was time to come alive again, to live again, to blot out the agonies of the past, to build a future on the ecstasy of this magic hour.

Jozsef hungrily seized Erzsebet into the protective shelter of his arms, claiming her for his own upon a blanket of velvety moss.

MARRIAGE AND BIRTH

On Friday, April 10, 1953, Jozsef, age nineteen, and Erzsebet, age eighteen, exchanged wedding vows in a small, lackluster, magistrate's office in Budapest. Both sets of parents were present as witnesses. Jozsef stood handsomely in his white dress shirt, blue tie, and gray suit. Erzsebet, carrying a spray of colorful wildflowers, was glowingly lovely in a sky-blue dress.

Prior to the wedding, Erzsebet's parents, honored to have such an intelligent and talented young man join their family circle, had invited Jozsef to meet with them at their home on several occasions for dinner and outings. They admired Jozsef's work ethic, his sense of responsibility to family (having supported his parents since he was a young child) and could obviously see how devoted he was to their daughter.

Hermina had not taken the news of her son's impending marriage well, as his face beamed with the excitement of young, pure love during his announcement to marry a few months earlier, "Mama and Papa! Erzsebet and I are planning to be married in the spring! Do you not think she is the most beautiful and sweetest girl you have ever met?" Hermina felt a shiver down her spine. A sickening vibration twisted through Hermina's resentful body, turning her world upside-down. *That girl is taking my son away from me!* Hermina was jealous - very jealous of Erzsebet, for when her son married, it meant any extra money her son was giving to his parents for expenses would dwindle, or perhaps, become nonexistent.

Lying in bed together on the evening of the "big announcement," Hermina, in a casual tone of voice, trying not to arouse any suspicion, commented to her husband, "So, it seems our son will be leaving us very soon to marry Erzsebet?" Jozsef rolled toward her, their faces almost touching. He tenderly twirled a strand of her silken hair around his finger, "Yes, I know. How I will miss our son being here with us every day! But Hermina, I remember…do you not remember how it was with us? How very much we wanted and needed each other, all the time?" Yes, she remembered. After all this time Hermina was still very much in love with her husband. Did she love her son? Perhaps, but not in the conventional way mothers loved their sons. She was proud of his accomplishments, for his notoriety reflected well upon her. She basked in the limelight shed on the family name because of her son's genius.

Hermina spoke gently, trying to hide her resentment of the entire idea, "I *just* want him to be happy. I was hoping he would meet someone from *our* more refined circle of friends instead a girl coming from a family of farmers and carpenters."

"Of course, Hermina, as did I," replied Jozsef, "But, you and I very well know we cannot control the emotions of one's heart. He has lost his heart to Erzsebet as I lost mine to you all those years ago. We cannot keep our son forever. He must live his own life. We will go to the wedding and be happy for them. Now, try to go to sleep. It is late." With those final words, he kissed his wife's cheek and rolled over.

Hermina's worried mind raked the darkness. She had worried about much since the early days of the war. She had worried through all the repulsive things brought into their lives by the war. The *war* was the destructive force leading to the downfall of her once perfect world. The beautiful apartment she had spent painstaking hours decorating (and painstaking amounts of money to achieve the desired effect) was gone … destroyed, as were thousands of other people's homes.

Hermina found her current living situation not only intolerable, but embarrassing, for she now lived on the outskirts of Budapest in one of the "abandoned homes" set high on concrete blocks: a small, three-room, beige-colored structure with a flat roof, behind a door with peeling blue paint. It was a small structure with a small living room that also served as a bedroom: the bed was the couch, and the couch was the bed. In the corner of the room was a fold-out cot used as a bed for their son. The kitchen was tiny, holding a wood stove, serving both to heat the house and for cooking meals. The washroom was separated from the kitchen by a ceiling-to-floor curtain. It was a primitive room only providing a chipped porcelain sink and a wall mirror filled with tiny cracks. In the corner sat a large galvanized tub used for bathing. Water was pumped via hand pump in the kitchen sink and carried to the tub in buckets for bathing. A tube connected to a drain under the tub "drained" the water through a hole in the floor beneath the tub to the underside of the house.

The worst part of the dwelling was that it had no indoor toilet – Hermina was appalled each time she used the outhouse in the tiny backyard. *Everyone knows my most intimate moments.* Hermina also fretted over her limited dress collection. There was no money for a fashionable wardrobe these days. And what did it matter what she wore anyway, for her social life was nearly nonexistent. Most of her high-society acquaintances had "vanished" during the war. Several of her husband's male friends were forced to serve in the many labor camps set up all over the country. Her most sickening memories were those of dear friends rounded up by the Arrow Cross Party and taken to the concentration camps where they had met their untimely demise in gas chambers. Even their friends who were not Jewish, but dissidents against the government, had been taken away. And, one by one, over time, their neighborhood had grown smaller and smaller, until there was only a few hundred where there had once been a thousand.

Professor Bognar still managed to perform limited concert engagements, as well as giving music lessons for small groups of students. The family had enough for everyday necessities but little more. If it had not been for their son contributing funds to the household, they would not have what they have today.

Hermina lived in a self-imposed, cursed world of gloomy hardship, woe, and despair. What would become of her now? Where would this dreary existence lead her? The lithe, supple, slim body she so highly coveted had evaporated, and now where lean lines of sleekness once reigned, bulging folds of flesh lived in their stead. But Hermina was not alone: such was the case for the many once beautifully-bodied women and men of the country, for the everyday sustenance of the Hungarian in this time of want consisted mainly of a cheap, starchy fare.

The "life in the limelight" she had planned so well for, schemed so well for, had, bit by bit, been pillaged from beneath her. Now, she was simply an ordinary woman leading a simple, ordinary life, except her husband still bore the title of "Professor." *What good is my husband's title without all the fun and excitement that used to come with it? And now… now, the child I birthed to gain a good life is leaving me. What good has all this planning and conniving done for me? I am nothing but a pauper living in a shack!*

She lay in bed listening to her husband's soft snoring. Rays of sun signaling the beginning of a new day were distending their strained arms through the manifolds of small cracks in the aged wood shutters. Testily, Hermina whispered into her pillow, "The new day comes, but it brings no joy to me."

Erzsebet had obtained her certificate in pediatric nursing and currently worked in the children's ward of a local hospital. At age eighteen, Jozsef had been drafted into the Hungarian army (now the Soviet Army since their occupation of Hungary) as was demanded of all young men.

During his year of military service, Jozsef performed numerous concerts in the country's largest military symphony. When able to catch a bus or train, Erzsebet attended his musical performances whenever possible, and every weekend, during that year, Jozsef commuted home from the *Felsogalla* train station to be with his sweetheart. But their weekend visits were far too brief. It took Jozsef all Friday night to arrive by early Saturday morning, and by late Sunday afternoon he would be on the train heading back to his post. But each stolen moment they had together was a treasure, a treasure waiting impatiently to be plundered, savored, and relished. Each time Erzsebet saw Jozsef bounding from the steps of the train, each time she saw him running toward her, each time he contained her within his quivering arms filled with unabashed love and longing, her very breath and heart stopped as she died in the embrace of delirious desire, only coming back to life when her true love's lips parted her own, filling her inner essence with his sweet breath of resurrection.

With the monies Jozsef had scrimped to obtain during the already, too many, harsh working years of his young life, he had secured a tiny, dilapidated apartment, its only furnishings a bed, and a kitchen table with two chairs.

The apartment was very old, with a battle-scarred exterior, as were most buildings in the city - a gloomy reminder of the war. The living room and bedroom was just one room with a bed and closet. The kitchen adjoined a tiny bath with a toilet and tub, but no sink. Hand washing, shaving, and brushing teeth were done in the kitchen basin. A coal stove in the kitchen easily heated the small rooms during the winter. A small gas stove and oven was available, as well as a tiny refrigerator that could barely hold more than two quarts of milk. Despite the cheerless, dreary setting of their apartment, the couple was happy beyond words – because it was all theirs and its walls radiated with love. *It was beautiful!*

Neither of their families were aware of the couple's private dwelling; therefore, immediately after the train's arrival, the infatuates would expeditiously elope to their enchanted sanctuary, where after a few splendorous hours of savagely fierce passion, each returned to their respective parent's homes, determined to let no one know of their secret haven.

Church marriages were ignored by communist Hungary for the regime did not recognize them as legal. The only recognizable marriage was the state civil ceremony - a ceremony performed without the mention of love, or God.

Erzsebet's father solemnly observed the lifeless ceremony with eyes wet with joy and sadness. Yes, he was overjoyed of his daughter's choice for a husband, but his thoughts drifted to how different this day could have been: *If the war had not come, we would have celebrated her marriage in the "Old World" style. If there was no war my daughter would have been married in her grandfather's grape orchard with many guests. Perhaps, he might still be alive if they had not taken his land? Who knows? There would have been wine, merriment, dancing to old Magyar rhapsodies, and the Czárdás played by a lively Cigány (gypsy) band. We would have feasted all night long! My Erzsebet deserves to have been married in a beautiful wedding dress and in elegant style. I have no money for any better. Not even the groom's family has money for anything finer. How much I wanted a real wedding day for her, not being married in this shabby government office by this fat Communist woman with cold eyes. The damn war! The war ruined everything. But look at them -see the way they gaze upon each other? One would think they were dressed in royal finery and being married in a grand cathedral! What can I say? They love each other. Please God, let them be happy....* Erzsebet's mother, sentimental and overcome by the day, cried tears of happiness into her handkerchief throughout the ceremony.

Jozsef's father stood straight, tall, and proud - proud of all his son had carried out in his young life, despite all the odds thrown at him by the world.

Hermina stood stoic, emotionless, in shock, because her son "actually went through with it." *Now there will be no more money for me. It will be spent on the wife.*

After the wedding, the couple retreated to the paradise of their tiny, divine apartment of *Eden*, (which the families believed Jozsef had recently acquired), and when night fell on the first day of their marriage, the eclipsing veil ensconcing their love was lifted, laying bare their consecrated famishment for one another.

With Erzsebet's wages as a pediatric nurse and Jozsef's musical performances for clubs and special state events, both solo, and with the Hungarian Symphony, they lived far above the country's average citizen. Jozsef's musical prowess had allowed him to rise to the highest heights of his symphonious profession: being asked to perform for visiting dignitaries at the Hungarian Parliament House, for he was considered one of the country's *"national treasures."*

Jozsef in the Hungarian (Soviet Army) playing his accordion at the Officer's Club

Jozsef performed several nights a week in the city's various clubs. On Friday nights, while Jozsef was working, Erzsebet went to sleep early to get her rest. This way she could be near the front of the line at the butcher shop when the doors opened at 5 a.m. Saturday morning to buy meat for their weekend meal. If she did not do this it would be impossible to get any meat, because in about an hour the supply would run out. When Jozsef finished work he would meet her in the food line. After their purchase they would go home, sleep till noon, and then cook their main meal.

One Saturday afternoon the couple window-shopped in downtown Budapest. Stopping by a local bakery, they indulged in a shared cup of coffee and a slice of *Dobosh* Torte. Afterwards, they came upon a shop specializing in Herend porcelain. Jozsef's attention was immediately drawn to a figure in the display window – an accordion player.

The "Herend Accordion Man," was exquisitely designed in the old style of Hungarian dress wearing a traditional cap, vest, and shirt with long flowing sleeves, holding a concertina with bellows open. The cap and pants were beautifully lacquered in black, the shirt creamy-white, and the vest and boots were tan-orange in color.

A black cap with a blue band around the brim adorned his head, and a yellow "feather" finished the ethnic costume. His cheeks were a rosy pink, and his mouth was poised in the shape of a happy "Ohhh," as he "sang" with his instrument. Erzsebet noticed the excitement and desire in Jozsef's eyes. "Let us go inside and look!"

She grasped Jozsef's hand and eagerly pulled him into the shop. Jozsef asked the owner if he could examine the statue. The shop owner gingerly lifted the piece from its cradle in the window and placed it upon a velvet cloth on the store's glass counter.

Jozsef cautiously lifted the happy player and held it in his hands, immediately captivated by the elegant beauty of the exquisite piece. Erzsebet and Jozsef were very much aware that the Herend brand was one the most distinctive porcelains in the world.

For almost two hundred years the Herend factory, in Herend, Hungary, created porcelain products sought by the world. The regal Queen Victoria had even purchased Herend dinnerware for her home in Windsor Castle!

The little accordion man had touched Erzsebet's heart. She viewed it as a replica of her Jozsef playing his accordion. But there was no way they could afford this masterpiece, the price too exorbitant for their purse. The owner overheard the young couple discussing finances in a corner. What a lovely couple they were! They reminded him of he and his wife many long years ago. It was difficult now-a-days for young people to make ends meet - for anyone to make ends meet in post-World War II Hungary. Life *was* more difficult than ever. How was anyone going to afford *anything*? Since the war his business had been on the downside. He needed the money as much as the young couple wanted the figurine.

The owner approached Jozsef and arranged a deal: they could make weekly payments and then the player would belong to them. Jozsef did a few, quick mental calculations, shaking hands with the owner to seal the bargain.

The Original Herend Accordion Player Man

Eight weeks later Erzsebet and Jozsef took their prize possession home. Sitting on the gray-colored kitchen table of their apartment, the little accordion player brought an air of chromaticity and nobility into their meager household, empowering Jozsef and Erzsebet to indeed feel as important as the Royals of Windsor! After hours of admiring their treasure, they wrapped the figurine in layers of soft cloth, placing it in a dresser drawer where no harm would come to it. Every Sunday they would again take the player out and place him on the kitchen table while they ate dinner allowing them to marvel upon their "royal" purchase. They had paid a steep price for their prize, having eaten many a meatless dinner, but they did not care.

It was late August of 1953, on a Sunday morning. Erzsebet had been cooking most of the morning, preparing one of Jozsef's favorite meals, "stuffed cabbage." The smell of the concoction was driving Jozsef's stomach to the breaking point. He was extra hungry today!

He entered the kitchen to inquire when the meal might be ready, only to find Erzsebet seated at the kitchen table, her complexion pale, and eyes downcast. He instantly rushed to her side. Grasping her pallid hands, Jozsef asked why Erzsebet was looking wane. "My *Edes*, are you sick?"

There was only silence, but the frightened look in his wife's eyes made him feel uneasy. "You *have* to tell me what is wrong. Are you ill? Do you need to go to the hospital? Please say something!"

A tiny whimper emanated from Erzsebet's throat releasing a cascade of tears. "My *Edes* Jozsef, I think we are going to have a baby – maybe in April. I have been waiting… wanting to make sure before I told you!" Erzsebet had remained silent about her suspicions, hoping it was not true, but now, with her darling husband kneeling at her feet, and the lovelight in his eyes burning into her soul, the pent-up worry and tension within her was released. She fell onto her Jozsef, weeping inconsolably upon his shoulder. "Our baby will starve!" she wailed, "We have so little! The baby will not even have diapers!"

Since their enchanted night under the Acacia tree they had taken excellent precautions to prevent pregnancy, but marriage had freed them from the "rules of society," and they now loved without abandon throwing all caution to the four winds. "This is a terrible time to have a baby! We are just getting started! Oh, Jozsef, what will we do?" Erzsebet's hands fumbled within the crinkles of her blue skirt, wringing the thin cotton fabric into a damp knot. "Our expenses are already strained, and now… with a child …"

Jozsef zealously held his sniveling wife in his firm arms, stroking her cheek with his fingertips. "What are we going to do you ask? We will be having a baby, and everything is going to be all right!" Jozsef pulled his wife more firmly to him, softly whispering into the strands of her waved hair, "Our baby will not go hungry or go without diapers!" Hot tears continued to drench Erzsebet's cheeks, her crying interrupted by Jozsef's lips touching her forehead, "My *Draga* Erzsebet, my accordion will make us the money we need. I promise!"

In the early morning hours of April 1, 1954, Erzsebet went into a grueling and exhausting labor. By American standards the hospital was pitifully primitive. The most the midwives could do for Erzsebet during her arduous labor was to drape her fatigued, sweaty body in cool cloths and give her verbal reassurances. Erzsebet's tiny pelvic frame made for a difficult delivery.

Jozsef sat, walked, and smoked for nearly forty-eight hours as the love of his life suffered to expel the life within her. Her screams and moans were heard in the far-off expecting father's waiting area. Her echoing cries of pain were driving him insane! This was so barbaric! He was totally helpless. He begged the nursing staff to stay close to his wife and help do whatever they could for his wife's comfort. The head nurse was a kind lady, who had seen many women in labor, but Jozsef's concern was so great, so sincere, she promised to pay extra close attention to Erzsebet, as best possible under the archaic conditions.

Jozsef's emotions ranged from fear, to panic, to agitation, to nausea, and then, as the contractions came closer, he begged for the child to come quickly and prayed his Erzsebet not die, for there was no life without her. There was *nothing* without her.

On April 3, 1954, at five o'clock in the morning, their daughter, Judit, entered the world. Erzsebet was in a delirium. Her tortured body was drained beyond exhaustion, and she mercifully sank into a deep, restorative, twelve-hour sleep.

Erzsebet's eyes fluttered open. It seemed to take forever for them to focus, but when they did, her sweet Jozsef was sitting by her bed. Even through the blurring light, Erzsebet could easily discern dark, hollow circles under her husband's shining orbs, telltale remnants of his fatigue and worry over her exhaustive labor. Erzsebet reached out her hand to her husband. He fervently reacted, grasping her slim fingers within his own, as she pleadingly inquired, "My love, my Jozsef, did we have a son?"

Son or no son – he did not care! Jozsef's only concern was the health of his lovely wife, the star of his world. His prayers had been answered. His wife was alive having come through her ordeal with no major complications. "My *Draga* Erzsebet, I have seen our beautiful daughter!" Erzsebet's tired face contorted in disbelief, her desolate voice filled with distress, "Jozsef, I *know* you wanted a son! I prayed for a son, I truly thought we would have a son …"

At that moment, the midwife entered the room with their precious bundle, placing the swaddled infant into the folds of Erzsebet's arms. It was the first time Erzsebet had seen their baby. Her dry throat constricted, unrestrained tears of elation flowed down her gaunt cheeks as she beheld the lovely child before her. "My sweet Jozsef, look… oh… look, she is perfectly beautiful. Look at our baby!"

Attempting to remain staunch, but unsuccessfully so, Jozsef's eyes filled to the brim with love and pride for his wife and child, "Yes, my *Draga*, she is absolutely exquisite, just like her mother!" Erzsebet's beaming face looked up toward her husband, pitifully inquiring, "Then…you are not upset you do not have a son?"

Jozsef leaned over his wife and little daughter, kissing his wife on the forehead, while the baby grasped one of his fingers within her tiny fist. "Upset? No! Do you not know boys are always more trouble! She is lovely like you, my sweetheart, I am happy beyond words!" Jozsef knelt by the bed throwing his arms about Erzsebet's legs, "I love you, thank you for our baby, I *love* you!" Erzsebet reached out a limp arm to her husband, "And I love you so much, my husband!"

Jozsef instantly brought Erzsebet's damp hand to his lips, kissing her cool fingers, his eyes swallowing the image of their beautiful baby girl in the arms of his darling wife. Jozsef was not only in love with Erzsebet, but also "in love" with his baby girl.

I never imagined how fulfilling it would feel to be a father. The moment I glimpsed my child's angelic face, I knew I would fight and kill for her. I will kiss my baby when she is awake and sleeping. She will know she is loved. How could my mother not love an innocent baby? How could she not have this warm feeling in her heart for me when I was born, when I was growing up, as I do at this moment for my child? Father - how could you not see my mother did not love me? How could you not see how much I needed her love?

Tears flowed from Jozsef's weary eyes as he peered down upon the now sleeping mother and her babe. His Erzsebet was the nucleus, the crux, the lifeblood of his world, unconditionally filling the once clouded stygian of his soul. His Erzsebet's softness, strength, grittiness, and tenderness were the foundations of his valiancy, lighting up the dark void of a past life unknown to a mother's affection.

Judit was christened at the end of the month with both sets of grandparents in attendance.

The birth of their granddaughter brought Erzsebet's parents and Jozsef's father much happiness, but Hermina, was not thrilled to be a grandmother, and not at all grateful as she should have been for her son's continued monetary support, "With the baby, I am sure the money will dwindle as the child's expenses increase."

Even when Hermina held the gentle softness of her little granddaughter for the first time, she denied herself the joy of primal, instinctual love for the innocent life in her arms, her selfish mind too preoccupied with jealousy for the "New Mrs. Bognar" and her "in-the-way" child.

REVOLUTION!

In the early 1950's Hungary's citizens were struggling to forge new lives after the war, but there was never a doubt Russia still ruled the country since "freeing them" from the Nazis in 1945. The evidence was everywhere - thousands of Russian troops and tanks still occupied the land, and the abhorrent Red Star of communist oppression remained mounted atop the country's major buildings.

The Russians had promised the Hungarian people a better way of life: better products, better wages, better medical care, better education, and a shorter workweek; however, many years later, life in Hungary was worse all the way around. A high percentage of goods produced by Hungary including vegetables, milk, mining products, machine goods, and more were being sent to Russia for *their* enjoyment - enjoyment brought to them by the sweat of the Hungarian worker. The Russians had offered more of everything, but instead, the country was in a chokehold, slowly, but surely, strangling amidst mighty waves of oppression and destitution.

The communist authority seeped into every facet of Hungarian citizens lives with the creation of the AVO (*Allamvedelmi Osztaly*), Hungary's State Security Agency – the most dreaded and despised secret police. This police force was comprised of not only Russians, but also Hungarian citizens, who were given special treatment and privileges if they agreed to spy on their friends and neighbors. The AVO set up sadistic centers of torture to penalize those who disagreed with the new government. Many Hungarians were banished to Siberia and never heard from again.

The Hungarian people could no longer trust anyone, not even friends or family, fearing they were secretly part of the AVO.

In early 1956 the general population, and especially students, held many peaceful rallies of protest in the city of Budapest against Russian occupation, with thousands of citizens throughout the country speaking out against the depravation of their liberty. Groups of freedom fighters were forming in secret. It was time to take back their country!

Jozsef was flagrantly outspoken against the Red Tyranny engulfing Hungary. His speeches against "the system" stirred up much dissent, empowering hundreds, then thousands of citizens to take his side. The people needed a leader, a hero, and the fatigued souls of the ravaged land were strengthened by Jozsef's forthright views about establishing a new, free, self-governing Hungary. The country's citizens did not think their demands were unreasonable. They asked only for the simple basics wanted by all human beings, but such thoughts were treasonous to their torturers: freedom, food, fuel, and dispersal of the secret police and Russian troops from their country, as well as the reinstatement of their government official, Premier Imre Nagy.

Jozsef was blindly unaware that his speeches and movements were being closely scrutinized by those in higher authority, who were truly in a dilemma on how to "bring down" the young, hot-headed activist.

Jozsef's musical talent was the pride of the country: he ranked as a highly admired, respected accordionist - considered a "National Treasure." Nikita Khrushchev, First Secretary of the Communist Party of the Soviet Union, had on many prior occasions, personally *"asked"* Jozsef to play *on demand* for his political functions in the Hungarian Parliament house, and on those occasions, Jozsef played hours on end for the Soviet elite, unpaid and unfed throughout each performance.

The Soviet government's quandary regarding Jozsef was a simple one: if they "silenced" him, Jozsef's political followers could create mammoth civil unrest, energizing, even further, the growing fires of resentment among the masses. They *last thing* they wanted to do was make Jozsef a martyr. Therefore, in lieu of the contributions Jozsef had made to the country through his musical genius, the government officials agreed to give him a "mild punishment" for his outspoken behaviors; however, as far as Jozsef was concerned, they might as well have sent him to the gallows. His punishment? Jozsef was forbidden to play his accordion or any musical instrument for one year, and during that year, he was sentenced to work in the sooty chasms of the Tatabanya coal mines.

Tatabanya, the small town where Jozsef's godmother lived, was extremely poverty-stricken. Coal mining was the lifeblood of the town. Practically every man old enough to carry a pick and shovel worked in the mines. The working conditions in the mines were archaic, reminiscent of the early 1900's in America, with little to no thought given to safety regulations.

Jozsef left for work as the first shining rays of the sun appeared over the horizon, joining the ranks of the town's exhausted miners, lowered away to work in a darkness that was darker than any darkness imaginable. And, every day, he and his fellow miners waded through water seepage, fighting off hungry rats, and living in fear of instantaneous death if the cribbage supports failed, for if they did not hold, thousands of pounds of earth and rock would rain down upon them. Other deathly phantoms looming in the mines included methane gas and microscopic particles of coal dust seeping into the miner's lungs. One volatile spark in a pocket of unseen methane gas could start a fire. There was nowhere to run if a fire broke out, every soul in the pit would be lost in seconds as the flaming inferno swirled its blazing fingers into every crevice of the grimy caverns. If the supports, rats, and fires did not quickly kill the miners, then most certainly, after years of inhaling the tiny specks of coal dust, many miners would die the slow death of a life-threatening respiratory illness.

Each day, Jozsef came home in the twilight of early evening, as the last golden spray of the sun's rays lowered behind the mountains overlooking the town. He rarely saw the light of full day. How he missed the warmth of the sun's heavenly body! It was cold in the hollow fissures beneath the ground, but the coldness of living without his beloved accordion, the "sun of his heart" was even colder. *The damn Communists did not give me a death sentence – but, they hope I will die in this black hole to save them from hiring an executioner. I will show them. I will survive this. I will beat them. Someday, somewhere, my family and I will have a life in the sun!*

Despite the dangerous, demeaning work - a far cry from playing music in the glamorous parliament house, Jozsef was grateful for the many good friends he made in the mines, and grateful that he and his family were able to live with his godmother in her small, humble home.

His *punishment* also meant a severe decrease in wages, making it difficult to purchase even the bare basics for everyday living. The family scraped by on minimum foodstuffs, determined to keep their apartment in the outskirts of Budapest, hoping against hope, that somehow, they would be able to return to their little home one day. Over the past year, they had been fortunate in being able to accumulate extra furnishings, but now being forced to live in Tatabanya, they had no choice but to sell whatever they could to help with expenses, keeping only the baby's mattress, their mattress, and the table and chairs in the kitchen. And, even if they had to eat weed soup again, they were determined to keep their little "accordion man."

Erzsebet thanked God every day for sparing her husband's life, but did *they* kill him anyway by confiscating his accordion? Erzsebet was devastated for Jozsef being sent to the mines, and not only worried about her husband's physical health as he worked under such dangerous conditions, but worried as much for his emotional well-being. Music was the portal to Jozsef's essence, the lifegiving elixir lighting his inner fire, the vital ingredient fueling his zest for life, and the inspirational force for his spiritual creativity. Jozsef's fingers had touched the ivory keys of an accordion every day of his life since he had been a small child. He would go crazy being torn from his instrument!

Everything they had struggled for had been taken away. Could the government be trusted to keep its promise to release her husband from the mines after one year? How could they possibly continue to make ends meet with their severely reduced income? Unfortunately, to her benefit and detriment, the reply to Erzsebet's questions would be answered from a most unlikely messenger.

Protest gatherings against the communist regime were increasing in number all over the country, with crowds becoming intensely more agitated and violent. Jozsef and Erzsebet could sense that something terrible was on the horizon.

Like pawns on a chessboard, they, and millions of others in their revered land of Hungary, were but little game pieces caught up in a game that would ultimately end in violence, blood, and death.

Tuesday, October 23, 1956, started out as a chilly morning. A light frost coated the shrubbery about the city of Budapest, and a hint of fog spread its misty tentacles above the ground. As the sun slowly rose, a cloudless sky promised a warmer than usual day for the time of year.

In the late afternoon, thousands of students, and workers, wearing red-white-and-green armbands (the colors of the Hungarian flag), held a protest march against the Soviet Government demanding democracy and reform.

The procession began at the Statue of Petofi (a beloved poet of Hungary), proceeding to the Statue of Bern, while singing the Hungarian National Anthem and the Kossuth Song. The student's goal was to gain access to the radio station on Brody Sandor Street to broadcast their demands for freedom and rally other nations to their plight.

The crowd eventually expanded to over one-hundred-thousand strong. In protest to the bonds of slavery imposed upon them by the communist regime, innumerable hands joined in the tearing down of a colossal statue of Joseph Stalin, the former leader of Russia, and greatly hated, ruthless dictator of the Hungarian people. The radio station, patrolled by the Hungarian Secret Police (AVO) allowed a few representatives of the protesters inside the radio station; however, after a few hours, there was no sign of the small group who had entered the building. Those waiting outside were concerned for the safety and welfare of the protestors inside.

The terrifying deeds of the AVO was one major reason for the Hungarian Revolt. This group of private police, through their works of systematic torture of rebels, created a constant climate of trepidation and dread. This, combined with the sore monetary conditions existing in Hungary, caused tensions to overflow into absolute insurgence.

The headquarters of the AVO was 60, Andrassy Street in Budapest, otherwise known amongst Hungary's citizens as the "Terror House," for within its formidable walls were chambers of torture. How convenient for the AVO – for this address had once been the command center for the Hungarian Nazi Arrow Cross faction during the time of the Nazi occupation of Hungary during World War II.

The mission of the AVO was to hunt out anyone: man, woman, or child even remotely against Russian rule of Hungary. The leader of the AVO was a Hungarian named Gabor Péter – a cruel man intent on finding "evidence" on those who were against the communist party. During the

1945 elections, the Hungarian Communist Party received only a small part of the vote, with the preferred Smallholders party receiving the winning vote. By the vote tally, Hungarians showed opposition to communist rule. But Gabor was enraged due to the high votes given to the Smallholders party, and he intended to do everything necessary to force communist domination in Hungary. The motto of the AVO was, "Whatever it takes to make them confess." Many innocents were subjected to unspeakable acts of persecution including the pulling out of fingernails with pliers and people being dipped in tubs of hydrochloric acid.

Russian dictator Nikita Khrushchev denounced Stalin's rule hoping to soften the revolt, and the AVO's name was changed to the AVH (*Allamvedelmi Hatosag*) but changing the name of a skunk to a more pleasant-sounding name does not change its odorous nature.

Initially, the police attempted to break up the crowd outside the radio station using teargas, but this only further agitated the masses who kept chanting for the small party inside the radio station to be released, resulting in calls for assistance of the Hungarian army to disperse the crowds; however, the Hungarian army refused to fight against their own countrymen, and linked forces with the dissenters, supplying the desperate fighters with their personal firearms and ammunition. Night descended upon the chaos with the spattering sounds of sporadic gunfire sprayed upon the masses by the AVO. Hope arrived for the fighters when truckloads of desperately needed reinforcements of grenades, rifles and machine guns were delivered from the ammunition factory at Csepel Island, and distributed among the protestors, who returned like firepower against the enemy. In angry response, the AVO rained down a more intense barrage of bullets into the furious populace. A handful of fighters had been killed in the earlier fighting, but now, hundreds upon hundreds of Hungarians began dying – the florid, noble blood of the oppressed weeping into the streets. Refusing to be stopped, the multitude gathered forces and lunged forward to get past the AVO's mechanized assault. Scores were cut down, but hundreds, and then thousands, using the crushing force of their own bodies, stoically pushed forward, overpowered the AVO, confiscated their weapons, and marched fearlessly toward the radio building, broadcasting their dire situation to all of Hungary and all the world.

The broadcast of the massacre spread rapidly. Disgruntled workers stormed factories where they had formerly made weapons for the Russians, helping themselves to the arms held there, distributing weapons to the frantic hordes, and by late evening, over two-hundred thousand had answered the call to freedom.

The wrath of the Hungarian citizenship was fierce, and systematically, they sought out the evil adversaries who had snuffed out the lives of the valiant ones, shooting their oppressors and hanging the bodies of the "beasts" from trees and lamp posts in the city as a warning to all who would attempt to terrorize Hungary – "Leave or suffer the fate of your fellow monsters!"

But such demonstrations did not stop the cruel onslaught oppressed upon the people by the "Red Devils." As the days of the Revolution would continue, individual revolutionaries would be chased down, unmercifully beaten, and left for dead. Thousands would be arrested and never seen again, and those trying to help injured freedom fighters would be fired upon.

The bloody Hungarian revolution had officially begun.

The news of the revolution spread within hours by the radio broadcasts to the small town of Tatabanya, where the men of the town found themselves in dire straits. With the massive unrest in Budapest there was no way to collect their pay that week from the office in the city. It would be suicide for anyone traveling the roads to Budapest to collect the payroll for the miners. Despite the ongoing revolution, goods could still be obtained if money was placed into the palms of "the right people."

Jozsef's blood boiled with insurgence. Was it not enough that he and his fellow miners were already living on substandard wages? Would there be no end to the death of fellow Hungarians as they relentlessly fought with every measure of their might to stave off the insane madness of the Red Army?

There had been too many losses in his life, too many losses for his loved ones and for Hungary, and Jozsef could not help but recount them all in his anger towards the Soviet swarm.

When would the suffering stop? When would the hunger stop? No one had enough to eat, except those who pledged allegiance to the communist party. The country remained in shambles since the end of World War II. When would the beauty of Hungary return? So many friends and family had been brutally exterminated during that war – his own beloved grandfather dying in the war's bombing raids, and now, at this very moment, the barbarous, inhuman Soviet Army was in control of his country!

Was it not enough *they* had taken his Hungary, taken his government, massacred his Jewish friends, taken his music and livelihood from him, taken his wife's land inheritance and the life of her grandfather and his grandfather, bombed them out of their homes – *they* had taken everything!

In the early afternoon of October 24, 1956, after a prior restless night of soul-searching, Jozsef stormed out the door of the Tatabanya mining office in a fit of antagonized rage. A ragged motorcycle with saddle-bags draped across the fender of the back wheel was parked outside. Jozsef did not know who the cycle belonged to, nor did he care. Without even checking if there was fuel in the tank, Jozsef mounted the bike, engaged the engine, and pulled off in a noisy cloud of tawny, golden dust and exhaust fumes. Above the noise of the cycle, Jozsef shouted out to his coalmining friends as he rode past them in the streets, "I am going to get your payroll money - if it is the last thing I do!" The shocked and astonished men watched Jozsef ride away on the tattered cycle. Some began to cry tears of fear for their brave friend, and others cried tears of shame - for their own cowardice in allowing Jozsef to strike out alone and defenseless against the certain hellfire he was to encounter. And, some simply cried. Then, out of all the cries of despair, came the comforting strains of the Hungarian National Anthem, as the workers joined voices to rally hope within the walls of their own haggard souls, and to steel Jozsef onward, their eyes following a crazy young man riding away on a set of suicidal wheels bound for Budapest.

Jozsef had given no thought to the precarious and unstable situation in the city. He was unarmed and unprepared for the Armageddon ahead. As he approached the outskirts of Budapest, dark plumes of smoke rose from the many fires set off by explosive barrages projected from Soviet tanks, and the explosions rendered by countless Molotov cocktails used by the revolutionaries against the invaders. The Freedom Fighters used a glass bottle half-filled with gasoline, or some form of alcohol, such as methanol or ethanol. They would stop-up the mouth of the bottle with a cork, or anything that would create an air-tight seal, with a cloth rag affixed around the mouth of the bottle. The rag would first be soaked in flammable liquid. Just before using it, the rag would be lit, and the fighters would then throw the bottle at the target. On impact, the bottle would shatter, spilling the flammable liquid over the target, igniting the object.

Amid the chaos of the burning city was the irrefutable sound of rapid gunfire and Jozsef knew it meant his fellow citizens were dying. Sudden nausea gripped him, and despite the cover of a cool, cloudy day, steamy streams of sweat exuded from his body. With gutsy determination, he drove the cycle into the midst of the fray, steering his way amongst the acrid odor of fuel and smoke. He swerved his bike between colossal tanks, enemy combatants and Freedom Fighters, his ears painfully aware of his countrymen's bloodcurdling screams as they breathed their last. Countless times, projectiles narrowly missed striking the young vindicator. Armed Hungarian men and women were all about, in the streets, atop tanks, behind buildings, on the tops of buildings, and lying on the ground - shooting at the enemy and nearly shooting him! The air was smoky from gunpowder and burning buildings. The dead and the dying were behind him and in front of him as he indefatigably pushed forward, determined to make it to the payroll office – if it was still there.

The door to the payroll office was hanging half off its hinges. The payroll staff, not knowing what to do, or where to go, was holding out in the back of the building attempting to avoid the pandemonium in the streets. Jozsef skidded his cycle through the narrow doorway breaking the hooks off the door causing it to fall inwards. Without shutting off the motorcycle engine, he shouted to the payroll master, "Hurry, give me the pay for the mine workers!" The paymaster stared incredulously at Jozsef's sweaty, grimy face and dust-ridden clothes. How had he survived the assault of bullets and "tank fire" all the way from Tatabanya? He remembered Jozsef as a young boy when he and his father performed accordion concerts, knowing all too well why Jozsef was condemned to the Tatabanya mines.

With no doubt in his mind that the young musician's request was a veritable one, the paymaster scrambled to the safe, and stuffed stacks of currency into the saddle bags, not even bothering to count if he had overpaid the workers. Rather the mine workers get the money than the enemy! Jozsef sent forth a relieved look of thanks to the paymaster, revved the motorbike's engine to the mechanism's limit, and once more whipped the steel beast into the melee of despair.

During the fleeting time Jozsef had been inside the payroll office, conditions in the streets had deteriorated rapidly, buffeting a new terrifying reality against Jozsef's already frayed nerves - how was he going to stay alive for the almost forty miles back to Tatabanya!

Insurmountable chaos encompassed Jozsef's surroundings as he plowed his cycle through, and around, jumbled heaps and piles of fiery rubble, as showers of angry bullets whizzed over his head. But even as he swerved about the mayhem, Jozsef's only thought was a wish for silence, deafening silence, to block out the hundreds of agonizing screams and cries of tormenting pain as maelstroms of piercing bullets penetrated their brave targets.

Jozsef's heart was convulsing without mercy within his chest, the pumping of his own blood echoing erosive swishing noises in his ears, as the stifling odor of scorching smoke and caustic chemicals engulfed his nostrils and throat, sending feverish, searing heat into the depths of his lungs. As hard as he tried to hold his breath for relief, he eventually had to exhale, having no choice but to breathe in more of the toxic mess. But far worse, was the heaviness in his gut, the sick feeling of revulsion as he twisted and turned his cycle around, and in-between, the mangled, bloody remains of hundreds of men, women, and small children strewn in the streets.

The pitiless conquerors had mowed down everyone and anyone in their path. Many wounded victims begged for Jozsef's help as he jetted past them. God forgive him - he could not help! He could not stop! If he stopped to help the wounded, he would end up a fearless, dead hero, no good to anyone. Hell had come to earth!

But what kind of a man would he be if he did not try to help? How would he ever live with himself - if he did live, to live with himself? He had to do something!

Jozsef slid the cycle behind the remains of a disempowered tank, landing beside the body of a thin girl, probably not more than fifteen or sixteen years of age, her disheveled blonde hair streaked red from where scraps of shrapnel had cut through her skull. Jozsef lurched his head from the view, his unbelieving eyes wanting to escape the tragic waste of such beautiful youth.

Screaming shots rang out from above, most likely from one of the upper story windows of the surrounding buildings.

Jozsef then watched in horror as a young boy, not even in his teens, carrying a machine gun, ran toward the cover of his hiding place behind the tank. The boy suddenly stuttered and stumbled as bits of sharp steel entered the softness of his young form, his body falling only an arm's length away from Jozsef - the young hero's innocent ruby essence spewing over Jozsef's face and clothes, officially knighting him, "Freedom Fighter."

Raw with rage, Jozsef grabbed the boy's weapon and ripped off the extra set of bullets encircling the boy's neck. Jozsef took aim towards the sounds of sniper fire coming from the upper window across the street. As his shaking finger pulled the trigger in rapid succession, the riveting recoil of the rifle butt tore into his shoulder after each successful strike.

In the meantime, dozens of screeching tanks had entrenched the street, their cannons aimed to take down buildings filled with the counterfires of the desperate masses. Jozsef frenziedly glanced about for a way to stop the brutal behemoths of death. His eyes latched onto the waist of the dead girl - two grenades were fastened to her belt. They would have to do. Grabbing the grenades, Jozsef left his protective shelter, and then, ducking low, he zig-zagged his way through the mayhem of smoke and bullets, grabbing onto the ice-cold tracks of a tank with an open turret. He pulled his way up to the opening, yanked the pins out of both grenades, and threw them into the hold. Within seconds, he was on the ground, tumbling, rolling over and over, landing behind a shielding mound of fallen rubble as the earsplitting thunder of his triumph blasted the atmosphere.

He had to get out! Fast! He had no more ammunition, and he had to find his way back to Tatabanya before nightfall!

Guided by unseen powers, Jozsef's "payroll cycle," miraculously escaped the *Gates of Hell*, arriving safely back in Tatabanya before the last streams of daylight shed their glimmer over the tiny town, where the sweaty and blood-spattered hero was immediately surrounded and greeted by an assemblage of jubilant, cheering miners and their families. Intoxicated cheers of elation resounded in Jozsef's ears as he victoriously cast the leather satchels holding the fruit of the men's labors into their exhilarated hands.

Jozsef's beaten body and mind could take no more. His knees broke beneath him as the adrenaline powering his cause rapidly faded away, and as the realization of what he had done in the past few hours crashed in on him. How in the world had he accomplished what could not be accomplished? His body trembled as the memory of the exploit overwhelmed his senses. Had he died, what would have become of his wife and daughter? He did not even remember making the decision to do what he had done.

Jozsef had won his own private war that day, however, it was a small victory in the greater scheme of things, but a victory all the same.

Erzsebet, holding little Judit in her arms, ran out to meet her husband, crying hysterically, "My Jozsef, my love, why did you do it? Why did you leave us? I thought you would be killed! I thought you were dead!" Waiting all day to know if her husband was dead or alive, and unbelieving that he *was* alive, and was here with her in the flesh, was too much for Erzsebet's worn mind to assimilate, and she gratefully allowed herself to collapse against the haven of her husband's bloodied chest.

The miners assisted the war-torn Jozsef and his little family home. Upon seeing her precious boy, the godmother's face beamed bright with love and pride. "Now, now, Jozsef, come in. Wash. Rest. Eat. Everything will be good now! You are home and safe with us. You are the bravest man I have ever known."

Late that night, as the mining town celebrated their financial victory, Jozsef and Erzsebet escaped to a shed behind the godmother's tiny hut. There, within its cold, bleak walls, lying on a narrow cot, and covered with only a thin, worn blanket, they lay entwined as Erzsebet held Jozsef close to her breast, showering him with butterfly kisses over his entire body, unbelieving her Jozsef had returned to her unblemished and unscathed.

No words needed to be said between them. Their love for one another said it all. And, after nothing was said, and everything expressed, they fell into an exhausted slumber.

The next day, Jozsef returned to The City, valiantly fighting alongside thousands of the country's courageous revolutionaries, battling to destroy the detestable abomination spreading over their land. Jozsef prepared Molotov cocktails, and, with the aid of fellow combatants, threw countless bottles of liquid lightening against enemy tanks and vehicles. He and other fellow revolutionaries tore down Hungarian flags containing the symbol of Russian oppression overlaid upon the brave colors of red, white and green, cutting away the hated insignia, as well as tearing down the crest of the despised Red Star adorning the buildings of Budapest, and then, riding with countless other fighters upon confiscated Russian tanks, Jozsef held the Hungarian flag, now barren of the ugly Russian motif, high over his head to show the enemy they would no longer be victims of their treacherous rule. Jozsef seized rifles from the dead fingers of the enemy, and pried weapons from the arms of his slain companions, as he fought his way through the streets of Budapest, opening fire upon any Russian soldier in his path, pushing forward into the embattled fracas with a countenance of fiery anger and unbridled rage, with only one burning thought – "Freedom for my country!"

Across the land Freedom Fighters took hold of Soviet tanks, weapon warehouses and government factories, and the fighting between the insurgents and the Russian Army increased in intensity.

A Budapest prison was captured by the Hungarian warriors and all political prisoners were released, and at long last, the public was shown the truth about the tortuous beatings inflicted within its walls.

Because of the increasing riots against the government, as a patronizing gesture, Russia gave in to the people's demands, reappointing the Hungarian-born Imre Nagy as the new Prime Minister of Hungary and Janos Kadar as foreign minister, attempting to appease the protestors.

Then the Russian army pulled out of the country allowing Imre Nagy to allow the formation of a new government. Moscow also released Cardinal Mindszenty from a Russian prison, an enormous "sacrifice," as the doctrine of communism "outlawed religious thought," viewing religion as "capitalist." However, the Soviets hoped that by releasing Mindszenty, one of the most religious men in Hungary to criticize the Russian government, the revolt could be quelled.

The Hungarian people were overjoyed, and for twelve, resplendent days, they danced and sang in the streets celebrating the defeat of the Soviet occupation of Hungary. The head, atop Stalin's statue, toppled by the angry crowd which lay on the ground, was decimated as the victorious fighters cut the statue's despised face into pieces. But their days of celebration were numbered.

On October 31st, 1956, Imre Nagy, used his newly given power to announce Hungary's withdrawal from the Warsaw Pact. As for the Russians, this was the "straw that broke the camel's back."

Then, the unthinkable happened. At dawn, on Sunday, November 4, 1956, the screeching metal of one thousand Soviet tanks roaringly crashed their way into Budapest to "restore order." This marked the beginning of suffering for untold numbers of Hungary's populace. Those fighting for Hungary's freedom would now pay the ultimate price: thousands would die, and thousands would be forced to leave their beloved homeland towards havens of safety.

Hungarian radio desperately put forth broadcasts imploringly begging help from the United States and from the United Nations, beseeching the world to castigate the Russians for their actions toward Hungary. The Hungarian radio announcer's last message to the world ended with the chilling words, "We will hold on to the last drop of our blood."

Messages from President Eisenhower of the United States, were heard over the radio, expressing his feelings of deep sadness for the Hungarian people. The president said, "Hungary can count on us."

A surge of hope spread amongst the Hungarian people upon learning the United States would support their cause, but their elation quickly dissipated when it was realized they were only being offered moral support, as no tangible help appeared from the West. The Great United States of America did not come to their aid as the Hungarians believed it would.

But aid to Hungary was not as simple to give as it appeared. After much exploration on how the United States could help Hungary, the American government realized the geographic location of Hungary was not ideal.

Hungary was surrounded by other countries controlled by the Soviets. If the United States helped Hungary, they would have to fight their way through many Russian-controlled countries, which could possibly lead to an all-out war with Russia.

America and Russia both had nuclear power arsenals. The thought of going into combat, with the knowledge of this reality, made the consequences of such an action too hazardous to contemplate. The United States considered an economic boycott of the Soviet Union, but the Russians would not care, for it ravaged what resources it needed from the countries it occupied.

To further complicate matters, Hungary's revolution was unknowingly ill-timed, for the United States was involved in the Suez Crisis – a matter needing more urgent attention than the revolution in Hungary.

The number of lives lost during the 1956 Hungarian Revolution were beyond comprehension. The revolutionaries, ranging in age from seven to ninety, fought the enemy with anything they could make and find: homemade grenades, rocks, clubs, and bottles filled with gasoline.

These fighters were everyday people with no military training engaging in desperate acts for desperate times. If conquered by the Soviets their freedom would be lost. They had nothing to lose for without freedom there was no life. Fighters barely in their teens, many younger, without regard for their own lives, crawled onto tank tops throwing *Molotov* cocktails down the turrets. In the bravest of acts, many young people strapped several grenades to their bodies, throwing themselves into the bellies of the iron monsters, obliterating their lives as they decimated the depraved murderers within.

Jozsef's tormented eyes witnessed the ruthless killing spree and immense savagery set upon his people by the impudent, heartless Red soldiers, as they resorted to even slaughtering Hungary's helpless wounded lying in the streets.

But the thirst of the captor's bloodlust was still not satisfied, as they proved by reveling in more of their disgusting delights, causing Jozsef's stomach to turn-over in revulsion, as he observed the *Evil Ones* tying the slain remains of Hungarian revolutionaries to their monstrous tanks, dragging the heroes sacred bodies through the avenues of Budapest as a warning to those who would oppose the enemy's might, as well as spitefully hanging the bodies of Hungary's patriots on the bridges spanning the Danube River.

Even Hungarian citizens who had aided the Freedom Fighters in any form or fashion were taken to railroad stations and shoved into overcrowded cattle cars for transport to somewhere in Russia for execution – most were under the age of twenty.

The conquerors shot everyone and everything in their sights, and the populace watched in horror as Freedom Forces consisting of the very old to the very young, were sought out and lined up against buildings, only to have their lives extinguished by the deafening bombardment of machine-gun fire. Despite their best efforts, the Freedom Fighters were not winning the battle. They were under-armed, under-fed, and out-flanked. Many Hungarians had already fled the country, with the United States sending planes and ships to Austria and Germany promising asylum to the refugees who could make it that far.

But Jozsef and Erzsebet had held out, praying for a miracle that would never come, and by the second week of November 1956, except for a few isolated incidences of a skirmish here and there, the fighting was at a standstill. The Soviets had won.

Jozsef and Erzsebet went to check on their Budapest apartment – to see if it had survived the conflict.

To hell with the coalmine!

The lower half of the building was riddled with the sprayed pattern of new bullet holes, now haphazardly mixed in with the ones remaining from those inherited from "The War." The windows on the lower level were shot out; however, their apartment on the third floor, was miraculously spared. Glass was cracked in the window panes, but everything else was still there. There really was not much for anyone to pillage as their dwelling was practically barren upon their departure.

Leaving Erzsebet and Judit in the apartment, Jozsef went out, and with a "few connections," gathered a meager amount of bread, some scraps of vegetables, paprika, eggs, and unbelievably, milk for little Judit. From these paltry rations, Erzsebet made a huge pot of watered-down soup that could last for a few days. Refrigeration was not a problem. The weather was cold, allowing the soup to be kept on the flower box outside the kitchen window to prevent spoilage. A little coal was still available for their stove, and at night, they pulled their mattress next to it for warmth.

The week of November 12, 1956, with their country in tatters, and the enemy crushing hope for any decent kind of life, Jozsef and Erzsebet thought hard about their future. They had very few options in their favor. Each was thinking the unthinkable and unspeakable – they must leave the country, but how and when was the pressing question. One thing they did know: there was a high likelihood that they would either be killed or captured by the enemy during their escape, but what was life if you could not "live it" anyway? What was life if you were told what to do, when and how to do it, never being able to trust friends or family, and knowing your children would be educated (brainwashed) by "the system" to conspire against their own parents "for the good of the country." No - they did not want their little girl to go through life in that way. They decided they would rather die together than live forever repressed.

With mortality staring them in the face, they chose to have a family portrait made by a photographer friend. Their reasoning was this: they would give the photographer the address of Jozsef's parents and have the photograph mailed there. If they made it to safety, they would later contact Jozsef's parents and give them an address to which they could send the portrait; however, if they died, then at least their parents would have one final picture of them as a family.

Their friend had offered them a complimentary family portrait session many times, but they never seemed to have time to take up his kind offer. If the studio had survived the Revolution, they would make the time.

And it had survived. They dressed in their best clothes. Jozsef wore his gray suit, and Erzsebet, a dark blue suit with a white blouse. Judit wore a pale pink dress with a background pattern of white flowers. Erzsebet placed a small cameo necklace about Judit's tiny neck and curled her daughter's silky blonde hair with pipe cleaners and did the same to her own hair.

With Judit in his arms, Jozsef and Erzsebet walked the short distance to the photography studio with the solemnity of a funeral procession, each thinking the same thought: this may be the last photograph they would ever have made together, for perhaps, in a few days they would all be dead.

Jozsef and Erzsebet sat on the photography bench with their little daughter cradled between them. Judit was tired and leaned her head against her mother's shoulder. Try as she might, Erzsebet found it impossible to smile, her somber eyes reflecting the thoughts of her tortured mind and soul. How was her little girl going to survive such an arduous escape? Would they all die? Her morbid contemplation was captured by the clicking sound of the camera's shutter.

This was it: the family was now forever captured in this one immortalized moment in time. For better, or for worse, only God knew their fate.

In the early evening hours of November 16, 1956, there was an urgent pounding on their apartment door. Jozsef's cousin, Ferenc was standing in the hallway, shaking with cold, his eyes wide with fear. "Jozsef!" he breathlessly let out, "They are starting to round up the leaders of the Revolution and executing them – *you* are on the list - they will be coming soon to get you!" Jozsef had known it was only a matter of time before "they" got around to him.

Our family portrait made a few days prior to escaping from Hungary – November 1956

The breath was crushed out of Erzsebet. She stood frozen at the doorway, her eyes glued on Ferenc. Deep in her heart she knew what had to be done, but this soon? The thought of what was to come sapped the strength from her legs. Tears welled in her eyes. She leaned her back against a wall for support, and with Judit in her arms, slowly lowered herself and the child to the floor.

The family's very existence in Hungary was rapidly disintegrating, for the world they had been born into was shattering and splintering around them, scouring away all evidence of their presence on *Magyar* soil. The road of life that had led them to this point in time was being rapidly decimated and savagely consumed behind them by the unrelenting appetites of both fate and destiny. There was no passage back to their prior existence. Fate had stepped in forcefully urging the three towards an unknown realm seething with every imaginable risk and peril.

It was time to disappear into the dark shroud of night - it was time to run!

ESCAPE!

The Red Warmongers had succeeded in obliterating the Magyar's once fruitful homeland and in their victory the "iron hand" of communist oppression clamped its choking hold about Hungary, suffocating the hopes, dreams, and lifeblood from the captives held within its borders.

Thousands had made the difficult decision to leave the country for a wondrous place called "Andau." Andau -where freedom was real and waiting - waiting for those with the courage and strength to make the perilous journey.

Ferenc had given Jozsef and Erzsebet a crudely-drawn map outlining their route to Andau, Austria, including instructions about the "freedom truck" pickup route run by an underground network to take as many citizens to freedom as was possible. Ferenc looked at his dear cousin, his boyhood friend, and companion. How he would miss him, but on this momentous evening, his mission was to assure safe passage for his beloved friend and his family. As much as Ferenc wished Jozsef could remain he begged him to leave quickly, "Jozsef, there is no time left, you must go. You must leave tonight and very soon!"

The enormity of the situation was incomprehensible. Jozsef and Erzsebet had hoped the United States would come to Hungary's aid, and now, with Ferenc's disastrous news, even if help came from the West, it would be too late for them. They had to get out now! Erzsebet's heart twisted as if massive steel chains were squeezing the blood from its arteries. With tear-filled eyes she pleaded to Jozsef, "I *must* say goodbye to my family - my mother - my father!" Her face grimaced, its stressed contours reflecting the pain in her soul. "No, no, my love," Jozsef insisted, "There is no time for goodbye. We can tell no one we are leaving. No one! Once we leave there is no turning back. Someday, somehow, if we survive our escape, we will see our families again. I promise you. We will." He held Erzsebet close to his chest, stroking her hair, softly whispering in her ear, "It is time now, we must go." Jozsef knew his political actions had put his family in harm's way. The secret police *would* find him and *them*!

Despite the price they had to pay – to leave their country, their home, Jozsef and Erzsebet would not have done things differently. The Soviet regime had made their lives intolerable and things would not get better.

Jozsef and Erzsebet's reasons for leaving Hungary were the same as the nearly two hundred thousand people who would make their exodus to borders of freedom. Since the communist party had taken control of Hungary in 1948, and until Stalin died in 1953, the people had lived under a ruthless and harsh dictatorship. Innocent people were falsely accused of "crimes" against the State. Orphaned children were taken to State orphanages to be raised as "Good Communists." Many of Hungary's political leaders were put to death. And worst of all, no one could be trusted, not even family. By the early 1950's, most of the domestic products produced by the Hungarian people were confiscated and sent to supply the needs of the Soviet Union. The Hungarian people were producing plenty, but with the current system, they were slowly starving.

Upon Stalin's death, Khrushchev, the new Soviet leader, condemned Stalin's actions, and there was a slight decline in the cruel and callous treatment of the Hungarian people. But it was not enough. People continued to live in constant fear, for the heartless and vicious acts of the government were still in place.

As Jozsef and Erzsebet speculated on their plan of escape, they thought of their little girl. She was so very small and frail for her age of two-and-a-half, the result of an inadequate diet. And no wonder! With all the rationing in place, a family was fortunate to get a loaf of bread and cooking oil to last them for a week! Both parents shared the same unsaid fear: How was their little girl going to survive the journey? How long would it take them to reach the Austrian border? What if something caused delays and they missed their truck? They had so little food to bring with them! How many belongings could they possibly pack? How were they supposed to carry their small child in the cold inclement weather walking over miles of territory exposed to patrolling Russian troops? How was she going to stay warm? Would they be captured? Would they all die, and how? So many questions invaded their thoughts, but there was no time to ponder over the answers.

Erzsebet's mind swam in circles as she glanced around their simple apartment. Suddenly, the gray, drab walls glistened as if made of gold. Despite its plainness, it was beautiful, because it was *their* place. They had worked themselves into utter exhaustion to keep the apartment after Jozsef was sent to the mines. When they left here tonight, what would become of their home? Who would move in? Erzsebet's eyes glazed with tears, but her thoughts quickly snapped back to the situation at hand, her mind whirring frantically. What would they pack for their journey? They had only two sets of arms, and one set of those arms had to carry the child.

Adrenaline suddenly surged through Erzsebet's body, quickening her senses, prompting her to dart about the apartment, madly sifting through drawers and cabinets. She gathered bread, a loop of dried sausage (*kolbasz*), and a small, glass bottle of milk, wrapping each in a thick cloth to protect the precious cargo. There was not much else to pack in the way of foodstuffs. She grabbed personal items: Judit's coat, hat, gloves, boots, and scarf, and the same for her and Jozsef.

Jozsef collected their identification papers to be shown on their arrival at Andau, secured their professional certificates to prove they were college-educated people, and gathered his personal music books and original, handwritten pieces of sheet music. Erzsebet checked the closet. On the floor, wrapped in a thick bundle, were at least one hundred love letters: the sweet moving stanzas of unashamed confessions of love that she and Jozsef had left for each other under their "Special Rock." But tonight, under their surreal circumstances, the lovely spring night under the Acacia tree seemed to be a dream dreamt an eternity ago. The inviolability of their love existed in those letters and how she cherished them!

In the kitchen, Jozsef was packing his already over-stuffed attaché case with important documents, as well as filling the knapsack with the food Erzsebet had put together. "The accordion player!" shouted Erzsebet. They had almost forgotten their "Royal" Herend treasure. After all they had gone through to obtain "him" the thought of leaving without the player was inconceivable. She gathered a bed sheet and rolled the small statuette in the pale linen.

Erzsebet hurriedly dressed Judit in her winter clothes. After she and Jozsef donned their coats and boots, Jozsef placed the heavily-filled knapsack on Erzsebet's back and placed the attaché case strap over his shoulder and across his chest.

The love letters! Erzsebet remembered they were not packed! But where was she going to put them all? She had no pockets in her coat and neither did Jozsef. If there had been time, she would have ripped out the lining of their coats and sewed the love letters inside, but there was no time to spare. Jozsef and Erzsebet stood frozen in place, their eyes flashing anguished looks towards one another as to "what must be done." After taking one last lingering look at the bundle holding dozens of enchanting love poems, intimate sentiments, and beautiful expressions of their undying devotion, they each took turns placing a handful of letters into the fiery belly of the coal stove. With stuttering breath, Erzsebet spoke her thoughts aloud, "If…we cannot take them with us… then…no one else will have them!"

The parchments of love burst into a brilliant red flame, igniting instantly in the fiery furnace, just as their hearts had burned immediately for each other the moment they had met. It only took seconds for their "love" to be obliterated into nothingness as Erzsebet watched on, her slight shoulders shuddering from the cries of regret ripping through her body. How much Erzsebet wanted the luxury of being allowed to have a good, hard cry; and how much she wanted the comfort of collapsing into Jozsef's strong arms, to hear her husband murmur words of love and support, but there was no time! Jozsef pressingly grasped Erzsebet by her shoulders, "My *Edes*, listen to me, there will be more letters, I will write you a love letter every day of your life, but right now, please do not cry. I love you, but we must leave *now*!"

Ferenc was waiting in the hallway outside the apartment to escort the family to a safe area where they were to begin their journey. Jozsef gathered Judit in his right arm. With his left arm around Erzsebet's waist they walked out the door of their apartment. Jozsef looked straight ahead, his mind filled with the many things needing to be done in a few hours.

But, upon exiting the apartment door, Erzsebet looked back over her shoulder, wanting one final look at their home. Stinging tears blurred everything into a shapeless, colorless mass. *I should never have looked back. It strangles my heart.*

Unbeknownst to Erzsebet, Jozsef had conspired with Ferenc to set-up a "Booby-trap" at the door of their apartment. After the family set out on their journey, Ferenc returned to the apartment, setting devices in place that would make sure the *Evil Ones* would breathe their last when they opened the apartment door.

On the cold, foggy evening of November 16, 1956, the Jozsef and Erzsebet Bognar Family closed the door on their life in Hungary, their birthplace, the land of their ancestors, the place where Jozsef's music and rhapsodies had taken hold - the Citadel of their Love.

The life they had hoped to build was never to be, at least not on *Magyar* soil. With heavy hearts the reluctant fugitives began their trek into the great unknown.

Several families embarking on the same pilgrimage crossed their path, and like Jozsef and Erzsebet, carried all they owned on their backs, in their arms, and in their hearts. To avoid detection by Russian troops, many parents had given their little ones sleeping draughts to suppress their whimpering and cries.

It was a slow, chilly, damp, five-mile walk to the check-point where Ferenc had instructed them to wait for a Russian Army truck (stolen by the Freedom Fighters) to transport the refugees the nearly one hundred miles to Andau – a distance impossible to walk in one night. The truck was their lifeline.

The family and other refugees rode in the back area of the truck for seemingly countless hours, before coming to a stop near a wooded area approximately fifty miles from the Austrian border. Everyone disembarked. The driver gave the group a general heading to follow through a dense set of woods where they would meet up with another truck on a different section of road.

Erzsebet, and Jozsef carrying little Judit, including the two other families, disappeared into the sheltering embrace of a tight cluster of trees.

The cool, foggy night was becoming more frigid, their circumstances made even more dismal by the muddy ground left from a prior rain.

The weather was the best and the worse scenario: the fog made it difficult for them to spot Russian squads making rounds in the area; however, the fog also served as a protective veil to avoid being seen, and that *was* a miracle considering there was nearly a full moon! After several hours of walking in the black gunk, their feet became numb due to the cold and damp.

Judit started to cry, and no wonder - she was just a little girl who was cold and hungry. How could she possibly understand why she was in a dark forest at nighttime and not in her bed? Jozsef held her close and whispered a Hungarian nursery rhyme to quiet her, "Little squirrel, little squirrel, he climbed up a tree. He fell down … he fell down … and he broke his knee. Oh, oh, oh, oh, nice doctor man, please make the little squirrel well again."

The family trudged onward, albeit slowly, for the forest floor was sticky and sludge-like, making each step an effort. The black-brown ooze seeped over the cuffs of their ankle-high boots, permeating their socks with the near-frozen mush. Judit tired of being carried, fidgeted in her father's arms, but Jozsef refused to set her down into the cold slush. He pitied her discomfort.

The other passengers who had disembarked from the truck with them must have fallen behind or become lost, for Jozsef and Erzsebet suddenly became acutely aware of no longer being able to see or hear them.

They walked on through the thick trees in the direction pointed out by the driver. It was eerily quiet, not a sound of life stirred about them, except for the sucking sounds made by their feet as they stepped in and out of the sticky mud.

Then… out of nowhere, high-pitched, blood curdling, gut-wrenching screams of men, women and children resounded through the placidity of the imperturbable forest, signaling the angels of retribution to swoop down and carry their torn, broken souls into the chambers of Heaven, to forever leave behind the caustic, razor-sharp echoes of gunfire that had extinguished the final spark of life from their bodies.

Why was it a crime to want to live in Freedom? Why was it an offense to yearn for the clean winds of free air to flow through your lungs?

The Red Tyranny had consumed their homeland of Hungary, the occupiers laying down the law of the land, having determined that any thoughts of freedom, any thoughts of not wanting to live under the Iron Fist of the Soviet Regime, any thought of free enterprise was a travesty unto itself, an abomination so great, so filled with debauchery that one should no longer be allowed to draw another breath. The distant, hellish-red glow of reverberating machine gunfire jarred Jozsef and Erzsebet into a burning, all-consuming, profound panic, for now, the nightmarish demise of their companions would certainly become their reality as the mordant, scathing voices of the patrolling Russian soldiers approached their inept hiding place. There was no way to go back now, no safe way home, and even if they could go back home, there was no home left to go to.

Witnessing the terrifying murder of their countrymen churned Erzsebet's bowels, and try as she might not to vomit, her plagued mind was in no condition to control her ravaged body, and she relieved her retching gut behind a nearby tree.

This is no time to lose control! Jozsef repeated over and over to himself. But Jozsef's addled, crestfallen body refused to listen to reason, and then, as he stood immobilized by dread, riveted in place beside his ailing wife, Jozsef's bruised psyche separated from his deadened bones.

Jozsef found himself swirling above a sanctuary of graceful tall timbers, gratefully reeling, blissfully floating away to a more peaceful place upon the elusive arms of cool, invisible winds. It was all so beautiful, fantastically beautiful, to lose all track of one's loathsome surroundings; it was so peaceful and beautiful to be able to escape to an enchanting place far from the realities of an ugly world.

Indeed, Jozsef's alter ego was pridefully working a marvelous illusion of beguiling deceit about him, blanketing his essence under a velvety cloak of fraudulent armor. And, Jozsef exulted in its facade, reveled in its comfort, and basked in its protection until … Until the shrieking wails of little Judit broke the magical mirror of his haven into a thousand pieces - her cries had sealed their death sentence!

Shaken from his self-aggrandizement, Jozsef heaved off his cumbrous mantle of betrayal, berating himself, hating himself, and despising himself - how could he have been so incomprehensibly irresponsible to let his guard down at this, the most critical, the most perilous moment of their lives? If the enemy found them now, it was because of him… and because of his flippancy, an agonizing end awaited those he loved more than anything in the world, more than life itself. The weight of his sin catapulted the piercing weight of a million-ton dagger through his chest, causing his knees to fold beneath him as he bent into the soil of the slimy earth.

No, no, no! We will not end this way! As a last dogged attempt to save his family, Jozsef vaulted into the deranged actions of a madman, grabbing Erzsebet's arm, viciously tugging and pulling her and little Judit behind a thick stance of timber, a trembling finger placed upon his lips signaling them to be silent.

As she held her bawling baby daughter close to her petrified heart, sickening shudders of an inky-black, faceless, soulless doom clouded Erzsebet's terrified mind as it unwillingly flashed grotesque images of three, ravaged, bullet-riddled bodies sprawled about the forest floor, the last warm, oozing remains of their valorous blood gathering thickly about their lifeless forms, as the viscera of the earth beneath them inhaled the crimson-colored juice of their trickling souls, the burgundy liquid seeking to nourish the buried seeds of the forest, perhaps to reincarnate into the veins of forest-green seedlings and saplings that would one day live again in the warmth of the sun - for no one would ever find them here, in this thick, muddy muck to give them a decent burial. No one.

Hardly able to take in even a shallow breath, Erzsebet dropped her knees into the slush of the cold, brown ooze, clasping Jozsef and her crying baby daughter close, whispering an anguished prayer of desperation towards the moon-filled sky, "Please God, be merciful – take our souls swiftly and do not let my baby suffer!"

Jozsef was not so quick to give in. Determined to save his family, he drew in a deep breath, as an uncontrolled animal instinct for survival overrode his fear. He snatched Judit to him, and with all his might covered her mouth with both his hands, as he tucked her tiny head under his coat, into the deepest depths of his armpit to muffle her whining.

The vociferate voices in the distance were coming closer *and* louder. Judit struggled under her father's coat, but Jozsef gripped her even tighter, burying his daughter's face deeper under his arm. Then Judit became silent. The family squatted in the cold sludge behind a dense set of brush to avoid detection by the shadowed soldiers who had halted in the opaque, misty darkness, no more than thirty feet from the crouching family.

A few moments, that felt more like hours passed, when at last, the faceless enemy strode in the opposite direction, disappearing into the foggy gray banks of mist. The fading sound of a car engine in the far-off distance confirmed the interceptors had departed, but that meant the road to their truck connection had to be near!

But, Jozsef and Erzsebet could not move, their minds and bodies bereft of strength to rise from their groveled position. After an unknown lapse of time, Jozsef's consciousness launched him into a morbid reality, nearly strangling the life from his heart, as a sickening revulsion spread throughout his limbs - *He had forgotten about Judit*!

Jozsef's bleary eyes nearly blinded him as he moved to gently disengage Judit from his armpit. His little girl's eyes were closed, and her body hung limp in his arms. He had smothered his daughter! Erzsebet glared upon her baby's sagging form as Jozsef helplessly held out their child to her. Her lungs ached to scream out the painful denial of her baby's suffocation, but the prior intense encounter had paralyzed her vocal cords.

Her husband could not have suffocated her baby – he loved her beyond all reason! Her baby cannot be dead! *Dear God…no, not my baby…let her live, she must live!* With stifled movements of halting uncertainty, Erzsebet rested the flushed cheeks of her wind-chapped face against Judit's thin chest straining to hear a heartbeat. "Jozsef!" she hoarsely whispered, "Look! See! – Judit's stomach is going up and down! Our baby is asleep… she is breathing, she is sleeping… she is *only* sleeping!" Holding their child between them, the exhausted and terrified young family huddled close to one another on the wet, frigid, forest floor. "My baby girl, forgive me for hurting you!" Jozsef's guilt-ridden figure shook heavily in-between deep groping breaths of remorse and repentance, his hot tears of relief tumbling onto the face of his sleeping daughter.

The young father covered his little girl with a thin blanket pulled from the knapsack, cradling her close to the warmth of his chest. No longer able to hold in the stinging lacerations of her emotions, Erzsebet wept heavily, her expended and rattled body shuddering from the abhorrence of all that had happened in such a short stance of time.

After regaining their fortitude, Jozsef edgily scanned his watch. An hour had gone by! "Hurry Erzsebet, hurry! We must make it in time for the truck!"

The family continued their flight, picking up their pace through the unwelcoming woods, at last coming upon the road leading to their pickup point. One other couple also met them there, informing Jozsef and

Erzsebet of a family positioned only about two hundred feet away from their location being captured, forced into a Russian truck, and taken away.

The unmistakable roar of an engine boomed through the deceiving tranquility of the evening signaling the cautious defectors to retreat to the safety of the tree line. The truck appeared to be the same one as before, but was it? Was it supposed to be another type of truck? The vehicle stopped.

The moon was high, and by its light, they could see it was the same man who had transported them earlier. The driver called out from the vehicle to the unnerved group, "Hurry, we do not have much time - get in!" Jozsef was apprehensive. It could be a trap! The driver could have been captured and forced to drive to the pickup point to gather escapees while Russian soldiers hid in the covered back compartment waiting to capture them.

Despite his misgivings, Jozsef knew the remaining distance to Andau was too far to walk in what few hours of darkness remained. Soon, it would be daylight, and the cloak of night was necessary to elude their pursuers. They had to take the chance. Jozsef cautiously pulled aside the canvas covering the back of the truck. It was empty! The reassured refugees clambered inside and within seconds were on their way.

After seemingly endless hours had passed, the vehicle made a hard stop jolting all on board awake. Jozsef rubbed his eyes, "I wonder where we are?" With cold, stiff bodies and throbbing heads, the passengers disembarked from the rear of the truck into the ominous solitude.

The faint light of daybreak barely illuminated the dispiriting landscape. In every direction there was nothing more than a wide expanse of desolate, marsh-like, swampy land. The driver pointed his finger "Go that way, you will see the bridge." With those last words he drove away. The earth was soft and oozing with wetness. The last remnants of a dissipating fog swirled about them, and with each step, their feet sank even more deeply into the gooey soil of the wetlands, but they no longer cared, their emotions too raw, and their bodies too depleted to worry anymore about cold feet or wet clothes.

Erzsebet had fed Judit milk, earlier, so she was pacified and sleeping in Jozsef's arms. Despite feeling nauseated from all they had gone through, the couple had forced themselves to eat the *kolbasz*, knowing they needed its sustenance to maintain their energy.

With exhaustion pressing upon every molecule of their being, the family stumbled forward, but then, without warning, Jozsef stopped abruptly in his tracks, his finger pointing to a dreamlike image up ahead, "Look, Erzsebet!" Out of the billowing mist, the ghost-like forms of a few, then several more, and then even more, sodden men, women, and children, emerged, each making their way towards the promising icon of hope awaiting the spent travelers. The glowing sun rose higher in the early morning sky, spreading its feathery, bright, powdery-pink streaks of a new dawn across the horizon. *It must be God sending a ray of light for us to follow*, thought Erzsebet. And He did. The Bridge of Andau was directly in front of them!

As the life-giving star spread its first yellow, warming rays upon the icy earth, faintly illuminated forms of fellow Hungarians materialized upon the planks of the small, ramshackle, rickety, wooden bridge spanning the narrow Einser Canal.

Jozsef and Erzsebet hearts fluttered with a rush of eagerness and excitement as a surge of exhilarating energy spread through their expended limbs, urging them to join the hundreds of pairs of shabby, muddy shoes marching upon the beams of hope stretching into the free border of Austria. Jozsef spirited little Judit to his chest. And, holding Erzsebet's hand in his, they ran on frozen feet toward the narrow stretch of wooden supports.

Then…they were there - standing at the threshold of a New World.

The realization of all they had been through bared down on their enervated, distressed bodies. Erzsebet flung herself into the sanctuary of Jozsef's arms, their baby held between them - crying tears of joy for the new life awaiting them, tears of mournfulness for all they were forced to leave behind, and tears of eternal thanks to God in the blessed heavens. "Come Erzsebet" Jozsef euphorically proclaimed, "This is no time to cry! All the crying time is gone! It is time for us to live again, really live! We made it! We are free!"

The unknown *Realm of Freedom was* a mere footstep away, and with little Judit standing between them, Jozsef and Erzsebet grasped her tiny hands and stepped onto the bridge of dreams.

FREE AIR

The people of Andau, Austria opened their country, hearts and arms to thousands of Hungarian refugees, housing and feeding the bedraggled, dirty, hungry, confused, and bewildered sea of humanity.

In the United States, community centers were gearing up for the arrival of thousands of refugees, organizing their efforts in every available building including schools and movie theatres, offering food, shelter, and bathing facilities to the Hungarian people. The selfless Americans donated countless articles of clothing to those who had no more to wear than the soiled garments in which they had escaped the invasion of their homeland. After a brief recuperation in the centers, the war-beaten refugees were transported by bus or other means to scores of refugee camps set up across the United States.

President Eisenhower had sent an open invitation to the Hungarian refugees to come to America for resettlement, sending several army ships, including the USS General Haan, to Bremerhaven, Germany to transport thousands to the United States. The General Haan was designed for about seven hundred troops and there were almost two thousand Hungarians on-board! The carrier was scheduled to arrive with its passengers in New York, from where, many would be transferred to Camp Kilmer, New Jersey, an Army camp originally built for staging American troops. Camp Kilmer had been closed after the Korean War but had been re-opened in 1956 to await the arrival of almost thirty thousand Hungarian refugees.

For the past month, Jozsef, Erzsebet, and Judit had taken refuge in the camps at Andau, and at last, were transported to the German port city of

Bremerhaven. It was impossible for the couple to comprehend the overwhelming series of events coming upon them in such a short time. It was as if they were watching themselves in a movie show running in slow motion: dismounting the bus, walking up the boardwalk onto the ship and undergoing the necessary paperwork and processing. The family had survived against all odds. Despite the horror, hunger, fear, and torments they had witnessed and endured, they were on their way to a new world where their feet would walk on untrodden roads.

But, on this incredible evening, renewed strength engulfed their battered bodies, for the three of them were on-board the USS General Haan set to steam across the Atlantic towards America. More than a thousand tightly packed Hungarians stood on the deck of the Freedom Ship as it made its way out of Bremerhaven Harbor towards the open sea, the little family standing in the center of the crowded platform mesmerized by the wide expanse of rippling ocean before them, the flaming hope of freedom flooding their veins.

Somewhere, amidst the massive crowd of refugees, a joyful chorus of Hungarian voices singing "Silent Night" floated through the air. At first, Erzsebet was certain a company of angels had descended upon them, because upon hearing the singing, she realized it was the most sacred of all days, "Jozsef, I forgot - it is Christmas Eve!" The agonizing sequence of events had made them lose all concept of dates or time. "Do you think the Americans planned it this way, planned that we depart for America on this night as a Christmas gift to the refugees?" Jozsef placed his arm about his wife's slight shoulders, "Yes, my *Draga*, I do believe they planned it this way. It is their way of blessing our new lives."

The ship's crew worked diligently seeing to the comfort of the immigrants. Hot meals were served and there were plenty of blankets.

Women and children received the best quarters on the ship. The men were separated from the women and children, placed wherever there was space available. The families would meet on deck during the day, or in common areas on the ship, but had to retire to their respective parts of the vessel at dusk.

Jozsef's quarters were in the bow of the ship, under the water line. Having only a straight razor to use for shaving, Jozsef soon discovered shaving to be a perilous undertaking. With a straight razor in hand, Jozsef would "dance," keeping pace with the fore and aft rocking of the boat to prevent himself from falling on his own razor.

It would be an approximately fourteen-day voyage by the time they reached New York. This winter, the sea was unusually treacherous and stormy, and even the captain remarked it was one of the worst seas he had ever navigated. The volatile sea crested waves of unbelievable proportions; however, Jozsef, with his bold and adventurous nature, and dreadfully bored by listless days of inactivity, stole away, unseen, to the upper deck to take part of the spectacular scene.

The cold misty sea spray and forceful winds swelled against Jozsef as he held fast to the railing in the centermost part of the ship. Here it came - a huge wave, maybe thirty feet high – up went the ship to the very top of the wave. As the watery coil passed under the vessel, a hollow opening was left beneath the ship, leaving it suspended in mid-air for milliseconds. Moments later, the vessel crashed straight down into the roaring tempest, rumbling, and shaking every bit of her iron frame. Jozsef laughed at the thrill of the ocean's assault upon the vessel and his person. The merciless onslaught of waves was nothing compared to the torments that had pervaded his former life.

Despite the winter cold, the assaulting challenge of brisk winds and mighty waves refreshed his spirit, as jolts of invigorating excitement filled his being with each drop of the ship into the briny brew, the ship speaking to Jozsef through its moans and groans as the watery hammers dared the metal conveyance to burst apart.

The stormy swells continued for days and days.

Almost every passenger, including the captain, succumbed to sea sickness. "Throw up bags" were distributed for emergencies. Erzsebet was having an especially difficult time with massive bouts of emesis, being barely able to lift her head off her bed. Little Judit, concerned for her mother's well-being, held an emesis bag under her mother's chin, "Here Mama, you can throw up right in here," and Erzsebet made very good use of it.

The anticipation of setting foot in America made the winter days and nights long. Time was passed by playing cards, walking the deck on better days, sleeping, and most of all, dreaming about where the winds of fate would take them.

On January 7, 1957, the USS General Haan steamed past New York harbor. Despite shivering temperatures, the elated and high-spirited Hungarian refugees crowded the ship's deck shouting, cheering, and waving the Hungarian flag, celebrating their victorious arrival to America. But, suddenly, as if on cue, all on board became quiet – a peaceful, respectful, somber stillness filled the air, as thousands of Hungarian eyes froze in place, spellbound by a shining, towering object in the distance, standing beautiful, strong and proud – a symbol of hope for all the war-torn souls on board – The Statue of Liberty.

The ship's spokesperson quoted the inscription at the base of the statue to the entranced masses: "*Give me your tired, your poor, your huddled masses, yearning to be free, the wretched refuse of your teeming shore, send these, the homeless, tempest-tossed to me, I lift my lamp beside the golden door.*"

Standing in silent awe amongst those on the crowded deck were Erzsebet and Jozsef, with Judit riding high on her father's shoulders. The ship slowed down as it approached the female colossus rising from the sea, the Lady's presence confirming they were truly in the Land of the Free. The jubilant family hugged, cried, kissed, and laughed at the same time, unable to contain the exuberant rapture emanating from their souls.

The Lady's message was exceptionally meaningful to Erzsebet, penetrating her to the point of being unable to contain her joy, the message bursting the very seams of her heart, as if the statue were speaking only to her: *Here we are huddled on a ship with those who yearn for freedom, exiles of our native country, very homeless and very tempest-tossed!* But, one poignant line of the poem ignited a fire within her soul, "*I lift my lamp beside the golden door.*"

"I know the meaning of these words!" Erzsebet's voice quivered with excitement, her face glowing with exhilaration. "Jozsef! The Golden Door *is* America! We are free, Jozsef, we are at last free! We have crossed *through* the Golden Door!" And then she cried the most beautiful tears she had ever cried before – the tears of a free woman.

In early November 1956, an Army facility in New Jersey, named Camp Kilmer, was readying itself for the arrival and processing of thousands of Hungarians through the invocation of "Operation Mercy," ordered by President Eisenhower. The American Red Cross, The Committee for Hungarian Refugee Relief, and other volunteer services and government agencies, assisted in assembling everything needed to embark on such an immense undertaking, with a goal to resettle the immigrants all over the United States through the assistance of innumerable charitable and religious groups. The United States Employment Service took part in matching the refugee's skills to jobs all over the country.

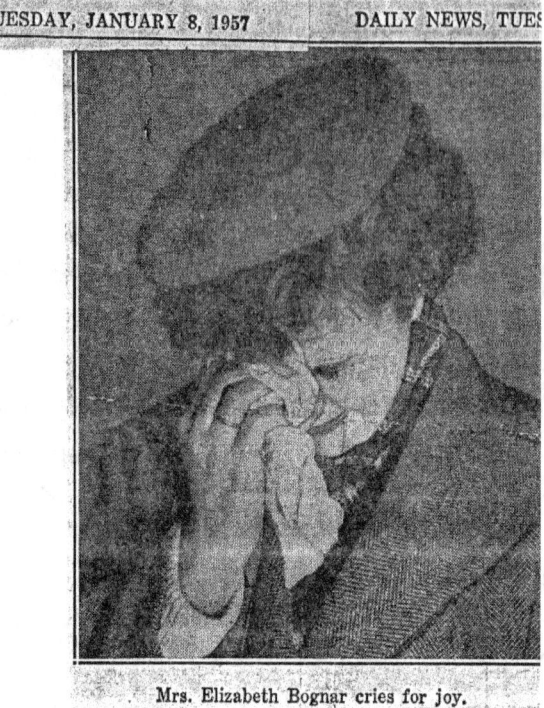

Newspaper article showing my mother crying upon her arrival to the United States

Sponsoring American families were also sought-after for a lifegiving mission: To take refugee families into their homes with the purpose of helping the newcomers learn a trade, educate them about American culture, and to assist the refugees in learning the English language, thus, enabling the refugees to assimilate into becoming self-sufficient residents within the borders of their new country.

The generous American people poured out their hearts to the refugees, and with their sponsorship, nearly thirty-two thousand refugees were relocated all over the United States.

After leaving the ship, numerous buses, planes, and trains were waiting to take refugees to settlement centers throughout the United States - Erzsebet, Jozsef, and little Judit were taken to Camp Kilmer where the young family was settled into temporary housing within the barracks.

Even in a refugee camp outside news can travel fast. Erzsebet and Jozsef learned that nearly seventy thousand Hungarian refugees had crossed over the tiny bridge of Andau before it was destroyed by Soviet Troops on November 21, 1956.

A cold shudder jolted through Erzsebet upon hearing their lifeline to freedom had been destroyed. *If we had not ran that very night, if we had delayed, we probably would not be alive.* The thought was too much for her to bear and she quickly tore it from her mind.

But now, a new peril encroached upon their happiness.

Despite all the delicious food readily available to her, little Judit was not interested in eating. Her loss of appetite had started during the latter days of their voyage, attributed to the unsettling movements of the ship; however, on dry land, with a warm bed to sleep in, and ample food, the little girl was failing to thrive, was feverish, coughing deeply, and her already gaunt features more pronounced.

A thorough medical examination by an army physician determined Judit to be suffering from an unalterable case of pneumonia. Through long, brutal days and nights, the child's unrelenting fever, cough, and malaise defied a series of penicillin injections. The young army doctor had committed a crime – the crime of compassion, the crime of being too involved with a patient, the crime of grief for a dying child.

His guilt-ridden conscious nagged him to the bottom of his mettle as he said the words that should be unspeakable to any parent. "I am so very sorry, but your daughter…your daughter is dying."

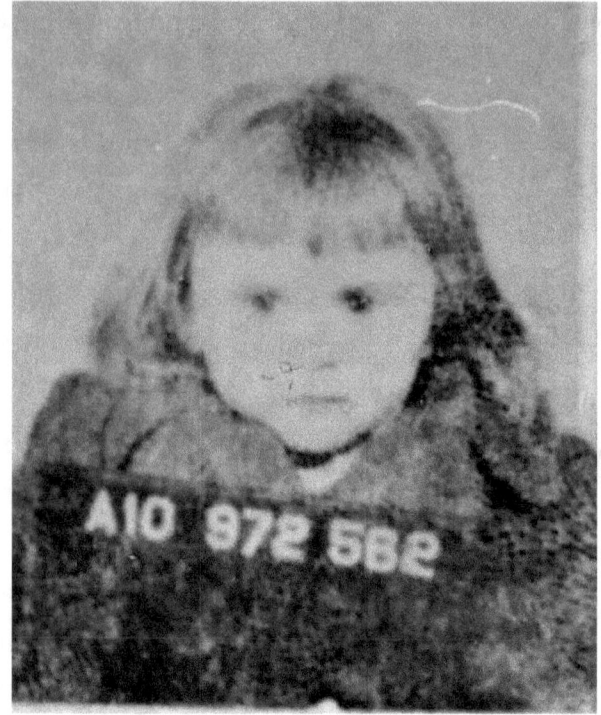

*Judit's (the author's) picture taken upon her arrival to the
United States - January 1957*

Coming to America was to be the realization of all Erzsebet's and Jozsef's hopes and dreams, and now, after all the dreadful and unspeakable hardships the family had faced, their little girl was dying! If she left this earth there would be no more dreams, no more freedom, no more of nothing, for her death would be their death sentence. There was no life without her.

As the sunrises and sunsets came and went over their withering daughter, torrid tentacles of grievous pain encircled Erzsebet's heart, smothering her senses in darkness, strangling her mind in limbo's hell.

When at last her incensed soul could no longer tolerate the soft, yet nerve-wracking rattles and mewing noises emanating from her daughter's chest, she screamed a scream of an anguished animal, vehemently grabbing the lapel of her husband's coat, her tear-stained faced grimaced in disconsolate pain, "We should have *all* died together in the woods on that awful night! I cannot live without my baby! I do not want to go on without her!"

Jozsef's armor of courage disintegrated, his arms carnivorously crushing his grieving wife to his chest. Leaning on what boulders of strength remained within him, Jozsef knew he must bite through his wife's wedge of pain.

"Sit down! Sit there on the bed beside Judit! Place your hand on her heart, *her* heart. Do you *feel* it beating? Do you *feel* the warmth of her? We will give her the strength to *live,* for as long as we *live,* she *lives.* We did not come this far to lose her!" As the faint ethereal beating of her daughter's life beat against her desperate palm, Erzsebet sent an imploring gaze, a gaze beseeching strength from her husband's fragile eyes. "You are right Jozsef, you are right, we have to pray Jozsef, we *have* to pray. God is our only hope!"

Jozsef gently rearranged the warm army blanket about his daughter's diminutive form, as Erzsebet, in a pose of heartbreak and defeat, clasped her hands tightly in prayer and knelt beside Judit's bed. Jozsef dropped to his knees beside her, holding the limp hand of their baby.

"Dear God," began Erzsebet, her voice tired, cracked and barely audible, "I will make a pact with you - if you will make my little girl well, I will never care how hard I must work in this life, I will never care if I have no more than I have today. Dear God, you may use me in any way you wish, just please make my baby well."

All through the following week, a week filled with unforgiving days and nights, Jozsef and Erzsebet alternated vigils over their baby girl; and, despite the doctor's grim prognosis, the practitioner battled against insurmountable odds for the child's survival, continuing the penicillin – continuing the wait for a miracle.

Somewhere in-between the travailing, measureless, sunsets and sunrises of her little girl's illness, Erzsebet's twenty-second birthday came and went, but she forgot to remember.

Another day of endless eternity was on the horizon, and with it, the first blush of daylight strained into the young family's shelter of despair. Why was a child crying? Jozsef ran toward the sound... and then awoke from his dream. But the crying continued even as Jozsef sat upright in his chair. It was Judit! His throat constricted. *Was this the end? Was his baby dying?* He leaned over Judit's bed, gathering his tiny daughter into the protective shelter of his arms. "My little one, it is Papa, tell me what is wrong, talk to Papa!"

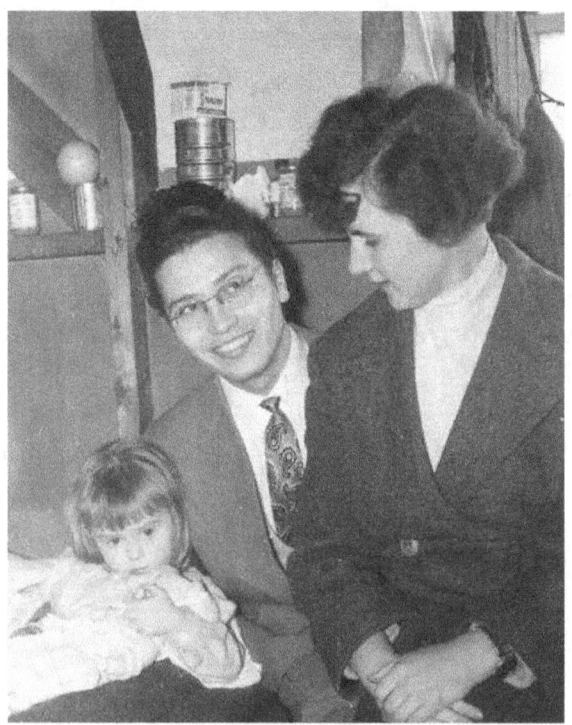

Judit in Camp Kilmer with her mother and father - photo taken soon after recovering from pneumonia, late January 1957

Jozsef stroked the softness of his little girl's cheek, but something had changed! His heart quickened as he placed a hand over Judit's forehead. There was no more fever! He stared incredulously into the hopeful depths of two sparkling diamonds casting their brightness about the dim room as the melodious sound of heavenly bells resounded in his ears, "I am hungry Papa..." Jozsef scrambled to the makeshift cot at the foot of Judit's bed. "Wake up my *Edes*, Erzsebet, wake up! We have our miracle - Judit is hungry!"

The story of the "little Hungarian girl who was going to live," accelerated through the barracks, reaching Sister Maria, a nun from Catholic Services, who joined with the family in giving praises of thanks for God's divine intervention; however, before leaving their happy circle, she bestowed upon them a sacred gift: a small, wooden cross, about six inches in length, adorned with an ivory figure of Jesus, "Please keep this cross as a testament of God's goodness, mercy, and love."

And, their blessings continued: the day after Sister Maria's visit, Jozsef was summoned to the refugee processing office to complete the documents required for their official entry to the United States and to fill out work experience forms. Jozsef was also issued a social security card and number listing his address as *Camp Kilmer*.

It was a sparkling, cool morning in early February 1957. A Hungarian interpreter introduced a gentleman to Jozsef by the name of Mr. Briggon, who had come to ask Jozsef an important question.

"Jozsef, I've been told of your musical genius and your ability to mend and restore a variety of musical instruments. I would very much like you and your family to come live with me and my family in our home in Greenfield, Massachusetts. I own a musical instrument store and am in urgent need of a knowledgeable instrument repairman. I see by your credentials that you are the best in your field. I'll pay you every week and help you find a home for your family. I'll help you learn English. You wife can assist with some housecleaning and can also be a nanny to my little boy. Please let me know what you think of my offer."

Jozsef was speechless. His mind whirred as he quickly processed the proposal. Accepting Mr. Briggon's offer would mean the end of their long nightmare and the beginning of a new life. It did not take long for Jozsef to make his decision as he reached out to shake his benefactor's hand, "I will be happy to work for you and I will be the finest repairman you have ever had!"

"I have to leave for home today," explained Mr. Briggon, "Do you think your family can be readied to leave within the next couple of hours?"

The original cross given to Jozsef and Erzsebet upon Judit's recovery

Mr. Briggon transported the happy, but awestruck family to Greenfield, Massachusetts. Never having owned a car, and their only transport in Hungary being by train, bus, bicycle, or walking, the thrill of riding in an American automobile was exciting beyond words. The road signs along the road written in English held the stunned family spellbound. The scenery along the roadways looked vastly different than Budapest. There were no highways like this in Hungary with such a frenzy of cars coming and going! And the family realized one intriguing thing among the landscape: none of the buildings were battered, torn, blasted by bombs, or riddled with bullet holes. Everything was clean and fresh – like the new life awaiting them.

At the edge of twilight, after a nearly four-hour drive, they arrived at the Briggon's eloquent homestead. Erzsebet was overcome by the unfamiliar, yet strikingly beautiful style and size of the home, along with its well-maintained acreage. She had never seen such a lovely house, she had never imagined such wealth to exist in the world. The New England-style home with its two-stories, large, covered wrap-around porch, small diamond-paned windows, and two imposing chimneys dominating the steep-sloping roof, silently beckoned them to enter. *Look at this house – it is a castle!*

With travel-weary souls and hearts filled with oceans of uncertainty and anticipation, the emigres followed behind their sponsor to the home's front door.

As they set foot upon the front porch, the entryway suddenly burst open, and a comforting yellow light beamed about the dwelling's happy occupants who emerged from within, greeting their guests with a jovial chorus of well-practiced Hungarian, "*Isten hozott,*" meaning, "God has brought you," but also meaning a heartfelt "Welcome!"

MASSACHUSETTS

Mr. Briggon's household strived to make the refugees comfortable. The family's bedroom was bright and cheerful with a lovely view of the immaculate grounds from behind the yellow Priscilla curtains gracing the bedroom's two front windows. When first entering their room, Erzsebet's eyes were drawn to a large mahogany dresser with a matching mirror. Never in her life had she seen such luxurious furniture! A four-poster double-bed with a white chenille bedspread was a welcome sight for their tired bodies. "Look Jozsef, there is a little bed for Judit at the foot of our bed! This kind family has thought of everything to make us comfortable in our new home!" Adjoining the bedroom was a private full-bath. "Oh, Erzsebet! Look here – a real bathtub with hot and cold water ready to use and an indoor toilet with real toilet paper!" Erzsebet picked up a square of bar soap inhaling the sweet-perfume to her nostrils.

"Oh Jozsef, this is how people should live, not like we were forced to live – our families lived like animals!" Erzsebet cried, and then they both cried in-between the walls of the bathroom, the remembrance of only having sponge baths for as long as they could remember clouding their thoughts. It had been many years since either had enjoyed the luxury of a relaxing soak in a hot bathtub, of using any soap other than those made of the harshest lye on their hair and bodies, and most disgusting of all - having to salvage whatever scraps of used, unsanitary cloth, leafy plants, and even worthless paper money to clean themselves after using the toilet. And, as refreshing as the hot showers were in the camps, and the little bars of soap provided for them there, nothing could compare to the sensation of one's entire body being enveloped in warm water on a cold evening, with the smell of sweetly perfumed milled soap floating through the air.

After the three enjoyed a bone-warming, sumptuous soak in the tub, Jozsef and Erzsebet lay in bed with full tummies and clean, refreshed bodies, comfortably covered up to their chins under the wrappings of crisp white sheets, a warm, feathery-soft blanket, and the chenille bedspread turned down to cover their feet. Little Judit slept peacefully in her tiny bed.

It had been a whirlwind day. Fate had stepped in, and in the blink of an eye, transported the family far from the torment, fear, and uncertainty of their former lives. Tonight, they were spending their first night in an American home.

Holding close to her husband, Erzsebet took in a deep quivering breath. Speech came with great difficulty for her throat was tight, and tiny rivulets of tears trickled down her cheeks.

The implications of their first night in this special home overwhelmed her senses. "Jozsef, I cannot believe all that has happened in only a few hours. Yesterday, we had no idea where we would call home, and now, here we are … *home*. But this house is immense, like a palace. I am afraid I will get lost in it! I like the family, they are kind and good. But still, I am frightened. We do not know anything about this new place. We cannot speak their language. I have no idea where we will go from here - we must be the only Hungarian people in this town!"

Jozsef held his sweetheart close to him, the warming security of his arm giving Erzsebet comfort. "*My baby wife, my Draga*, we have been given this chance, a new chance, to make something wonderful out of all the disasters in our lives. Just think of it - out of all the pain and horror we have endured the unendurable! The winds of change kept blowing against us, pushing against us, urging against all odds to carry us to this place, to this time.

And through it all, we held on to one another to slowly be set down in this faraway place." Jozsef glanced down into the strained face of his frightened wife, "My *Draga* one, you must believe with all your heart that we will blend in with America, that we will throw out all the doubts and fears of our former selves, that our determination for a new life will cut into the very crust of our new country's soil, into the very spine of this new land. I know one thing for sure, *for sure*, my most precious Erzsebet, I am going to work hard, *work hard with all the strength my body will hold,* to build us a life only envisioned in our dreams – the life you and our daughter deserve!"

Judit made a moaning sound in her sleep, prompting Erzsebet to lean toward the foot of the bed to check on her. "She is only dreaming." Reassured, she settled back into the crook of her husband's arm, her husband's words easing her fears.

The windows of Erzsebet's young face looked upward into the fern-colored valleys of her husband's eyes, knowing all the answers to their uncertain future lay within his glistening orbs. "My Jozsef, just *say everything will be all right* for us from now on, and I will believe you."

Jozsef squeezed his wife's soft hand, "My *Edes*, everything *will* be all right. This is America, remember? Where anything is possible, and I promise you, on my life, I will try harder than anyone has ever tried before. One day you will have a fine home like this house, with beautiful clothes, lovely jewelry, and even your own automobile!"

Erzsebet, at last assured, let out a happy laugh, "Oh Jozsef, really? I do not think we will have that much, but whatever we do have, I will be happy as a Queen, because I will have you with me, always."

The little refugee family could not have imagined the multitude of new sights and sounds awaiting them when Mr. Briggon engaged the family on a "grand tour" of the town. Such a high standard of living was not thought possible in their wildest dreams.

Having lived in want all their young lives, Erzsebet and Jozsef now had access to everything they needed *and* wanted.

"Jozsef, I never envisioned such opulence and grandeur existed in the world!" exclaimed Erzsebet as they passed by numerous storefronts displaying wares of clothes washers, clothes dryers, refrigerators, televisions, (no one had their own television in Hungary, at least no one they had ever known), electric irons, hair dryers, telephones, fine furniture, car lots, food stores, drug stores, radios, perfume, makeup, elegant clothes and jewelry.

"Everyone has their own home," remarked Jozsef, "And look, see all the nice apartments, also!"

"Everyone has a beautiful car!" observed Erzsebet, as car after car with their fortunate occupants passed by them down Main Street.

The Briggon's had a clothes washer and dryer in their home. The first time Erzsebet washed her family's clothes in the machine, she pulled up a chair to listen to the mechanical sounds of "cleaning." Its rhythmic pace carried her thoughts back to her childhood, remembering the austere poverty of her former life.

My Mama scrubbing clothes on her wood washboard outside in the heat of summer and in the cold of winter. My Mama hanging clothes over a line strung between two trees. How fresh the clothes smelled in the spring and summer! But how frozen and blue were Mama's fingers as she hung clothes outside in the winter months. And the clothes ... the clothes were frozen stiff! How red and cracked were my own hands after washing Judit's diapers in a wooden tub.

Jozsef was astonished by the variety of musical instruments available for purchase at Mr. Briggon's music store. *This is a dream come true ... I will be surrounded by what I love ... music.* A familiar-looking case struck his eye.

Carefully opening the latch, a wondrous thing appeared – an accordion, but not just any accordion, but a *Giulietti* accordion - one of the finest in the world. Jozsef gently ran his fingers across the ebony and ivory keys, his fingertips treasuring the feel of the stately piece.

Jozsef had not felt the weight of an accordion against his chest for a long time – a very long time. How he yearned to feel the pull of his arm against the bellows, the vibration of notes through his soul, but he dared not take the chance of removing the accordion from its cradle. Resting a hand upon the gleaming black casing of the instrument, Jozsef let out a mournful breath of desperate want and longing, "One day, my beauty, one day, you will be mine." Jozsef, lost in his daydream, was unaware of a shadowy witness to his pathetic scene.

Life eventually settled into a comfortable pattern: After making breakfast for the three of them, Erzsebet waved goodbye to Jozsef as he and his sponsor drove off to the music store. Erzsebet's days were spent as nanny and housekeeper, cleaning and dusting the many rooms of beautiful furniture, waxing, vacuuming, and mopping, and caring for Judit and Mr. Briggon's little boy who was about Judit's age.

Staying busy while Jozsef was at work made time go by quickly for Erzsebet, and before she could count the days, March was upon them, bringing with it the emerald green grass of spring and Jozsef's twenty-third birthday.

Judit's third birthday was celebrated in April.

Since the night of their escape, the family had known only cool days and cold nights, but with spring's warm temperatures and bright, clear sunlight, the weather was perfect for Erzsebet to take her young ward and Judit outside to play about the yard, where Erzsebet recovered her "lost childhood," learning to play hide and seek, Red Rover, kickball, croquet, and badminton, much to the delight of the children, and herself.

One shimmering afternoon, on the Briggon's wide expanse of green turf, Jozsef lay on a plaid blanket with Erzsebet, the sun's warmth seeping into the tiniest crevices of his bones, spreading its luxurious warmth throughout his body. How wonderful it was to do absolutely nothing on a dazzling Sunday, but to bask in the lustrous incandescence of sunshine. With closed eyes, Jozsef could not help but reminisce about the vow he had made while toiling in the bowels of the cold, black Tatabanya coalmines: *One day, my family and I will have a life in the sun.* "I made it..." sighed Jozsef, "We have our life in the sun."

Jozsef happy at work at the music store – early 1957

Judit glowed with health. With a nutritious diet, her despairingly thin frame was filling out. Erzsebet also noticed changes in her own being, having more energy than she could ever remember, and, playing with the children outside made her feel as if she had been granted a second childhood.

How fortunate the children in America are – they can play and romp without worrying about revolution, hunger, bombs, and the evil that comes with war on their native soil.

A typical evening with the Briggon family included the playing of word games to broaden the refugee's vocabulary, watching television, especially looking forward to their favorite show, "The Wonderful World of Disney" every Sunday evening. In this enjoyable, yet effective way, Jozsef and Erzsebet soon learned sufficient English to express their basic wants and needs.

News of the Hungarian refugee family making their home in Greenfield spread quickly, bringing two unexpected visitors to the Briggon's home that May of 1957: A gentleman who was an English/Hungarian interpreter, and a lady who owned a local nursery school. After formal introductions, the owner of the school came right to the point – she was interested in Judit attending her facility. Through the interpreter, it was explained how the school would allow Judit to make new friends, develop social skills, and learn the English language allowing Judit to easily transition into American culture. The owner emphasized how each child was treated as a unique person and given individual attention. Children received snacks and lunch. Three school station wagons made rounds every morning to pick up the children and took them home in the afternoon, therefore, transportation would not be a problem.

Erzsebet and Jozsef certainly wanted their daughter to have every advantage in adjusting to American life; however, they explained, through the interpreter, of not having money to pay for the school's service. Sensing the worry in Erzsebet's eyes, the owner quickly interjected, "I am not going to charge for your daughter's tuition. I came here only with the best of intentions. I would like your daughter to have a good start with her life in the United States."

There was a moment of silence as Erzsebet processed all she had heard. Her eyes welled with moisture and a lump formed in her throat. "Thank you!" Erzsebet responded in English, as she rose from her chair to give the generous lady a heartfelt hug. It was final: Judit would start her first day of school the following Monday!

The morning of the big "American school day" was soon upon them. Erzsebet explained all the details to Judit, assuring her she would have fun-filled days playing with children, making lots of friends and learning fascinating things. But Judit was extremely anxious about going to an unknown place without her mother, and her "nerves" would not allow her to take in even a small breakfast of toast and milk, with Judit making it to the bathroom just in time to regurgitate her breakfast.

Judit apprehensively clung to her mother's knees as the door to the station wagon opened welcoming her to board. Judit observed a little girl sitting in the backseat playing with a red and blue pinwheel. Judit had never seen such a thing, and without even kissing her mother goodbye, she quickly climbed into the backseat where another red and blue pinwheel was waiting just for her. Erzsebet waved as the school wagon went on its way, as the pinwheel Judit held out the car window spun round and round.

The one-story nursery school, with its deep green lawn dotted with large, shady trees, was situated on approximately an acre of land. Sun poured into the classrooms through large picture windows. Everything was child-sized from the chairs and tables to the countertops. The students were curious about the little girl who spoke no English and Judit was curious about the children who spoke no Hungarian.

But the language barrier rapidly dissolved, for the teachers involved Judit in all activities and the children were eager to teach her "all the words." The most enjoyable time of the day for Judit was snack-time and lunch-time, where she drank all the delicious, creamy milk she could swallow and all the new and exciting foods she could devour.

Upon arriving home from her first day at school, Judit excitedly prattled about her day. Erzsebet's eyes darted over her child's face as her little girl described her adventures at school. *How full of life and happiness she is. Look at her shining eyes. Sending her to this school was the right thing to do.*

On the second day of nursery school the staff played patriotic American songs on the record player. In the large front room, the children were asked to march single-file in a circle to the beat of the music, each holding a different musical instrument to simulate playing along with the recording. Instead of an instrument, Judit was asked to march holding a small American flag. After the parade, snacks of milk and cookies were served.

Judit in the nursery school parade proudly carrying the flag of her new country – mid- 1957

After her snack, Judit noticed a piano against a far wall. She had not noticed it the day before. Judit plucked out a made-up tune singing a made-up story for each note. Out of the corner of her eye she spied a girl riding on the back of a wooden rocking horse. How much she wanted to ride the horse – and at that very moment! Unable to ask the girl in English if she could take her turn on the horse, Judit, in frustration, attempted to push her off the rocker; however, the girl sat strong in her seat. Judit determinedly grabbed hold of the horse's head stopping its rocking motion, at last succeeding to dismount the girl from the saddle. Judit victoriously climbed onto the horse, urging the fine steed to carry her away to beautiful imaginary places and lands.

Unknown to Judit, a reporter from the local newspaper had been at the school all morning photographing Judit during all her activities. The following day numerous pictures of Judit were published in the local newspaper. Her parent's favorite photo was the one of Judit carrying the American flag. The caption under the picture read, "Carrying the flag of her new country."

Jozsef spent his days diligently restoring and refurbishing each client's instruments as if they were his own. Intermingling with the store's clients enabled Jozsef to learn English faster than he ever thought possible. Erzsebet continued to clean house and watch over the Briggon's little boy, always looking forward to the afternoon when her Judit would come home from school.

After approximately six months of living with the Briggon family, Jozsef had sufficient funds set aside to buy a used car and to rent an apartment. The four-room apartment was at ground level. Another renter lived above them. The dwelling had a large, covered, wrap-around porch, with a neat, fenced-in yard where Judit could play.

Mr. Briggon arranged help to move the family making sure their new home was well-stocked with donated furniture, kitchenware, linens, and food for the fridge and pantry.

When all their belongings were placed inside the apartment, Mr. Briggon called Jozsef out to his car. He opened the trunk of his car revealing a large case. Mr. Briggon asked Jozsef to open it. "Unlatch the snaps - it is your gift from me."

Jozsef swallowed hard. He remembered seeing this case on his first day at the music store and then the case had disappeared. He had believed it to be sold. His trembling hands hesitantly pushed the snaps open. Jozsef slowly raised the cover and pulled back the protective black velvet cloth, revealing the treasure contained within - it was *the* beautiful *Giulietti* accordion!

The communist government had confiscated Jozsef's accordion when they forced him to work in the coalmines. Jozsef had given up all hope of ever replacing it. How could he possibly accept such a generous, expensive gift? Unable to hold back his emotions, Jozsef's eyes filled with tears. Joyous emotion caused Jozsef's body to wobble, and he placed his hand on the car, leaning into it for support, his shoulders shaking as he cried out of pure happiness.

Mr. Briggon was taken aback, unprepared and overwhelmed by the scene unfolding before him. He had expected Jozsef to be excited and happy upon receiving the instrument, but not to this degree of emotion. But, how could Mr. Briggon know…how could he ever imagine how his unselfish act of kindness had "brought Jozsef back to life," for without his accordion, Jozsef had become only half the man he once was.

The realization of what the gift of the accordion truly meant to Jozsef suddenly rushed over Mr. Briggon, and, with gentle empathy, he assisted Jozsef to an upright position, placing an arm about his heaving shoulders.

"Jozsef, listen. Jozsef, *please* don't cry. You have *more* than earned this instrument, not only with all you have had to endure in coming to America..." and then, trying to put some humor into the subject to help Jozsef stop crying, "Look ... You *really* do deserve this. You have done such a wonderful job repairing and refurbishing my client's instruments I have had a steady stream of new customers for weeks - I don't know how you have been able to keep up with all the work!" Jozsef took a deep breath, as he regained his composure, and began wiping the moisture from his eyes with a handkerchief.

Mr. Briggon was relieved to see Jozsef's tears subside. "I know the accordion will give you a fresh start - a way to realize your dreams. But right now, it's time for you to be happy, and time to get settled in your new home!" Mr. Briggon lifted the accordion case out of the car trunk and walked with Jozsef to the apartment's porch. After setting the accordion down, the mentor assured Jozsef, "My entire purpose in bringing you and your family to my home was to assist you in assimilating into the American way of life and to be able to take care of yourselves. I must say, you have far exceeded even your own expectations! Don't you think so? Look how far you have come already!" He shook Jozsef's hand and told him he would see him at work the next day.

It was a jubilant July evening. One year ago, they never could have imagined they would be living in the United States in their own apartment and own their own car! It had been another monumental day. So much had happened since morning! As tired as they were from all the day's excitement, the couple found it difficult to think about sleep even though the donated bed was wonderfully comfortable.

An electric fan placed near the window provided a cooling breeze, enough so, to accommodate the use of a light blanket. Once more their lives had taken an unbelievable turn for the better in a short amount of time! Jozsef held Erzsebet close, "From now on things will only get better. I could never have come this far without your help. You have worked too hard."

Placing her hand in Jozsef's, Erzsebet stroked the calloused fingers, "My sweet Jozsef, my everything - we did it together. How did Mr. Briggon know about the accordion?" Jozsef held her small hand to his chin, "I do not know how he discovered my yearning for *that* accordion, but somehow, he knew everything, my *Draga*. He knew everything."

The next day, with Jozsef at work and Judit at school, Erzsebet decided it was time to explore the boundaries of her neighborhood. Union Street was lined with apartment homes and houses similar in design to their own dwelling. The street of their apartment led to an unnamed road in the opposite direction. Erzsebet followed the street, as it gently rose to a low knoll, upon which was a big building with a sign on the roof set in large red letters. Erzsebet sounded out the name of the store, Foo-oood, *Food*.

Upon entering the store Erzsebet's eyes widened, "A food store – A place to buy food so close to my house!" Not being able to contain her excitement, she was determined to "try out the store." Erzsebet observed other women getting their shopping carts and did the same.

In the Briggon's Home, the groceries were brought in by their sponsor from a store somewhere near the house, but from where, she was not sure. There had always been a variety of wonderful foods to consume while living with the Briggon Family, but today, Erzsebet would make her own selections. There was food everywhere and the meat counter was full!

"Thank you, God, for making sure I will not have to wake up early to fight crowds before the food runs out! I will buy a few things for dinner - a real *Magyar* dinner that came from an American food store!"

Erzsebet valiantly walked home with her small bag of groceries with a singing heart and flying feet. As she approached her porch steps, she heard a conversation spoken in Hungarian! The voices were coming from the apartment house directly across from hers. On the veranda, a woman was talking to a man in the *Magyar* language! Erzsebet placed her groceries on the steps of her porch and quickly ran over to the woman and man across the way. "Are you *Magyar* (Hungarian) as I am?" she asked in her native language.

The young woman appeared happily startled, "Yes! We came to America this January of 1957 on a ship called the *USS General Haan*."

Emmy and her husband Laszlo were also taken to Camp Kilmer and sponsored by a family in Greenfield. Laszlo was a machinist. Emmy spent her days tending her home, and baby son, born in America - a real American citizen. Erzsebet and Emmy now would have the company of each other, and together, could learn more of the culture and language of their adopted country.

Finding Emmy was an unbelievable stroke of luck, for through her, Erzsebet and Jozsef discovered many communities of Hungarian people within a fifty-mile radius. Their isolation was at an end. They were not alone!

Jozsef, Erzsebet, Judit, Laszlo and Emmy spent many weekends during the summer visiting other Hungarian families in the area. Within this newfound circle of friends, they were introduced to what was "beyond the town," discovering the Green River (a popular swimming place) and picnicking in the beautiful mountains of the Mohawk Trail.

Coming home one Saturday afternoon they stumbled upon an A&W Root Beer stand and discovered the Great American Hotdog. "Jozsef," exclaimed Erzsebet, her mouth full as she bit into her second hotdog smothered in ketchup, "Did you ever think we would have food served to us from a tray perched on our own car window!"

Erzsebet and Jozsef at the Green River

It was a warm Friday morning. Tired of playing with her dolls on the porch, Judit yearned to do something more exciting. Inside her heart was the flame of her father's adventurous spirit and she wanted *more than just the porch*. She had the perfect place to explore – downtown Greenfield, and maybe more. Downtown was one of her most favorite places. The hustle and bustle of the town with its mixture of noisy cars and sidewalk conversations was thrilling to her young heart and mind. It was an easy walk, not more than one mile from her house.

Erzsebet went to check on Judit. Opening the front door to the porch she called to her daughter, "Judit it is time for lunch. Come and eat now!" There was no reply. Erzsebet checked the front of the apartment, the yard, and even checked with Emmy, but Judit was not there. Erzsebet panicked -where was Judit! Straining her eyes down the long expanse of sidewalk a shopping cart was magically making its way toward her with no one pushing it along. As the cart came closer a blonde head of hair came into view just above the grips of the cart. It was Judit - pushing a cart full of groceries! How did Judit go to the grocery store? She had no money? Erzsebet heard the unmistakable sound of Judit crying. The closer Judit got the louder the sobbing.

Judit and her father picnicking at the Green River - 1957

Judit *did* have an adventure. On her way home from her downtown trip, she decided to help her mother by doing the weekly grocery shopping. Judit had always accompanied her mother to the grocery store and knew every item her mother placed in the cart. Judit had gone up and down the aisles of the grocery store, loading up on cottage cheese, sour cream, meats, fruit, bread, soda, and milk. Pushing the cart out the door of the grocery store, Judit made her trek home.

How did a tiny three-year-old girl manage such an exhausting feat? Judit ran toward her mother with tears streaming down her face. A much-relieved Erzsebet pulled Judit to her chest only to discover her daughter was covered in sour cream and cottage cheese!

On questioning her daughter, Judit explained she wanted to bring the groceries home to her mother because she wanted to "surprise her." *Well, she certainly did surprise me! But how in the world did she become covered in sour cream and cottage cheese?*

"A big dog tried to hurt me on the way home. I thought if I gave him something to eat, he would leave me alone. I opened the sour cream and cottage cheese and tried to feed it to him, but he jumped up on my chest and the food spilled on me and fell on the ground. When the dog started to eat the food on the ground I ran away and pushed the cart home. I was very scared!"

As much as Erzsebet wanted to scold her daughter it was all she could do to keep from laughing as she envisioned the story unfolding in her mind. But what troubled her conscious was the food – it was not paid for. When Jozsef came home from work Erzsebet explained the "dog story" to her husband. Jozsef was both amused and upset. The food would have to go back to the store, and they would have to pay for what could not be returned. He would do his best to explain that his daughter did not understand her wrongdoing.

Jozsef pushed the cart back to the store loaded with whatever food could be salvaged. After Jozsef's explanation of the situation to the store manager, the manager burst into laughter as he envisioned the young child's epic adventure. The manager questioned the store's staff and learned a cashier had assisted in holding the door open for Judit to push the loaded food cart outside - the groceries were never even placed in bags! The manager found the entire scenario hilarious. The manager shook Jozsef's hand and told him to bring the food back home with him. It was "perfectly okay for this one time." Then, the manager patted Judit's head and made his way back to the store office. The family put the remaining groceries in bags and went home.

Judit sitting on the porch at Union Street

That evening, due to Judit's "inappropriate actions," the family enjoyed a "most appropriate" dinner made from the "doggy cart groceries."

The next time Judit played on the front porch Erzsebet wrapped one end of rope about Judit's ankle and wrapped the other end over the porch railing. Judit was now "trapped" and could not leave home. There would be no more adventures. Unbeknownst to Judit she could have escaped from her bonds at any time. Had she just given a little tug on the rope, she would have found the ropes were never tied, but only loosely draped in place over the porch rails.

"There has to be a kinder way to keep her home," Jozsef reflected, as he observed his sullen daughter "tied to the porch." In a flash, his mind whipped up an ideal solution. With the help of Laszlo's truck, a shiny blue swing and slide set was purchased, and within an hour of getting it home, was put together, with Judit ecstatically swinging and sliding away.

She not only had a swing to play on, but also a sparkling red tricycle with a bell on the handle. Judit rode up and down the sidewalk ringing her bell to make sure everyone saw her new bike. Jozsef made it very clear to Judit that she must never wander off her street again or the swing and bike would be taken away.

As they watched their daughter contentedly play, Erzsebet's heart lightened, relieved of no longer having to "tie" her daughter to the porch. "Jozsef, how did you managed to buy all this for Judit? It costs far more than we could afford this week!" Jozsef hugged Erzsebet, lifting her feet off the ground and swinging her around and around. "It was easy! I have found out how to buy something when you have no money – I charged it!"

Soon the Fall of 1957 was upon them; however, this October was not a "normal October." The month of fall colors and celebration of the Autumn Season in America marked a tragic remembrance for Jozsef and Erzsebet: October 23,1957 marked the one-year anniversary of the Hungarian Uprising.

The couple had received a letter from relatives in early October describing how the citizens of Budapest were to symbolically wear black on the anniversary of that fateful day as Hungary's demonstration to the world that their country remained in mourning for the thousands of lives lost in the dreadful days between October twenty-third and mid-November of 1956.

Sitting at their kitchen table, Jozsef read the letter out loud, translated into broken English, the letter read: "During this time of mourning we stay home. We not go movie house or out to coffee. We grieve as one people on anniversary death of our country. One day we win when God knows it will be the time. How we miss you, think of you each day, wondering when we see you again…" As he recited the last lines on the page, Erzsebet's insides churned with grief for her family and lost country. Her helpless cries of despondency filled the air of their apartment as Jozsef powerlessly held her close, sharing her pain. *Who would not cry for the loss of one's country, family, and friends?* Erzsebet's overwrought eyes piercingly searched her husband's face, "My *Draga* Jozsef, I miss our family! Will we ever see them again?"

"I do not have an answer for you my *Edes*," professed Jozsef, "I wish I could tell you when." Erzsebet, not receiving the response she had hoped for, threw herself upon her husband's chest with a face full of tears. But Jozsef truly had no answer to give. Trying again to reassure Erzsebet, he held her even more tightly, "I miss them also my *Draga*…I *miss* them. I do not know how we will, but somehow, someway, one day, we will see our families once more. I am sorry… I cannot read any more of the letter to you, it hurts me too much." Jozsef placed the letter on the table and wiped his wet spectacles. Later, Erzsebet read the final line of the letter to herself, "Pray for us."

In late October, Judit told her mother about a day the children called "Halloween."

"Mommy, I am to put on a scary costume or paint my face to look ugly, and then go to houses and knock on doors at nighttime, and… if I say Trick or Treat, people will put candy in a bag that I am to carry. Why do I have to do this to get candy?"

Erzsebet, uncertain of this strange American custom could not give her daughter an answer, but thought it would be fun to participate, wanting her daughter to try "All fun things done by American children." Jozsef would not be home on Halloween night; fortunately, he had been hired to play his accordion at a party. He not only needed the money, but it would be a chance for him to show off his musical ability and perhaps gain more playing jobs.

By Halloween night Judit had changed her mind about going trick-or-treating. The thought of making herself "ugly" just to get candy felt odd. "Mommy, I will stay at home and we will hand out the candy to the children who come to our house." As darkness settled in, Erzsebet and Judit placed candy in little bags, lining them up on the kitchen counter waiting for the "Trick or Treat."

Watching from their kitchen door, they observed children in costumes going from door-to-door on their street and across the street. Judit could hardly stand the suspense as she waited for her first trick-or-treater to knock on their door!

Across the way they could see Emmy sitting on her porch holding a large bowl of Tootsie Rolls on her lap. As the sun exited for the day the peals of children's laughter echoed throughout the neighborhood. Erzsebet was quite caught up in all the excitement, her stomach pent up with all the anticipation of a small child about to celebrate her first Halloween in America!

Judit and her mother peeked out from behind the curtain covering the window of their kitchen door. A little boy dressed as a pirate was making his way to their porch! Judit's excitement bubbled over as she sprang to the countertop to grab a bag of candy to give the boy.

A woman, apparently the boy's mother, came running up behind him, pulled his hand, and promptly escorted him back onto the sidewalk and walked in the opposite direction. Erzsebet observed the same scenario as children approached Emmy's place. The parents were intentionally not allowing children to come to their homes! Every time a child made his way to her walkway, or to Emmy's, the child's guardian diverted him back to the main sidewalk. Erzsebet and Emmy locked eyes with each other in the dim light, but even the darkness of the evening could not hide the disappointment in their faces.

By now, Judit had retreated to a little stool in the kitchen, the bag of candy spilt on the floor, crying a confused river of tears. The phone rang. It was Emmy. "Erzsebet, I know why parents not let children visit our house. It is good I learn English. I hear parents talking they not trust foreigners. They say our candy make children sick!" Not wanting Judit to know the gist of the conversation, Erzsebet briskly thanked Emmy. "I will talk more tomorrow." After hanging up the phone, Erzsebet clutched her queasy stomach. What a terrible disappointment for her little girl! Judit had planned on this night for the last week! How could she explain the actions of ignorant gossipmongers to an innocent child? As she glanced into the forlorn eyes of her little girl, the perfect solution to the night's dilemma flashed through her mind.

She told Judit to stay put and not to move from her stool. Erzsebet went into her bedroom closet and found exactly what she was looking for. About two minutes later, Erzsebet peeped around the corner to make sure Judit had not moved from her seat. On stockinged tip-toes, Erzsebet sneaked unobserved into the kitchen shrieking out a scary "Booooo!" Judit jumped from her stool, screaming for her mother's help as a ghostly apparition made its way toward her. Erzsebet lifted the white sheet covering her from head to foot, with holes cut out for her eyes.

"Do not cry Judit! Come with me. We will play Trick or Treat!" Judit jumped up and down in relieved excitement, "Yes Mama, we will play!" Erzsebet went outside on the front porch and had Judit close the kitchen door. She then knocked loudly on the door, and said in English, "Trick or Treat!" Judit opened the door and dropped a bag of candy into a paper bag held out by her mother. Judit then put the sheet on her head and did the same, and her mother put candy in her bag.

They played in this manner until all the bags of candy had been distributed between them, but, the best part was yet to come: in the glow of flickering candlelight, mother and daughter sat cross-legged on the floor in front of the television reveling in their cornucopia of treats. Next year, Erzsebet was determined to have her daughter go trick-or-treating. *If she wears a mask and does not speak with an accent no one will know she is a foreigner.*

The remainder of 1957 evaporated between the demands of home and work, and with the arrival of a crisp, white snow in early December, the town geared up for the hopeful promise of a "White Christmas."

Erzsebet and Judit decorated their apartment with homemade garland and snowflake cut-outs made of colorful paper. Everything had to be extra special for their first Christmas in America!

Erzsebet went into a "baking mania," preparing Jozsef's favorite - walnut and poppy seed strudels. In Hungary, it was the custom to put up and decorate the Christmas tree on Christmas Eve. Jozsef carried their evergreen tree from the car placing it in the corner by the window in the living room. After all the lights and decorations had been positioned "just so," the family stepped back to admire their creation. Without warning, Jozsef blurted out, "Judit, I hear some noise outside! Erzsebet take Judit with you to the front porch to see what it could be, and I will check the back door!" When Erzsebet and Judit returned inside to let Jozsef know they had not found the source of the noise, they found him sound "asleep" on the couch.

Suddenly, Erzsebet heard her daughter squeal with joy, for under the tree were several brightly wrapped packages, Santa had come! Judit shook her father till he "woke up."

"Daddy, Santa Claus came!" shouted a very excited Judit. Jozsef feigned a yawn, "Santa must have been the one making the noise outside and then used magic to make me fall asleep, so he could place the presents under the tree!"

After Judit had "played herself out into exhaustion" and was fast asleep, Jozsef and Erzsebet snuggled together on the living room couch. The late evening was exquisitely peaceful and lovely – the only light in the room provided by the colorful bulbs on the Christmas tree. It had been the most beautiful and wonderful day for the three of them - celebrating their first Christmas Eve in America!

It had also been an emotional, overwhelming day, as it was one year ago, when they had stood on the deck of the USS General Hahn, with bewildered hearts and vanquished dreams, awaiting the ship's departure to America. On that evening of mixed hopes, how could they have ever imagined the wonderful life waiting for them across the wide expanse of ocean?

But it was a bittersweet happiness. The couple thought of all those who did not make it to America - the ones who had died during the Revolution, and the ones who had died during their escape for freedom. Clinging close to one another, the couple cried quiet tears of sadness for those who were now with God, and for their parents and relatives who were unable to share in the joy of this most extraordinary day.

Christmas-time also meant the arrival of the New Year, and on New Year's Eve of 1957, in their small living room, Jozsef and Erzsebet, surrounded by several of their newfound Hungarian friends, raised their glasses in a toast to give thanks for being in a free country where they could do and be whatever they chose to do, and to be whatever they wanted to be. They gave thanks to their sponsor, Mr. Briggon, and a toast to President Eisenhower for giving the Hungarians refuge from a tyrannical, oppressive, communist government. If the blessings of 1958, were anything like the blessings they had received in 1957, it would be a very good New Year, indeed.

April of 1958 marked the month of Erzsebet's and Jozsef's fifth wedding anniversary. Through Hungarian friends they learned of a Hungarian church in Fairfield, Connecticut, called the Calvin Reformed Church, and within its hallowed walls, on April 10, 1958, with their Hungarian friends in attendance, and four-year-old Judit standing between them, Jozsef and Erzsebet were "truly married," this time with the blessing of the Church, and the mention of Love.

It was a busy year with Jozsef working at the music store, Judit at nursery school, and Erzsebet diligently working to disguise the dingy, faded green-tinted walls of their apartment with colorful wallpaper, refreshing the worn window casings with fresh paint, and planting cheerful flowers at the base of the porch to add color to the entranceway.

Every two weeks, on a Tuesday afternoon, Erzsebet took Judit for ballet and tap lessons at one of the finest dance schools in the area. She joined the other mothers who sat in folding chairs along the walls of the large room observing their daughter's tutorials.

The little girls wore black leotards and black tights. Wrapped about their waists were the most colorful array of tutus. All little sets of feet were adorned with tap shoes or ballet slippers depending on the lesson at hand. The school was expensive. Costumes and shoes needed to be purchased and each lesson cost two dollars - enough to buy ten loaves of bread!

Judit had seen a ballerina on television and wanted to "dance like a ballerina." Erzsebet never had the opportunity to pursue her childhood dreams and she was determined to make sure Judit would have a chance to follow hers.

Erzsebet painting her apartment on Union Street

Sacrifices had to be made to cover the cost of such an extravagance; therefore, Erzsebet saved money by only purchasing the simplest, most inexpensive clothes and foregoing any luxuries for herself. What did the choice of her wardrobe matter or being able to wear silk stockings, when it came to her little girl getting all the chances she never had? Besides, her clothes, even now, were still a hundred times prettier than the outfit she had worn the night she met Jozsef at the school dance. But, by American standards, she still looked poor.

The other mothers from "higher society," dressed in their latest regalia, chatted amongst each other about their child's performances, about their shopping sprees, and town gossip. Erzsebet tried to engage in a conversation here and there; however, as soon as she opened her mouth, her heavy Hungarian accent compounded with its broken English engaged disapproving looks on the women's faces, their stony expressions sending a clear message of not being at all interested in what a "stupid foreigner" had to say. Erzsebet felt small, out of place, and uncomfortable as several sets of cold eyes callously, wordlessly, scrutinized and raked over her person. But Erzsebet suffered in silence for her Judit's sake. *I can withstand anything if it means my daughter's happiness.*

Judit had been practicing her ballet routine at home for the upcoming dance school's *Recital*. All week she had pirouetted about the apartment in her lilac tutu.

Erzsebet's chosen dress for the recital was an elegant, tasteful sheath-style garment, silvery-purple in color to match Judit's tutu. Jozsef had purchased the dress for his wife using his famous "credit plan." After Erzsebet slipped into the shimmering sheath, she stood in front of her mirror, but was unable to recognize the woman before her.

Judit on the evening of her ballet recital

The dress was the most beautiful she had ever owned, and, she was the most beautiful she had been in her entire life. Now, with a proper diet, and no longer living "on the edge," her skin and hair had become healthy and vibrant. Her hazel eyes sparkled with health. Jozsef stood behind her, the mirror sharing their reflection. "You will be the most beautiful woman there." Feeling left out, Judit wiggled her way between her parents "I think we all look beautiful!"

"Yes, we do!" agreed Jozsef.

The days of 1958 came and went. On warm evenings, Jozsef played his accordion under the cover of the apartment's large porch. Swirling breezes carried his classical melodies to the distant corners of Union street.

Many visits were made with other Hungarian families who had also fled Hungary in 1956. Each weekend guaranteed a road trip, a picnic, an excursion to the mountains or a nearby river.

One highlight of the year was when a prominent family in the area had taken interest in Jozsef's musical genius. Hoping Jozsef could land a recording contract, they arranged for a local radio station to feature Jozsef on a live radio program. Erzsebet watched the performance from the "wings," her heart bursting with love and pride, as Jozsef, the love of her life, performed many of his most beautiful and difficult pieces. It was a triumphant moment for Jozsef. He had played on Hungarian radio often, and now, he was on American radio! Unfortunately, although Jozsef's performance was well received, it did not stir an interest with any recording moguls.

In early February of 1959, the demand for instrument repair had slowed. Needing more income, Jozsef regretfully told Mr. Briggon of accepting a job with a roofing company. Mr. Briggon had anticipated this day. He knew the birds would eventually leave the safety of the nest to explore the world in their own way. After all, this is what his sponsorship and friendship to the family was all about; helping them find self-reliance in their new country. With a grateful heart, Jozsef thanked Mr. Briggon for seeking him out at Camp Kilmer, for taking his family into his home, for the gift of the accordion, and for giving them the chance for a real life – a life that without his help may never have come into existence. He gave the man who had shown him the greatest of kindnesses a grateful hug, assuring Mr. Briggon that he would remain in touch and Mr. Briggon assured Jozsef of the same.

It was time to seek out new adventures.

Roofing paid well, but it was hard, backbreaking, and demanding work. Determined to prove his worth, Jozsef pushed himself to catch on quickly. He came home tired, but happy, because everything he lived for was waiting for him behind his front door. Judit and Erzsebet were his world. He had nothing else. He would do whatever it took to provide for his family and pride was never a factor.

In mid-February of 1959, Erzsebet was feeling emotionally tired and uneasy. She had been harboring a secret from Jozsef, not knowing how he would react to her news. She did not want to upset her husband, for he was always exhausted after a backbreaking day of nailing shingles; however, Erzsebet knew she could not wait much longer. On the evening of Valentine's Day, 1959, Erzsebet told Jozsef she was going to have a baby. Amazingly, Jozsef was calm and took it in stride. Erzsebet was his foundation, the very essence of what kept him going. Many days he felt he could not possibly hit one more nail into a rooftop, but knowing she was there at the end of every long day, holding him, loving him, giving herself to him completely, made the worries and hardships of everyday life melt away. "I am very happy my *Edes*, another baby! Do you realize this baby will be our firstborn child in America? A real American Citizen! This is truly a day to celebrate!"

It was an unusually warm Sunday afternoon in the late spring of 1959, when Mr. Briggon paid an unexpected visit to congratulate Jozsef and Erzsebet on their news of another baby on the way; however, his visit was two-fold: He had a special surprise for his protégées - a single-family house on Maple Street. With a second child on the way Mr. Briggon realized the family needed growing room. He had spoken with a realtor friend about an older house that had been on the market for over three years with no takers. Mr. Briggon explained the family's history to the realtor, who agreed to sell the home to Jozsef, but Jozsef would have to sign the paperwork within two days of moving in. It appeared Jozsef would have no say in the matter for Mr. Briggon had already given the broker a small down payment on the house. Jozsef and Erzsebet were elated, but dumbfounded - A real home of their own!

An impromptu farewell party was held that night at Emmy's house. Emmy had to act fast for Mr. Briggon had arranged to have the new home's electricity and phone service turned on. The family was to move into their house the very next day!

Jozsef's mind spun about, unable to fully comprehend what was happening - He would be a homeowner! This would be the third roof over their heads since arriving in the United States. *Mr. Briggon certainly believes in doing things at the last minute – first the move to this apartment and now into a real house!* That evening was spent with close friends and Mr. Briggon, where glasses were clinked together in celebration of freedom, long life, health, happiness, and a special heartfelt toast to their benefactor.

The following day, the move to their new home was accomplished with a minimum of fuss. Laszlo and Mr. Briggon arranged to have friends with pickup trucks assist in the transportation of the family's belongings. Within three hours the apartment was empty, and by evening, everything in the new home was in order, including dinner which consisted of the Goulash and homemade bread Erzsebet had brought from the apartment.

Early the next morning, Judit woke up in her new bedroom. She quietly crept into her parent's room directly across from hers, but they were not in bed. She continued downstairs but could not find them. Judit was frightened. It was barely daylight. The house was dark and creepy. She did not even know where a light switch was located. Judit cried. She believed the house had made her parents disappear!

After about thirty minutes of sniveling and whimpering, an exhausted, cried-out Judit, heard a rumbling noise outside. She climbed onto the couch placed beneath the front room window to get a better view. Her parents were in the driveway sitting in the front seat of a truck driven by Emmy's husband, Laszlo. In the back of the truck was her swing set! In their quick retreat from the apartment the family had left the swing set behind.

Owning their own home was too good to be true. Erzsebet spent her first days wandering from room to room amazed by their good fortune. *I believed our apartment in Budapest was beautiful, but this house truly is.* The home, built in the late 1900's, was gray concrete with a stucco finish. In the summer, the front of the wrap-around porch would be encircled by lovely blue hydrangea bushes.

Upon entering the foyer, a staircase on the right led to the second level containing three bedrooms and a bath. The foyer was large enough to accommodate a desk which Jozsef used as his office space. To the left of the foyer was a formal living room, and straight ahead was a large eat-in kitchen with a good-sized pantry. A door in the kitchen led to a covered, enclosed porch, leading out to a beautiful, large back yard filled with blooming flowers. There was also a detached garage. To the left of the kitchen was a formal dining room. Several windows on all floors ensured the house would be light and airy. And, to Erzsebet's delight, there was a wringer washer in the basement!

Another stroke of good luck was Jozsef finding additional income to maintain his new home by playing his accordion in several local venues including a ski lodge in Mount Snow, Vermont.

Jozsef and Erzsebet had frequently written to their parents in Hungary about their many new adventures in America, sending pictures of their new home, of their granddaughter, and word of a new grandchild on the way!

A reply came in June of 1959, when the mail carrier delivered a large, stiff envelope, addressed from Jozsef's parents in Hungary. Erzsebet had waited for Jozsef to come home that evening before opening it. Sitting at the kitchen table, Jozsef hurriedly tore open the envelope revealing its hidden contents: it was their family photograph taken before fleeing Hungary! How beautiful they were! But their eyes could not conceal the misery, sorrow, and pain of the escape they were planning.

Erzsebet gazed upon the portrait. *How much prettier and happier I would have been on this picture if I could have known about the beautiful life awaiting me in America. Our only thoughts at the time were focused on death or capture.*

Liquid carriers of uncontrollable sadness flowed down Erzsebet's cheeks as she stared at the photograph before her. Jozsef got up from his chair, and stood behind his wife, wrapping his protective arms about her shoulders. Jozsef gently wiped away her tears with his fingertips, "We *have* come a long way since the day of this photograph. But we survived my *Edes, we survived* together!"

Holding the picture in his hand, he raised the photo high in the air, waving the image triumphantly, "Tomorrow we must have it framed, to always remember, to never forget, that with love and courage we achieved the impossible!"

September of 1959 was the first public school year for Judit. She was to begin Kindergarten! Judit had soaked up the English language like a sponge at nursery school, and in her interactions with her playmates, and began public school speaking English as well as any American-born child - *without* an accent. The local bank had a school program where it assisted children in opening savings accounts. Every week a lady from the bank came to collect money from the children to place in their accounts. Jozsef would not be outdone by the other American family's weekly contributions and made sure his daughter could deposit at least twenty-five cents per week, and each week, Judit proudly held out her passbook as the "bank lady" stamped in the amount of her deposit.

On October 25, 1959, Erzsebet gave birth to an exquisite baby girl. *Again*, Erzsebet was disconcerted about not giving Jozsef a son, and *again*, Jozsef kissed his Erzsebet and told her, "You *know* how much I love little girls. She is lovely, perfect and I adore her. How much more I love you for giving me another beautiful daughter!"

Despite her husband's encouraging words, Erzsebet remained sullen and glum after the birth of her second daughter, still brooding about not giving her husband a son. Jozsef knew the perfect cure for his wife's postpartum depression: a full-length faux fur coat with a genuine mink collar, (purchased on a payment plan.) Jozsef found the curative power of mink astonishing!

After her baby sister, Kuki, came home from the hospital, Judit had difficulty adjusting to no longer being the center of attention. For five beautiful years *she had been the baby*. And, for five beautiful years her mother had devoted all her time and attention to *her*, but now her mother was "too busy with the baby."

Erzsebet in her coat with the mink collar - Winter of 1959

On a Saturday afternoon, about a month after Kuki's birth, Erzsebet came downstairs after putting her new little daughter down for her nap. To her shock, she found Judit sitting among the Priscilla curtains that had originally hung in the living room.

Judit had taken scissors and had cut numerous holes in *every single curtain*. Judit was also sucking on the baby's juice bottle draining its contents to the dregs. Erzsebet's first reaction was one of anger. How could her daughter do this? She had scrimped to afford those curtains!

"Why, Judit? Why did you do this!" She scolded her firstborn, pulling her up from the floor and spanking her hard on the bottom. "I wanted you to spend time with meeeee!" sobbed Judit, her reddened face twisted in sadness. Erzsebet took hold of her daughter's hand, "I do spend time with you Judit, every day. I am here for you!" Judit's frustration burst forth with the truth of her emotions, "But Mama, I love you so much, but the baby keeps you away from me most of the time!"

Erzsebet was bewildered. It was true. Judit had *been the baby* for a long time. It had been the only way of life her daughter had known. Erzsebet's mind worked quickly to render a solution. "Judit, how would you like to help me take care of the baby?" Judit stared intently as her mother continued, "Well, as you can see, it takes a lot of time to take care of a baby. You are such a big girl now and very smart. Would you like to help me feed, bathe, and dress the baby whenever you can? This way, I would have more time to be with you if we take care of her together?"

"It is a very good idea, Mama. I want to help. I can be a really good big sister." Judit took her big sister role very seriously, helping her mother with her little sister every chance she could, and in no time, the two sisters were inseparable.

One afternoon, Judit had bathed her baby sister in a plastic tub placed in the kitchen sink, and after drying and dressing her, concluded her little sister looked like a tiny doll; therefore, she bundled her sister in a blanket and placed her in the center of Jozsef's recliner to admire her. "Come Mama, look… see how pretty and tiny Kuki is? She is as tiny as a little pill!" And that is how it came to be that Kuki was bestowed her nickname of "Pilvia."

In early December of 1959, Jozsef returned home from work, finding Erzsebet sitting on the couch, her eyes puffy and red, with Judit and Kuki on the floor huddled about her feet. Erzsebet handed Jozsef a letter from her mother in Hungary. Her sister Magda, who had been living in Sydney, Australia, had died from a lingering illness. Erzsebet had been frozen in place since receiving the news, sitting on the sofa all afternoon reminiscing about childhood days spent with her sister. Her sister's loss only compounded her wish to be able to see her family, and she asked the question of her husband that she had asked at least a hundred times before, "Jozsef, will I ever see my family again?"

Jozsef pulled his crying wife onto his lap, cradling her in his arms. As the peace of sleep enveloped Erzsebet, he carefully loosened his wife's grip from about his neck, lowered her onto the couch, and placed a blanket about his sweetheart for warmth.

After making a quiet, quick dinner for Judit, and giving Pilvia a bottle, he put the children to bed. Worn out, he took a pillow and blanket downstairs making himself a pallet on the floor beside the couch. Exhaustion of the tumultuous day overwhelmed him, not only was his work day exhausting, but now, he was overcome in grief for the loss of his sister-in-law.

As he stretched out on his makeshift floor-bed, Erzsebet's question about seeing their loved ones in Hungary resounded in his head. *I have no idea if we will ever see any of our family again. Right now, I have no way of knowing how we could ever accomplish such a thing. It is a high price to pay for freedom, this bitter sadness of being separated from those we love.*

Jozsef reached for Erzsebet's hand and fell into instant slumber.

With his expanding family, Jozsef worked three jobs: a roofer, a weekend accordion player, and as a salesman for the Fuller-Brush Company.

Fuller-Brush produced various cleaning products for everything a housewife needed to maintain her abode. The company provided their door-to-door salesmen with product-filled suitcases to be demonstrated in client's homes. It was strictly commission-based, cold-call selling. Jozsef walked door-to-door in different neighborhoods, knocking on doors, asking housewives to allow him to come in and show them how *easy* it was to clean their homes with his products.

In mid-December of 1959, Jozsef had experienced an extraordinarily difficult day demonstrating the company's products, cleaning several homes from counters to carpets. The women allowed Jozsef to show off the efficacy of his products; however, after hours spent cleaning, the ladies declared they were "Just not interested, right now."

Feeling used and unappreciated, Jozsef stormed home. *Those women simply used me as a maid – an unpaid maid!* It had been one of the most awful, tiring, and stressful days he had experienced in this line of work. "All that cleaning for absolutely nothing," grumbled Jozsef, as he parked his car in the driveway.

Coming up the steps, Jozsef's overworked, empty stomach growled at the delicious aroma of Erzsebet's *Chicken Paprika* wafting out the open front door. Having the door open was a usual practice for Erzsebet, for she believed in "airing out the house" regardless of the time of year.

A high-pitched, harsh screeching noise echoed down the front hallway into the kitchen, surprising Erzsebet, as it glided swiftly by her feet. And, just barely missing little Kuki's bassinette, came the Fuller-Brush suitcase, which Jozsef had angrily thrown into the kitchen, with the utmost of precision, all the way from the open front door. And just like that… Jozsef's Fuller Brush career days were over.

Jozsef had enough of "cleaning," and was determined to come up with a better way of providing for his family. Roofing was not steady work, and obviously, it was not an occupation he could continue to do into his old age. With the Fuller-Brush job ending in disaster, Jozsef decided it was time to use the power of his brain instead of his back.

That evening, Jozsef sat at his desk in the foyer, his shoulders slumped, his hands holding up his tired, foggy head. With closed eyes, his brain whirled about fantasizing several different job scenarios. Suddenly, everything became clear. Jozsef stood up, his hands crossed behind his back, as he paced quickly up and down the short hallway.

During the past year-and-a-half, Jozsef had met several accomplished accordionists during his travels, and he, himself, was a musical master. Why had he not thought of this before? He would work for himself!

Coordinating with five fellow accordionists, Jozsef formed the *School of Modern Music* in Greenfield, Massachusetts. He and the other instructors would be giving in-home accordion lessons to students of all ages. The music school was advertised in local and surrounding county newspapers. The response was overwhelming and Jozsef was on the road to success.

The Christmas of 1959 was one of great rejoicing. They lived in freedom, owned a real home, had two beautiful children, and the accordion school pupils were pouring in. New Year's Eve arrived, spent with devoted Hungarian friends wishing success for all with toasts of *real* American beer, and the lighting of *real* American cigarettes for the menfolk. Life could not be better.

The year of 1960 started out busy and prosperous. Jozsef's music was gaining popularity! He had received several invitations to play his accordion for various events throughout Massachusetts, Connecticut, and Vermont. In addition, he still operated his school of music in conjunction with the other instructors.

Judit and little Pilvia were inseparable. Judit loved being a little mother to her small sister. Erzsebet was totally immersed in her role of motherhood and housewife. Each day she would go down to the basement to wash clothes in her wringer washing machine and hang them out on the clothes line with meticulous precision. When dry, Erzsebet fastidiously ironed the clothes, taking fierce pride to make sure her family's appearance outshined all others. As a little girl, Erzsebet did not have the luxury of pretty clothes, shiny new shoes, or hair ribbons. As she pushed her iron back and forth over the lovely dresses of her daughters, she remembered back upon her childhood days. *How much I had wished to wear silky dresses and glossy ribbons in my hair, but the war took all those dreams away.* Because of her lost childhood, Erzsebet took great care when dressing her daughters, living her little girl dreams of being dressed up like a princess through them, making sure their dresses were dainty, crisp, clean, and always tying thick, shiny ribbons in their hair - *even if they were only going out to play.*

Jozsef during his School of Modern Music days – 1960

On warm afternoons and early evenings, Jozsef's favorite time was sitting on his front porch, with closed eyes, playing his accordion. The gentle breezes carried his repertoire of classical pieces down the sidewalks of Maple Street. At times, inquisitive neighbors gathered to listen in front of the home mesmerized by Jozsef's flying fingers moving effortlessly over the black and white array.

Jozsef purchased a child-size, ivory-white, Giulietti accordion, with white and blue keys for Judit, and each week he gave her an accordion lesson.

How would it look if the daughter of the accordion teacher did not play the accordion? Judit reluctantly, but obediently, spent hours each week practicing lessons to please her father.

The weight of the accordion was uncomfortable against her chest, too heavy in her lap, and the straps dug into her shoulders. Judit would much rather have been out in the backyard burning ants with a magnifying glass than taking accordion lessons!

Jozsef was a critical teacher and treated his daughter no differently than he would a paying student. Judit loved listening to her father play the accordion and admired her father's musical ability, but the instrument did not come naturally to her as it did for him. Despite her feelings of awkwardness, she took her accordion practice seriously, wanting to please her father and make him proud of her. Downstairs, Jozsef could hear Judit practicing in her room. *Maybe one day, Judit will realize that reading and playing music is a wonderful gift.*

The first School of Modern Music Accordion Recital was held in the spring of 1960. Jozsef rented the auditorium of a local high school. It was an ideal venue with a large seating capacity and a substantial stage.

The newspapers announced the event and tickets were sold to the public. The player's proud parents and outside patrons packed the auditorium to revel in the music of the student's accomplishments. Each student had practiced a selected piece for their performance, including Judit, who had chosen to play "The Marine's Hymn." She had chosen the piece for three reasons: it was short, easy, and she could get off the stage quickly! The night was perfect. Jozsef's students were a compliment to his musical talent, but Jozsef's greatest moment was when his little Judit performed her flawless solo.

With the monies earned from the accordion recital, accordion lessons, and the work Jozsef picked up from private events, the family's finances were looking up. They were always mindful of their spending, but, at last, had money to spend on a few luxuries.

Since he was a boy, Jozsef had been intrigued by spy novels where the hero drove an elegant sports car. Erzsebet and Jozsef had gone "window-shopping" on a Saturday afternoon and "somehow" Jozsef drove to a Renault sports car dealership. On the showroom floor was a two-seater, red Renault sports car. When Jozsef took the seat behind the wheel he knew he had found the car of his dreams. His eyes met Erzsebet's, asking silent permission to buy the car, and Erzsebet would not deny him his dream. Memories of childhood deprivation and endless want clouded her mind, and this time, Jozsef would not be deprived. They would worry about paying for it later. After all this was America, and like Jozsef always told her, "Anything was possible!"

A favorite weekend activity was Jozsef taking his family for a long ride in the red Renault. There was technically no back seat, only a space behind the driver and passenger seat for luggage, but it was just large enough to accommodate the children. Jozsef was "King" behind the wheel of his Crimson auto, scooting to the mountains for picnics or the Green River for swimming.

Erzsebet had met a very kind fifteen-year-old girl named Grace. At least once a month, Grace stayed with the children, allowing Erzsebet and Jozsef time to escape from the world's prying eyes, the red Renault swerving towards their private realm located somewhere beyond the twisted backroads of Vermont.

In early June of 1960, Jozsef was standing on a ladder repairing shingles on the upper story of their home. Erzsebet was in the kitchen preparing Jozsef's favorite cold drink – iced coffee. The day was warm, sparkling, and sunny, and as usual, Erzsebet had every window open to allow soft gusts of fresh air to circulate through her home.

Erzsebet had placed two glasses of iced coffee on a tray to refresh her husband. She was in the process of carefully balancing the glasses to prevent the contents from spilling, but as she reached the archway of the front door, the high-pitched screech of metal resounded through the air, mixed with Jozsef's cries for help.

Erzsebet quickly made her way to the front door leading to the porch, just as Jozsef's ladder slipped side-ways, crashing to the ground with Jozsef still holding onto the rails. Erzsebet dropped her tray to the ground and rushed to where Jozsef lay. His face was twisted in pain, and Jozsef had severe pain in his back and was not able to move his neck.

Erzsebet did not know how to drive a car. She called an ambulance to take Jozsef and her to the hospital, and then phoned Grace to come watch the children.

In addition to Jozsef's severe neck and back pain, he also had intermittent numbness of the fingers of both hands and bilateral legs, explained by the doctors as possible "pinched nerves." Out of concern for possible bleeding in Jozsef's brain and, or, a spinal injury, doctors performed a lumbar puncture and numerous other tests. No bleeding was found in the brain, but Jozsef was diagnosed with a herniated disk. After the lumbar puncture, Jozsef experienced violent and unrelenting headaches, along with nausea and vomiting due to a type of dye administered during the test.

Three weeks after the ladder accident, Jozsef remained in the hospital, his pain barely diminished. Jozsef was not used to inactivity. He was always on the go and heading toward new goals. Being confined to an uncomfortable hospital bed, with nothing to do all day, was a miserable existence, one that only reminded him more about his misfortune. How could he have been so careless? How in the world did he fall? He had done countless roofing jobs for strangers without event and then injures himself on his own roof! He thought about the expense of the hospital stay and losing his income to provide for his family, and compounding all this, was an intense fear, the fear of not being able to hold and play his accordion again.

Erzsebet visited Jozsef in the hospital every day, bringing her husband homemade food. It was about a mile walk to the hospital. Erzsebet walked the distance pushing Pilvia in her carriage with Judit by her side. While Erzsebet visited with Jozsef, Judit tended Pilvia in the waiting room.

Jozsef questioned Erzsebet about their finances, knowing she always kept a "little extra" hidden away in case of an emergency. Putting on her sweetest smile, Erzsebet gently held Jozsef's hand, "My *Edes*, everything is doing well at home. You know the children do not eat much and I can eat the same thing every day and do not care. There is still plenty in the money jar."

Lying to Jozsef was difficult, he could always detect the slightest deflection in her tone of voice, but apparently with his pain, he was not attuned as usual, and was happy with her answer. But nothing could have been further from the truth. The nearly-barren pantry and refrigerator was proof. What was she going to do?

Erzsebet made sure Jozsef had water by his bedside and gave him a salami and rye sandwich she had hidden in her purse for his nighttime snack. She lovingly adjusted his pillow, straightened the wrinkled sheets and blankets, and kissed her sweetheart goodbye for the day.

On the walk home Erzsebet's thoughts were as gray and dim as the dark clouds building on the horizon.

The rainy weather cleared later in the afternoon. Only a few droplets of rain balanced themselves on the green blades of grass in the front yard, as the sun's glowing yellow rays broke through the remaining clouds. Judit was in her room playing with Pilvia. Erzsebet was glad the girls could entertain each other, because she needed some quiet time to figure out how to buy food with a nearly empty purse.

With the sunshine came a sticky dampness, and soon, the house had become too warm for her comfort. Erzsebet went outside to the front porch and sat down on its steps. A deep empty feeling rushed through her, bringing with it devastated feelings of hopelessness and helplessness.

If Jozsef did not recover soon there was a possibility of losing everything. She *could* get work as a maid. Rich people *always* needed a maid. She *could* at least get a job for a couple of weeks, but how could she leave her two young children alone all day?

Maybe she could ask Grace to help watch the children while she worked and could pay her later? She decided to ask a neighbor for a newspaper and look through the jobs. She needed to feed her children. She had to do what she had to do.

Her thoughts were broken by a twinkling, merry tune, emanating from a traveling ice cream truck that frequented the neighborhoods in the summertime. The truck appeared randomly with no set day or time of arrival. Of all days, why today? Erzsebet heard the happy squeals of the neighborhood children yelling in delight, their taste buds primed and ready to consume the cool confection. The price of an ice cream cone was five cents.

Nearly every child on the street was lining up for the tasty treat. *Please do not let Judit hear him coming!* But it was too late. Having left Pilvia sleeping in her crib, Judit happily skipped down the stairs making her way to see her mother. Speaking in English, Judit asked, "Mommy, may I please have ice cream? I have been good, haven't I?" Erzsebet hugged her little girl tightly with both arms and eyes moist with tears, and replying to her daughter in English, she explained, "My baby, you are always good. I want to buy you the ice cream, but I have no money for it." Judit's mother had always bought her a cone. Why could she not buy her one today? Judit was only six years old, not yet old enough to comprehend the complex problems of the adult world, or the circumstances responsible for the family's financial crisis. Judit's face turned red and her little eyes flooded with tears.

Erzsebet's heart twisted with remorse, remembering only too well the many times she had gone without as a child, and now her little girl was feeling the same pain of deprivation. Erzsebet had never wanted her children to go without life's simplest joys - not in America. But today it could not be helped.

Through her distress, Judit heard her name being called. She turned toward the voice. It was a lady who lived down the street. She had an ice cream cone in her hand. "Come here!" she called to Judit and handed her the biggest ice cream cone Judit had ever seen - a double scoop! The neighbor looked deep into both Judit's and Erzsebet's tear-stained faces. She had been standing on the sidewalk near the ice cream truck. It was easy for her to hear the interaction between the mother and daughter for Erzsebet's front steps were a mere few feet from the curb where the ice cream truck had made its stop.

Not wanting to pry into another's business, and not wanting to make her gesture seem as charity, the neighbor shouted over to Erzsebet, "I bought the cone for me, but he gave me the wrong flavor, so I figured your little girl might want it!" Erzsebet gratefully waved to the woman and mouthed a heartfelt "Thank you" to her. Other than the kindness shown to them by Mr. Briggon, it was the nicest thing anyone had ever done for them since they moved to Maple Street.

That evening, a despondent and forlorn Erzsebet sat down with Judit to explain the reason for their miserable state. Judit did not seem sad at all upon hearing why they had no money. On the contrary, Judit's face lit up with excitement, "Mommy, do not worry, I have lots of money!" Erzsebet was puzzled, "My baby, how can you have a lot of money, you are just a little girl?" Judit quickly disappeared upstairs and ran back down again. In her hand was her savings passbook. She had twenty-five dollars in her account! "Mommy," Judit exclaimed, "We can buy food and you will not have to cry!"

Early the next morning, with Pilvia in her carriage, Erzsebet and Judit quietly walked a very long mile to the downtown bank. Erzsebet was overwhelmed and grateful for her little daughter's quick thinking and innocent generosity, but understandably, felt pangs of guilt and shame - Parents were to provide for their children not the other way around.

Erzsebet had never set foot inside a bank. She had no idea it would be such an extremely formal-looking institution. She observed customers going in and out of its revolving doors. The men sported tailored suits and expensive haberdashery, and the women appeared as if they had stepped out of the pages of a high fashion magazine.

Erzsebet always took great care in her appearance when leaving the house for any occasion, but on this day, she felt severely underdressed compared to the bank's elite clientele. Perhaps, she should have dressed more "elegantly," but right now her mind was on more important things. Besides, her visit was of a practical and pressing nature. *I will be in and out quickly. No one will notice us.* She straightened her posture and stoically pushed Pilvia's carriage through the turnstile door with Judit following behind.

Judit tiptoed to reach the teller's counter and handed her passbook to a wrinkly-faced woman, whose eyeglasses were seated on the mid-portion of her large nose. The woman's gray hair was severely pulled back into a "bun" behind her head. She wore a dark, fitted suit, with a white blouse buttoned nearly to her chin. The woman's eyes darted about quickly assessing the little family in front of her. Erzsebet wondered why the woman kept staring at them. *Does she only see us as poor people compared to the other people here?*

"I would like to take out all my savings money!" announced a very excited Judit. The woman questioned, "All of it? Why?" Erzsebet interjected, "For personal reasons." Judit tiptoed even higher trying to look over the tall counter. The teller began the transaction, and after what seemed like an eternity, the icy-eyed woman handed Judit her savings money.

Judit was exhilarated – this was the best thing she had ever done in her entire young life. Her body felt energized and thrilled for helping her parents during their difficult time.

Not being able to contain her elated emotions, she turned away from the teller window, and shouted very loudly for all to hear, her voice reverberating through the large, granite halls of the lobby. "I am going to buy food for my mother and take money to my father in the hospital!"

The upper crust bank patrons shook their heads disapprovingly as they stared at Erzsebet, their disgusted facial expressions saying what their mouths did not: *Why does this bank allow people like that woman and children in here!*

Erzsebet may not have been dressed in her finest attire, but today, she felt as if she were the richest woman in the world. She bent down and hugged Judit. She then stood proudly erect, looking about her, staring directly into the blaring eyes of the cold, callous clients, "My daughter has more honor in her small body than any of you will ever have in all your lives!" With her head held high, and moving with the dignity of a queen, Erzsebet maneuvered Pilvia's carriage through the unaccommodating revolving door, her mind spinning in disbelief as she realized what she had done.

The words had just tumbled out – and in *good English*! She would not allow a bunch of "old crows" to stare-down her little girl. Finally, free of the stuffy building, Erzsebet pushed Pilvia along in her stroller with Judit proudly marching ahead, eager to fulfill her mission.

Erzsebet pleaded with the front desk clerk at the hospital to allow Judit and Pilvia permission to see their father as they had not seen him in a long time, but the clerk's stern reply of "they are under-age," caused Judit's heart to sink with devastation. She had wanted to give her father the money herself and see the happiness on his face. "I want to give Daddy the money!" she wailed, her eyes swollen with tears.

With her adrenaline still flowing from the bank encounter, Erzsebet was determined to find a way. "Do not cry, my baby, I will make sure you will see your father!" Erzsebet was distraught. She remembered how happy Judit was in the bank, how the cold-hearted bank customers disapproved of them, and how much they both had cried over the past two days. Judit *would* see her father. She had to have a moment to think.

She took the children outside and turned to face the front entrance of the hospital. She stood motionless surveying the grounds. "I know what to do!"

Erzsebet firmly took hold of Pilvia's baby carriage and urged Judit to follow her. With much difficulty, she pushed the bulky, baby buggy over the green grass of the hospital's bumpy front lawn.

Jozsef's hospital room was on the first floor, at the very corner of the building. There was no air conditioning, therefore, the room's large windows, barely four feet above the ground, were open.

Erzsebet pushed Pilvia's carriage under the window. She waved her hands in front of the window and called Jozsef's name. Jozsef cautiously made his way to the window ledge, painfully leaning over the old wood frame.

He reached out his arm to hold his wife's moist hand. "Why are you outside, are you all right?" Erzsebet could at last release her secret financial burden. "We are fine, my *Draga*. The children wanted to see you, and this was the only way. I must tell you something. Remember when you asked if we had any money left? I could not tell you the truth. You were very sick, and I did not want to burden your mind while your body was healing. We did not have hardly any money. I did not know how to buy food for us. But your little girl has a present to give you!"

"Open your hand Daddy!" Bewildered, not knowing what to make of the scene before him, Jozsef obediently lowered his arm down toward his daughter. "Open your hand wider, Daddy!" Judit placed five dollars into her father's hand, as she did so, she spoke in a lilting way, as if singing a tune, "I alread-eee gave mom-meeee twen-teeee dollars to buy food on the way home! This money is for you in case you need it!"

Jozsef stared incredulously at his little girl, "But … how did you do this?" Judit, not being able to contain her joy, jumped up toward the window ledge, "It is my school savings money!"

Jozsef's heart was overcome with pride and love for his young daughter, but at the same time, was in despair, for he felt worthless as a provider. For weeks his family had been doing without, worrying about how to put food on the table, but still bringing *him* food at the hospital! Today, his little Judit had saved them all. "Erzsebet, *Edes*, hold Judit up to the window!" Judit found herself quickly boosted up by her mother's proud arms, eye level with her father. Jozsef kissed his daughter's bright cheeks. "I love you my little Judit. Thank you for helping your mother and me. I promise you things will be better one day, soon, for all of us."

After his family departed, Jozsef weakly crumpled onto his hospital bed, clutching the five-dollar bill within his palm. Tears stung his eyes. *I must get out of this place!*

After nearly five weeks in the hospital, a very weak and debilitated Jozsef came home. Thankfully, it was a lovely sunny day for his homecoming.

Erzsebet placed her exhausted husband in a lawn chaise in the backyard, covering him with a light blanket, hoping the sun's revitalizing rays would soak deep into his body and give him strength. The healing sunshine warmed his worn essence, and Jozsef quickly fell into a peaceful, healing slumber, dreaming of better days to come.

With the love and affection lavished upon him by Erzsebet and his little daughters, Jozsef's health regenerated quickly, allowing his strength to return, and his pain and numbness to disappear. Not too long after coming home, the sweet strains of Jozsef's music once again floated through the air down the sidewalks of Maple Street.

The late summer days sailed swiftly by and memories of Jozsef's accident faded away. The family spent many pleasant days by the river, taking drives to the mountains, and taking the children to Mountain Park, an amusement center in Holyoke, Massachusetts, one of the most popular places for family fun. There were expansive groves for picnics, a Kiddie-Land area for the children, a train ride that wound through the parks large acreage, and over twenty other types of rides, including a wooden roller coaster.

But for the couple, the most romantic part of the day was when Erzsebet and Jozsef embarked on a trip through "The Tunnel-of-Love." As the little boat made its way through the dark passageway, even with the children seated between them, no one could see them kissing.

The political background of Jozsef and Erzsebet's youth was one of chaos, turbulence, civil unrest, evil corruption, and social and economic instability and mayhem. Political views were oppressed upon the populace and no one had a say as to whom the governing body of their country would be.

But now, in America, a wonderful new type of day was approaching - Election Day. Although they had not yet become American Citizens, Jozsef and Erzsebet were fascinated by the electoral process. The two candidates running for president in 1960 were John Kennedy and Richard Nixon. Kennedy won the Democratic nomination and Nixon won the Republican nomination.

On September 26, 1960, Jozsef and Erzsebet were among the nearly seventy million Americans watching the first debate between Nixon and Kennedy on television. Nixon and President Eisenhower were close to their hearts, for President Eisenhower had sent the "freedom ships" to Bremerhaven to pick up the Hungarian refugees and had sent the USS General Hahn to bring them to America. Nixon had come to visit the Hungarian refugees in Camp Kilmer showing great kindness to all the refugees, but especially to the children.

Kennedy was a "good man," according to Jozsef, and he genuinely liked both candidates. He agreed with the Election Day pollsters that this election could be a toss-up. While watching one of the presidential debates, Jozsef remarked to his wife, "I do like Kennedy, however, if we could vote, I know you and I would vote for Nixon, for his kindness to the refugees." Erzsebet quietly reflected, "There is no doubt."

Another life-changing event was on the way: in mid-October of 1960, Erzsebet told Jozsef they were having another baby. "Jozsef, I do hope we will have a baby boy. I do so want you to have a son."

John Fitzgerald Kennedy was elected on November 8, 1960, in what was one of the closest elections in the history of the United States. "The next time," Jozsef thought, "The next time there is an election, we will be citizens and able to vote." The very thought burned a yearning fire deep within Jozsef, knowing that soon, he and his wife would have a say in the governing of their new country.

Jozsef nervously paced the halls of the hospital maternity wing. Erzsebet had gone into a sudden, hard labor just after midnight. The pain was too great for her to ambulate, forcing Jozsef to carry his very pregnant wife down the stairs of their home into the open back area of the station wagon where she could lay down on her way to the hospital. There was no time to call a babysitter and it was too late into the night to bother anyone. He had no choice but to leave his sleeping daughters at home and lock the door behind him. The baby was coming quickly; however, there were complications. The baby was in an awkward position for delivery. Erzsebet was in terrible pain; therefore, the obstetrician sedated her to perform manual manipulation. In the early morning hours of July 30, 1961, their third child entered the world.

Jozsef watched Erzsebet sleeping in her faintly lighted hospital room. Even after the suffering of her labor, she was so beautiful!

His thoughts flew back to the night they met at the dance. How in the world did he find this perfect woman? She was not only beautiful outside, but full of goodness. She had such determination, strength and resilience. She never complained through all their struggles and hardships, always putting herself last, her family first, the most loving and devoted wife and mother. Jozsef felt blessed among all men.

He gently pushed Erzsebet's damp hair away from her forehead. He *was* the luckiest man in the world. There could be no other woman in the world as wonderful as his Erzsebet. She was a fighter in every way, and it was her strength that gave Jozsef the will to endure anything. Jozsef gently kissed his sleeping wife's hand and left the room to take care of some very important business.

He quickly called Grace to ask if she could come over to the house, get the spare key from its hiding place, and stay with the girls till he returned home. When Grace arrived, the girls were safe, and happy to see her.

Jozsef was walking on air as he energetically made his way to the hospital gift shop to purchase the largest box of cigars available. He then swiftly proceeded down the halls of the hospital cramming cigars into the hands of anyone he met along the way.

This was one of the best days of his life and he was bursting to tell the whole world *he had a son* - a little boy! Jozsef swore to all things holy that his son would always be loved as he himself should have been loved.

Erzsebet awakened to the sound of Jozsef calling her name. Fighting the effects of deep sedation, it was difficult for her to fully open her eyes. With a tired, hoarse voice, she bade Jozsef to lie down beside her on the bed "for a little while." Jozsef balanced himself beside Erzsebet on the narrow hospital bed. With an exhausted, weary voice, echoed in defeat, Erzsebet questioned her husband, "We had another girl, did we not …?" *She did not know!* Jozsef leaned in towards his wife to hold her tightly. Slowly and tenderly, he kissed her cheeks, forehead, and lips with delicate butterfly kisses. "My *Draga, my Pillango,* my everything … you have given me a son - we *have a son*!" Through gushes of wet, grateful tears, and a dry throat, Jozsef repeated himself over again, almost whispering, "We have a beautiful *son*!" Erzsebet weakly reached for Jozsef's trembling hand, her tired voice coming to life, "Oh, my *Edes*, my love, now my purpose for life is complete!" And, she cried - deeply.

Jozsef then tenderly placed a dozen, red, sweet-smelling roses onto Erzsebet's lap. His damp eyes met her tear-filled hazel pools, and he dried the jubilant droplets cascading down Erzsebet's cheeks with his already damp handkerchief.

The exhaustion of her traumatic childbirth coupled with the news of at last bearing a son, was overwhelming for her wrecked, debilitated body. "Jozsef, I am very tired and sleepy, but I am very happy. I love you with all my heart." Before drifting off into dream-filled clouds of slumber,

Erzsebet heard a faint voice coming from a misty void - *You are my love, my precious, my wife, my world!*

Despite her own misgivings, Erzsebet had painted the baby's room blue, hoping that somehow, it would grant her heart's desire, a baby boy, and Divine Providence had granted her wish. Friends and neighbors came to visit baby Sonny upon his arrival home. Erzsebet sat in her comfortable recliner admiring her Jozsef as he strutted proudly about the living room holding his little baby boy up high for all to see. Her husband, at last, had *his* son. Erzsebet's heart was bursting with happiness. "I wish my little boy to be a wonderful, brave, strong man with a loving heart and soul like his father!"

After the guests departed, the significance of the monumental day was upon them. It was the first time all the bedrooms were occupied: the girls in their room, their son in the nursery, and Jozsef and Erzsebet in their bed, holding each other close. They reminisced upon their meeting eleven years ago and could not believe all that had happened in their lives since the night of splendor under the Acacia tree, and at long last, Jozsef had a son to carry on the family name.

"Restaurant for sale – owner will finance," the words jumped out at Jozsef as he read the Sunday paper one early morning in September of 1961.

Jozsef had not told Erzsebet, but the *School of Modern Music* had seen the last of its better days. His students were performing wonderfully, but to his credit and demise, he had taught them all *too well*. Armed with the knowledge given to them by their master they were now ready to show the world the fruits of their music teacher's labors. Jozsef and his instructors had taught themselves right out of work! Not enough new students were signing up to replace the ones moving on. The school had given him a good income, but now, it was time to explore other options - before finances became desperate. Jozsef was a born entrepreneur and the thought of working for someone else did not sit well with him. He had enjoyed his "boss-free-state" with the music school and was determined to keep it that way.

This restaurant might be the opportunity he was seeking. Jozsef figured it would not hurt to look at the restaurant and he decided to explore the business around noontime the next day.

The eatery was located across the street from a high school. Jozsef could see many students entering and leaving the establishment. Once inside, he observed the restaurant filled nearly to capacity. Good - it was a busy place, and very nice and clean! There were booths along both walls and a soda fountain counter with swivel seating. He found an available seat at the counter and asked the man serving sodas if the owner was available to speak with. "You are looking at him," said a kind-looking man, appearing to be in his late fifties.

"I saw your ad in the paper," said Jozsef, "I would like to buy your restaurant – what are my options?"

By mid-October of 1961, Jozsef was the official proprietor of the restaurant. The former owner had wanted to sell the establishment quickly for medical reasons. The owner self-financed the property allowing Jozsef to make his monthly payments directly to him.

From hamburgers, hotdogs, fries, chili, shakes and countless other concoctions, Jozsef and Erzsebet mastered the preparation of America's favorite mouthwatering entrees.

With time, Jozsef discovered the restaurant's pulse: Throngs of teenagers invaded the restaurant for malts, shakes, and fries at the end of the school day, loading the juke box with the latest Rock-and-Roll hits. The older clientele frequented the restaurant in the mornings and evenings filling the restaurant with the melodies of *Moon River* and *Yellow Bird*. The older patrons especially enjoyed the new Hungarian specialty dishes introduced by Erzsebet: pastries, potato soup, goulash, and chicken paprika. At the end of the day Erzsebet's pots were always empty.

Judit's school was down the street from the restaurant, allowing her to walk there for lunch. Mostly raised on a Hungarian diet, her taste buds were newly awakened, exploring tasty treats she never knew existed. Judit, always a picky eater, now ate heartily!

The staff consisted of two waitresses: one to cover the day shift and one to cover the evening shift. Erzsebet assisted wherever she was needed. She waited tables, cooked, and cleaned. They were open from 9 a.m. to 9 p.m. every day, but closed Sunday. The hours were long, but they did not mind, for Jozsef and Erzsebet toiled only for themselves and their dreams.

October 25, 1961 was the date of little Pilvia's second birthday, and her birthday party was held with friends in the restaurant. Jozsef played the accordion for the occasion giving his own rendition of the "Happy Birthday" song. Plenty of American food and birthday cake was eaten, topped off with a celebratory cheer of success for their restaurant. With the income from a bustling restaurant and with monies earned from whatever accordion gigs Jozsef squeezed in here and there, the family's future looked secure.

It was Christmas Eve of 1961. The restaurant had closed its doors at 3 p.m. Outside, the snowy streets were quiet, but inside, the sounds of laughter, the beat of rock and roll music emanating from the juke box, and the jingle of traditional Christmas melodies, courtesy of Joe's flying fingers filled the air.

It was a night of nights: Jozsef and Erzsebet had invited all their friends and employees to their first official restaurant Christmas Eve party.

Sitting on swivel seats at the food counter, watching their children and friends dancing away to "Rockin' Around the Christmas Tree," Jozsef and Erzsebet were still in awe of being restaurant owners. Five years ago, on Christmas Eve of 1956, they were but poor refugees shivering on the deck of the USS General Hahn without a clue where destiny would take them. Not in their most fantastic dreams could they have envisioned, that they, poor, penniless immigrants, would own a restaurant in the United States! It *was* a night to celebrate. With closed eyes, Jozsef danced "The Christmas Song," with his lovely Erzsebet.

Holding his wife firmly against him, Jozsef could not help but remember how wonderful it was to hold her for the first time in the moonlight, where destiny had made her his own, forever. His Erzsebet was beautiful then, but at this moment, she was even more beautiful than ever, as he gazed upon her shining ebony hair, reflecting the glow of the colorful Christmas lights upon her dark, silken tendrils, the facets of light serenading her luminously radiant face.

And in that moment, Jozsef could also not help but remember the promise he had made his wife during their early days in America, and lovingly reminded her of a promise kept, "I told you my *Pillango*, remember? I told you one day, you would have a house, a car, and pretty clothes, but I forgot to mention that you would also have a restaurant!" Erzsebet giggled with happiness and excitement and pulled her husband near.

Monday, New Year's Day of 1962, had been spent playing with the children and resting up for the next day of work at the restaurant. It was 9:30 p.m. The house was quiet, the children asleep in their beds, worn out from a hard day playing with Christmas toys.

Jozsef and Erzsebet, wrapped in the blissful comfort of matching Chenille robes, cuddled together on the floor in front of their Christmas tree, with Jozsef's right arm possessively placed about the shoulder of his lovely Erzsebet.

The colorful lights on the Christmas tree bounced and flitted off the walls casting a mystical glow about the darkened living room. It was serene, calm, and quiet, a time to simply enjoy the closeness of one another.

However, Jozsef's heart was troubled, on this, the first day of the New Year. After purchasing the restaurant, he had written his relatives in Hungary of being the owner of a restaurant in America. He had written the letter quickly on the restaurant's counter before beginning his prep work for the day, and had given the return address as the restaurant, and it was there where he had received a reply.

He had not told Erzsebet, but the letter was from a cousin in Hungary informing Jozsef that his father was having increasing difficulty with his vision, making it difficult for him to do the simplest tasks, greatly inhibiting his father's ability to earn a living. After much deliberation, Jozsef decided to ask Erzsebet's permission to have his parents come to America and live with them.

How could he tell her his plan? The tree lights cast a glimmer of exquisite color on her lovely face. She had never looked so radiant. How could he spoil the mood of the evening? He knew his mother was never on good terms with his wife. She was not even a good mother to him! It was a lot to ask of Erzsebet, but he mainly was asking for his father's sake. One thing for sure, he would not go against his wife's wishes. If she said no, then it would be no. His own family had to come first.

Pulling Erzsebet closer, Jozsef seized his chance, "My *Draga*, I need to tell you something. You may not understand or agree, but please listen." Squeezing his hand, Erzsebet searched her husband's face. "Jozsef, what is wrong? You look worried."

Jozsef laid out his idea, explaining the tremendous, costly undertaking. Lawyers would have to be hired both in Hungary and America to handle the correspondence with the Soviet government. The family would have to be very frugal with their spending as every extra dime had to be put aside, not only for the lawyers, but his parent's airfare. Erzsebet had already entertained the idea of Jozsef wanting to bring his parents to live with them. She had "read between the lines" of many former letters sent to them by family and friends in Hungary, informing them, even as far as a year back, of Jozsef's father having problems with his sight, cataracts. She was hoping, however, to delay that day as much as possible. Not that Erzsebet minded the fact of having two extra persons in the household, but Hermina was always hateful toward her. No matter how hard Erzsebet had tried to be a good daughter-in-law and a good wife, Hermina had always maintained a cool, yet "respectful distance" from her.

Fortunately, Erzsebet's parents were both in good health. Her father had been contracted recently for a long-term construction project to build a new soccer stadium in Hungary, assuring he and his wife a source of financial flow for a good while.

Erzsebet knew if the situation were reversed, and if her parents were ill, or wanted to leave their homeland, Jozsef would help them. "Jozsef, it will be very difficult for us, but if it eases your mind, and gives your sick father peace in his later years, we will find a way." It was too late now - the words had been said. She could only pray the ends justified the means.

In the early spring of 1962, aided by lawyers in both New York and Hungary, permission was granted from the Hungarian (Soviet) government to allow Jozsef's parents to leave Hungary. The Hungarian lawyer told Jozsef it had not been a difficult decision. "The government was only too glad to relieve themselves of an old, sick man, who, no longer, in their opinion, was productive to the common welfare, and whose medical condition was, and would always be, a continual drain on the finances of the state."

Jozsef decided to leave the restaurant in the care of one trusted employee during his absence, as he would be away for up to two weeks helping his parents get settled.

The night before their trip to the airport Jozsef and Erzsebet were awakened by a terrible screaming and rattling noise coming from their bedroom. Jozsef bounced out of bed with a baseball bat prepared for the worst. They found their little son standing straight up in his bed, screaming at the top of his lungs, shaking the bars of his crib with such strength that the bars had come out of their sockets onto the floor, nearly causing him to tumble out of the crib onto the hard surface below. (The crib had been placed in their bedroom as Jozsef's parents were to sleep in the baby's former room). Erzsebet moved quickly to catch her baby as he wavered close to the unrestrained edge of his mattress. "How in the world did he do that! How can a little baby destroy an entire crib! It's impossible!" yelled an exasperated Jozsef. Dumbfounded by what she had seen and heard, Erzsebet checked her son's diaper and offered him a bottle, of which he took a little. He had no fever or rashes. She looked at her husband and shrugged her shoulders, "I think he had a terrible temper tantrum!" Since the crib was destroyed, they placed Sonny between them in their bed and tried to get what sleep they could as the next day would be a very long one.

In the early morning hours, on a late April morning in 1962, Jozsef, Erzsebet, and the children departed for the airport. They made the children a bed in the back of the station wagon to allow them to sleep until they arrived at their destination.

The family waited anxiously in the terminal building of the Idlewild Airport, in New York, with Jozsef listening attentively to the loud speaker for the announcement of his parent's flight. Jozsef looked proudly upon his children: Judit was now eight years of age, Pilvia was almost three, and Sonny would be one-year old in the coming July.

Jozsef squeezed Erzsebet's hand, his mind buzzing, thinking about the exciting new life his parents would have in America - hoping they would be happy. Erzsebet was nervous, because, from this day forth their lives would forever change. Their privacy would be at a minimum; however, she was sure the grandparents would love their grandchildren, and, it would be good for the children to know at least one set of grandparents.

Erzsebet's thoughts came to a brusque stop as the loudspeaker announced the arrival of her in-law's flight. After all the hugs, kisses, and tears of joy were exhausted at the terminal gate, and the luggage located, a jubilant Jozsef escorted his entire family to the Chevy station wagon. Jozsef had reserved a large hotel room at the airport for the family to spend the night, as it would be too late in the day for the long drive home.

Jozsef ordered dinner through room service. The room was very large, containing two double beds, fold out cots for Pilvia and Judit, and a crib for Sonny. Erzsebet spread out a blanket on the carpet and divided the meal amongst her husband, children, and in-laws. The food was good and hot. Jozsef watched his father dig hungrily into his meal; however, Jozsef's mother elected to sit in a chair apart from the others. Her whiny voice shrieked across the room, "Jozsef, you have brought your father and me all the way to America to live in one room and eat off the floor?" She was still the same Hermina, never satisfied, and still wanting to be the center of attention!

On the way to the hotel, Jozsef had clearly explained the reason for their hotel stay, but Hermina had a way of conveniently not hearing things she chose not to hear. Erzsebet's throat tightened and her stomach felt heavy. She took in a deep breath. *This is not a good sign.*

They arrived home the afternoon of the next day. The weather had cleared, and the warm sun crept through peaks of white clouds. Jozsef was eager to show his parent's their new home and their bedroom. Jozsef's mother had always adored cats. Her pet cat was fluffy and orange-striped like a tiger, but unfortunately, she could not bring it with her, and was forced to leave it behind with friends in Budapest.

Upon entering her bedroom Hermina broke down in an inconsolable array of tears. First, Jozsef thought she was simply overwhelmed with happiness when she saw his efforts to paper the nursery walls with pink and blue "kitty-cat" wallpaper, for his mother's enjoyment; however, it only reminded Hermina of the pet she left behind.

The only comment she made towards her son's efforts was, "I miss my cat!" Jozsef's father put his arm around his son's shoulder, "We like the room very much - very much, and we will be very happy here."

Not at any one time from the airport, or at any time since her arrival, had Hermina said anything positive regarding the children. She *had* placed her hands on their heads, stroking their hair at the airport, but had not showed any sign of great emotion in seeing her grandchildren. She had not even commented on her son's home or the car she was riding in. She said nothing about anything. Within the first hour of having Hermina in her home Erzsebet wished she had never agreed to have her live with them. Too bad they could not have just brought Jozsef's father to America and left Hermina back in the old country!

The evening of arriving in their son's home, Jozsef took his father aside, explaining that he had arranged for his father to have cataract removal surgery the next day. The thought of his father living in a world of darkness and shadows had weighed heavily on Jozsef's heart for too long.

He wanted his father to enjoy his life in America, but how could he enjoy anything without his sight? Jozsef was hesitant in breaking the news of the pending surgery this quickly. His father barely had been in America for twenty-four hours!

But, like Jozsef, his father was a practical man, and did not want to be a burden on his son and his family as a "blind man." Professor Bognar was also very much aware that such a procedure was very expensive. Sitting at the kitchen table, he extended his arms out to his son. "Jozsef, how can you do this? You have placed yourself in a precarious financial situation bringing your mother and me here to live with you. Now - you have made plans for my eye surgery. Of course, I want to have it done, but I do not know how you will be able to afford it." His father's shoulders slumped in resignation as he shook his head from side to side. "No, no, now is not a good time."

Jozsef, pulled up a chair to sit beside his father. "Now is the best time! I cannot stand by and watch you plummet into darkness, never seeing the light of day again! Please, father, please!" Tears flowed from the older man's clouded eyes knowing what his son said was true. "I will do it Jozsef. I love you my dear son."

After a two-week hospital stay, Jozsef's father was home recovering well from his cataract surgery. The surgery was a successful one, but not a comfortable one; however, Professor Bognar, grateful for his regained sight, made slight of his past discomfort. "I felt like I was going to block a dam with those sandbags piled on my head to keep me still!" With his contact lenses in place, the music master's vision had improved to nearly 20/15.

As the weeks passed, Hermina dutifully, but reluctantly, helped Erzsebet prepare meals, watch the children, and other household chores. "Well, at least she is *trying* to be part of the family," thought Erzsebet, breathing a small sigh of relief.

Jozsef had always wanted a family business. He had seen the success of the Greek and Asian families when everyone worked together in their restaurants. Jozsef envisioned the same scenario for his family, and now, with many helping hands, he was sure the restaurant would grow. He might even open another one!

Jozsef's father had nothing constructive to do during the day. He was a quiet, kind man, and never complained. He patiently sat, watching the children play, throwing a ball to them, and listened to "woman-talk."

Knowing his father had to be bored with nothing interesting to do with his time, Jozsef asked his father if he wanted to work with him at the restaurant. "Father, working together we can make the restaurant better than ever!" From then on, Jozsef's father accompanied Jozsef to the restaurant every day.

Jozsef let his father choose his own light duties such as sweeping the floor, washing the sinks in the bathrooms, refilling the salt and pepper shakers, washing soiled towels in the washing machine, folding table linens, and washing out the coffee pots.

Jozsef asked his mother if she could watch the children during the day to allow Erzsebet to assist him at the restaurant. He relied on Erzsebet's specialty dishes of goulash, chicken paprika, and strudels, as the customers looked forward to the days when these items were available. Eventually, everyone had a routine: Hermina watched the children, Jozsef and his father worked together at the restaurant, with Erzsebet's days divided between home and work.

July of 1962 had found Jozsef and Erzsebet exhausted - the strain of bringing Jozsef's parents to the states, the long days spent working at the restaurant, the nights Jozsef worked in the basement doing musical instrument repair for extra income, and Jozsef playing the accordion for special events, had taken its toll on the couple. Jozsef explained to his parents the need for his family to have a few days away to refresh their bodies and minds after a very difficult, tension-filled year.

Since Sonny was very young, Jozsef did not want Erzsebet spending her vacation worrying about diapers and formula. Jozsef's parents agreed to care for Sonny while the rest of the family took a brief holiday. They would return home in time for Sonny's first birthday.

Jozsef drove to Canada via New York-way. After their long drive, Jozsef noticed the flashing lights of a motel up ahead called the "Rainbow Motel." Everyone was tired from the drive. "This looks like a good place to stay," and Jozsef pulled into the parking lot of the motel.

Jozsef asked the motel desk clerk where they could find a good place to eat nearby and were told of a little Hungarian restaurant down the road. After a satisfying dinner, they retired for the night to begin their Niagara Falls adventure.

Bright and early the next morning the family made their way to ride an antique cable car suspended from six, sturdy cables. The cable car traveled over a deep gorge, offering a mesmerizing, frightening, but unforgettable experience of a natural phenomenon, called the Niagara Whirlpool. The whirlpool formed at the end of the rapids, where the gorge turned abruptly counterclockwise, forcing torrents of water through the narrowest part of the gorge. Suspended above the world in their cable car, the family was awestruck by the breathtaking and panoramic view. The air was refreshingly cool, crisp, and invigorating!

Rays of sun permeated the misty water droplets hovering in the air, creating a playground of colorful prisms spreading their colors across the sky. Jozsef and Erzsebet held hands, and now and then, gave each other quick, light kisses. At that moment, all their cares lifted away to the far corners of the earth by the vaporous breeze. They planned to spend three days at Niagara, each to be filled with new sights and sounds. There were many different falls to be discovered, but their favorite was Horseshoe Falls being named after its naturally-formed shape.

Their second evening at Niagara, Jozsef and Erzsebet put a very mature, eight-year-old Judit "in charge," to stay in the motel room with Pilvia, for they longed to spend one evening at Niagara alone.

One of the area's largest attractions was "The Walk Behind the Falls" tour. Niagara was beautiful beyond words during the daytime, but at night, it was transformed into a fairyland with an array of brilliantly colored lights streaming out from behind the falls. Visitors put on raincoats to protect their hair and clothing from the water shower and then led through caves hidden behind the falls. The roar of the water was deafening. The water's mammoth force shook the very ground they walked upon. Jozsef's adventurous nature urged him to lean over the protective railing to photograph the watercolor marvel. Longing for a time to be alone, the couple briefly stole away from the tour group to share tender kisses and embraces in a tiny alcove in the rear of the falls.

The parents found the television playing, every light burning, dolls and coloring books strewn upon bedspreads upon their return to the hotel. Judit and Pilvia were sound asleep.

The following day, the family visited a water garden park filled with the soothing sounds of trickling brooks, miniature waterfalls covered with arched foot bridges, mosses, ferns, and flowers, and plus, the famous Clock of Flowers, a huge floral timepiece with colorful blooms outlining the shape of each number on the clock.

Jozsef had saved the best part of their trip for last.

The *Maid of the Mist* was docked at the passenger boarding area in a calm inlet. Niagara Falls had been providing boat tours to the base of the falls for nearly one hundred years. Jozsef was determined to get as near to the falls as possible to obtain a closeup photograph. On deck, the passengers were provided rain ponchos as they were going to get very wet!

"The Maid" engaged her engines and chugged away to the base of the *American Falls*. The passengers quickly discovered why the ship was named "The Maid of the Mist." The boat floated as if it were suspended on a massive, misty cloudbank. The falls, crashing into the river around them, created the scenario of a windy, rainy hurricane.

The churning waters pressed against the sides of the boat, rocking her back and forth. Waves poured over the railings as she made her way near the foothold of the falls, while jutted rock formations peaked in and out of the watery nest daring the boat to come nearer. It was overwhelming and frightening for his daughters, but rather the opposite for Jozsef.

Jozsef and Erzsebet at Niagara Falls 1962

Why should he be afraid? He had stood on deck of the USS General Haan as the ship was catapulted thirty feet into the air! This was just child's play! Jozsef shouted to his daughters, "This is a tiny thing compared to what we experienced on the ship coming to America!" But no one could hear him. There was no use in trying to carry out a conversation, for the thundering, shuddering, reverberation of the noisy waterfall blocked out any noise, other than its own, as the watery arms slammed their mighty force to the very depths of the river basin.

At last, the vessel headed for calmer waters, making its final round to the basin of Horseshoe Falls, and then pulled into port to unload its soggy passengers. The family agreed: the boat ride was the most exciting, spine-tingling, and thrilling experience of their vacation!

The day before Sonny's birthday, the family honked the car horn in their driveway alerting Jozsef's parents of their arrival home. Much to their dismay, little Sonny toddled out the front door, alone, to greet them. Erzsebet scooped her son up in her arms, kissing him repeatedly from head to toe, but noticed an odd odor about him. Just as she was about to check the reason for the strange smell, Jozsef excitedly presented his son with a huge, blue, inflatable elephant bought for him at *The Falls*. Sonny gurgled with delight as he carried the elephant around the yard. Where were Jozsef's parents? Why had they not come outside with Sonny?

Erzsebet walked in through the kitchen door and observed Hermina sitting at the kitchen table drinking a soda. Jozsef's father was taking a nap upstairs, not aware of his son's arrival home. Erzsebet wondered why Sonny came out of the house unsupervised. "Hermina, why did the baby walk outside unattended?" Hermina defensively responded, "The child needs to learn to take care of himself!" Erzsebet felt her face heat and her palms sweat. How she wanted to strangle that woman! Without a word, she took Sonny upstairs to find out why her son smelled so sour. As she made her way up the stairs, she could hear Jozsef reprimanding his mother in Hungarian for sitting inside while allowing his son to promenade outside without adult supervision. "He could have walked into the street and been hit by a car!"

His mother's voice and Jozsef's voice became louder and angrier. Erzsebet shut the door of her bedroom to blot out the noise. All that nice relaxed-feeling from Niagara Falls was gone out the window. She was more tired now than ever.

A few minutes after Erzsebet had secured herself and Sonny in her bedroom, Jozsef heard his wife calling for him. The tone of her voice suggested urgency. Jozsef quickly made his way upstairs to their bedroom.

Sonny was lying naked on a towel in the center of their bed. Erzsebet gently grasped both of Sonny's ankles together, pulling his legs up into the air to expose his tiny buttocks. Jozsef cringed at myriads of ugly blisters, filled with pustules, mixed with areas of raw-looking skin, and crusted, dried stool. Elizabeth had found the front of her little boy's diaper soaking wet, but had not felt the wetness earlier, because Sonny had a plastic "panty" pulled over his diaper. Upset, worried, and being beyond angry with his mother, Jozsef grabbed the phone in his bedroom to phone their children's doctor. Within thirty minutes the physician's vehicle pulled into the driveway. Further fueling Jozsef's rage was discovering that his mother had fed Sonny breakfasts consisting of soda poured over his cereal instead of milk. "Why did you give the baby soda and cereal for breakfast?" Hermina defiantly straightened her shoulders, "Because he liked it that way."

Their doctor had visited the home several times in the past to treat the girls for tonsillitis and Erzsebet for "milk fever," after she had given birth to Pilvia. His bedside manner was always professional, assuring, and calm; however, upon laying eyes on little Sonny's buttocks he was visibly shaken. He knew Erzsebet was a wonderful mother. He had been Erzsebet's doctor through her pregnancy with Pilvia and Sonny. The children were always squeaky-clean and neat. Jozsef, ashamed to tell the doctor the truth about his mother, explained that Sonny had been under the care of a young babysitter while they were out of town, who apparently was "inexperienced in changing diapers," assuring the doctor he would "Never hire her again!"

The physician prescribed Sonny a medicinal cream to be applied three times a day, advising Erzsebet not to place a diaper on Sonny and to "Expose the area to as much air as possible."

While Erzsebet tended Sonny, Jozsef walked the doctor to the door and paid him for his services.

Weary and worn-out, Jozsef slowly walked back to the house. His mother remained seated at the kitchen table as if nothing of significance had taken place in the last hour. Meanwhile, his father, awakened by all the commotion, had made his way downstairs to the kitchen. On seeing his son, he gave Jozsef a big hug, which Jozsef genuinely returned in kind. Then, without saying a word to his mother, only giving her a piercing, angry glance, Jozsef told his father he was tired from his trip, hugged him, and loudly stomped upstairs for the night.

By early September of 1962, Hermina had become increasingly withdrawn from the family, spending most of her time either on the front porch or in her room. One evening after dinner, in the privacy of their bedroom, Hermina declared to her husband, "We must have our own place to live. I have no privacy!" The impetus for her request was Judit's intrusion into the bathroom to use the toilet while Hermina was bathing in the tub, complaining Judit had "seen her naked." Hermina had screamed for Erzsebet to come upstairs to remove Judit from the bathroom. Erzsebet explained to Hermina that had she only locked the door the incident would not have happened. Erzsebet did not give a care if the entire world had walked in on her mother-in-law – she deserved it! Besides, Erzsebet noticed Hermina was wearing a bra and panties in the tub – *who can wash their body wearing underwear?* Obviously, Judit had seen nothing important!

Poor Grandpa Jozsef, when not at the restaurant helping his son, was usually found sitting, slumped low in his lawn chair or porch swing, listening to Hermina's tirade, not arguing against her, allowing her to pound him with her shrieking tones. Unbeknownst to either of his parents, Jozsef had overheard several of his mother's rants, but had held his temper. His dreams of a loving family working and living together had proved to be a farce.

Jozsef bit his lip in anger and tightly clenched his fists. Did his mother not realize what sacrifices his wife had made to allow him to bring her to this country? She had pinched pennies by not buying herself anything decent to wear for a long time and had eaten only "poor food" consumed in the old country. His wife had done all this to save money for *her!* Even Judit had announced she wanted nothing for her birthday or Christmas if it meant her father could see his parents again. His little Pilvia, well, she was still too young to understand anything. And worst of all, his sweet little boy had been under his mother's "care" while the rest of the family spent carefree days in Canada. How could his mother think a one-year-old could be left alone to tend to his own needs? His mother had shown her grandson the same loving care she had shown her own son – none.

As if Jozsef's relationship with his mother was not already strained to the breaking point, one day, completely out of the blue, Hermina callously announced, "Jozsef, your parents should really be more important to you than your family, just leave them and come back to Hungary and take care of us like you used to!"

That did it! His mother was even more cold-hearted and selfish than he had ever imagined. She could have the moon in her hand and still want more. How could his father love her! He had to do something before she *did* ruin his marriage.

The next day Jozsef contacted his friend Ray who owned a small, brick, two-story apartment building on the main street of downtown Greenfield.

After listening to the drama of Jozsef's household dilemma, and Jozsef's explanation of not being able to afford an expensive rental for his parents, Ray gave Jozsef a deal he could not refuse on one of his older, fully-furnished, first-floor apartments, complete with electricity and water. Hermina had only to move in.

Jozsef's heart went out to his father, who spoke with his son before moving to the apartment. "I am leaving my son, but it is not because I do not love you and your family, but I am leaving because I do love all of you. I want you to have a peaceful life. I know you find it difficult to understand why I love your mother. When I met her, it was as if a fresh spring breeze blew into my heart. I could not help myself and I have been in her spell ever since. Yes, I see how she is, but even if I did want to leave her, where am I to go? Also, where would she go? It is best I stay with your mother. Odd as it seems, we do understand each other. My heart still loves the woman she once was. There are days when I would be perfectly content to send Hermina back to Hungary to be taken care of by her relatives and live out the rest of my days with you, Erzsebet, and my grandchildren in the *kitty-cat room*, but I cannot do it to her. I cannot do it to myself."

Jozsef's parents moved into their new apartment with a minimum of effort, only needing to move the bedroom furniture, dishware, pots, silverware, clothes, bedding, and towels. The day after her in-laws moved out, and with the "help" of her children, Erzsebet stripped the wallpaper from the "cat room," sanded down the walls, and painted the room with the leftover blue nursery paint to create a playroom for the children, also doubling as a bedroom for Sonny.

Upon returning home that evening from a long day at the restaurant, Jozsef viewed the result of Erzsebet's labors. With arms akimbo, he took in his wife's efforts. "Erzsebet, you are an incredible woman! A playroom is just what the children needed!" Jozsef pulled Erzsebet close to him watching their children enjoy the spaciousness of the play space.

Jozsef longed to make up to his wife for the intense hurt caused by the decision to bring his parents to the states, but he could not think clearly, his mind was overloaded, and his body tired. Erzsebet was strong and resilient. Even when the bottom fell out of her life, she did not spend time complaining, but simply bounced back with more determination than before. She was Jozsef's role model, his strength, his everything. When Jozsef viewed how she had toiled fixing up the "cat room" his heart filled with guilt and shame. How could she not be angry with him for wasting all his efforts and money on a mother who did not appreciate his or her efforts? He never wanted to see or hear a cat again!

After Jozsef's parents moved out, the family quickly resumed their normal routine. Pilvia had been enrolled in the same nursery school as her sister had attended. Judit was in elementary school. Sonny was at home.

Jozsef's father had decided not to come back to work with his son at the restaurant. He had been happily productive while helping his son's business succeed; however, not wanting to argue with Hermina any further, he told Jozsef it was best he stayed home.

On a Saturday afternoon in mid-September 1962, Jozsef received a call from his father. "Jozsef, my boy, I am lonely. I miss you and the grandchildren. I came to America to be with you and your family. Hermina is now much happier since she has her own apartment and is much more amenable. Please do an old man a favor in his aged years and let us have dinner with you tonight. Hermina is aware of my calling you and has agreed to come with me and behave if you will have us."

Erzsebet believed in second chances. Perhaps Hermina would be different now that she had her own place to live? Perhaps, now that Hermina was more adjusted to her life in America things would be better? Besides, it was only dinner, and after dinner, Erzsebet would have her life back. If Jozsef wanted to see his parents, especially, sweet Grandpa Jozsef, she did not mind if her in-laws came to dinner.

The dinner had gone amazingly well. Hermina was polite and reserved in her mannerism, but that was her usual demeanor. Erzsebet thoroughly "divorced herself," from her mother-in-law's mood during the meal focusing her attentions on Grandpa Jozsef.

It was relatively warm for the time of year and day, and a dim glimmer of light glowed outside just before the sunset. Grandpa Jozsef asked if he could go outside and throw ball with the children. The lawn chairs had been put up for the season, therefore, Jozsef let down the back gate of the Chevy wagon, assisting his mother to sit on the tailgate to observe her husband and grandchildren play.

Surprisingly, everyone *was* having a wonderful time. Grandpa Jozsef was immensely enjoying his visit. Hermina grew tired of sitting and stood up beside the tailgate as her husband and grandchildren played "Wonder Ball." It was Sonny's turn to catch the ball, but it slipped past him and rolled toward the car, stopping under the tailgate. Sonny squatted down to pick it up, but the tailgate was over his head and he could not stand up. He pushed upward on the gate with both arms over his head slamming the gate shut. What happened next was an unreal chain of events, occurring so quickly, there was no time to change the outcome. Hermina's agonizing screams echoed through the yard, as strong streams of blood squirted from her right hand into the eerie twilight. When Sonny pushed up on the tailgate, Hermina's "pointer" finger had been severed below the first joint: her hand was resting on the metal locking mechanism in the rear of the wagon, exactly at the point where the bottom tailgate latch caught the upper lock. Erzsebet bolted into the house, grabbed a stack of kitchen towels, running back to a hysterical Hermina, securing a bundle of towels over Hermina's bloodied hand. Placing Hermina in the back seat of the station wagon, Jozsef and Erzsebet tore out of the driveway headed toward the hospital.

The bloody scene terrified Judit and her siblings. In the pale light of dusk, she watched her grandfather pick up his wife's severed finger with his handkerchief. It was a scary-looking thing - just a nub of pale flesh, attached to a long, red, shiny fingernail. Judit observed her grandfather slowly making his way toward Sonny, and before she realized what was about to happen, the old patriarch firmly struck Sonny on his buttocks, causing the little boy to be knocked down upon the gravel driveway and he immediately began to cry. The grandfather was raising his hand to strike Sonny again, but Judit swiftly ran to her little brother, frantically scooping him up within one arm, and with her free hand, speedily pulled little Pilvia along, running toward the shelter of the free-standing garage in the backyard where her father housed his Renault, approximately fifty feet away from the driveway. Confused and upset, the grandfather did not see where the children had exited.

Once in the safety of the garage, Judit placed Pilvia and Sonny in the backseat area of the Renault. By now, the fullness of night had settled in, and with it, colder air. Judit covered her sister and brother with a blanket her father kept in the car for outings. It was pitch-black in the garage, and Judit was afraid, but not of the dark.

About three hours after their hurried departure, Jozsef and Erzsebet came home with a drained, enervated Hermina. Unfortunately, had they thought of bringing the severed finger with them, the doctors may have had a chance of reattaching it. But, now, it was too late to think about that possibility. All the doctors could do was to give Hermina pain medication, antibiotics, and suture and bandage her finger.

As Erzsebet assisted an exhausted Hermina into the house, Jozsef found his father sitting alone in the darkness on the front porch holding Hermina's detached finger in his handkerchief. The old professor looked worn out, appearing older than ever, as if all the life within his body had been drained away.

Jozsef did not hear or see the children. "Father, where are the kids?" His father stared at Jozsef with blank eyes and spoke with a voice lacking expression. "They ran away. They were afraid of me." Waves of fear and anguish swept through Jozsef, as his voice nearly cracked asking what had to be asked, "Why did the children run away? Why are they afraid of you?" Erzsebet had heard all, and a paralyzing nausea instantly gripped her heart as she thought the most terrible thoughts parents think when their children disappear. She began frantically running through both levels of the house, around the perimeter of the home, the basement, but no children were found. Her heart pounded fiercely in her ears as she dashed into the blackness of the backyard towards the children's swing set breathlessly calling their names. The fullness of night made it impossible to delineate her boundaries. She should have brought a flashlight! Torrents of tears only made her vision worse. Her clenched, dry throat made it almost impossible to call out; however, she threw out one, last, loud exasperated shout for her children, her ears straining to hear a response. Out of the shadowy gloom she heard Judit's voice, "Mommy! We are in the garage!"

Erzsebet took the children upstairs to her bedroom, checking each child from head to toe, especially little Sonny. Other than being cold and hungry he appeared physically all right with no bruises or cuts.

Erzsebet made her children hot chicken noodle soup to warm them up and then tucked them in for the night. Jozsef drove his parents to their apartment. No one spoke a word, not even when his parents made their departure toward their dwelling. It was just as well, for Jozsef had nothing good to say, and neither did they.

It was early October of 1962. Jozsef awakened to a cloudy Sunday morning, getting up early to mend a few instruments, determined to get the repairs out of the way to allow him extra time to spend with his family that day.

Jozsef had taken up repairing musical instruments in the basement on Sunday mornings - his long wooden work bench stocked full of musical repair parts for many instruments. Jozsef conjured up any repair work possible to make extra money, still trying to make up for the large monetary losses incurred during his botched attempt to make his parents happy. If there were no instruments to repair, he played his accordion on Sunday's for special events. Jozsef was always working. And yes, he was always tired, but he could endure all the tiredness in the world if it meant his children would have a better life than he had in Hungary.

Jozsef glanced over at his very exhausted sleeping Erzsebet, his heart heavy, as he recalled the strife she had endured with his mother. Today, Jozsef was determined to let his wife sleep in as late as she wanted.

He quietly slipped out of bed and made his way to check on the children. The girls were already awake, playing with their Barbie dolls in bed. With a quick "Shhhh," and speaking low, he asked the girls to go down to the kitchen. He was going to make them breakfast today because "Mommy was very tired." He went to the nursery to check on Sonny. He changed his diaper and carried him downstairs.

Since owning his restaurant, Jozsef had become quite a fine chef, and in no time at all, the children were fed. After breakfast he announced to his children that it was time for them to accompany him down to the basement. Jozsef spread out a blanket on the basement floor in front of the cast-iron radiator heater near his workbench. He had to find a way to entertain his kids, but there were no toys in the cellar. His eyes quickly searched about, and his mind worked up a plan.

Holding Sonny in his left arm, Jozsef heated up his soldering iron, asking the children to watch him carefully. With precise, slow movements, using his right arm and hand, Jozsef used the smoldering iron to engrave each child's name into his workbench. The heat from the red-hot iron created billows of smoke swirling into the air as his hand worked easily and steadily forming the pattern of his children's names: Judit, Kuki, and Sonny. The girls hugged their father as he explained, "Seeing your names here while I work will make me happy every day."

But, Jozsef had more tricks up his sleeve. He produced a quarter out of his pocket, placed it in his palm, and when he opened his palm the quarter was gone! "I know where it is!" Jozsef exclaimed, as he "found" the quarter behind each child's ear. The children begged their father to repeat the quarter trick often, and each time, the quarter was found in their hair or under their chin.

When the magic show was over, Jozsef had the children giggling with delight, as he wiggled his ears, his nose, and moved his eyebrows up and down, while making every funny face he could think of. Just when Jozsef was running out of ideas, he heard Erzsebet calling, "Where is everyone?" It turned out to be the most perfect of days.

In 1962, the Soviet Union and the United States were in an arms race. The Soviets had nuclear missiles that were only powerful enough to extend into Europe, but the Soviet government officials were fearful, for the missiles of the United States could strike targets throughout the Soviet Union. Even as early as April of 1962, Soviet Premier Nikita Khrushchev (for whom Jozsef had played his accordion in the Hungarian Parliament house), had entertained the idea of placing missiles in Cuba that could be deployed against the United States, hoping to deter the United States from forming a potential attack against the Soviet Union.

Fidel Castro, Cuba's dictator, saw this nuclear missile placement to be advantageous. Since the United States inspired failed Bay of Pigs invasion of 1961, to oust Castro from power, Castro felt the United States could attack again at any time; therefore, all summer long in 1962, cloaked in secrecy, Castro conspired with the Soviet Union to build nuclear missile installations on the island of Cuba.

The "Cuban Missile Crisis" began in early October of 1962, when reconnaissance photos revealed Soviet missile construction sites based in Cuba – only ninety miles off the United States coastline.

President John Kennedy met over a period of seven days with the upper levels of government. It was decided the United States would place a naval quarantine around Cuba hoping to prevent any more missile building supplies to reach the island.

Just a few days before Pilvia's third birthday, the family was watching television when their program was interrupted for a special public announcement by President Kennedy. On October 22, 1962, he told the citizens of the United States that Soviet nuclear missile installations had been discovered on the island of Cuba and a missile launch toward the United States from Cuba would be considered an act of war upon America. President Kennedy demanded the Soviets to step down and withdraw their missiles from the island.

By October 25, 1962, on Pilvia's third birthday, President Kennedy raised United States military readiness to DEFCON 2, placing the United States in a state of war readiness, only one level below DEFCON 1, meaning war was imminent. So, that night, instead of having a birthday party for Pilvia, Jozsef and his family were at the grocery store, along with what seemed to be the entire population of the town. Everyone felt that war could break out at any time. People were rushing to stores to stock up on canned food, powdered milk, medicine, and other supplies in the event *Martial Law* was declared.

Jozsef had prepared a "bunker" for the family in the basement. Having lived through bombing raids, Jozsef and Erzsebet knew only too well how to prepare for the worst. This was an unbelievable turn of events: the nuclear missile crisis coincided with the date when the Hungarian Revolution began in 1956. It was such irony, thought Jozsef, that six years later, he and

Erzsebet were again facing a battle to save their country and maybe their lives.

Before leaving with the family to the grocery store, Jozsef had a heartfelt talk with Judit explaining that if a missile attack occurred, she must be strong and brave, as they would need her help with the children, assuring her they would do everything possible to keep them all safe.

Judit asked her father if she could bring her pet bunnies with her in the basement, but Jozsef explained there was only enough air and food for the family. "We are going to be confined in a tight space and the stench of the rabbits, with our already not too pleasant living situation, would make things much worse." The thought of her pet bunny rabbits being burned to a crisp by nuclear flames made Judit sick. She began to dry-heave and quickly made her way to the bathroom.

October 27, 1962 was a terrible day. A U2 fighter was missing over Alaska, feared to have strayed into Soviet territory, another U2 American spy plane was shot down over Cuban airspace, and Khrushchev demanded the United States remove their missiles from Turkey in exchange for the Soviet missiles in Cuba.

For several days Jozsef and his family existed on the edge of a living nightmare; although, the public feared what missiles could do to their country, very few Americans had lived through the terror of real bombs destroying everything you had, or the nauseated feeling of seeing death all around, or having to eat scraps of half-rotted food found in the streets. Erzsebet and Jozsef had lived through it all.

On October 28, 1962, in a strange turn of events, the United States breathed a huge sigh of relief; finally, Khrushchev announced he was removing the missile installations and transport missiles back to the Soviet Union, as the United States had promised not to invade Cuba.

Upon hearing the news of the Soviet withdrawal, Jozsef and Erzsebet clung to each other and their children, grateful for peace; however, the stress had been a tremendous strain for them, and that night, in the privacy of their bedroom, the horror of what could have been, all the terrible memories, all the old buried feelings of fear and desperation thought to be long gone was reawakened. Erzsebet held her husband tightly, "Jozsef, please hold me, hold me tight!" Jozsef curled up to his wife's back, enveloping her in his arms, wrapping his legs about her icy feet to keep her warm. Her breathing soon quieted. Jozsef felt her tense body go limp with sleep. *Dear God, please do not let it start all over again, not in America.*

It was Halloween night of 1962. Judit and Pilvia had not yet decided on their costumes. Judit finally chose to wear one of her mother's discarded voile dresses, complete with old costume jewelry and a matching hat with a little veil that came over her eyes to the bridge of her nose. Pilvia was made up to be a "princess." Judit bedecked her with strands of colorful beads and made up her face using her mother's lipstick and eye shadow.

Sonny was too small to go out with them. He was still in diapers and way too wobbly and slow. Anyway, Judit did not want to babysit during her trick-or-treating. Erzsebet sent the girls off with big pillowcases in which to place their stash of treats.

It was a surprisingly warm night for the end of October. This pleased Judit immensely. There was nothing worse than wearing a costume no one could see because it was covered by a bulky winter coat! About an hour and a half later, exhausted from walking up and down the sidewalks of Maple Street, Judit and Pilvia made their way up the steps to their front door. The door slowly opened and out jumped a big white ghost with a mass of blonde curly hair. Its body was entwined with what seemed to be endless strands of rope wound through the handles of at least ten pots and pans of various sizes. The ghost shouted "Booooo, how do you like my costume!"

It was their mother in disguise, draped in a sheet, and tied up in pots and pans, wearing her old blonde wig! Erzsebet's childhood had been sad and drab. She had missed out on too many things that children did for fun. Her heart yearned to be "out there" in the big adventure of it all. She wanted to experience this "trick-or-treating" just once in her life, for she felt young, and was young.

Judit stayed home watching over Sonny and Kuki, her ears acutely aware of nearly every dog in the neighborhood howling and yelping at a big white ghost making its way up and down the sidewalks of their street. The clamoring, banging, and tinny sounds of Erzsebet's pots and pans striking the concrete walkway was enough to "wake up the dead." Erzsebet giggled under her sheets, "No wonder the kids love to do this, and the best part is…no one knows it is me!"

Between the Cuban missile crisis, the restaurant, and everyday life, Jozsef nearly forgot the most important day of his life in America: His American Citizenship swearing-in ceremony!

On November 8, 1962, six years after leaving his native Hungary, Jozsef raised his right hand to take his pledge of allegiance and oath of citizenship to the United States in a Boston, Massachusetts courtroom. Jozsef's thoughts whirled as the reality of what his United States citizenship meant new job opportunities, being able to vote and serve on a jury, but most important, a sense of belonging to a country, again - his country - America. Jozsef loved the United States for giving him a home when he and his family had nowhere to go after *The Revolution*. As Jozsef waited for his name to be called to take the citizenship oath, his mind drifted back to the dark days of communist rule in Hungary, of living in the pits of a coalmine as punishment for speaking out for what all humans desire and deserve.

Jozsef's thoughts turned in silent remembrance of all the Hungarians who had died for the very honor he was to receive today: To be a citizen of a free country. With that thought in mind, and now, with the title of "American Citizen" behind his name, Jozsef was intensely aware of how fortunate he was to be a servant of the greatest country on earth, the United States, and he swore from this day forward to honor, fight for, and love *his* new country every day of his life.

After the ceremony, Jozsef excitably hugged his wife and children. With eyes filled with tumbling tears and a throat tight with emotion, Jozsef declared, "We are Americans now, my Erzsebet! We are truly home and truly *free*, and to show the world we are really Americans, we will buy a flag and display it outside our house, and no matter where we live in the future, we will always have an American flag flying outside our home!"

Once a week, Jozsef purchased and delivered groceries to his parents, as well as giving his father a stipend for incidentals he and his mother may need. At the end of each month he mailed Ray a rent check for the apartment. That was the best Jozsef could do under the circumstances. If his parents needed anything in the interim, the grocery and drug stores were just outside their apartment door on Main Street.

Ever since Jozsef had brought his parents out of Hungary, things had gone wrong. First the chaos caused by Hermina in their home, then the missile crisis, and now, a new terror lurked on the horizon, but it was one he could not fight.

Something *was* terribly wrong. Where was everyone? Friday mornings were usually one of his busiest! Jozsef leaned on the counter of the restaurant looking out the large glass windows facing the street.

A few of his elderly customers were sitting in their usual spots sipping coffee and reading the November 15, 1963, morning news. Joseph's mind wandered as he prepped the store for the day's business. Tomorrow, November sixteenth, would mark the seventh year of their escape to America.

Jozsef's photo on his United States Citizenship Certificate

Today, should have been a day to celebrate their bravery in coming to a new country. But, Jozsef did not feel celebratory, for since September, patronage from both his elderly and younger clientele had been dwindling. Jozsef carefully looked over his menu. It was not repetitious. He had always provided a wide variety of foods to please every palate. He had maintained reasonable prices and high standards of food quality.

Every Friday and Saturday when business was at its zenith, he made sure there was always a new entre for his customers to try. And, every Friday, he had several fish entrees for clientele of the Catholic faith.

He meticulously cleaned the fryers, making sure the oil was fresh for his fried foods, and the fish had their own vat to avoid imparting a "fishy taste" to his other cuisines. The floors were washed every night before closing and the tables and chairs were also wiped clean.

One of his regular breakfast clients was Ray. He was a laid-back, thin man in his early fifties, with kind, slanted blue eyes and a gray mustache, who moved slowly, and talked even slower than he moved - the man who rented the apartment to Jozsef's parents.

At his usual arrival time of 9:30 a.m., Ray casually walked in through the gleaming glass doors of the restaurant and seated himself at the counter to order his "usual." After a sip of java, Ray asked Jozsef why he was looking so glum.

Jozsef explained to Ray about his business "dropping off," and for the life of him, he did not understand why. There were only a very few good restaurants in town, and his was one of them. Ray set down his coffee cup, "Jozsef, I need to speak with you. That's why I'm here. I've heard talk."

Life is strange and full of quirks: when you are on the bottom, down and out - everyone feels sorry for you. They are kind and generous and try to help you achieve a better way of life. But then, when you are doing better in life due to *their* voluntary kindness and generosity, the *same* people who wanted to help you create a better life end up disliking you when you are doing well in your endeavors – *doing better than them.*

According to Ray, the townspeople were "upset that foreigners were becoming more successful and earning more money than the Americans born right here in the good old U.S.A." Jozsef was confused, "Why do they feel that way Ray? You know my money did not come easy. Running this restaurant is exhausting. Erzsebet and I *had* to learn the restaurant business. We never did anything like this before. We both stuck our noses to the grindstone and persevered together to build a business. Everyone in the family has made sacrifices. It has taken every bit of our guts and determination to build a good reputation for our business!"

What could Ray say, for all Jozsef said was true. Ray watched Jozsef and Erzsebet work three times harder to earn their money than the guy sitting behind a desk pushing a pen. He had watched the couple extract money "from scratch" with no extra hands to help, except the hands attached to their own two arms.

The barbershop in town was as old-timey as they came. One pleasure Ray indulged in was lying back in the barber's chair with a hot, wet towel covering his face to soften his tough bristles.

"Jozsef, the other day, while I was 'steaming' under a face towel, at the barber shop, I overheard some folks discussing your restaurant."

Ray related the following tidbits of conversation to Joe, "They couldn't see my face under the hot towel, which is good, for I couldn't believe what I heard."

Those Hungarians believe they are better than the rest of us in this town.

They dress their girls in prissy dresses just to go out and ride a bike.

Yeah, and what about that fancy sports car and scooter-cycle the man drives? Even I can't afford one of those.

I know what you mean, my wife commented that the owner's wife wears a real mink coat!

Joe furiously interjected, "Only the collar is real mink!"

"Now Joe," Ray smoothly and quietly drawled, "Hear me out," and continued describing the covert conversations.

If they think they are so much better than us, then we can show them they aren't.

The breath was nearly knocked out of Jozsef as he listened to the morbid plan of his destruction.

I know how we'll do that! We'll make sure they don't make any more money! Tell your kids not to go there after school and tell your friends to eat at that other place across town."

Jozsef held up his trembling hand signaling Ray to stop, for his heart felt tight, as if he had just received news of his own death – a living death. He thanked Ray for his honesty and shook his hand. "Ray, you are probably the only decent person left in town." Ray saw tears building in his friend's eyes. He patted Jozsef on the back, "I'll be around if you need me." Ray continued to sip his coffee.

With a quick "Thanks Ray," Jozsef found his feet running out the restaurant's back door making his way down several sets of concrete steps into the nearly empty parking lot. Jozsef stood in the back of the building, his shaking hands lighting a cigarette that he had no intention of smoking.

He had been filled with such great dreams and hopes, but nothing seemed to be working out for him in this town. He and Erzsebet had worked unearthly hours to build this restaurant. Even Judit helped mop floors on Sundays. His father, bless his heart, enjoyed working with him, until his mother's selfish whining convinced him to stay at home. He thought of all the things his dear Erzsebet had gone without to bring his parents to live with them.

He had tried countless times to sell the Renault, trying to get out of the monthly payments to make things easier, but she had absolutely refused to think of it. She loved her husband too much to have another childhood dream taken away from him. She told him she would work day and night, but he would have his dreams. *She could be so stubborn*, but he loved her even more for it.

Erzsebet had no idea the restaurant business had come to a crawl, for with three children, and at her husband's insistence, she now spent most of her days at home. He was amazed that Erzsebet never complained. She took each day as it was given her, not expecting more than what came with it. He, on the other hand, took each day and wanted to mold it into something bigger and better.

It appeared, however, that Joe's efforts would be in vain. He could not fight an entire town. The few loyal customers, and there were some, would not provide a sufficient income to keep the business afloat forever. Jozsef punched his fist into the restaurant's trash dumpster, feeling as worthless as the refuse contained within. Jozsef reluctantly walked back inside the restaurant, his mind and body numb, no longer caring if he succeeded or failed. He found Ray still sitting at the counter, aimlessly pushing around some toast crumbs on his plate.

Ray signaled for Jozsef to come over to sit with him. Ray was anxious as Jozsef approached for he had another issue to discuss with his friend. He felt guilty about distressing Jozsef further, but what he had to say, had to be said and could not wait. Besides, he would rather be the one to tell Jozsef the news than to have him find out through malicious gossip.

With carefully chosen words, Ray explained he was walking downtown the day before, and noticed Jozsef's parents through the front window of the Welfare Office, waiting to speak to a representative. Ray was curious and walked inside to ask if they were okay. Jozsef's father, in broken English, explained to Ray they were there to obtain the agency's assistance in helping them find transportation back to Hungary because Hermina did not want to live in the United States anymore.

Ray asked the old professor if his son knew he was returning to Hungary, but Jozsef's father shook his head, adamantly telling Ray, as best as he could explain, that he did not want his son's money to help them return to the old country.

The author sitting with her father on his scooter in front of the Maple Street house

Upon further probing, Ray learned it was their second visit to the agency, for the Welfare Office had contacted the American and Hungarian Embassies, and somehow, arrangements were in the works to send them home, but Ray did not understand exactly by what means or when they were leaving.

This news sent Jozsef's emotions over the edge. For the first time since he had opened the doors of his restaurant, Jozsef hung a "closed due to illness" sign on the door and locked up the business in the middle of the day. Jozsef pulled into the driveway of his home. His head felt swollen and his emotions were reeling from the morning's stressful events. He was wrung-out. His mother was urging his father to move back to Hungary! Since she could not break up Jozsef's marriage and have her son all to herself, she would simply take her husband away from any happiness in the United States, back to a life he did not want, to a life that offered him no hope.

It had been one of the worst days Jozsef had experienced in years. How in the world was he going to tell Erzsebet the truth about the restaurant and their finances? The only news that Erzsebet would call "good" was that his self-centered mother would be out of their lives at last. Jozsef gathered his strength, deciding to put on a "happy face," for now, and explain the situation later. He would tell Erzsebet he was "feeling under the weather," and had closed the restaurant for the day to get his strength back.

He was not sure if she would believe him, but it *was* really the truth. He needed to feel Erzsebet's nurturing closeness. He needed to sit down to one of her great dinners, have her soak his sore feet in a tub of warm water, as she did every day, and then spend blissful peaceful hours in her arms.

The next day was a cool, but sunny morning. It was a Saturday, and the children were huddled in front of the television watching "Mighty Mouse" cartoons and would be occupied for at least an hour with their favorite shows. The night prior, he and Erzsebet had enjoyed a most romantic evening. He did feel calmer, and more clear-headed this morning, and Joe figured it would be as good a time as any to speak with his wife about the business and his parents.

Erzsebet sat motionless on their bed as Jozsef explained the news relayed to him by Ray.

Although, she was young, with a child-like spirit, and could be naïve, she was not entirely so. Erzsebet had suspected things were not well with them financially, and the situation regarding her husband's parents, especially Hermina, was not surprising. Whether by choice or a quirk of circumstances, Hermina had never adapted to her life in the states. In addition, she became more embittered when her plan to win her son back did not pan out as she desired.

Regardless, both Jozsef and Erzsebet were relieved she would be out of their lives; however, their hearts went out to Jozsef's father for his plight. Jozsef's parents had decided to return to Hungary, and their fate was no longer one he could help them with. The most important thing now was to find a way to keep his own family's existence afloat.

On a dreary and cloudy Sunday, while Erzsebet played with the children, Jozsef sat at his desk, pushing his penciled finances around to determine how bad things really were. He reasoned if the restaurant business did not slow down much more from their current earnings, and with the extra income from accordion jobs, they could pretty much make ends meet, barely.

He again approached Erzsebet about selling the Renault, and again, she stubbornly refused, stating she would rather go work as a maid then to let the people of the town take away her husband's car. How could he begrudge her dreams?

It was Erzsebet who encouraged him to persevere, her courage empowering him to trudge onward through the storms of life. Jozsef was determined. "I will make things work out for us, I have to."

On Friday, November 22, 1963, Jozsef heard an announcement coming over the radio: *President Kennedy is dead.* President John F. Kennedy had embodied many of Jozsef's own beliefs. The news struck Jozsef hard. It seemed that those who spoke up most loudly for truth and righteousness were always the first to be shot down.

It had happened to him …and now it happened to Kennedy.

Adding to his sadness, was a letter Jozsef received a few days after Kennedy's death from his mother's brother, Antal, announcing Jozsef's mother and father had returned to Hungary with funds supplied by his mother's two brothers. His parents had obtained a small, but adequate apartment in Budapest. Jozsef was relieved to hear his parents had found a way to return to their homeland; however, his relief soon turned to despair as he continued reading, "Dear Jozsef, your mother died not too soon after her return to Budapest from anesthesia complications during a routine tonsillectomy procedure."

His poor father! He had returned to Hungary for Hermina, the love of his young and old life, and now, it was for nothing. His father was alone. After speaking with Erzsebet, and with her blessing, Jozsef wrote Antal, "Please tell my father to come back to America to live with me and my family."

Jozsef received a rapid response from his father, a letter politely turning down his son's offer to bring him back to America. "My dearest only son, you need to concentrate on your own family. I will be fine with the help of Hermina's brothers. They take turns caring for my needs. Jozsef, thank you from the depths of my heart for everything you did for your mother and me in trying to give us a better life. I very much regret your mother's selfish and cruel actions toward you and your family while in America, but also, when you were a little boy. I *should* have noticed that something was not correct in the way she treated you as a child. My striking your little son after Hermina lost her finger is unforgiveable. My only excuse is that I was not in my right mind due to the shock of the situation. I love you Jozsef. Perhaps, one day, if God is willing, I will see you and my grandchildren once more. Try to forgive your mother ... and me."

His father's letter continued with the ramblings of a sad, tired old man beaten down by the world. The news struck Jozsef hard, and he could read no more.

He kissed his father's scribbled signature, folded the letter, and placed it inside his Hungarian bible. His mother was dead. A strange, bewildering, and sick sensation gripped his chest, along with a tightening of his throat.

No matter what kind of a mother Hermina had been to him, she was the *only mother* he would *ever* have, and for that one reason, he allowed himself the blissful relief of deep, grievous tears.

In the days to follow there would be no more time for mourning, for dark clouds were on the horizon, and strength had to be preserved for the struggles to come.

The business was failing miserably. The mortgage payment was behind. The payment on the business was behind. The car payment was behind. The house had been on the market since a week after Ray's news "about the town." Not one person had come to view the home. No, the people of Greenfield were not even going to let him make money to get out of town.

The last waitress was reluctantly let go. Jozsef and Erzsebet operated the restaurant on their own. Jozsef did the cooking and waiting tables during the day and Erzsebet joined Jozsef in the evenings to cook, wait tables, and clean up for the night.

As soon as Judit came home from school every afternoon at three o'clock, her mother was going out the door to work at the restaurant with her father.

Erzsebet cooked a meal ahead of time for Judit to warm either on the stove or in the oven. Judit set up a card table in the living room where the children dined while watching afternoon cartoons or the early evening movie. After dinner Sonny and Pilvia played together while Judit washed dishes in the sink. The kitchen sink was a good three feet across, and almost two feet deep, a very old design. After scouring the sink with powdered cleanser, she first bathed Pilvia and then Sonny, diapering her little brother, and dressing both siblings in their night clothes. After the baths were done, Judit played with Sonny and Pilvia, and watched television with them until 8:30 p.m. which was their official bedtime. Judit would then lock the doors, help the little ones brush their teeth, and at last, after a very long day for a nine-year-old girl, she tucked her brother and sister into bed for the night.

There was no one to tuck Judit in, she was responsible for herself, but it could not be helped. It was simply the way things were due to her family's predicament, and she gave no thought to the fact that the responsibilities of an adult world had come upon her before their due time. Her father would already be gone to work by the time Judit left for school in the morning, and her mother would be sleeping, because Erzsebet rarely settled down until the early morning hours after coming home from the restaurant.

Judit set her own alarm clock to wake her up each day at 7 a.m. for school, and every morning Judit plugged in the coffee pot set up by her mother when she came in from work at night. Then, she made her own breakfast of toast, jam, and coffee, got dressed and walked the approximate one mile to her school.

Jozsef continued to have income from various accordion jobs he acquired. He had met several professional musicians and entertainers in the many clubs where he had performed including a husband and wife team, Al and Ann, both in their early forties. Al, a musician, played the clarinet, trumpet, and drums, and Ann, was a comedian. After one of Jozsef's nightclub performances, Al approached Jozsef with an offer. "You are way too good of a musician to waste your time in this town. I want to make you a business proposal."

The first week in February of 1964, Ray arrived at the Maple Street house with a moving van. He and two other men removed all the furniture from the home. Although, the children were told what was to take place that day, Jozsef asked Erzsebet to take the kids to lunch at the restaurant. He did not want his family to see all their possessions taken away. The house had not sold. There was no way they could remain in the home any longer. Jozsef had kept the restaurant running, but only barely, by a thread.

Everything had to be sold to make ends meet for the long trip ahead: Al and Ann were moving to Florida and had asked Jozsef and his family to move there with them to start a fresh life in the *Sunshine State*.

Al had contacted several clubs in the Tampa Bay area, assuring Jozsef there was plenty of money to be made in the music and entertainment industry. He called it the "Land of Plenty." As a matter of fact, he had already touched base with several club managers and had lined up "gigs" for Ann, him, and Jozsef to work as a team.

Jozsef felt he had nothing to lose. Making a living in Greenfield was no longer an option – a new start was exactly what the family needed.

Jozsef kept the Renault upon Erzsebet's insistence as she was sure he would be a great success in his new musical undertakings. They kept only the most necessary items, but other than the Renault and Chevy station wagon, everything else was sold, including the children's toys. Every bit of money was needed for the venture ahead.

Ray gave Jozsef a lump sum for the home's contents. He could use the household items for his rental apartments. He paid Jozsef more than the contents were worth. Ray was determined to make sure the family had enough money for travel expenses until they could get settled somewhere. Jozsef was grateful for Ray, as he was just about the only person in town who cared about him losing all he had worked for, except for one other person - Mr. Briggon.

Jozsef paid Mr. Briggon a visit to thank him for being a good mentor and friend to his family, explaining he was leaving for Florida to begin a new life. The two men hugged each other with true affection. "You will succeed Jozsef, I have faith in you," sighed a sad Mr. Briggon as he sent Jozsef on his way, knowing he would never see the little refugee family again, wondering where the winds of chance and fate would take his young tutelage.

The move for Florida was planned to take place during the last week of February, with arrival in Tampa by sometime during the first week of March.

Jozsef had arranged temporary housing for the family in an old concrete hotel, *The Weldon Hotel*, built in 1905. The hotel was near the restaurant and Judit's school. Jozsef planned for his family to live there until their move.

There was no kitchen, only two bedrooms and one bath, with the family taking their meals at the restaurant. Judit could walk from the hotel to the restaurant for breakfast and from the school to the restaurant for lunch. An ice chest was kept in the parent's bedroom to store milk and juice. Cereal was kept on the nightstand by the couple's bed if the children needed a nighttime snack. The living quarters were tight at the hotel: the entrance to their accommodations went directly into the main bedroom where Jozsef and Erzsebet slept. From their bedroom was access to the bathroom. Another door opened from the parent's bedroom to a second bedroom where the children slept on two twin beds pulled together to create one large bed to fit all three kids lying side by side.

The difficult days of February flew by with work, worry, and planning for the move, and just as before, each day after school, Judit took over her role as "second mother," coming home to the hotel as Erzsebet was leaving to work at the restaurant. At dinner time, Erzsebet drove back to the hotel to bring the children to eat at the restaurant, and then brought them back to the hotel and returned to work.

Every night Judit bathed her siblings in the clawfoot tub and secured them in their big bed for the night. Jozsef and Erzsebet usually got back to the hotel around eleven o'clock every evening. Most times they ate dinner at work after closing the restaurant, and each night, the exhausted parents fell into bed to rest up for another long day.

Judit slept by the window in the children's bedroom, her alarm clock placed on the window sill, set to wake her at 7:00 a.m. Each school morning Judit walked silently through her parent's bedroom to gain access to the bathroom.

Her mother would be soundly sleeping, but her father would always have departed by 6:30 in the morning to prepare the restaurant for opening and prepping. Being as silent as possible, Judit brushed her teeth, dressed, and quietly opened the main door to the outside hallway, carefully turning the handle to a "locked" position before closing it shut. After eating breakfast at the restaurant, she walked the short distance to her school.

The restaurant had also been offered for sale but with no takers. Since the house and the restaurant were obviously not going to be sold any time soon, and knowing he had to soon leave town for Florida, Jozsef realized his only option was to abandon their home and business.

There is no need for me to waste any more money on payments to anyone. We need the money in our pockets right now for the move. Besides, we will be long gone before the creditors realize we are no longer living in town.

The morning of the move was cool and overcast. A U-Haul trailer filled with kitchenware, clothing, and several miscellaneous items to set up housekeeping, as well as Jozsef's tools for instrument repair was hooked to the Chevy wagon. Judit, Sonny, and Pilvia waited in the hotel's parking lot by the car while their parents checked out of the hotel.

The back seat of the Chevy station wagon had been folded down and made into a comfortable bed area to allow the children a place to sleep during the journey. Jozsef had secured his accordion on the passenger seat of the Renault and stored his music books in the small rear section.

It was decided that Jozsef would lead the drive and Erzsebet would follow.

A million thoughts raced through Jozsef's head as he hugged and kissed his family before their departure. Here he was, seven years out of Hungary, when at that time, his little family had risked their lives to find freedom from a life of Soviet communistic oppression, and, this morning, he and his family were "escaping" from a town bent on suffocating their livelihood. Jozsef had no idea where in the world they would end up after their escape from Hungary. And, on this cloudy morning, they once more faced an uncertain future as they fled Greenfield.

But this time things were different: he now had a wife and *three* children. And, unlike when they had a few material things to leave behind on their exodus from Hungary, they had, in the past seven years, amassed a home, furniture, cars, and a business. All those things had been lost - except the cars.

Jozsef worried about the future consequences of abandoning the restaurant and his home, mainly on how it would affect his ability to build a new life. He had no choice. He was backed into a corner. He made the only decision possible under the circumstances. What else could he have done? Not one soul offered to purchase either their home or business.

All his dreams of "making it big" were dust in the wind. He had to do what he had to do.

Determined his family would not be persecuted by townspeople in Florida as they had been in Greenfield, Jozsef decided that all "Old Hungarian ways must be left behind." The family was to associate only with Americans and was not to focus on finding other Hungarian communities.

Jozsef emphatically told Erzsebet, "No one will know we are foreigners if I can help it! We will do our best to lose our foreign accent by only speaking English!"

That morning of February 29, 1964 (a leap year,) the family was "reborn." Jozsef proclaimed, "Starting today, each of us will go by an *American name*. I will go by Joseph, or Joe. Erzsebet, you will be called Elizabeth, or Liz. Judit, your name will be Judy, as far as Kuki and Sonny, their names can stay the same because they sound more American, anyway."

Jozsef gave a staunch performance during his announcement, but upon his shoulders was the weight of a thousand worlds. Not wanting his family to glimpse even a wrinkle of doubt upon his brow, he flashed a brilliant, white smile, "Everyone in the car! Florida here we come!"

FLORIDA

A few miles into their journey, Joe was driving his Renault through a green light at an intersection. A pickup truck pulling a horse trailer coming from the other direction did not stop at their red light. The truck plowed into the passenger side of the Renault forcing it to spin round twice before coming to a halt. Liz and the children were following directly behind Joe as the nightmarish scene unfolded before them.

Pushing her brake pedal to the floor, Liz brought the Chevy to a scabrous stop. Bolting from the car to aid her husband, her mind raced with the worst of thoughts as she sent up a silent prayer, "God, please do not let my Joe be hurt!"

Joe sat rigid in his car seat, eyes fixed straight head, his knuckles blanched white from his tight grip on the steering wheel. "Joe are you okay? Joe!" In shock, Joe was oblivious to his wife's calls, his mind still reeling from the hard impact. Liz jerked the car door open and grabbed Joe's shoulders. He slowly became cognizant of her voice, his glazed eyes meeting those of his anxious wife. "The car is crushed!" he moaned, "Is my accordion ruined?" Joe's accordion, the lifeblood for his family had to be safe. Without it, there would be no money to be made in Florida, and nowhere to go. Groggy from the surreal series of events, Joe slowly emerged from his car apprehensively approaching the passenger side. The damage was extensive. The entire side of the car was crushed inward. As Joe was surveying the damage to the car, Liz quickly assessed the condition of the accordion. She crawled over the driver's seat to check the instrument. Her heart thumped wildly in her chest, "Joe! Your accordion is perfect! It is not harmed!" Rushing to her side, Joe cautiously peeped over her shoulder to confirm her words. Liz's small frame was trembling from the ordeal. Joe placed an arm about her slumped shoulders. She was a pitiful sight with her ebony hair blowing about in the sudden, cool, swirling winds about them. Her head was downcast to where it was nearly touching her chest. Joe gently placed his hands on both sides of her frightened face. Her eyes were squeezed shut trying to hold back cascades of tears escaping their lidded confines. "Joe, what are we going to do?" Joe wiped her cheek with his fingers, "Don't worry, my butterfly," assured Joe, holding his petite wife close. "Somehow, everything will work out. I will make sure of it!"

The local police station was only two blocks away. The investigation revealed the truck driver was heavily intoxicated. The police asked Joe if he wanted to file charges. Joe's heart sank. Of course, he wanted to file charges! Yes! He wanted to see justice done, but Joe had no time. He had to leave and soon! Regretfully, Joe decided to leave the "idiot drunk," to the police. He was two hours behind schedule and already totally exhausted. The Renault appeared drivable. After Joe helped Liz and the kids settle into the Chevy, he signaled for Liz to follow him in the Renault and the family resumed their drive.

No more than twenty minutes into their journey, Joe heard a loud thumping and bumping emanating from the passenger front wheel section of the Renault. He signaled to Liz that he was pulling over to the side of the road and she pulled her car in behind. Joe brought his car to a slow halt. The unbelievable chain of events started taking their toll on Joe. His insides were shaky, nausea teased his gut.

Liz fared no better. She had almost lost her husband, her only love. The thought of what would have happened to her and the children had Joe died was incomprehensible. She had little money and nowhere to live.

She steeled her mind to clear it of all negative thoughts to allow her to focus on the problem at hand. Joe deduced the car was too crippled to continue the journey, painstakingly deciding to drive it to the nearest Renault dealership where he would park his treasured vehicle on the car lot and leave it to the fates. The car was fixable, but Joe had no time to wait for repairs. His only choice was to leave the car at the dealership with a note on the dashboard detailing why it had been abandoned. "They will fix the car, sell it and still get money to make up for me not paying them," reasoned Joe. He parked the vehicle a good distance from the main display building and left a handwritten note on the car's dashboard. With a heavy sigh, Joe's eyes swam over the crumpled form of his dream car. Gently, in almost a reverent gesture, he ran his hand along its sleek, shiny hood. His silent thoughts revealed the pain of his ravaged heart. *My sweet Erzsebet, she had worked so hard to keep this car for me, because I loved it, and it has all been for nothing. All that money spent on payments and there is nothing!* Joe could not help but be embittered. Was there anything else he would have to abandon? He had lost his country, his parents, his home, his business, almost all his possessions, and now his treasured Renault. It seemed the entire world was against him. The only bit of luck he had was no one observing him abandoning the vehicle on the car lot.

Joe took over the wheel of the Chevy. With Liz seated by his side, the children lying in the back of the car, with U-Haul in tow, he headed toward I-95 South.

It took the family four days to make the trip to Tampa, Florida. With three children aboard, there was always one who had to eat, drink, or go to the bathroom. To save money, Liz had brought along a coffee pot, toaster and an electric fry pan and made their breakfast and dinner in the motel rooms along the way. Every morning she would pull eggs out of the ice chest, scramble them up, and serve them with bacon, and toast. She and Joe would drink coffee and the children would drink milk. In the evenings, an easy, but filling meal was beans and hog dogs and cookies for dessert. At lunchtime each day, they would locate a grocery store and purchase staples needed for their morning and evening meals, placing these in the ice chest for storage. Lunch was eaten in roadside diners. At the end of each grueling day a beaten and exhausted Joe and Liz fell into bed to dream of better days to come.

The last golden rays of sun shown its soft light upon Florida's tropical landscape as the family arrived at their Tampa destination. Al had given Joe directions to a kitchenette-type motel in the area where he and Ann would also stay upon their arrival in a couple of days. Al had booked them several gigs for the next few weeks and Joe was hoping to earn enough money to find the family a rental home by the end of the month. The motel was a one-story, pink stucco structure, enabling Joe to pull the car up to the front door of their unit. The family was surprised to find a very large, clean room, touting two double beds, crib, bath, and a kitchenette with table and chairs. A courtyard in the center of the motel parking lot contained several concrete picnic tables with benches and a few charcoal grills for cooking out. Masses of colorful flowers were planted about the property.

Judy was sitting on a concrete bench one morning watching her brother and sister as they played "tag" in the courtyard. A motel worker was watering the surrounding foliage. "What is the name of that big orange flower over there?" asked Judy as she pointed to the plant in question. "That flower is called the Bird of Paradise," replied the worker.

"Why is it called the Bird of Paradise?"

"Well," replied the kind-looking older gentleman, "Because many people think the flower looks like the head of a tropical bird." Judy studied the elegant yellow and orange flower. "It *does* look like a lovely bird. Paradise is a good name for it." Judy felt the cool mist of liquid spray blowing through the air as the man continued watering the plants. Her spirit was light and happy. All the gloominess of Greenfield was quickly fading away. "Paradise, that's where I am now," sighed Judy, "Florida is my paradise."

Over the next few days the family explored the city. Judy felt as if she had been transported to another planet. Tampa looked no bit like conservative, small-town Greenfield. It was a large place where everything was tall, modern, and shiny. Even the sunshine was brighter! The weather was cool when they left Massachusetts, forcing the family to wear coats or sweaters, but here, the sun was bright, warm, and the skies the loveliest shade of blue. From the moment the family arrived in Tampa, all the cares and stress of their old life vanished. No one spoke of Massachusetts and that seemed to suit everyone just fine.

Joe, Al, and Ann, put on their first performance that very week in a small club not far from the motel. The club owner apparently liked what he heard and asked them to perform every night for the next five days, which was perfect, because after that timeframe, there was another job to move on to. On work nights, Joe would leave the motel at about 7 p.m. Sometimes, in the early morning hours, Judy awoke to the sound of keys jiggling the lock of the motel room door when her father came in from work.

Because of his late work hours, Joe always slept till nearly lunchtime, or later. Judy and her mother worked diligently to make sure Pilvia and Sonny were entertained with food, quiet games, and outside walks until Joe woke up; however, it was becoming quite difficult for Liz to entertain the little ones, and sometimes, even herself. They could not play the television for fear of waking up the patriarch of the family and there were no toys to play with since they all had been sold with the house.

It was nearing their third week of motel living. On a most beautiful, clear Saturday morning Joe awoke in a good mood and happily announced to the family, "We are going shopping!" The children did not understand where they would be going, but at least it meant they would have something to do other than staying at the motel.

The burden of stripping their children of all their playthings had troubled Liz and Joe since the day Ray had taken away all their household possessions in his truck. They knew the children were bored and restless. Joe was determined to remedy the situation. Al had told Joe about a store called "J.M. Fields," a discount department store with one of the biggest toy selections in the area. With money finally in his hands, Joe told his children, "Pick out the toys you would like to have!" None of the children questioned their father's authority on that subject and did a fine job of making a decent dent in their father's budget. Watching their children selecting new toys was one of the most relaxing and happiest days Joe and Liz had experienced in months.

Al had failed to tell Joe one very important detail, and the detail was what *genre* of nightclubs they would perform in – "strip clubs." When Al said there would be plenty of work, he meant it. Tampa had plenty of "Gentleman's Clubs." Joe really did not care *where* he worked. He just wanted the money to take care of his family.

Liz discovered her husband's "secret life," quite by accident. Joe was polishing his accordion on the kitchen table with its open case on the floor at Joe's feet. Liz happened to glance down at the case and saw - a "pasty," (a circular, adhesive covering placed over the nipples of female strippers). From it dangled a long, shimmering, silver tassel. Liz did not know what it was (she was still rather naïve to the ways of the world). Joe, however, did not know that *she did not know* what it was. "My butterfly, I did not want you to think that I *enjoyed* working in those cheap establishments, but as you know, we needed money, and it was the only venue Al could book us into quickly. I took the jobs because the pay is great, and besides, those strippers are all old and dried up, not much to look at. I have no idea how that *thing* even got into my case! You have nothing to worry about! I love you, and only you!"

Liz kept a blank expression at Joe's remark. It was the first time Liz had heard about the "strippers," and was quite taken aback for a moment. As her mother was digesting this bit of unexpected news, Judy's thoughts went back to the time she had seen a movie in 1962 called "Gypsy." Apparently, her father did no research about the film, for he believed it was a movie about real gypsies. Judy wanted to go see the movie because her father had told her that somewhere down the line, "We have gypsy blood in us." He said, "Go have fun and watch how your ancestors lived." Judy was in for a surprise, because it was not the sort of gypsies her father had in mind. As it turned out the film was based on the life of Gypsy Rose Lee, one of the most famous strippers of her day. To Judy's eight-year-old eyes, the film provoked many tantalizing thoughts and questions as she envisioned her father playing his accordion for a bunch of wiggling women, wearing only "underwear."

Collecting her emotions, Liz looked deep into her husband's anxious face. He loved his family more than anything in the world. How could she hold her husband accountable for the clubs he had to work in? She knew he was trying his best to make a living anyway possible. Joe was surprised at his wife's reaction to his confession, as if it was simply a mere matter-of-fact statement; however, although Liz was earnestly trying to appear unshaken by the unexpected revelation, she *was* a little jealous. What wife would not be? But she would never let Joe know. Retaining her self-composure, she responded the only way she knew how to retain her dignity (and her husband's) under the circumstances, forcing the sweetest smile she could assemble, "My *Draga*, Joe, please bring me another one of these, I need two, you know!"

Living in the motel was a great adventure for Judy. As much as she wanted her mother and father to find a new home, she also feared starting a new school. Motel life was a wonderful break from the miserable days spent in her Greenfield classroom.

Judy had thought little about Massachusetts since arriving in Florida; however, school had always been a dreaded thing for her. The longer her father delayed in finding them a home the longer she could stay away from a "mean teacher."

Judy could not help about being afraid of school, for her former teacher was a miserable old woman whose face was permanently molded into a "sour-face." The vicious creature had made it known to Judy that she did not like "foreigners." Her attacks toward her young tutelage ranged from accusing Judy of not doing her homework, even mailing letters to her parents to that regard. Judy's father knew this could not be true for he personally helped his daughter with her homework - especially with arithmetic. He concluded that whatever knowledge his daughter had absorbed, was due to *his own efforts*, and not from the teachings of Judy's instructor. Judy's parents visited the school at least once a month to have a "conference" with the "educator" on subjects ranging from homework, sleeping in class, and not doing her assigned workbook tasks. On each visit Judy's father proved the teacher wrong.

Tiring of the game, Joe met with the "witch," as he now called her, one final time. "You will no longer intimidate or accuse my daughter falsely again. If you do, I will pull her out of school." The dried prune of a woman glared angrily at Judy's father with her slanted, squinted eyes and twisted, red blotchy face, "You can do no such thing, I am *also* the principal of this school. I *mak*e the rules here!"

"Just watch me," countered Joe.

After the showdown between Judy's father and teacher, things became worse. It all started when Judy had an outbreak of at least twenty "boils on her bottom," which, unfortunately, had to be lanced by her family physician. She could barely sit down due to the discomfort. The day after the lancing, Judy was very sore and told her mother she did not think she could sit on the hard chair at school. Therefore, her mother had sent Judy to school with a small pillow to sit on to "cushion her behind." The teacher was infuriated. She asked Judy who had given her the pillow to which she replied, "My mother." The teacher inquired why Judy needed to use a pillow in her chair. Reluctantly, Judy told her the story of the boils, the lancing, and how painful it all was. The teacher did not believe one word of it. She insisted Judy had brought the pillow to school because she felt "superior to the other students." Judy insisted she was telling the truth. "We'll see," the teacher retorted. She gave the class a reading assignment and promptly escorted Judy outside in the hallway where she lifted the back of Judy's dress and pulled down Judy's panties exposing her blistered buttocks to the world. Judy's only saving moment, was that her "front" was covered by the fall of her dress. The teacher could not deny that Judy had spoken the truth, as both her buttocks were covered with a myriad of red, swollen, scabbed-over boils. The pain of her "behind" quickly faded replaced by a greater pain of emotional torment. To add insult to her injury, Judy was further embarrassed when a male student and teacher from another class came into the hall witnessing the scene. At that moment, Judy wanted to run and hide from the world, but there was nowhere to run, nowhere to go, except back to her schoolroom "cell."

But destiny had intervened in determining that Judy would not have to see her teacher again. The family was moving to Florida.

The day before their move. Joe had instructed his daughter not to attend school, and to spend the day with her mother and siblings at the restaurant. He was on a mission to confront the teacher personally, to make sure she would never again torture another student as she had his daughter.

Joe arrived early, before school started for the day, approaching the teacher in her classroom as she was preparing for lessons. Without knocking on the classroom door, he stealthily approached his target, "You will never touch my child again, or any child again. Your days are numbered in this facility. You are *not* the final authority for I have met with, and have spoken with, the *utmost* authority. Now, you will have to answer to him.

You forget one thing - we have witnesses as to what you have done to my child." The cruel, wrinkled sow pushed a long skinny finger into the lapel of Joe's coat, "How dare you speak to me in this manner, I will remove your child from this institution!"

"I have already done that job for you!" Joe vehemently replied, "She *is* removed, permanently! Now, *remove* your finger from my chest or you won't have a hand to use that finger with – I dealt with evil such as yours when I was a child in Europe during World War II and during the Hungarian Revolution of 1956. My people and I sent *your* kind of evil to hell. I am not afraid to send you there to *join them*!" With those final fiery words, Joe spun around and strode out of the brick fortress leaving the "old bat" standing with her mouth gaping. He already had Judy's school transcript in the car from his meeting the day prior with the school superintendent to present to her new school in Florida.

Now, on this sparkling, sunny, Florida morning, Judy's vacation from school was to soon be over, for after an extremely difficult search for the right size home, at the right price, Joe had rented a home on Regnas Avenue in Tampa.

The small rent house was situated at the end of a long, dead-end, gravel road. A sparse number of neighboring houses were scattered along the street. The house rent was ninety dollars a month! Liz was appalled at this discovery, urging Joe to "Try to find a less expensive home." Frustrated with her not understanding the stress he had been through to find *a home in this low price-range*, Joe could only respond back with the truth, as much as he did not want to believe it himself, "But Liz *Edes*, this was the *cheapest* house I could find!" A small compensating factor for the rent was that the house sat directly across from an orange grove, no more than fifty feet from their front yard. There would be plenty of fresh fruit! Another perk was that due to its isolated spot on the street, there was no traffic, making it an ideal spot for the children to play outside.

The home was a one-story, typical "Florida home," complete with jalousie windows. The main entrance was a door entering the kitchen. The kitchen was very small, barely able to contain the table and chairs within it, and storage space was at a premium; however, the kitchen opened into an airy-feeling, sun-filled living room with windows on two sides. A large circulatory oil heater was situated in the short hallway. Down the hall were two bedrooms and one bathroom. The house was furnished including a small black and white television on a rolling stand in the living room. The parent's room had two twin beds covered with sheets and bedspreads; however, for some odd reason, the children's room contained only lawn furniture!

No sooner had Joe deposited his family at the house along with a supply of groceries, he immediately drove off to buy beds for the children. This was fine with Liz, as it would take her and Judy a while to take the household items out of the U-Haul and make the house look more like a home. Fortunately, they could work in peace, for Sonny and Pilvia, worn out from the excitement, were napping in the parent's bedroom.

It was late afternoon when Joe pulled the Chevy into the driveway. He called Liz and Judy out to the car to help him bring in the beds. At first, Judy was confused when she saw the beds her father had purchased for them. When she peeped into the back of the Chevy wagon, she saw three, fold-out cots with thin camping-type cushions. Her first reaction was to say, "These are not real beds!" But she could not say it. Her father looked so happy at that moment. He also looked very worn and tired with black circles under his eyes. Even though she was only nine years old she was no stranger to the financial plight of the family. Many a night she had overheard her parent's hushed conversations on how the family was "living on fumes." Blinking back tears of disappointment, Judy helped her father take the cots into the second bedroom. "Oh, Daddy, thank you so much, this is the best bed I ever had!" Joe's eyes blurred over as he hugged his daughter tightly. She was quite the little actress. Her voice could not disguise the sadness in her eyes. At that moment Joe felt inadequate as a father. Sensing her father's insecurity, Judy quickly gushed, "Daddy, I do really *love* my bed, it's the best!"

The family had mainly devoted their attentions to the interior of the home, to where they had neglected to appreciate what the outside yard offered. To Joe's amazement the small backyard shed had built-in countertops, and two good-sized windows. It was an unbelievable stroke of luck: Joe had a place to repair musical instruments to help supplement the family's income!

To that end, Joe sought additional employment as a musical instrument repairman and found a job with a music store in Clearwater. It was a good distance from the house, but it was an extra job. With the nightclub performances and the new musical instrument repair opportunities, Joe was determined to make a new start.

Joe had gone over the route to her new school with Judy several times until she could easily find her own way. Judy still had her *English Racer* bicycle and decided she would ride her bike to school. Soon after moving into the rent house, a nice family who lived across the street came to introduce themselves to the newcomers. They had a child near Judy's age and offered to drive Judy to school with their child during inclement weather, or anytime, if Judy did not feel like riding her bike.

It was a Friday, an odd day to start school, but at least she would have the weekend to recuperate if she didn't like the place. The day was bright, warm and sunny as Judy breezed her bicycle toward her new hall of learning. She had been apprehensive that morning, full of fear and doubts, uneasy in her stomach, worried if she would have another "creepy" teacher. Joe had instructed Judy to proceed directly to the school office where a counselor would meet with her to escort her to class.

The school had an unusually attractive layout: classrooms were connected by covered breezeways whose borders were lined with green grass and flowers. Stately palm trees lined both sides of the walks. Each classroom had a wall lined with open Jalousie windows allowing lots of sun and fresh air to flow through the rooms. Two huge fans were blowing air from the back of Judy's classroom sending refreshing cool air towards the front of the room. The most amazing sight was a television set in the classroom! Students were intensely observing an instructor on the television directing a mathematics lesson.

The counselor introduced Judy to her teacher, a slightly plump lady with light brown hair, and twinkling blue eyes. The teacher greeted Judy with a warm, genuine smile. She turned down the volume on the television, announcing Judy's arrival to her new classmates. A myriad of cheerful greetings and handfuls of waves burst from the room. Judy was elated with the upbeat attitude of her teacher and class. The heavy burden and fear of not liking her new school quickly evaporated. As she settled behind her desk, the words her father said the night before echoed in her mind, "I *know* you will like your new school and teacher," Her father was correct, but how did he *know*?

Joe was still at work when Judy arrived at home from school that afternoon. As she walked through the kitchen door, Judy was met by her mother, brother, and sister, excitedly chanting, "Happy Birthday!" With all the excitement of moving into their new house and school, Judy had forgotten all about her tenth birthday! It was April 3, 1964.

Joe had no trouble fitting in at the music store. His strong work ethic and sense of pride was affixed to each musical instrument he repaired. The owner of the store patted himself on the back for hiring him – business had picked up with Joe around. Liz, however, felt guilty about not contributing to their finances. Finding a job was difficult when she had two young children at home to care for and no second car; however, Liz was still determined to find a way to bring in more money.

One morning the words to her dilemma appeared directly in front of her for the perfect job. Liz knew she was absolutely qualified for the position. The newspaper want-ad read: "Cook needed for college cafeteria, must be able to work nights."

Liz had made friends with a delightful, kind woman named Pat who lived a few houses down the road. She called Pat asking if she could drive her and the children to the college early that afternoon to apply for the job. It was still early in the day and Joe would not be home for hours.

Joe returned home that evening where a fine dinner of roasted chicken and parsley potatoes awaited him. After the children were settled in for the night the couple sat cuddled up on the couch watching an old western movie. During a commercial, Liz nonchalantly informed Joe of accepting a position as a cook in a nearby college cafeteria. Joe was apprehensive, but he could not say no to Liz for wanting to work. They sure needed the extra money. "But how will you drive there? We only have the one car?" Liz, smiled, evidently very proud and excited of her idea, "As I will be working a night shift, I will take the car when you arrive home. I will watch the children during the day, and you will take care of them in the evening!" Joe could see the happy glow emanating from Liz's face at her accomplishment. He also knew when Liz decided to do something it was pointless to get her to change her mind. She was a *determined* woman.

With damp eyes Joe grasped his wife's soft hands in his calloused ones, "What have I done to deserve the most wonderful wife a man could have?" Liz rested her head on Joe's shoulder, "You have done everything my darling, everything. It has been such a long day. Do you want to go to bed now?" Liz held her hand out to Joe and pulled him up off the sofa.

The following week Joe and Liz worked out their schedules. As soon as Joe arrived home in the evening, Liz gave him a kiss and a hug and drove the car to work at the cafeteria. She would have supper partially prepared on the stove and

Judy would finalize the odds and ends of putting the dinner together, serve it to her father and siblings, wash and dry the dishes, and then set the pots and pans to soak in the sink for her mother to wash upon coming home. While Judy cleaned up from dinner, Joe went to the backyard shed to commence repairing the instruments brought home from work to get a head start on the next day. The more instruments he repaired, the more he earned.

Despite their dizzying schedules, on Friday, May 15, 1964, after seven years in America, Liz, and Judy, proudly and reverently, took their naturalization Oath of Allegiance to the United States of America at the Tampa Courthouse.

Afterwards, in the courthouse lobby, Liz, Joe and all three children happily embraced. "Now, my *Edes* family, we all belong to this country, exclaimed an ecstatic Liz, "We are all citizens at last!" Upon arriving home Joe and Liz hung an American flag at the entrance of the house.

Erzsebet's photo on her United States Citizenship Certificate - 1964

A week after Sonny's third birthday, in early August of 1964, a strange car pulled into the driveway. Two unknown men emerged and knocked on the door. It was an overcast, muggy Saturday morning. Joe had woken up early to take care of the children, so Liz could sleep in as she had come home from work after midnight the night before.

Joe peeped out through the Jalousie frames and then opened the kitchen door. He stepped outside on the adjacent concrete patio where the two men greeted Joe, "Sir, we have been hired by the bank to repossess your Chevrolet station wagon." Joe felt as if the ground was caving in beneath his feet and his stomach felt as if a pound of hot bricks were searing into his gut. "You signed the car over as collateral in the event your loan on the restaurant went into default." Joe shuddered. He did use the car as collateral. At the time he never imagined he would be in the situation he was in now! How in the world did they find him here in Tampa, especially on dusty, old Regnas Avenue! "How did you know where I lived?" The men would not disclose the information. One man reached into his suit pocket and produced the legal documentation. Joe had no choice. He had to let them take the car. But if the men took the Chevy now, he and Liz would have no transportation to go to work!

With the extra instrument repairs, Joe had saved a good sum of money hidden inside a jar of nails in one of the upper kitchen cabinets. It was his private "stash." Even Liz did not know he had it, because it was for a "rainy day," and this day was as rainy as it would get. Joe told the men he would let them take the car but asked if they could first drive him to a used car dealer about four miles away, explaining he had to buy another car quickly so he could go to work. Surprisingly, they obliged his request.

Joe did not have the heart to wake Liz about the repossessed car. "Judy, I want you to watch the children. I'll be home in about a couple of hours or so. Please let your mother sleep. She is exhausted." From the living room, Judy saw her father open a kitchen cabinet, spill a lot of nails onto the counter, and then gather a bundle of money into his pants pocket. She watched her father get into the strange men's car. She could barely discern the back of their vehicle for the giant cloud of dust left in its wake as it sped down the gravel road.

It was after the noon hour, when at long last, Judy saw a pale blue car coming down the road with large "fins" emanating from the rear of the vehicle. The finned car pulled into the driveway. The stranger's car pulled in behind. She noticed the word "Dodge" on the blue car. Joe got out of the blue-finned car and slowly went through the movements of removing his personal belongings from the Chevy. Joe moved mechanically, as if someone else were moving his limbs for him. Everything in this moment of time felt unreal, as he recalled all the wonderful times the family had spent in the Chevy; however, his reverie was abruptly assaulted by the other men's voices telling him to "hurry it up." With trembling hands, Joe surrendered the keys to the taller of the men, his eyes following the assailant as he seated himself in the driver's seat of Joe's Chevy wagon. The other man got in his own car. Joe stood stoically silent, his eyes barely able to make out the shape of his former car as it disappeared forever into swirling clouds of dusty brown powder.

Judy had awakened her mother immediately after her father left to explain what had happened, for she was afraid, having never seen such a terrified look on the face of her father. "Mommy, I saw Daddy open a kitchen cabinet and pull out a glass jar with big nails in it, but also in the jar was a lot of paper money. Daddy grabbed the money and got in the car with the men."

After his last glimpse of the Chevy, Joe was too exhausted, shaken and embarrassed to come inside the house. He needed to be alone. He opened the door of the Dodge, sat down at the wheel, staring blankly into nothingness. He had lost his precious Renault, and now, they had taken his Chevy wagon. The car had been there when both Kuki and Sonny were born – the only car they had ever known. The Chevy had brought them all safely to Florida.

Joe's mind spun in circles, again reiterating the losses in his life: his country, his parents, his home, his business, his household possessions, his Renault, *and now, his Chevy*. No, it did not *seem* the world was against him, it *was* against him. He was at rock-bottom - again! He limply laid his sweaty forehead face-down on the steering wheel.

Liz had been watching Joe through the windows of the kitchen door, her heart awash with love, sorrow, and admiration for her embattled husband. *My poor, sweet, Jozsef, my love, my darling, my everything, please do not let them destroy you!* Liz slowly made her way toward the car. As if he could sense his wife's presence, Joe lethargically lifted his head from its resting place. Liz leaned into the car window smiling gently at her sweetheart. Not saying a word, she opened the driver's side door.

"Come my love, come inside. It will be all right." She pulled her husband out of the vehicle, her grip from his wrist nearly slipping from the stressful moisture exuding from his skin.

Once inside the house, she locked eyes with Judy, giving her "a serious look" that meant "Do as I say." The *look* that Judy knew all too well not to ignore or question. "Judy, *please* play with your brother and sister for about an hour. Your father is not feeling well. I need to help him get better."

"Of course, Mommy," Judy replied, not understanding the scene before her. Judy's eyes followed her mother and father. Liz placed her shoulder under Joe's armpit supporting his slumping weight and led him to their bedroom. She closed the door and Judy heard the "click" of the lock.

Life went on. Joe worked in the world of music during the day and Liz worked in the world of food at night.

Joe's Chevy Wagon in Massachusetts

When possible, on either a Saturday or Sunday, Joe and Liz packed the car with a picnic basket, blankets, towels, diving masks, radio, plastic buckets and shovels, and drove the family for an adventurous, sundrenched day on the beautiful white sands of Clearwater Beach.

The clean ocean breezes relaxed their tired spirits, engulfing their senses with fresh hope for better days. The children delighted playing in the greenish-blue waves of the shallow shoreline, gathering shells, building sandcastles, watching tiny schools of fish, collecting sand dollars and observing the colorful Coquina clams. One of the children's most enjoyable activities was watching the tides come and go, and with each ripple of waves a Coquina clam would put forth a little "arm" to dig itself deeply into the soft wet sand. Each roll of a wave brought forth hundreds of these little living shells, akin to a colorful wet rainbow of yellow, white, purple and pink stretching for miles along the water's edge.

After a glorious sunlit day at the ocean the family gathered seawater in several plastic pails and headed for the car. In the parking lot Joe poured water over everyone's feet to wash off the sand. Liz placed a towel on the back seat for "wet bottoms" and then they would head for home.

Often, after an afternoon at the beach, Joe treated the children to an "outdoor movie." He would place lawn chairs on the concrete patio outside the kitchen door, open the Jalousie windows, and pull the black and white television on its stand up to the kitchen door allowing the children to watch wrestling through the door with their father, while feasting on hotdogs, beans, and ice cream cones. It was a simple thing to do, but it brought the children much happiness and Joe looked forward to doing this whenever possible.

In late October, Al phoned Joe on a warm, Sunday afternoon. Al spoke so quickly that Joe had a difficult time discerning or comprehending what Al was trying to say. "Joe, I heard through the grapevine that Mr. Busch, the big beer magnet, is seeking a strolling classical accordion player to entertain the guests in the dining room of his restaurant. This is your opportunity to get into finer circles and show off your talents! I know you can get the job!"

Joe was exhilarated. This was truly the opportunity of a lifetime – performing in a prestigious setting owned by a millionaire! "Thanks, Al. I'm going to contact Mr. Busch and convince him I'm the man for his restaurant!"

In March of 1959, Mr. August A. Busch, Jr. a beer-brewer, opened a "beer garden" (offering free beer – and a free hospitality center for the City of Tampa), along with a complementary wild bird show at his newly-opened brewery. He designed the beer garden to resemble a lush tropical island, offering free beer to his patrons as they departed from a fun-filled day within the walls of his "Hospitality House."

One of the focal points of his facility was a restaurant designed after the famous Old Swiss House in Lucerne, Switzerland, owned by his wife's brother.

Mr. Busch, Jr., built the "second" Old Swiss House in Tampa, Florida, as a gift for his wife, opening the facility in 1964. The restaurant was one of the finest and most elegant places to dine in the Tampa area, with clientele and prices to match the ambiance.

A couple of days before Halloween, Joe arrived at the Old Swiss House for his "performance interview," where Mr. Busch warmly greeted his client, "Your friend tells me a lot of great things about you, Joe. Please, play whatever tunes you like!" Mr. Busch then seated himself on a deeply-cushioned, high-backed chair in the elegant dining room, eagerly awaiting to hear Joe's talent. With his beloved instrument strapped upon his shoulders, Joe leisurely strolled through the grand accommodation, weaving his way between the guest tables of the empty dining room as he belted out a foot-tapping Bavarian drinking song, as well as two more classically-styled pieces, much to the delight of his interviewer.

Mr. Busch was elated, "Joe, you are definitely hired! What a performance! Are you available to start next weekend, and every weekend after that? Perhaps every Friday, Saturday, and Sunday?"

Things were looking up! With Liz working at the college cafeteria, his repair jobs, the weekly job at the music store, and the night work at the Old Swiss House, Joe was able to purchase a small, second car for Liz. "Oh! What a wonderful feeling to be free!" Liz exclaimed, as she sat behind the wheel of her maroon-colored Chevy Impala. "At last, I will be able to go shopping and take the children places during the day!"

In the late fall, on many a Sunday or Saturday afternoon, Joe took the family to the lush grounds of Busch Gardens, where the children played on the fun-filled playground and watched the colorful parrot show. Joe and Liz drank free beer at the Hospitality House and the children sipped on sodas. The garden's grounds were majestic and inviting, filled with just about every authentic tropical plant and tree the islands offered. It was the perfect place to escape the drudgery of everyday life and enjoy spending time together as a family.

After the Chevy had been repossessed, Joe believed the Greenfield nightmare to finally be over. But it was not to be. The men who picked up the car must have told Joe's whereabouts to every creditor he owed. Threatening letters were in the mailbox on an almost daily basis: the banks wanted money for payments on the house, restaurant, Renault, department store accounts, and countless petty bills. Now, that the creditors knew where he lived, Joe was fretful other collectors would come knocking on his door. Joe could no longer take the stress of his situation, and with a heavy heart, filed for bankruptcy.

It was close to Christmas-time in Florida, and unlike the cold, snowy winters in Massachusetts, the grass was bright and green, the scent of seasonal flowers filled the air, and the breezes blew warm. But despite the lovely day promised by the sun's yellow rays, Joe's thoughts were elsewhere. This Saturday morning, Joe had awakened early, creeping quietly out of the house to take care of an issue wearing on his mind and soul. He had left a note on the kitchen table for Liz stating he had to take care of a "business matter," and would be home around noontime.

About one o'clock in the afternoon Liz heard Joe's tires crunching down the gravel driveway. She had prepared a lunch/dinner combination for their main meal consisting of fried chicken, mashed potatoes, and corn on the cob. *I'm so glad Joe is home - he must be starving! He never eats breakfast!* She peered out the kitchen window. Something was wrong. Joe was walking very slowly toward the kitchen door. His shoulders were rounded and slouched. As he came closer, she noticed his eyes were red and his nostrils swollen. "Judy, watch the kids. Do not come outside!" ordered a panicked Liz as she made her way to her husband.

Liz met Joe on the driveway. He was in tremendous physical distress. He was crying. The day had become unusually hot and humid for the time of year and sweat exuded from every pore of Joe's body. Liz pulled her husband into her arms, and just in time, for his knees buckled beneath him. It took all the strength Liz had to keep Joe from crumpling to the ground. As he sank closer to the earth, he sobbed uncontrollably. Liz held him tighter, raising him up, and walked him to the house.

The children were frightened and bewildered at the sight of their father's condition. Liz signaled them to *"be quiet."* She lay Joe down on the narrow couch in the living room, propping his feet up with several throw pillows. She placed a cold cloth on his forehead. She kissed his tear-stained face. "Please, my Love, tell me what happened?"

Between wracking sobs and a few gulps of ice water, Joe explained he had been to a department store to try to buy something, *anything*. He needed to re-establish his credit and had to start somewhere to create a fresh credit history.

Joe told Liz he had asked to speak privately with the store manager and had "begged" the manager to allow him to purchase any item on credit. Joe detailed how he had "spilled his guts" to the manager, detailing everything about his life in Hungary, about what happened in Massachusetts, and how he came to be in his current financial predicament.

The store manager had remained stony-faced during Joe's tearful tirade; however, something must have touched the manager's heart, for as Joe continued his story, the harsh lines of the man's face softened, culminating in him shaking Joe's hand about opening a charge account.

Since he knew Joe was a musician, the manager recommended Joe purchase the latest Hi-Fi "stereo" record player/radio just recently introduced to the store. The stunning walnut floor cabinet gave the appearance of fine furniture with an accompanying fine price of two hundred dollars!

The manager arranged payments of ten dollars a month for the stereo. Help was arranged to place the cabinet in the trunk of the 'fin car," but it was too large, and the trunk had to be secured with a rope to prevent the stereo from falling out. As happy as Joe was that he had succeeded in his mission, the ordeal was overpowering for his body, causing his emotions to cave in on the drive home, as the enormity of what he had accomplished became clear. *I don't care if I cried, if I begged. I don't care if other store patrons heard about my troubles. There are times in one's life when pride is of no importance, and at this point in my life, I have no more pride. But I don't care, for now I will be able to establish new credit!*

With Liz's attentive, soothing, loving care, Joe's crushed spirit quickly rejuvenated - how very proud Liz was of *her* husband. She kissed and hugged him for fighting for his family, exclaiming, "Oh, how I wish I could have been there to see you in action!" With his nerves calmed down, Joe realized he was starving! He had not had anything to eat or drink all day, except for the few sips of ice water offered by Liz. After happily feasting on his fried chicken and slurping down several glasses of iced tea with lemon, Joe perked up, "Everyone, go outside and help me bring in the new record player from the car!"

The Regnas Avenue Christmas Eve of 1964 was a happy one. Christmas records were played on the "Dad-stereo record player," as Joe and Liz watched their children tear into their presents. Despite all its battles, life was very much worth living, for as long as they had each other, anything was endurable. Joe was determined to build a new life in Florida, and it would happen in the New Year of 1965.

Joe was still commuting to the music store in Clearwater. It was near a drug store, a convenient spot not only to pick up prescriptions, but also a quick place to pick up a few incidentals for Liz on his way home. It was late spring, around 5 p.m., on a busy Friday. The music store had closed for the day and Joe went to the drug store to pick up some items before settling in for the congested drive home. He hurriedly exited the drug store heading for his parked car when he heard his name being called. He spun around and saw his boss waving for him to come back to the shop. Joe was in a hurry. He wanted to get on the road before the traffic got any worse, but curiosity got the best of him. He walked back to the music store where his boss asked Joe if he could step inside to "talk with him for a minute."

Joe's head was swirling in a happy daze all the way home. Life sure had its way of surprising you when you least expected it, for beside him on the car seat was a newspaper ad, a phone number, and one hundred dollars in cash! Joe and his boss had exchanged several "discussions" since Joe started working at the store.

All in all, Joe's boss had pieced together a good idea of Joe's past life and struggles. It did "bother him" that Joe spent a lot of time commuting to and from work. He was a businessman and reasoned that if he could get Joe to live closer to the store, he would also be a more productive employee. His customer base had increased since hiring Joe, and without him spending a dime on advertising! His customers had done a fine job of spreading the word that he had the best musical instrument repairman in the area, and, all his clients insisted for "Joe to fix it!" He reasoned the more Joe could "fix," the more money he would make! But he was not at all callous. He was a good man, and the "human side" of him cringed at the thought of Joe and his family living in an expensive, tiny rent house so far away from Joe's work.

That evening, after he had signaled for Joe to come back to the shop, he had told Joe about a newspaper ad detailing a nice house for sale in

Clearwater. It was a new FHA home only requiring a modest down payment.

The boss told Joe the house was perfect for him and his family and wished he could have discovered the home before Christmas, as it would have made the perfect gift for them.

But now Christmas would come early in 1965, for he personally knew the people who owned the realty company and had arranged for Joe to see the house the next day. If Joe liked the house, he was to hand over the cash for the down payment and sign the papers!

Joe was reluctant to take money from his boss, even though he was bursting inside with excitement. "I cannot take this charity," explained Joe when his boss placed the money into his hand. "Look Joe," replied his well-intentioned employer, "This is not charity, this is a chance - consider the one hundred dollars a loan and you can pay it back some each payday."

Driving home along the Clearwater Causeway, memories of all the kind people in Joe's life filled his mind: Mr. Briggon, who had sought him out in Camp Kilmer as their sponsor, had found their first apartment, and who had also given him a down payment for the house on Maple Street. There was good old Ray, who understood him more than anyone else in Greenfield, and had helped his parents find an affordable apartment, and assisted helping Joe move the family out of Massachusetts.

And now, fate, if there was such a thing, had intervened to move them out of the Regnas Avenue rent house. A real house would be a definite improvement over their present lodging. The monthly payments would also be less, by at least thirty dollars – enough to buy a whole week's worth of groceries!

Joe quickly analyzed the situation: he would drive directly from his music repair job in Clearwater to the Old Swiss House in Tampa on Friday's to save time, having already placed a change of clothes and his accordion into the car, and when he had to work Saturdays at the music store, he could do the same to save time and money. By the time Joe arrived home he had it all worked out.

Saturday morning was filled with anticipation as the family drove to the open-house in Clearwater. Joe and Liz were pleasantly shocked when their car drove onto the home's large concrete driveway. Standing proudly before them was a new, dark-red, brick, ranch-style home, touting a big picture window in the front and a set of white, double-doors for the main entry. The driveway led into a huge, over-sized garage. A kindly, older couple, who were real estate agents, were sitting in lawn chairs in the garage, greeted the family, "We have been expecting you!" Beyond the front door was the most beautiful, 1700 square foot, modern home Liz had ever entered. The foyer led to a large living room/dining room combination. Off the dining room area to the right, was the door to the garage, and to the left was the entry to a large, eat-in kitchen, complete with all appliances, including a dishwasher! Off the kitchen was the door to a nice-sized backyard, large enough for a swing set for the kids. A hallway led to a laundry room complete with washer and dryer.

From the living room, another hallway led to a bedroom on the left, a bath to the right, another bedroom to the left, and directly across from it, the master bedroom, complete with its own bath and large dressing area. There was closet space galore, and best of all, the house had central air-conditioning and heating. No more window air conditioning units and circulatory oil heaters.

In less than a week they were the official owners of the house in Clearwater on Long Street. There was only one problem: they had no furniture! Not one chair of their own. The real estate people told Joe and Liz about a very nice, upscale furniture store, with low-scale prices.

The next week, after a quick lunch at a Sandy's fast food hamburger place, Joe took his family to the furniture store. The store featured types of furniture they had never seen or even knew existed.

For the living and dining rooms, Joe and Liz decided on a living room suite in the Danish Modern style, with burnt orange cushions for the couch and recliners, with matching dining furniture, with Danish modern table, and padded, green, swivel chairs. The kitchen was perfect to accommodate a comfortable, corner-style, sleek yellow and white, breakfast bench and nook set.

They chose a single bed made of maple for Sonny's room with a matching dresser (he was too young to know what he wanted). However, the girls knew *exactly* what they wanted: A French provincial bedroom, consisting of two twin beds, one long dresser, and one tall dresser, complete with matching headboards. For their bedroom, Joe and Liz, again, picked out a bedroom suite in the Danish-style. They had chosen all the furnishings, but still had no lamps. After the lamps were selected for each room, Joe seated himself in the sales office to sign the sale papers. He charged everything and arranged for the furniture to be delivered the following Saturday. No one said he had bad credit and no questions were asked.

Before moving day, Liz had given the cafeteria notice, having found work in a Howard Johnsons' restaurant in Clearwater. Liz was an intelligent woman and had sought employment as a pediatric nurse (her occupation in Hungary) but was told her nursing certification from another country could not be honored in the United States and she would have to re-obtain her degree by attending college in the states. College was not an option. Unfortunately, the only job option readily available was an occupation she excelled in: working in a restaurant.

With every bit of good luck always comes some bad. Liz's car gave up its life just after the move to Long Street. Besides needing a new car, Joe had forgotten to buy a very important item – a television! Joe decided to try his luck at the same department store where he had purchased his stereo cabinet. His payments on the Hi-Fi stereo had always been made on time, and he often had even made double payments. The stereo had been paid off sooner than required.

The store's television showroom had a collection of the latest color televisions. The children were locked in place in front of the moving pictures amazed by the colorful display. Joe saw the delighted expressions on his children's faces and was a little delighted himself. He told the salesman he would like to "charge it," and without a hitch, he was the proud owner of a color television.

After purchasing the television, Joe placed the family into the trusty "fin car," and drove to the Chevrolet car dealership in Clearwater to find a car he could afford. They were just there to look. One week later, on a Sunday, Joe returned to the car lot at four o'clock in the afternoon. Joe was a master in "dealing." After all, the place where cars are sold is called a *dealership,* and Joe was determined to strike a good one. Joe did not leave with his new yellow Chevrolet Impala until six o'clock that evening.

In those two hours he had the salesman go back and forth with his "offers" to the management. They would refuse his offer and *he* would refuse their offer.

Knowing the dealership closed early on Sundays. Joe was determined to wear the management down until the last minute before closing. Joe planned to make them so exhausted with "the game," that they would give in, and they did give in ... and Joe got "his deal."

Joe placed the key in the ignition of his new Chevy happily realizing, "I'm the first person this car's valves have ever pumped for!" Liz followed Joe home in the *fin-car* with the children in tow. It made her heart glad to see

Joe in a new vehicle, again, bringing back the happy memories of when he had purchased his shiny, red Renault; however, she quickly pushed the Renault out of mind. She would think only happy thoughts. *They deserved only happy thoughts.*

Within two weeks, the family had accumulated a new home, new furniture, a new television, and a new car! Joe was not sure how they would pay for it all, but he would have plenty of time to figure it out later.

Joe turned the garage into a workshop for his musical instrument repair. He placed an ad in the newspaper to that effect, and much to his relief, the calls started pouring in, and that was a good thing, for he would need every extra dollar to cover all the new and unexpected expenses.

School began in September. Little Sonny was the only child home during the day. The days were lovely and warm. Liz filled up Sonny's wading pool, playing and immersing herself in the water with him, until it was time to clean house and get herself ready for work, but Liz was miserable at the Howard Johnson's restaurant. Things had started out slowly, but she surmised it was just "a slow time." As it turned out, every day was "a slow time." Liz relied solely on tips as she was only paid sixty cents an hour as a waitress.

One weekend in October, after working a double-shift (covering lunch and dinner on both days) she had put in sixteen hours and the only thing she had to show for her efforts was five dollars, and that paltry amount was squeezed out of her tiny tips of pennies, nickels, dimes and quarters. Liz gave her notice and came home.

That evening, Joe helped his wife peruse the classifieds to locate another place to work. A waitress was needed at a seafood restaurant in Indian Shores. Seafood restaurants were always open late.

Liz picked up the phone, inquired about the job, and spoke with "Joanie." Joanie told Liz they were "desperate" for an experienced server, "This restaurant is always swamped with customers *and* the tips are great!" She asked if Liz would mind driving over that night to talk about the position. Within one minute of hanging up the phone, Joe and Liz were on their way to Indian Shores about a twelve-mile drive from the house. Joanie and Liz struck it off immediately and Liz was to start her job the next day.

At six o'clock in the evening on August 18, 1967, in a filled-to-capacity school auditorium, four rows back from the stage, sat Liz with her children. She glanced over to admire her little family: Sonny was adorably dressed in a suit with a bowtie and the girls arrayed in new dresses.

This night was monumental: Ten years after arriving in America, Joe was receiving his electronics certification from a vocational technical institute. It had not been easy, but between all his jobs, Joe had squeezed in two nights a week to attend the institute to train in the field of electronics. Joe's wandering spirit was driving him on to try new ventures. He needed a steady weekly income with an employer who could provide a job with a chance of a promotion and medical and dental benefits for his family. He had no health insurance, but fortunately, no one in the family had required hospitalization since their move to Florida.

Within a month of graduation, Joe landed a position as an in-home television repairman for a nationwide department store specializing in all types of home appliances and televisions. The company provided many opportunities for career advancement, a decent salary, uniforms, and health insurance.

Every morning Joe left the house at 7 a.m. to begin his repair route at 8 a.m. He parked his car at the service center lot and proceeded to the office to obtain his route sheet reflecting the scheduled repairs for the day. He then sat behind the wheel of his blue repair van filled with every part imaginable to fix a television.

Judy came home from school at around 3 p.m. meeting her mother as she walked out the front door departing for her restaurant job wearing her standard uniform: a crisp white blouse, blue skirt, white "nursing" shoes (because they had very cushioned soles), and a black linen apron. Liz picked up Pilvia from school at two o'clock. By the time Judy got home, the kids were usually in Sonny's room playing with blocks or puzzles.

After Liz gave Judy instructions for preparing the evening meal, she kissed the children goodbye and drove away. Assuring Sonny and Pilvia were entertained, Judy then proceeded with her daily routine of putting away the freshly-washed clothes her mother had neatly placed on each family member's bed. She then would set the table for dinner and make iced tea. Judy took time to play with her siblings before she needed to start cooking dinner for the usual 5:30 p.m. meal.

Her father was always on time, and always hungry, when he walked in the door from a hard day at work. Despite her young age, Judy was quite a self-sufficient and efficient housekeeper: cooking, ironing, and cleaning house as well as any grown woman.

One evening, Judy's father came home from work extremely stressed. All the repair jobs Joe had been assigned for the day had been awfully difficult. He dubbed such difficult television repair jobs with the nickname of "dogs." Joe was worried because he could not complete all the jobs on his route that day. Afraid to turn in an incomplete route sheet, Joe had driven the repair van home that night as he intended to go back out after dinner to complete his work.

With all the side jobs Joe was doing to support his family, he felt guilty about leaving the children home alone, as unfortunately, they had to be left at home alone quite often due to his working extra jobs in the evenings while Liz was at work. "Would you like to come to work with me tonight in the work van?" Joe's children, like their father, loved adventure, and all yelled a resounding "Yes!"

After dinner, Joe sat the children on the floor in the rear of the van and took off to finish his service calls. While Joe was inside the client's homes fixing their televisions, the children stayed huddled in the van, playing the "quiet game," because Joe told them they *had* to be quiet.

Joe made two service calls that evening, arriving back home close to 9:30 p.m. He would have to leave for work extra early the next morning to make sure the service vehicle was parked in its spot at opening time.

Sonny and Pilvia were especially excited about the entire escapade as they always had to be in bed by 8 p.m. Joe knew Liz would not be pleased to learn he had toted the children with him to work after hours. She would chide him and remind him it was "not a good idea and not safe."

Joe explained to his children that the "nighttime ride" must always be their secret so he would "Not get in trouble with Mommy." All agreed, kissed their father goodnight, thanking him for a most exciting time and went straight to bed, tucking their father's secret safely away in their hearts.

Joe attended several company training programs and was well-versed in not only television repair, but also the inside workings of washers, dryers, garage doors, stoves, radios, television antennas, refrigerators, and water heaters. His accomplishments had not gone unnoticed by management and Joe was invited to participate in the management training program. Once again fate was knocking on the door of Joe's heart and he bade it to enter.

Later that year, the company sent Joe to various management training classes, not only in Florida, but as far away as Texas and Atlanta, sometimes, for up to one week at a time. Joe took advantage of every class offered, excelling even beyond his own expectations.

Liz was very happy with her job at the restaurant and had made numerous friends among her fellow employees who respected and admired Liz for her strong work ethic and her kind persona.

The restaurant was large, airy, and sunny, its walls composed of huge windows that allowed natural light to flow through its rooms. In the evening, colored lights placed among the foliage outside the windows reflected their gentle glow into the dining rooms. As nice a place as it was, Liz rarely had time to take it all in, she was just too busy, and being busy at work meant *money*.

In the fall of 1967, Judy was thirteen and starting eighth grade at John F. Kennedy Junior High School, a large, two-story building, located just kitty-corner to her house on Long Street. It took only five minutes to walk onto the school's campus. On her first day of school, she sat in her homeroom classroom waiting for the teacher to enter. The rear of the classroom had a "wall" made of heavy folding screen partitions, sectioning it off from another large classroom. All morning Judy had been concerned as to what type of teacher, or teachers, she would have this year.

Judy's question about "teachers" was answered only too soon: He was an old, stern, miserable-sort, appearing to be annoyed with anyone younger than himself. He gruffly announced to the students, "I am not only your homeroom teacher, but your history teacher. I will not tolerate any misconduct or foolishness in my class!" He hit a ruler against his desk, yelling as if all the students were deaf, "As I call your name, please rise so I may identify who you are!"

"He reminds me of my mean teacher in Massachusetts," thought a disheartened Judy. "I don't like the atmosphere in this room at all."

Author on her bike in front of the Long Street House - 1965

She had no sooner finished her thoughts, when another teacher entered the room making an announcement: "These students were registered to the other classroom behind the screen divider, will all students proceed to their correct location."

What a refreshing difference! The new classroom was huge with a large movie screen in front of the room. A shapely middle-aged woman, with neatly coiffed blonde hair, announced she was their history and homeroom teacher. She welcomed everyone, assuring the class they would have a wonderful year together.

The history classroom contained ten rows of desks stretched across the width of the classroom, with at least ten desks behind each of the ten rows. The first student in every row was handed a stack of orientation papers to hand out to each person in their row. Judy sat up front. After the papers were handed to her, she made her way down the avenue of desks in her row, shyly handing each student a stapled information packet.

As the first few weeks of school progressed, Judy fell into the rhythm of each class, but her favorite class was history. Two days a week, the room was darkened, and the subject matter taught using documentary-type films projected onto the movie screen. After each film, students took a quiz to assess their knowledge of the material presented.

About a month after the school year began, Judy's world was to be transformed, for a bright spark of change, hidden in the ebony shadows was making its way toward her.

Feeling a tap upon her back, Judy glanced around, and found herself being handed a folded piece of paper by the student seated behind her. Judy unfolded the note, but the darkness made it impossible to read - she would have to wait till the lights came on after the film.

The once interesting history lesson now became boring. Judy fidgeted in her seat. She had not made friends with anyone in this class or even bothered to get acquainted with the students sitting behind her. Who in the world would be sending her a note? At last, the lights switched on, enabling Judy to intently study the mysterious message, which read: "You are beautiful! Turn around and I'll wave to you!" Judy turned her head back over her left shoulder, trying her best to be inconspicuous. In the row opposite, on her left, about three seats back, sat a young man wearing a yellow, long-sleeved shirt with a pointed button-down collar, brown cords, and brown loafers. He was holding his right arm low in the aisle as he subtly waved his hand. Judy took in his attractive features. *He is so good-looking!*

A sudden surge of warmth spread to her cheeks as she quickly assessed her admirer. He had striking features: sea-green sparkling eyes, thick sandy-colored hair with a stray wispy lock sweeping above one eye, perfectly chiseled facial bones, a lean frame, and a dazzling smile that would have swept Judy off her feet had she not been sitting down.

When the bell rang for the next class Judy's wooer made his way over to her side. "I couldn't help notice you. I think you are the prettiest girl I've ever seen! I've been watching you since school started – I had to find out who you are!"

Judy's heart went aflutter. The clamor of students changing classes with their hoots and hollers made conversation tedious, requiring both to yell above the crowd, "My name is Judy! What's your name?"

The boy excitedly spilled out his identity, "Jay - my name is Jay, and you were meant for me!" Jay made his statement assuredly and nonchalantly, as he had already decided Judy should acknowledge that she was now "his girl."

Jay reached for Judy's hand. "Can I see you today - maybe between classes - at lunch?"

Judy caught her breath. Everything was moving so quickly! "Lunch is great! I'll meet you at the cafeteria door at 11:45." The words came off Judy's lips before she realized she had even spoken them. "I'll see you there!" Jay exclaimed, as he quickly bolted off to his next class, leaving Judy standing in the middle of the school's noisy hallway wondering, "What just happened?"

They met at the cafeteria door, both foregoing lunch – both too excited to think of food. The school had a courtyard with several park-style benches, and they settled there for their introductions.

Jay was an orphan. His mother had died in some mysterious way when he was about age four or five. No one in his family had a clear answer to the cause of her death.

He had never even seen a photograph of his mother. Judy found all this puzzling. "There was something strange in my parent's marriage or something on how the family accepted her, something weird like that, but I am not really sure about any of it." Jay explained, as he brushed away a long strand of hair from his eyes. "In any event, I really don't have a clear memory of her. Sometimes I have dreams. I think they may be about my mother, but they are so vague, so dark, it's hard to make out any details."

Jay took in a deep breath, "My dad died of lung cancer when I was about age seven. I do remember living in New York with my father. After he died, I went to live with my grandmother here in Florida. She's in her late seventies. Her brother, "Uncle Davey," who is about eighty, also lives with us in a neighborhood near Redington Beach. I love them a lot and they love me and take good care of me. I also have another uncle, but his job takes him around the world, something to do with government work. I have several cousins from his side of the family. What about you? Tell me about your family."

Judy gave Jay a quick synopsis of her background, about her brother and sister, and how she and her parents had come to the United States.

Jay looked longingly into the eyes of the girl who had stolen his heart. What was it about her that made him feel differently about her from other girls he had met? Yes, she was beautiful, sweet and kind, but there was something else. The answer came when he held her hand in his.

He clasped her fingers within his palm feeling the warmth of her skin. An easy peaceful feeling permeated his essence, like settling down in a cozy chair in front of a fireplace after being out in a cold wind. Her very touch soothed his spirit. "I've been looking for you all my life, I've come home," he whispered softly.

Judy and Jay, at the fair, soon after they met - 1967

Raising her hand to his lips he gently kissed her wrist, his hot breath sending a warm, weakening sensation through Judy's body, causing it to yearn for something she did not understand.

They sat close together after the "kiss" in total silence. The lunch hour would soon be over. Whatever had been left unsaid would have to wait until tomorrow. Judy struggled to find words to express her perplexed emotions. "Jay, I've never felt this way before. I've never had a boyfriend and have never been kissed. My insides feel all shaky, like everything is upside-down. When you touch me, when you are near me, I feel as though my legs won't hold me up, like I'm melting!" Jay traced the outline of her freshly kissed wrist, "Then, we're both melting together. I want to meet your family. Do you know when I could? It's unbelievable, I mean, all you told me about how you and your family got here to America, and now, through all that, *you* are here with me! Your family life sounds wonderful. I wish I had grown up with both parents. I have no idea what it's like to live with both a mother and father, especially parents like yours."

Jay's eyes watered over, and one elusive tear escaped down his cheek. He quickly wiped it away with his arm. "It's been a very empty life without a mother and father. Don't misunderstand, I love my grandmother and uncle, but I sometimes wish things would have been different. But, then again …if it had been different …I wouldn't be here with you. Would I?"

A whirlpool of emotions swirled within Judy's chest: a feeling of pity for Jay's "orphan-ness," and a magnificent and breathtaking emotion she could not quite identify. "Yes, oh, yes, Jay, you are right. I'm so happy we met, and I would love for you to meet my family! When I go home today, I'll ask when you can visit!"

The bell rang signaling the end of the lunch period. It was time to go on to the next class. Jay clasped Judy's hand tightly, pulled her close, and kissed her cheek. "I'll see you tomorrow, right here, at the same time." Judy's face blushed with excitement. "I'll be here waiting for you, Jay."

When school let out, Judy's legs could not carry her fast enough across the wide expanse of lawn separating the school from the street where she lived. As she neared her home, she could see her mother opening the car door, getting ready to leave for work at the restaurant, having already placed her apron and handbag on the bench seat. "Mommy, Mommy, I need to tell you something!" Judy shouted as she raced breathlessly toward her mother. "I met a boy today! I have a boyfriend, and he thinks I'm beautiful! He wants to meet you and Daddy!"

Liz observed the flaming color in her young daughter's cheeks and the happy sparkle in her eyes, her mind carrying her back to that treasured, miraculous point in time when she had met "Her Jozsef." Was it now her daughter's moment in time, her fate, her destiny reaching out to her? "Mommy, did you hear me? Judy urgently implored. "Can Jay come to meet you and Daddy?" Liz snapped out of her trance, "Of course!" She placed her arm around Judy, "You both come home for lunch tomorrow. I will make toasted egg salad sandwiches and soup!"

"Oh Mommy, thank you. You are really going to love him!"

And Liz did love the boy. She was overwhelmed by his gentle, sweet nature, and helpless little boy appeal. By the time lunch was over, it was decided Jay would visit the family next weekend. Liz leaned against the front door frame watching the young couple walk hand in hand back to school.

It's like me and Joe. We were only a little bit older than Judy and Jay. They love each other already - I know they do. Liz knew that love did not take time. She knew love did not require a "certain age to be when you fell into it." It just happened when you least expected it. How could she tell her daughter she could not know the meaning of love at her young age? It would be hypocritical.

As Liz cleaned up the lunch dishes it suddenly dawned on her: She had made all these arrangements without consulting her husband! "Oh well, I will tell him soon, right after I make him his favorite meal for dinner later this week on my day off!" Liz hummed happily as she finished washing the dishes.

Joe took an instant liking to the boy; however, he was not very pleased when Liz told him the "Kids were in love." Joe was not blind. He could see the special glances and smiles exchanged between the boy and his daughter. "They are too young right now. Judy is only thirteen and he is fourteen. They would have to wait at least four years to get married. The problem is …I am worried they "will not wait." Joe had *not* forgotten how it felt when he first met Liz. How she had enchanted every molecule of his being! How much he wanted to kiss her, to hold her, to touch her, and much more! It was the "much more" that made him uneasy about his daughter and Jay.

"Young first love - that magic spark – is a special feeling that fills one's heart only once in a lifetime. There may be many other loves, but there is only one first, everlasting love when souls entwine, when innocent lips touch for the first time, when fingertips tremble at the slightest touch. Oh, first love, oh magic love, please let it last." Judy's hand quivered as she penned the lines in her book of poems. Since meeting Jay, she had written several small poems about love. Judy had never thought about being in love before. She had never even paid much attention to her looks or her body. But now-a-days she spent a lot of time looking in her mirror, looking to see what *he* sees when looking at her.

Her heart-shaped face, typical of most Hungarian girls was graced by high cheekbones, her finely outlined lips were not too thin or too thick, and her light brown brows complemented eyes that seemed to change color from blue to more of a green depending on her mood. She *was* pretty. She *felt* pretty when she was with Jay, and most exquisite of all, was that Jay told her at every opportunity how much he loved her, how beautiful she was, that she was his "beauty queen."

She would soon be fourteen- come spring – almost a real woman. Her waist, once thick in her early childhood from an overindulgence of eating all foods placed in front of her was now slim. Her breasts were firm and not too big or too small. Her long hair, with bangs fringing her eyebrows, was golden blonde, falling to her mid-back.

School no longer felt like school. It was the place where she and Jay courted each other, where they held hands, sat close to one another, where they planned for a future they hoped would come soon. Judy did not remember taking a test, or hearing a lecture, or reading any required subject matter for school.

Liz standing in her yard on Long Street, Clearwater, Florida – 1967

Amazingly, Judy made good grades, most likely out of nothing but pure good luck on her exams. Her only thoughts, *his* only thoughts, were for one another, longing for the times when they could hold hands in the crowded school hallways between classes, for entwining legs while eating lunch in the school cafeteria, for walking arm and arm in the courtyard while waiting for Jay's school bus.

The end of the school day was always a sad time as Judy watched Jay press his face and hands against the glass window of the school bus, attempting to keep Judy in his view for as long as possible. Judy waved goodbye to Jay until his bus disappeared around the corner, and then walked the very short distance to her house from the schoolyard, her insides filled with an aching emptiness that could not be quenched until the moment they saw each other once more.

Life continued this way through the fall and winter. During Christmas break Jay went with his grandmother and uncle to visit with his out-of-town relatives. When school started again in January they continued in their old familiar pattern and routine with Jay visiting Judy's family on weekends.

It was Wednesday morning, April 3, 1968, just before the start of the school day. Jay walked Judy to her school locker. "I have something special for you!" With bright, mischievous eyes, he ordered, "Don't pick up your books yet, not till you see what I have for you!" He handed Judy two gifts exquisitely wrapped with fine paper found in high-priced gift shops. "Happy fourteenth birthday - I picked these out especially for you – please open them quickly before the bell rings for class!" Eagerly tearing off the delicate covering and ribbon, Judy discovered a beveled glass decanter of *Chanel No. 5* perfume, and another elegantly-designed bottle of *Wind Song* cologne. Jay excitedly asked, "I hope you like them - my grandmother said you would like them!" Judy was astonished, "Like them? I adore them! I have never had any perfume of my own before. Thank you for thinking of me, thank you for all the time you put into selecting such lovely birthday gifts for me!"

Judy's turquoise eyes locked onto Jay's sea-green ones. His face shown with happiness and contentment knowing he had done the right thing for the woman he loved. The hallway was crowded with students bustling to get to class. Lost from view in a corner near her locker, no one could observe Judy pulling Jay close to her, as she softly whispered in his ear, "I love you my sweet Jay." Empowered by her words, Jay moved Judy's hair away from her neck, "May I spray some perfume on you?" Judy was tingling from his touch, but nervously anticipating the bell to ring for the start of class. "Yes, please, but just a little bit for now!" Jay carefully sprayed a small amount of *Wind Song* perfume on Judy's neck and hair, the fragrance swirling in the air about them as he held her close, burying his face in her silken tresses. The warning bell sounded for class. Shouting "I love you!" above the noisy conglomerate, Jay then darted away, disappearing into the colorful sea of students.

The school's spring dance was coming up in late April. Judy's heart fluttered in excited anticipation at the thought of finally being alone with Jay. Well, almost alone…they would still be amongst hundreds of students, but at least no family members would be around! She and her mother had spent one entire Saturday searching for just the right dress and accessories for the occasion. Liz was equally excited for Judy recalling how exhilarating it was when she met her Joe at their school dance: now her daughter was going to a dance with the young man she loved.

Jay's grandmother offered to drive the young people to the dance. She arrived with Jay at Judy's home the evening of the dance, greeting Joe and Liz with sincere enthusiasm for the happiness of the young people and the fine night waiting for them. Jay sat anxiously in the living room waiting for Judy to come out to meet him.

Jay was more than rewarded for his patience when Judy appeared, for she was the loveliest thing he had ever seen in her scoop-neck, white silk dress, touting an overlay of fine lace, with "butterfly" sleeves, its elevated hem skimming her legs at mid-thigh. Judy had selected a waist-length necklace consisting of tiny yellow daisies, shiny yellow high heels and a yellow beaded purse. Her hair was styled in the popular "flip" fashion of the day, her eyes and lips revealing a tinge of mascara and lipstick.

Upon Judy's entrance, Jay immediately flew to her side, placing a protective arm about her shoulder. "You are the most beautiful girl I have ever seen." Joe, Liz, and the grandmother looked upon the youngsters with mixed feelings of happiness, and, a twinge of uneasiness. Jay and Judy were so young, yet so obviously in love. It was a happy time and a dangerous time for them. After Judy and Jay had departed, Joe turned to Liz with deep fatherly concern shadowed in his eyes, "I am very happy they love each other, but I am very worried their feelings will lead to complications in the future. I know he is an orphan and craves family. I know he loves us, and we love the boy too. You can't help but love him. We must be sure that they are never alone, I mean, alone like we were."

Liz took hold of her husband's hand, trying to assure Joe that his feelings were unfounded, "I know why you feel as you do. But we raised Judy the right way. She would not do anything like you fear. She confides all her feelings in me. If she ever mentioned anything that I felt would raise concern, I would immediately talk to her about it."

"Still," Joe sighed wearily, "It's a long time till they are of age to marry. We must just wait and see how it goes."

The cold aesthetics of the school gymnasium was transformed into a springtime wonderland. The only lights present were tiny sparkling glimmers abounding from small trees placed in planters in all corners of the room. Colorful streamers of every color in the rainbow rained down from the ceiling. Attached to the end of each streamer was a fanciful spring flower cutout.

The live band consisted of a bass guitar, lead guitar, drummer, saxophone and organist already playing the best songs of the year. Jay held Judy firmly against his chest during every slow song. It was the first time they had pressed their bodies together in such an intimate way. Pulses beat faster, and breaths became shallow, as if a secret switch had been turned on, activating every ion of pleasure within youth too innocent to know such pleasures. Jay pulled Judy even more firmly against him, feeling every curve of her young womanhood against his torso, their figures molding so tightly in unison, one could not tell where one body started and the other began, and, at that moment, Judy realized that Jay was not a boy, but a *real man*. The dimmed lights, and throngs of other dancers surrounding them, hid their passionate kisses from view. Jay pressed his lips into the softness of Judy's neck, unable to hold back his feelings, unable to contain his love for the girl in his arms, "My life was nothing, I was nothing, until you came into my world. I will wait for you - wait as long as it takes."

It was mid-summer of 1968, Judy was worried. She had not had a phone call from Jay in two weeks. He usually called every day and they would talk for at least an hour prior to Judy's bedtime. "Mommy, I don't think he cares for me anymore!" whined Judy. "Why hasn't Jay called me? Do you think he met someone else?" Liz gazed into her daughter's welling eyes, "Judy, you should call him. I know he loves you. Maybe something is wrong."

Judy twisted her shoulders in frustration and placed her hands on her hips, shaking her head from side to side in frustration, "But Mommy, why should I call, he's the guy, he's supposed to be the one to call!" Liz also felt something was not quite right in Jay not phoning. He was too kind and caring to ignore Judy, never mind ignoring the entire family. For the first time in all the years she had taught her daughter the *proper protocol* for "what a lady should and should not do," she wished Judy would not have taken her advice.

A few days later, on a Saturday, the phone rang. Judy immediately rushed to pick up the receiver, "Hello!" Jay's flat, toneless voice, replied, "Hello." Judy's pride was bruised, and she spoke stiffly to show her hurt, "Why haven't you called me? Have you been too busy?" Jay responded in monotone vocalizations, "Yes, I have been very busy."

Jay sounded distant, not like himself, at all. *What was wrong with him?* "My grandmother died. I've been in Pennsylvania for her funeral. I don't have anywhere to live anymore. Uncle Davey is too old to care for me. It's been decided that I'll be sent to live with my uncle in Panama." *Panama? Where in the world was Panama?* Judy's mind was racing as she tried to absorb the distressing facts and their implications.

"Jay, what does this all mean? Do you have to leave soon?" *Mama was right! I should have called him. I wasn't there for him when he needed me, and now he is going far away!* Jay's voice was faint, filled with distress, "My uncle is now my legal guardian. Oh, Judy, I love you! I don't want to go. It's not fair, just when I found true happiness with you, I have to go far away!" Judy's arm went limp and the corded phone fell to her side. Liz had overheard Judy's side of the conversation and quickly grabbed the receiver from her daughter's hand. "Jay, this is Mama Liz, what is wrong?"

Upon hearing his adopted mother's voice, Jay emotions overflowed, "Mama Liz, I have to go live with my uncle in Panama because my grandmother died. What am I going to do? What will Judy and I do? I love Judy, I love you all! I wish I could stay with your family. I asked my uncle if I could stay and live with you but was told I can't."

Liz's eyes swelled with tears. There was nothing she could do. She had no say where Jay could live even though she loved him as a son, for she had no legal claim on him.

"Don't worry Jay, we will find a way. There will be a way for you to see Judy, somehow." Unable to keep herself together, she wearily handed the phone back to her distraught daughter.

With a throat filled with tears, Judy pleaded, "Please, write me every week, please Jay, promise to write. I love you so much! What am I going to do without you?"

Jay tried to be strong and reassuring, "Even though I will be far away from you doesn't mean I don't love you. I will always love you. I promise to find a way to be with you soon. I *am* going to marry you!" Jay's final words sent Judy over the edge, "Jay, I wish we could get married today, then no one could tell you where to live! I promise to wait for you no matter how long it takes. I'll write you every week!"

Jay breathed a scratchy sigh into the phone's mouthpiece, "Well… I've got to go now, everyone is standing around, it's difficult to talk, and I've got to finish packing. I will write you often. Tell everyone I love them, but mostly … I love you …wait for me, please." With those final words the line went dead.

The next school year of 1969 arrived. Judy turned fifteen in April. As promised, Jay wrote Judy every week, and each week Judy sent her reply. The mail usually arrived around Judy's lunchtime at school, and everyday Judy waited on the front steps of her school during the lunch hour, looking for her mother's car. If there was a letter from Jay, Liz would always arrive before Judy's next class would begin. Seeing her mother driving up to the front of the school waving Jay's letter out the car window was the happiest time for Judy. As soon as Liz's car pulled up to the front of the building, she would quickly open the vehicle's door, sit beside her mother on the front bench seat, and share the letter's contents, then re-reading the same letter every night until the arrival of the next. Jay did the same for her correspondence - it was the only way to be near while so far apart.

One warm May morning, a friend of Liz's came to visit, bringing a surprise with her for the children. It was a curly, fluffy ball of warmth – a miniature black poodle! He nuzzled his way into Judy's arms and lavished her cheeks with wet kisses! "He is all yours!" announced Liz, (meaning the dog was for all her children), but try as they might, Sonny and Pilvia could not get the young puppy's attention, for he had made his choice to be best pals with Judy, so he was named, "Pal."

Pal and Judy were inseparable. He was a sweet and loving dog to everyone, but Judy was his favorite. Pal was Judy's comfort, keeping her company and offering a distraction from thinking about Jay being far away. Each day after dinner she and Pal would go on a lengthy walk around the neighborhood, the little poodle pulling her along the now routine route. They would rest at the half-way point on the banks of a small lake. Judy tied Pal off to a nearby tree under whose branches she would rest and dream about the day when she would see Jay once more.

Once a week, Judy gave Pal a "bath" in the large shower stall in the upstairs bathroom. First, Judy would shower and wash her hair, and then would hold Pal under the warm spray of water and apply a good amount of "human shampoo" to his charcoal coat. Pal was not at all pleased, but patiently tolerated the watery ordeal. Judy would then rub him down with a downy soft towel and blow-dry his coat until he was soft and silky. At last, free from his beautification regimen, Pal would bound out of the bathroom, run down the stairs, and roll about on the carpet trying to remove the last dregs of the "shampoo smell." The little poodle may have been small in stature, but large in mind. Each night, when Judy said "Goodnight" to her father and gave him his goodnight kiss, (mostly to her father because Liz was not yet home from work on Judy's school nights), Pal understood her words and would automatically rush upstairs, jump up on Judy's mattress, ready to curl up at his mistress's feet by the time she came to bed.

During Jay's absence everyone's routine remained in its usual circles with school, work, weekend trips to the beach and an occasional trip to visit friends. One of the family's favorite ways to spend a weekend afternoon was exploring model homes. Rutenberg homes were the pièce de résistance of model homes, with a "pièce de résistance" price to match; however, it was a "pipe dream" of Joe's to obtain such an elegant home. Joe had been doing a fine job in his role as a training manager at work, progressing rapidly through numerous programs and graduating with high scores. Joe dreamed of moving up the corporate ladder quickly to obtain the monetary rewards that would enable him to afford such a home.

In June of 1969, during a casual conversation with a coworker, one afternoon, Joe expressed his aspirations about owning a larger home. His coworker told Joe he had a friend, a building contractor, who was trying to sell an elegant two-story home, near the intercoastal waterway. The home had been on the market for two years without a buyer. There was nothing wrong with the home, just something wrong with the buyers! He offered to call the broker that day to see if he could meet with Joe the same day after work to tour the home.

The house, located in a tasteful development near the ocean, stood tall and proud amidst a mix of one-story and two-story homes. When Joe pulled up in front of the house something "snapped" inside him - this *was* the house he had been looking for! It was not in the Rutenberg style but had a unique style unto itself of simple sophistication. The two-story, two-thousand square foot structure revealed a sturdy concrete shingle-type roof, long concrete driveway, and a gracious front covered porch area with white columns, with brick-inlay flooring. A picture window occupied much of the front of the home and a large, front double-door welcomed him. To the left of the entrance was an oversized, double-car garage just perfect for an on-the-side television repair shop.

Upon entering the foyer, he was greeted by the owner/builder. After brief introductions, Joe inquired, "Why have you had so much difficulty selling the house?"

The builder twitched his shoulders, "Well, as you will notice, it is the largest home in the area. Most of the potential buyers felt the home looked awkward sitting in-between homes of lesser stature, but the neighborhood is a fine one, and all the homes are high quality, it's just that this house towers above the rest and costs more than the others. I had built the house for me and my family, but my wife decided she did not want to live here, and we moved elsewhere. Now, I have an over-sized, over-priced home with no buyer."

He looked Joe square in the eye, "Look - Sam is my friend, and he told me you were looking for a nice large family home. I'm willing to give you a super deal on this house if you would like to buy it." Joe was intrigued. "Do you mind if I give myself a tour. I won't be long and then we can talk?" The builder complied. "Sure, wander around. If you have any questions just let me know." Not wanting to seem overly pushy, the owner walked outside to smoke a cigarette in the driveway.

The foyer's long hallway branched off in three directions: to the right, a short hallway led to a half-bath, done in pink, and a doorway leading to the garage. On the left was a large living room. Straight ahead, a short hallway led to a large family room with an adjoining eat-in kitchen. The large modern kitchen had a pantry, under the stairs storage, and plenty of cabinet and countertop space. Off the kitchen was a doorway to a formal dining room with large sliding glass doors, and the family room displayed a large back wall of sliding glass doors opening to a huge back yard, large enough to put in a pool. Joe climbed the steps to the upper level.

At the top of the hallway, on the right, were two bedrooms: one facing the back of the home, and the other facing the front. To his left was the master suite with adjoining bath done in blue. There was a fourth bedroom to the left front of the house, and on the same end a full bath with yellow fixtures. The bedrooms had closet space to spare, including a good-sized guest closet on the upper landing. The home was spacious and stunning, with plenty of room for his family to grow and play. The question in Joe's mind, now, was whether he could afford the property. *A good deal to the builder may not seem like such a good deal to me.*

Joe went downstairs finding the builder leaning on the kitchen counter. "Well, what do you think? Is the house up to your expectations?"

"The house is perfect, but I hope the price is too," replied Joe.

Joe started the drive home with his head swimming with excitement. He had just purchased a home without consulting his wife! The builder had given him a deal of a lifetime, agreeing not only to personally finance the home, but also offering to help Joe sell his current home. The house payments were higher than Joe had anticipated, but Joe reasoned he could compensate the extra expense by doing a few extra television repair jobs and accordion gigs. He would find a way. Joe had signed his part of the papers and Liz had only to go by the builder's office and sign the contract. They could move in at any time.

As he drove home, Joe's heart sang, *"My precious Liz, I did it for you. You deserve this home for all the terrible things you have had to endure, for how hard you have worked, for never complaining, for loving me through everything."*

The following week, each day, as soon as Joe got off work, he and the children moved furniture and other household items to the new house, where Judy made sure all floors were scrubbed, bathrooms cleaned, and cabinets lined prior to placing their belongings. Liz did not want to take time off from work, for they needed to keep money coming in, especially now, with a larger house payment. Liz had opted not to see the new house, not until the day she would be moving in, stating, "I just want to be surprised!"

And surprised she would be, for Joe and the children assured her they would "Fix the house really nice."

The last day of living in the Long Street house was upon them before they knew it. Joe and the children gathered the last of their possessions in the late afternoon and bid farewell to the house in Clearwater for it had sold quickly.

The children were bubbling with excitement during the drive to their new home, hoping their mother would like the way they had cleaned and decorated. Liz had not wanted to say "goodbye" to the Long Street house as it would have been too sad for her. She had worked an earlier shift the day the family was moving to the new dwelling and was to meet them there at 6 p.m.

Liz arrived at her unseen abode as her anxious family waited for her on the front porch. "Welcome home!" they all chanted as she walked through the double front doors. Liz quietly made her way into the family room, the kitchen, dining and living rooms, the garage, and downstairs bath, remaining silent as she observed her surroundings. She explored the upstairs and slowly descended back down to the first floor, still not saying one word.

Liz's silence frayed Joe's nerves. Liz was absolutely quiet, standing in the middle of the family room, looking about her. Liz was speechless, because she was happy, and silent, because the incredulous enormity and reality of what her eyes beheld, the beauty of it all, knowing this would be her new home, the era of an astonishing new beginning, overwhelmed her.

Holding out her arms to her family, she beckoned them all into her embrace. "Oh, my Joe, my kiddies, it is the most beautiful house I have ever seen - that I ever will see in my life! I do not deserve it!" With those words she cried uncontrollably from pure happiness. Joe helped her sit down in a chair and wrapped his arms about her slight shoulders, "Yes, you *do* deserve this and so much more, my beautiful butterfly."

"My *Edes* kiddies, my *Draga* Joe, you worked very hard to make this home perfect for me," exclaimed an elated Liz, "Everything is spotless and organized, just like I would have done it. I adore my home and I adore you all. I am so happy! I want to live here forever!" The children hugged their mother all at once, burying her in a fury of kisses. "Let's celebrate," proclaimed Joe, "Who wants Pizza!"

It was a lovely, but very hot, sunlit Saturday afternoon in mid-August of 1969, Judy had settled down on the living room couch to read a newly arrived letter from Jay.

As Judy intently perused the letter's contents, not wanting to miss a single word, her stomach somersaulted as she came upon one line: "I've asked my uncle if he will pay my tuition to attend a military/boarding school. He's agreed to enroll me in Admiral Farragut Academy about twenty miles from your house. I'll be able to see you every weekend starting in September!" Judy let out a jubilant shout to her father in the family room, "Daddy! Daddy! Jay's coming home!"

Admiral Farragut Academy, a Naval Honor School, was named after Admiral David Glasgow Farragut. The all-boys school was established in St. Petersburg, Florida in 1945, on the shores of Boca Ciega Bay.

Beginning in mid-September of 1969, Jay visited the family every weekend. The academy required all cadets to be back in their barracks by 8 p.m. every weekend evening. Therefore, every Saturday and Sunday morning, the family drove to the academy to bring Jay to their home, and each Saturday and Sunday evening the family drove Jay back to his residence. Judy's life went from humdrum to lively and exciting.

Jay accompanied the family during their normal weekend routines, either at home or out shopping, and helping with any projects around the yard or inside the home. Judy and Jay took long walks around the neighborhood, talking and planning for their wedding in 1972, immediately after Judy's eighteenth birthday.

Jay had decided to pursue a career in oceanography and was to join the Navy upon his graduation. They planned a very simple marriage ceremony in Judy's home, after which they would live on whatever Naval base Jay was assigned. They had many dreams to dream and plans to plan. Life was wonderful, blissful and perfect!

Christmas-time was soon upon them. Liz and Joe looked forward to a real family Christmas, but Judy was the most excited of all - eagerly anticipating a romantic Christmas Eve spent in her family's parlor cuddled up to Jay in front of a twinkling, sparkling Christmas tree. Liz scurried about cooking her famous lasagna ahead of time and baking Hungarian pastries, freezing each delicacy for the big day, as well as going into a Christmas cleaning delirium. This would be the first Christmas Jay would be spending with them!

At last, everything was finally coming together in their lives: Joe was doing well in his career, Liz loved her job at the seafood restaurant, the kids were doing great in school, and, Judy would have her darling Jay for Christmas.

About two weeks before Christmas, the phone rang. Joe was at work and all the kids were in school. Liz answered the phone. It was Jay! "Mama Liz, I can't be there for Christmas!" His voice was trembling, as if he was about to break out in tears. "My uncle insists I fly back to Panama for the holidays and I won't be back until just before New Year's Day. I told him I didn't want to go, as it was originally planned for me to stay on at the academy during the holidays and spend Christmas with you, but now, he has changed his mind and my plane ticket has been already setup to return to Panama."

Liz's stomach heaved. She steeled her emotions, trying to keep calm, attempting to hold back tears, not wanting to further upset Jay with any emotional outburst on her behalf. "Jay! I am so sorry! Of course, all of us, and especially Judy, will be disappointed, but we know you must do as your family says. We will make our "own Christmas" when you return. I will keep all the goodies I baked right here in the freezer. They will still be perfect for eating when you get back. We will have Christmas in January!" Liz's voice was bright, a good disguise for the veil of sadness covering her heart.

"I love you Mama Liz - sorry, I have to hang up now. I'm short on change for the pay phone."

"Jay, I love you too. Everything will work out."

Then he was gone – again. Why could he not be with them this one Christmas? Perhaps it was because the uncle did not realize how much the little family in Florida loved his nephew? Perhaps, the uncle and his family wanted Jay with them because they loved him, too. Liz was only too aware that until Judy and Jay became of age to marry, Jay did not belong to their family. He was only theirs through the family's love for him. Things had to be this way until the time came when it could be different.

Joe and Liz in their dream home – Florida – early 1970's

By early February of 1970, temperatures were already in the mid-eighties. Joe glanced about the barren backyard, his engineering mind hard at work. "We need a swimming pool. I think I'll make a few calls."

A week later, on a Saturday, one of the area's most prestigious pool companies arrived on the scene with backhoes to dig a big hole in the backyard for the pool. Several dump trucks were lined up in front of the house to transport the excess dirt away from the yard. Joe had not yet figured out the logistics of making the payments on the pool, but, by now, Liz knew her husband never really planned on how he would pay for anything. He simply just "paid for everything." When Joe wanted something, he was determined to get it "now," and not years from "now." One of Joe's favorite sayings was, "What's the point of wanting something if you have to wait till you are too old to enjoy what you wanted?"

Within a few days the "pool hole" was dug and a team arrived to apply a mixture of cement and sand, called "Gunite." This mixture was then sprayed onto a wired cage surface inside the outline of the pool shell.

Joe didn't quite know the exact technology behind the application and asked one of the pool guys about the process. "This stuff is actually called dry-gunned concrete. It means we inject the cement and sand into an airstream through the hose nozzle. As we do this, we add water at the nozzle and control the water-cement ratio. The hose isn't heavy at all, though you think it would be. The mixture is light because the hose is filled mostly with air, dry cement and sand. It doesn't get thick or heavy till the water is added at the point when it's sprayed directly onto the pool frame. Here, give it a shot!" With that, he thrust the hose into Joe's hands and before he knew it, Joe was hard at work! The hands-on adventure satisfied Joe's curiosity. "This is going to be one tough pool! It's definitely not going anywhere!"

By afternoon the pool frame was filled in, giving it the appearance of a large, in-ground, concrete birdbath. It was a pleasing, "kidney-shape," which complemented the backyard well. The construction supervisor put his hardhat in the back of his truck, "This stuff should setup fine by tomorrow, noon, and then we'll be back to finish placing the coat over the Gunite. When that's done, you'll be swimming in no time!" With those last words the "pool people" left for the day.

That night, in the early hours before dawn, an unforeseen storm of ferocious strength hit the area. Thick clouds filled with lightning bolts and piercing forks of rain pelted the region. This was not an unusual occurrence in Florida. Storms were known to quickly "pop up" and then disappear quickly. Just as folks in California were not the least worried about "slight tremors" of the earth during the night, the same held true for how Floridians felt about the sudden "Florida nighttime storm."

By morning's light the storm had dissipated. Pilvia awoke in her canopy bed, stretching, and contemplating over things she needed to take care of that day. Her eyes expected bright rays of sun to peak between the curtains, but not today. "It's so dark outside, it looks like it will be a cloudy day, maybe more rain." She lazily sauntered out of bed and pulled aside the fabric from her upstairs bedroom window to assess the weather, but her view was blocked by a huge wall of "something."

"Daddy! Da-deeeee!" Pilvia screamed loudly. Joe did not understand what was happening, but Pilvia was screaming as if the house was on fire! Scrambling out of bed, he rushed to Pilvia's room, where he found her leaning out of her open bedroom window. "Daddy, the pool is standing on its side! It's almost touching the second floor of the house! Look! If you reach out far enough, you can just about touch it!"

Joe's heart froze. *What in the world was happening here?* He rushed for the phone. Within an hour a supervisor from the pool company arrived to survey the site. "Never in all my years have I seen anything like this!" That statement did not make Joe feel any better. "Well, I haven't seen anything like this either! My pool is standing on one end! How are you going to fix this mess?"

Water from the prior night's storm had gotten between the Gunite lining of the pool and outer dirt wall, floating the pool right up out of the hole. The larger, heavier end of the pool had filled with water, pushing it downward; therefore, the lighter end of the pool stood straight up out of the ground, causing the colossal structure to rise upward, with its length parallel to the upstairs bedroom windows. It was literally standing "at attention!"

The pool supervisor kept staring at the monstrous disaster. Joe could tell he was nervous. "Well, what do you think? What can be done to fix this," asked Joe anxiously. The pool guy ran his forearm over his sweaty brow, "We have to wait for your yard to dry out more, and then – then we'll have to break it all apart and start all over." Joe was fuming, "Break it apart and start all over? I can't believe this is happening!" Joe stared at his backyard. It looked like a plane had crashed nose-first in the muddy mire.

In a couple of days, a huge truck arrived with a "wrecker ball" swinging from it, along with several dump trucks lined up in a row in front of the house. But there was another problem, the pool shift had unsettled the ground, and now, the dirt under the house was washing away! The wet dirt around the pool had been slowly "chunking off" into the pool hole since the last rain. The heavily soaked ground had seeped far under the backside of the house, causing large clods of dirt to break away. The dirt foundation on which the house stood was disappearing!

Three things required immediate attention: First, the underside of the home had to be repaired; second, the pool had to be broken up into manageable pieces, and finally, the mammoth concrete portions had to be hauled away.

Hundreds of gallons of Gunite was forced under the backside of the family's dream home to support the structure, until at last, a mammoth excess of the gray matter leached far out into the yard.

"We need to let the Gunite setup under the house before we start breaking up the pool. We can't afford to shake up the house till the stuff hardens up." With that, the site supervisor, walked to his truck, but Joe could hear him talking to himself as he walked away, "Let's hope there isn't any more rain!"

Liz and the kids scurried to remove delicate items off shelves. Each time the wrecking ball collided with the pool, the walls of the home shook relentlessly! The crew had arrived early the next Saturday ready to begin their unremitting pounding to destroy the concrete monstrosity. The pool chunks were collected and hauled away in several dump trucks. Once again, there remained only a big dried-up hole in the backyard.

It was late March of 1970, on a perfect Sunday afternoon. The weather was sunny and warm. Joe and Liz relaxed on their back patio watching Judy, Jay, Sonny and Pilvia as they frolicked in the pool, doing headstands with only ankles and feet visible above the waterline.

The "swimming hole" had turned out more beautiful than Joe and Liz could ever have imagined. A smooth-surfaced, pebbled walkway had been installed around the pool's perimeter giving the entire project an air of upscale elegance. After all the damage had been repaired, and after the pool had been redone, and after Joe had received the bill, he was one of the happiest guys on the planet. And, no wonder! He had received a tremendous discount on the pool!

"Joe, please tell me how much the pool company charged us for the pool?"

"My sweet little Liz," Joe smiled, squeezing her hand in his. "Nothing at all!"

A stunned Liz stared unbelievingly into her husband's eyes, "What do you mean "nothing"? Please do not joke about this! We still owe *something*!"

Joe lay back in his lawn chair, legs propped up on a pillow, with both arms behind his head looking quite contented and pleased with himself. "Well, you see," he teasingly replied, "Things *do* happen for a reason!" Liz was becoming impatient, "Joe, *tell* me what it cost!" Joe leaned over and kissed his wife on the cheek, "It was literally *on-the-house*!"

Liz demanded a real answer, "Joe what does that mean? Tell me!" Despite all her years dealing with the public, Liz could still be quite naïve. "My little girl," Joe cooed, "It means it cost *nothing*. It was free!"

Afraid of bad publicity, the pool company had "buried the bill" deep within the concrete depths of the Gunite pit. Liz could see Joe was enormously satisfied and proud of himself. "I *told* you I would work it out!"

Liz leaned over and kissed Joe on the lips, "I knew you would, you *always* have and always will!"

The family pool in Florida- 1970

In mid-April of 1970, just after Judy's sixteenth birthday, Joe came home from work to find Liz's car still in the driveway. She had not left for work yet. Judy met him at the door with a worried expression on her face, "Mommy is upstairs. She was about to leave for work when she checked the mail. She got a letter that said her brother died!" Liz, still dressed in her work uniform, was lying on her bed staring at the ceiling. It was obvious she had been crying for her eyes and nose were red and swollen. "Liz, *Edes*, what's happened? Judy said your brother George died!" Joe had assumed it was George, for it was the only brother Liz had contact with. Liz's face contorted in pain, "No! It is Ferenc! He died in Corsica, of alcoholism!" Joe took a moment to gather his bearings. Ferenc? Then he knew. Ferenc was Liz's older brother, a dashingly handsome, tall, broad-shouldered young man. He had been very good to Liz when she was a little girl, and the two had been very close. Disillusioned with the political path of Hungary, Ferenc left Hungary to enlist in the French Foreign Legion. Since then, no one had heard from him. "May I see the letter?" asked Joe. Liz handed her husband a crumpled envelope, which contained a long correspondence filled with "ugly words from a landlady in Corsica," stating, "Your brother died in misery. He drank himself to death! He has been dead for a year and owed me months of rent money. I found addresses for his relatives in Hungary and asked them for the money, but they had no money, so they gave me your address, stating you lived in America. I know Americans have money. Pay me his back rent! Your brother was a bum alcoholic! When will I get my money?"

Joe's mind swam in a fog. Alcoholic? A bum? No, that did not describe Ferenc. But now, it would be impossible to find out what had happened to the good-looking young man who was kind of heart and gentle in spirit. How in the world did he end up in such wretched conditions leading to his pitiful death? Liz knew something terrible had happened to her brother, but whatever it was, she could not have changed the sad outcome. As if the pain of her brother's death was not enough, one week later, Liz received a letter from her father stating her mother had died of pneumonia.

It was late April 1971, on a Saturday. Judy was outside hanging freshly washed clothes on the clothesline. Jay sat at the family room dining table watching Liz cut up vegetables for the evening meal of beef stew. It was a mild day, and he was comfortable being barefoot, wearing shorts and a short-sleeved cotton shirt (having changed into "something more comfortable" after the family had picked him up from the academy earlier that morning for his usual weekend visit). "Mama Liz, I have something I need to ask you." Not wanting to cut her finger, Liz did not look up from the carrots on the cutting board, "What is it Jay?" Jay hesitantly proceeded, "Well, you see, the academy is having a formal military dress parade in celebration of Mother's Day, to honor the mothers of all the cadets." Jay's voice picked up with tones of excitement, "We've been practicing for several weeks getting all the rifle maneuvers correct and making sure our steps match. I think we've got it down really well now!" Liz continued looking down, now working on slicing up chunks of celery. "I had no idea the academy held a Mother's Day Parade! Is this something they have every year?" Jay honestly responded, "I'm not sure, I didn't ask, I was too excited when I heard about it. Will you please be *my* mother?"

Liz paused with her celery-cutting, her mind not fully comprehending Jay's request. Looking up into the boy's face, Liz sought confirmation of his statement. Jay looked deep into her questioning eyes. "I want you to be *my mother* at the parade. All the cadet's mothers will be sitting in the stands and waving to their sons as they march past. The cadets will halt in front of the stands and perform a special rifle maneuver program practiced just for their mothers."

Jay got up from his seat and walked over to the kitchen counter where Liz was standing with her vegetables. Out of nowhere, his face twisted into a painful expression of grief, his voice teetering and childlike, "You don't understand! You *have* to be there for me - I'm the only boy there *without* a mother!" Jay suddenly fell upon an astonished Liz's shoulder, his face tucked into the crook of her neck as he poured out the full extent of his innermost pain. Liz had never seen him cry!

Holding his thin, shuddering form, the full meaning of Jay's words sliced through Liz's heart as sharply as her knife had cut through her vegetables. He had *no* mother. *She was dead.* "Oh Jay, I understand! *Please* don't cry! I'll be there for you. I'll be your mother!"

They clung one to the another and wept: Jay for the loss of a mother he never knew, and Liz for the mother who had died long ago and would never know how wonderful and beautiful a son she had borne into the world.

It was a picture-perfect, radiantly sunny, Sunday morning, May 9, 1971. The review stand was bustling with over two-hundred mothers dressed in their Mother's Day finery.

Sitting in the stands amidst a sea of chiffon, silk and satin, was Liz in her yellow lace, knee-length empire dress, with its puffy "Cinderella-type" sleeves. The cadet band was playing loud and strong as she, Joe, Judy, Sonny and Pilvia, awaited the Admiral Farragut Cadet's entrance from far across the field. Judy could see the future soldiers massed together in the distance, their uniforms melding together into one blurred mass of blue and white.

"They all look the same from here, which one is Jay?" asked a bewildered Judy. "I do not know, my love, but I am sure as they get nearer, we will be able to tell," Liz assured her. "There are coming now! They look beautiful!" chirped Liz as she strained her eyes seeking out something that would differentiate Jay from the others.

The cadets rounded the corner of the field, and much to the family's delight, stopped dead-center in front of the mother's review stand to show off weeks of agonizing rifle drills. "Jay's right there! I see him," Judy quipped excitedly. "See! He's looking right at us. I know he can see us!"

Liz had a kerchief in her hand and waved it wildly above her head to let Jay know she was there. Of course, he could not reply, but Liz knew he could see her. Jay knew she was there for him. The band of cadets performed their drill with perfect execution.

"Will all mothers please stand!" came an order from an unseen loudspeaker. Liz, along with the other cadet's mothers stood proudly as their sons looked up at them. "Present arms!" The cadets tilted their rifles forward in an honorable salute to the mothers. Tears of happiness flowed down Liz's cheeks, and, tears of sadness. In a mere second Liz thought of Jay's mother, about her not being there to see her beautiful son: *Jay's mother, I am sorry I do not know your name. Please, do not be upset with me for standing here in your place. Jay begged me to be here for he wanted a "mother" to be here for him, same as the other boys. I am honored to represent you on this special occasion, on this Mother's Day.* Liz had a surreal moment: *What if I had never come to this country. What if I had never left Hungary? Jay would have never had met Judy. He would never have come to this academy if not for loving my daughter. Thank you, God for letting me live, for letting Judy live, so we could bring Jay happiness today, and thank you God for Jay meeting Judy so he could "have a family" here for him today. And, Jay's mother, thank you for allowing me to be part of your boy's life.*

Seconds feeling more like minutes passed. Liz was shaken out of her thoughts by a blaring whistle signaling the cadets to march off the grounds to the strains of a triumphant march. Staring straight ahead, in uniform precision, the "soldiers" left the field in finely tuned elegance.

If Liz had met a fortune teller on the day she disembarked from the USS General Haan to shelter in Camp Kilmer, telling her that in a few years she would be standing in the stands of a military school parade, as a "mother" for an orphaned boy in America, she would have thought her to be "crazy."

As Liz watched her "second son" march out of sight, she came to a startling conclusion, "It is fate. I had to come to America to be here for Jay, to be 'his mother' for this special moment in his life."

The family met Jay after the parade in the parking lot and took off for a nearby Mother's Day Dinner at the Big Boy Restaurant, and just in time, for everyone was famished!

Admiral Farragut Academy held several cotillions each school year and May signaled the last of the dances, with each cadet issuing an invitation for his special lady to be his guest in the academy's elegant ballroom.

This late May evening of 1971, proud cadets lined up along a long wall in the ballroom awaiting the entrance of their "special one." How handsome they all were sporting Navy-inspired dress uniforms consisting of a blue-colored, double-breasted jacket decked out with six, gold-colored buttons, crisp navy-blue slacks and long-sleeved, white dress shirt, and the distinctive bowtie.

Joe and Liz drove Judy to the academy's front entrance where a steward opened the car door and escorted her to the ballroom doorway. The hired band sent forth the romantic strains of *"Can't Take My Eyes Off You"* across the softly scented sea breezes of Boca Ciega Bay.

When Jay caught sight of Judy, his heart turned upside-down and his stomach tightened. She was beyond beautiful tonight! Not that he did not think she was beautiful, otherwise, for to him, she was the loveliest girl he had ever seen, but *Cotillion-time* was when Jay saw Judy at her finest.

The gowns she chose were feminine and alluring, accentuating the mature lines of her young figure. Her waist-long flaxen tresses for this dance were arranged in a stunning "up-do," her lovely face enhanced by the artful application of lipstick and eye shadow, transforming Jay's "everyday girl" into a vision of angel-like loveliness.

Strengthened by her presence, Jay broadly strode to Judy's side, grasping her outstretched gloved hand, squeezing it tightly and protectively. Judy's touch transported him to a far-away enchanted kingdom where he was her Prince and she was his Princess. Judy was the enchantress of his soul. Since their first meeting Jay's every waking and sleeping thought was only of "his Judy."

School would soon be over, they would graduate, marry, and the long wait to be together would be over. Upon hearing their favorite song, "*So Happy Together*," Jay lovingly placed his hand about Judy's waist and guided her onto the dance floor. Judy rested her head on Jay's shoulder, her lips tenderly kissing his neck as their bodies floated to the music.

The summer of 1971 was different. Jay stayed with Judy's family for two weeks in June before returning to the Dominican Republic where his uncle now resided. Those two weeks were enchanted moments in time.

Judy and Jay, first cotillion of the year at Admiral Farragut - 1971

Judy and Jay had been good, well almost good, both too frightened of the wrath of Judy's father to allow the heat of passion to take them to the *forbidden zone*.

But during those fourteen days, the two had taken many a leisurely walk, stealing away to a special wooded spot, under the shade of a mighty tree, allowing themselves the freedom to explore the restless feelings surging within them. Jay's warm hands caressed the soft fullness of his sweetheart's bosom, his fingers kneading the yielding, willing young flesh. Judy boldly undid her jeans, allowing Jay to explore her cool firm buttocks and the silky softness below her belly. Unbuttoning Jay's shirt, she ran her hands across his taunt abdomen, muscular chest, and daringly unzipped his jeans, her hands cupping the firmness formerly confined by blue denim. They kissed tender areas of skin unknown to the touch of fresh breezes or the light of day, driving each other to the brink of insatiable madness, drawing back before the inevitable would occur.

One day, during those breathtaking two weeks, Liz was unexpectedly asked to cover a day shift at the restaurant and Joe had an appointment to pick up a television to repair in his garage. Pilvia and Sonny were outside playing with the neighborhood kids. For the first time – ever, Judy and Jay found themselves alone in the house. Judy led Jay upstairs to her bedroom locking the door behind them. They eagerly helped each other undress and lay side by side on the bed, delighting in the sight and touch of each other. Their young bodies, entwined as vines, sought new places to explore, new places to expand their bounty. How they loved each other!

"Judy, if only we could run away, I would marry you tonight," whispered Jay as he buried his face in the tangles of her long hair. "You ARE my wife, there may be no minister here, but you will always be my wife."

"Jay, my love, you ARE my husband! I love you so much it hurts right here," exclaimed Judy, as she clutched her hands over her stomach and heart. "I had no idea how wonderful it would be to hold you like this, to feel your bare skin against me, to have you touch me as a husband touches his wife."

Judy lay on her left side with her head nestled on Jay's right shoulder. Jay lay contentedly, feeling the warmth of Judy's soft body against his bare skin, weaving his fingers through her golden hair, thinking his thoughts aloud, "Next year, in the summer of 1972, we'll be married. No one can stop us. I'll join the Navy and you'll live with me on the Navy base. We'll have at least two kids right away. You know that house just down the street from your parents? Hopefully, it will still be available when I get out of the service, I'll buy it and we will live right there, close to your family, I mean, *our family*." Judy pulled herself closer to Jay, allowing him to dream his dreams about their future. Being an orphan, always living with relatives and being moved from place to place, Jay craved the stability of family life - his *own* family. Jay ferociously claimed Judy's lips once more, and she willingly clung to him, never wanting to release herself from his arms. Their blood boiled with want and longing, a longing that could no longer be restrained. They were close, so close, to the brink of melding their souls. Now was the time to become one, at last!

The enchanted spell was broken by the rumbling of Joe's truck as it pulled into the garage directly beneath Judy's bedroom. Jay sprang up in a second, frantically gathered his clothes and rushed into the bathroom. Judy quickly dressed, combed her hair and applied lip gloss and ran downstairs.

By the time Joe started unloading a television from his truck, Jay greeted him in the garage, and assisted Joe in lifting the television onto the repair counter. When the two came inside, Judy was in the kitchen preparing the evening meal. Joe and Jay went outside to sit on the patio by the pool.

As Judy tended her stovetop, a feeling of "incompleteness" gnawed at her body. Everything had stopped too abruptly! Her insides remained full of a longing not fulfilled. *Why did Daddy have to come home right now? I can't help but wish ...wish we had done more.*

There was one thing Judy and Jay realized that afternoon: the odds of being alone again in the same manner until their honeymoon was nil. The couple had little of an appetite during dinner. Much to their relief, Joe did not notice. He enjoyed his supper, and miraculously, was oblivious to their escapade, his mind already working on how to "fix the dog of a television."

On a Sunday evening in late August of 1971, Judy received a long-distance phone call from Jay, as he had traveled back to the Dominican Republic for the remainder of his summer vacation. Jay's voice was strained, "I've got some good news and some not so good news." Jay hesitantly began their conversation. "My uncle is being transferred back to the states. He has a home in Virginia and is in the process of moving the family back there as we speak. Now that he's moving back to Virginia, he doesn't see the need to pay money for me to continue my education at the military academy, so he's already enrolled me in the local high school in Vienna, Virginia. I think I'll be moving there in about a week."

There was silence on the other end of the phone line. Not seeming to notice, he continued, "The good news is that at least I won't be overseas *somewhere* and just a few states away instead of an ocean away. Besides, next summer we will be married and living together on the Navy base." Jay was quite happy about that last thought and let out a slight chuckle.

Judy did not find this to be any laughing matter. The only thing Judy could think about was being together. "But when *can* we see each other again!"

Jay reassured her, "Don't worry, it's already been arranged that when school lets out for Christmas I'll be on the first plane down there and spend at least two weeks with you and the family before school starts again after the holidays, and this time, I promise I will be there no matter what!" Judy pondered on the thought, "Well, that is *only* four months from now."

Feeling guilty about her earlier, selfish attitude, Judy spoke tenderly to her sweetheart, "Don't worry Honey. We will just have to write and call each other a lot. You're right, soon, so soon, Jay my love, we'll be married, and be together every day. No more goodbyes. I love you so much." Judy heard Jay let out an exhaustive sigh of longing, "I love you too *Sugar*. I always will."

As promised Jay and Judy kept in touch with letters and phone calls, and between the demands of school and home responsibilities, early December was upon them quickly.

On the morning of Friday, December 3, 1971, everyone was either at work or school. Instead of her usual cleaning routine, Liz was determined to get in some serious Christmas shopping before going to work at the restaurant that afternoon.

There had been some unexpected repair expenses between cars and plumbing, so there was not as much money to spare for gifts as Liz had hoped; however, she was sure if she "shopped smart," the discounts provided by the many Christmas sales would lessen the severity of her small purse, for she yearned to buy her family, but especially Jay, some very nice gifts.

The mall was only a few miles from the house. Liz pulled into the parking lot, dropped the car keys in her purse and opened the car door. The sun poured in through the car windows with the temperatures high for early December. Liz placed her feet on the warm asphalt pavement, noticing a "lumpy feeling" under her left shoe. Liz lifted her foot. No! This could not be! A bundle of money held together by a rubber band lay at her feet. Liz quickly looked about to make sure no one would see her pick up the paper treasure. She swiftly grabbed the bundle and sat back in her car seat, closing and locking the car door. *How much money is there?* With trembling fingers, Liz excitedly undid the rubber band. The outer currency was a twenty-dollar bill, and beneath it, were several more twenties, and some ten and five-dollar bills. The remaining currency were one-dollar bills. But nevertheless, she had at least two-hundred dollars! Liz sprung out of her seat, locked up the car, and with her heart floating high, announced to the world, "Now I can buy Jay something special. Watch out stores, here I come!"

It was December 7, 1971, the anniversary of Pearl Harbor Day. The subject had been discussed in history class that morning; however, Judy found it difficult to concentrate on the day's lesson. She had awakened in a good mood, excited that Jay would be coming home for Christmas in two weeks; however, on the school bus ride to school, and after alighting from the bus at its destination, an uneasy sensation closed in about her. She had no reason to feel upset or nervous, but the oppressive force appeared out of nowhere. On walking to her first class around 8:30 a.m. she heard her name faintly being called by a male voice several times but could not determine the source in the noisy, crowded hallway of students. The feelings of anxiety, agitation and nervousness increased as the day went on. She could hardly wait for the day to be over.

Judy walked home from the bus stop at the end of the school day. When she had left the house that morning at 6:45, the day promised to be a warm one, enabling Judy to wear a bright green, short-sleeved shirt and hip-riding, white bell-bottom slacks. As she rounded the last corner of her walk, she could see her house up ahead on the left side of the street, but she could also see her father's car. *Why is Dad's car in the driveway? It's too early for him to be home? Mom's car is there too. That's so weird. Mom and Dad are never here when I get home!*

The disquieting feeling ailing her all day increased in intensity and she quickened her pace. As she neared the house, she noticed her father walking round-and-round the tall flag pole he had placed in the center of their circular driveway. The sea breezes were picking up, and the red, white and blue stripes of the American flag were extended almost completely horizontally.

Joe glanced up, at last locking eyes with his firstborn. *Why isn't Dad waving? I'm sure he can see me. Something is wrong!* Panicking, thinking some tragedy had befallen her mother or siblings, Judy ran the remaining short distance to the house, at last coming face-to-face with her father. His distress was evidenced by swollen, red eyes and beads of sweat pouring from his forehead. Her stomach tightened.

Desperate for answers, Judy frantically begged, "Daddy what's wrong? What's happened? Is it Mommy? Is it one of the kids?"

Joe reached out his arms to Judy, his mind racing through dozens of scenarios of "how to tell her." Joe placed his right arm around his daughter's shoulder. His calloused left hand stroked the strands of her long, wind-blown hair as he attempted to speak through a cracked and uneven voice. Clearing his throat, he again attempted to say what had to be said, "Judy, I need to …oh my baby girl, I have to tell you…something." With that, he threw both arms around his little girl and held her close to his damp chest, tears bursting from his eyes, "Jay… Oh Judy, my sweet baby girl, Jay died today – early this morning!" Judy's throat nearly swelled shut at his words, as she looked deep into the swollen, green pools of her father - the horrifying truth confirmed by his tortured glance. "Nooooo, Da-deee, Noooo!"

School books tumbled upon shining, green grass, as the warm, bright, yellow sun faded to cool shades of somber gray, forcing a mist of icy fog into Judy's heart, enshrining her soul in darkness. *Jay's dead! Jay's dead!* In a split second, the foreboding words ran through her mind a thousand times. Judy clung hard to her father's upper arm, her fingertips digging deep into his flesh, her eyes flashing wildly, her voice crazily and frantically pleading for a resolve he could not give her, "Daddy, pleeeeze, nooo, Daddeee! I love him so much! He can't be dead! Daddy, please! You must help me bring him back! We'll all bring him back! You know he's not really gone! It's a mistake! We are going be married! You said we could get married! You love him too, I know you do Daddy! He can't die because we all love him!"

Emitting a frightful, keening noise, Judy's legs buckled beneath her, and just before her slight frame collapsed upon the earth, Joe swept his daughter up in strong loving arms and carried her limp form inside the house.

That morning Liz was shaken out of her slumber by the ringing of an alarm clock sounding off somewhere in the house. She teetered out of bed seeking out the noise only to realize it was the incessant blaring of the telephone. Still half asleep, she picked up the receiver.

"Hello!"

An unknown woman's voice, spoke haltingly, "This is ... this is Jay's aunt." Liz thought hard, *Jay's aunt, she has never called here. I have never spoken with her before. Why is she calling me?*

"I ... I don't know how to, how to tell you, I'm so sorry, so sorry to tell you... our Jay was killed. He died this morning in a traffic accident!" Liz's felt her heart nearly explode as her stomach churned into bouts of nausea, thinking she was having a nightmare. But the voice was not a dream, it was a voice of tormenting reality. "But Jay cannot be dead!" she screamed into the phone, "He cannot be dead! They are supposed to get married! We all love him so much! Why are you saying this?" Liz clutched her tight chest as Jay's aunt relayed the sickening details.

A December in Florida was unlike a December in Virginia. Tuesday morning, December 7, 1971, in Florida, had brought with it pleasant, warm temperatures; however, four states above them, in Vienna, Virginia, the morning was cold, rainy and foggy. Jay always rode his motorcycle to school. His young cousin, the daughter of Jay's uncle, also resided in the same home. She was a passenger on the school bus traveling directly in front of Jay on his motorcycle.

The school bus applied its brakes, making a left turn towards the school. The exact logistics of the vehicle's movements was uncertain, but somehow, as the bus turned, Jay braked to slow down behind it. The cycle slid on the slick, wet roadway, forcing the bike onto its side, gliding the metal frame with its rider directly under the wheels of the bus.

As the deadly details were spoken, Liz stood frozen in place, the phone held firmly to her ear, her grief-stricken mind uncomprehending of what she had heard. *Why had Jay been allowed to ride his motorcycle under such weather conditions?*

An inconsolable Liz unloaded her painful rant at the unseen messenger of death at the other end of the phone line. "He should not have ridden a motorcycle to school in that weather, someone should have driven him in a car!" You killed him! You all killed him! None of you loved him like I did, like *we* did! If you had driven him to school, in the car, he would be alive!" Liz could not control the depth of her grief further. She let forth a deep moaning sound from the depths of her soul, awash with anguish, misery, and sorrow. Even in her deep emotional pain, her distraught state, Liz realized her accusations were unjustified, but she needed an outlet for her loss. Continuing to verbally assault the voice on the phone, she cried bitterly, "You destroyed *their* lives, *our* lives! It is *your* fault!" Liz continued spewing the splinters of her battered emotions into the phone's receiver, until, after an unknown lapse of time, she found the line had gone silent.

That evening Judy went in and out of an exhaustive emotional sleep. Despite being covered with several blankets, and the warmth of the evening, she shivered with cold. Joe and Liz sat on the bed by her side, as she moaned, burning with emotional pain and grief. "Mommy, Daddy, he can't be dead. It's all just a bad dream, isn't it? Her devastated parents could barely speak. "No, my baby," Joe quietly responded, "He is truly gone."

Since age thirteen Jay had been part of her world, and now, as their long wait to marry was nearly at an end he dies? "No, no, no, no!" Judy let out a piercing scream of anguished denial. Rigors overcame her body causing her body to shake violently. Joe pulled Judy to a sitting position, cradling and rocking her back and forth as he had done so many times when she was a little girl. Liz lay down beside Judy, trying to warm her child with her own body, "I am so sorry my baby. We loved Jay too, very much." Joe and Liz both besieged with the heartache of losing Jay, and the fear of what was to now become of their heartbroken daughter, broke down and cried, holding fast to each other with Judy nestled between them.

On December 9, 1971, the aunt called again, but this time, Joe answered the phone and the two spilled tears of sorrow as the aunt explained she would be mailing back all the gifts the family had given Jay, and all the "love letters" Judy had written Jay over the years. The aunt invited the family to a Memorial Service in Virginia to be held in Jay's memory, after which he would be cremated, and his remains taken to a family cemetery in Pennsylvania.

The prior year Judy had purchased Jay a fourteen-karat gold necklace with a matching gold cross with both their names engraved upon it. Jay had never taken it off from the moment Judy had placed it about his neck. Judy could not bring herself to speak personally to the aunt, but through her father, had requested the gold chain and cross be cremated with Jay "So they could always be together." The aunt promised to carry out Judy's wishes.

Joe offered to drive his daughter to Jay's funeral in Virginia, but she was adamant about "not wanting to see him that way," an easy way of denying the truth: not seeing his lifeless form meant he was not dead, "just away."

Joe and Liz sent a spray of red roses in Judy's name to be placed on Jay's casket for his remembrance ceremony.

Judy's subconscious shielded her from the shock of Jay's loss. She continued to go to the mailbox every day expecting a letter from her lost love, instinctively reaching for a ringing phone believing it was Jay calling her. At times, Joe and Liz believed her state of denial was a good thing, for their daughter was happier in that protective state and functioned as though nothing had happened; although, many evenings as they made their way upstairs to settle down for the night, Judy's muffled sobs and moans could be heard emanating from her bedroom.

The shock of Jay's death was both emotionally and physically draining for the entire family, even Sonny and Pilvia sensed a "dark cloud of grief" floating over their home, feeling helpless on how they could comfort their sister.

The first week or two after Jay's passing, Judy's mood ranged from anger towards Jay for "leaving her," anger towards God for taking away her young fiancé, regret for all the lost dreams she and Jay had dreamed to do together and suffering from bouts of insomnia and lack of appetite.

A few days before Christmas, Judy remembered *something*: The *voice*. The voice calling to her the morning of Jay's death was *his* voice: Jay had died at approximately 8:30 a.m. that December seventh morning – exactly the timeframe when Judy heard her name being called. Her Jay had reached out to her from "beyond" as he left this world.

Jay's cousin had written Judy a letter after Jay's accident informing her Jay had died on the way to the hospital in the ambulance of "neck injuries," telling her that the emergency medical personnel had asked, "Who is Judy?" The only words Jay repeated over and over before his death was Judy's name.

A sad, subdued Christmas of 1971 came and went. The tree had been set up and decorated the day Liz discovered the money bundle. On Christmas Eve, as was the family's tradition, they opened their gifts, trying to maintain some sense of normalcy. Liz and Joe were worried for Judy. She was straining to be cheerful for the sake of her family, but through each smile, a tear overflowed the boundaries of its eye.

The Monday after Christmas found a bereaved Liz at the nearby men's store returning several items of clothing and other gifts purchased at the establishment. Liz had intentionally arrived early before the store opened, parking her car in the original spot where she had found the money bundle. The salesman was unprepared for the answer of his question, "Was there anything wrong with the merchandise? Would you like to exchange the items?" Liz could not contain her grief. She ran her hands gently over the soft, velour fabric of the sweater she had carefully selected for Jay. "He is dead - that is why I am bringing it all back. Oh God! He is dead!" She slumped over on the sales counter in tears. The salesman rushed to aid the grief-stricken woman to a nearby chair. After a cup of ice water and condolences from the store's staff, Liz got her refund for the merchandise. When she got back to her vehicle, she kept the car door open. Sitting down on the car seat, she placed both feet on the pavement. "Now, it is all over – you are going back where I found you." With those words, Liz took the refund money, along with her own cash to equal the amount she had originally found, bound the cash with a rubber band, and placed the currency on the ground close to where she had first discovered it. "Please be found by someone who really needs you." She closed the car door, cranked the car engine and drove home.

On New Year's Eve, a Friday, a large box addressed to Judy and her family arrived on their doorstep. Joe was off that day, but Liz was scheduled to work later that night, which was good in its own way, for New Year's Eve brought in large parties of people, which meant large tips. Joe settled the box in the middle of the living room floor using a box cutter to split the container open.

Joe and Liz sat silently allowing Judy to sift through the time capsule of memories sent by Jay's aunt and uncle. Several stacks of letters tied with a twine-type material took up most of the box: letters Judy had written to Jay, words of love for the boy now forever lost to her. Beneath the letters were several gifts Judy had given Jay, and gifts given to Jay by the family. The container also held the Christmas present Jay had intended to give his sweetheart: an ivory cameo necklace with a watch on the reverse side.

Judy clasped the necklace in her hand, running her fingers over the cameo cut-out. "Her Jay" had touched this, he had selected this beautiful gift for her, was going to place it about her neck that very special Christmas Eve they were to spend together. But he was taken from her, too young, too soon. He never again would call her, never again would she feel his intimate touches, he would never marry her, she would never have his baby.

How I wish Jay and I had consummated our love on that summer day, if we had … I could possibly be carrying his child at this very moment, and then… he really would have been mine forever.

Suddenly, without warning, Judy rushed upstairs, leaving her parents in a quandary as to what she was doing. Once in her room, Judy quickly opened her dresser drawer and gathered up all the letters Jay had written her over the years and placed the letters into a blue suitcase kept under her bed. She hurriedly brought the case back down to where her parents were waiting.

She placed the suitcase on the floor, and immediately deposited the letters sent by Jay's aunt alongside her own letters. But, one envelope stood out

– a letter Jay had sent her only two weeks prior to his passing. Her fingers traced the swirling outline where he had penned her name. *His* hands had touched the pale envelope, *his* fingers had inked the love-filled passages on the sacred parchment tucked within. This is the closest she would ever come to "touching him" again.

Judy's moment of reckoning had at last come to pass. Her face winced in pain "It's really over, he's never coming back. Jay is gone, forever, isn't he?"

Judy gazed deep into the faces of her parent's strained faces waiting for an answer. The grief-filled eyes of her parents could not hide the truth. A deep shudder tore through Judy's essence. She wept unpretentiously and inexhaustibly, having wept for Jay's loss often, but not to this depth, for she had shielded herself from believing what she did not want to believe. All Joe and Liz could do at this point was to embrace their daughter, to hold her tightly. All three sat on the living room floor, holding fast to one another, at last allowing the pain within them all to be released through bleak, guttural rales.

The year of 1972 started quietly. Through the support of her family, Judy realized she must go on living her life, for in doing so, Jay would always be with her. Judy wrote in her diary: "As long as I live and breathe, Jay lives and breathes. Deep in my heart there is a special private place, a place where the time of our love will stand forever - to be treasured till my last breath, when once more he and I will be together."

The "bitter storm" of the winter of 1971 passed, giving way to a fresh new world, awash with bright sunshine and spectacular color. Eons of springs had brought new life, new hope, and new chances for the world. Judy was a "child of springtime," and with her eighteenth birthday approaching, Joe and Liz prayed their daughter would find a new purpose to her life.

On Saturday, April 1, 1972, two days before her eighteenth birthday, Judy responded to a knock resonating upon her front door. To her delight and surprise, a gentleman from a local florist shop stood before her holding a vase filled with eighteen, red, sweet-smelling, long-stemmed, roses. "Who would be sending me roses?" Judy apprehensively opened the card sent with the delicately scented bouquet. The card read, *"From Your First and Everlasting Admirer, Love Dad."* Judy held the card close to her heart and ran to find her father outside by the pool, where she wrapped her arms around him in a grateful embrace. "Daddy! The flowers are beautiful (it was the first time Judy had ever been sent flowers). Thank you for giving them to me!"

Joe hugged his "first baby" to his chest. With blurry eyes and words coming with difficulty through an emotionally dry throat, he beseeched his daughter, "Please, Judy, please be happy again. Your mother and I just want you to be happy! We have felt so utterly helpless these past few months. We don't know how to help you. All we can do is love you, no matter what. We love you so much!" Leaning into each other for comfort, Judy put her arms about her father and hugged him close. "Don't worry Daddy. I will be all right. Please don't be sad anymore. Jay would not want our family to be unhappy." Wanting to assure her father of her intentions to "feel better," Judy airily announced, "Daddy! I am going to put on a pretty dress, so you can take my picture with my birthday flowers!"

Judy graduated from high school the first Saturday in June of 1972. Helped by her customer service, business and typing classes in school, she was offered a teller position at a nearby bank and began work the first Monday after graduation day. Liz drove her to work in the mornings and Joe picked her up in the late afternoon on his way home from work.

Judy had taken driver's education in high school and had obtained her driver's license at age sixteen. Wanting to drive herself to work, Judy approached her father about buying a small, used car.

Joe obliged and purchased a "tank" for his daughter, a bulky, dark blue, late 1960's, Plymouth, whose sides were thick enough to take on an assault of "car fire." Joe stood beside his daughter at the driver's door on the car lot explaining why he felt the car was right for her, "It's not a very fancy car, but it will protect you!" Judy did not mind what kind of car she drove, as long she could drive where she needed to go, and Joe did not mind buying the car, but asked Judy to pay him back thirty-five dollars a month till the car was paid off and pay for her own car insurance. "Things are always appreciated more when you know how difficult it is to obtain them," he reminded her.

It was quite a strain on Liz having to rise early to take Sonny and Pilvia to school after getting home late from work. Most nights she did not get to bed until the early morning hours. September was the beginning of the school year for Sonny and Pilvia. Now, that she had a car, Judy announced, "I have an idea! Mommy, I'm going to drive Sonny and Pilvia to school in the mornings from now on and then drive myself on to work. You get home way too late at night from the restaurant and never get enough sleep because you drive the kids to school by eight o'clock. From now on you can get more rest!"

After school began, as per her new routine, Judy drove Sonny and Pilvia to their elementary school. One cloudy morning after dropping her siblings off at school, she was turning through an intersection when her car stalled. Judy could see a vehicle headed straight for her passenger side door. *Can't they see I'm not moving at all?* With that last thought, the oncoming car slammed into the front passenger door pushing her car deeper into the intersection, right into the path of another moving vehicle. Her driver's door crumpled inward.

Fortunately, a police cruiser in the vicinity came to the scene quickly. Judy was not injured, just shaken. She walked across the street to a local business to call her father at work, not even thinking to call her mother. "Daddy, I was in a car accident, but I'm not hurt! It's a good thing I was driving a tank!" Within a week the car had been repaired and the family was back in their usual morning routine. When Judy drove the car to work the first day after bringing it home from the repair shop, her father's words rang in her mind: *Not a fancy car, but it will protect you.*

Joe directed several types of training classes for his company ranging from television repair, home appliance servicing, and even garage door opener installations.

In the early fall, Joe was doing onsite garage door installation training with two new hires. The door was not yet properly secured to the mechanism on the garage ceiling. Joe asked one of the students in training to hold the door up for a moment while he checked the tension on the motor. Joe dropped his screwdriver and bent to retrieve it.

And then the unthinkable happened: the trainee absentmindedly loosened his grip on the garage door causing its full weight to fall upon Joe's lower back. The men quickly lifted the door and pulled Joe to safety. "Call for help, I can't move!" Joe lay painfully motionless on the customer's concrete driveway.

"You've got several crushed vertebrae in your lower back with a bunch of nerves in danger of being severed. We've got to get you to surgery immediately." Joe stared incredulously into the doctor's eyes. "I can't! I've got to work!" The doctor's blue eyes squinted, trying to convey the sincerity of his message, "You *won't* be working at all if you don't get to surgery soon. Do you understand my meaning?" Joe was overcome with worry at the devastating diagnosis, "I have to call my wife first, please."

Joe was in surgery for several hours. Liz waited impatiently for the neurosurgeon's verdict in the hospital waiting room. She was there alone, insisting that her children continue with school and work that day, "There is no sense in everyone just sitting around the waiting room."

Judy was very worried about her father, and about her mother being alone in the hospital. "Mommy, don't you want me to stay with you. You might need something?" Liz hugged her *Csimby*, "I promise I'll call you at work if anything happens."

The surgeons skillfully accomplished what needed to be done for Joe to have a good quality of life. The following day, Joe's doctor came to his bedside, "Okay Joe, it's time to get out of bed and walk!"

"Walk? I can't even stand up straight!" whined Joe as he attempted to take his first excruciatingly painful steps. Liz's heart ached as she observed her Joe leaning heavily on the arm of a nurse as he painfully walked up and down the hospital halls, bent and hunched over like a one-hundred-year-old man.

Joe spent one week in the hospital, making steady improvement. He was not yet able to stand completely upright on his return home. The healing process was slow, but with physical therapy, determination, and his family's loving care, Joe grew strong and healed quickly. It was time to get back to work and to living!

Judy found work as a pharmacy assistant in 1973 learning the ins and outs of the pharmaceutical world. The days were satisfying and fast-paced, finding herself involved with patients on the phone needing help with their prescriptions, learning the names and usages of hundreds of medications, and meeting the needs of pharmacy clients face-to-face.

The pharmacy staff was good to her, like a second family, and she enjoyed going to work every day. The best part of work was staying busy, which meant she didn't have time to think about the past, and making money was good. As the years passed, she had sufficient income to buy herself a racy, brand-new, off-the-showroom floor, Cobalt Blue, 1976 Mustang Cobra, go to a gym to stay in "bikini-shape" and afford beautifully tailored clothes (plus she insisted on paying "rent" to her parents as she wanted to prove her independence).

Unfortunately, the 1970's would be a difficult decade for Judy, filled with many turbulent, unsatisfying relationships, for Jay's loss had deeply scarred her heart. The more men she dated only confirmed Judy's heartache: the perfect innocent young love she and Jay had shared would probably never come again. There more than likely would only be "One Jay" in her lifetime, for try as she might, that "wonderful feeling" continued to elude her. Emotionally depleted by her failed romantic endeavors, Judy focused her energy toward creating a new career. In mid-1976, she enrolled in a medical transcription course at a local vocational college. Pilvia, soon to be seventeen, also signed on with Judy for the same. That year, Sonny would turn fifteen in July. He was an "A" student, very popular with his peers and involved in just about every club the high school offered.

Joe's career blossomed, eventually rising to the position of district training manager, with his training expertise extending as far away as Puerto Rico. With Joe's television repair business, his still lucrative musical career, his climb up the corporate ladder, and his beloved Liz's contribution from working at the restaurant, the family, at last, was in the best financial shape of their lives.

It was the first Saturday in June of 1976. Almost twenty years since the Hungarian Revolution. Joe wanted to get away with the family to "do something patriotically *American.*"

"Family meeting!" Joe's call rang through the house. His commanding voice urged all to be present. The family gathered around the long, rectangular, walnut dining table in the formal dining room. "This year will mark the twentieth year of the Hungarian Revolution, as well as mark the two hundredth birthday of the United States of America. In Hungary, we fought for our freedom, just as the Americans fought for their independence. In honor of *all* Freedom Fighters I have made hotel reservations for us. We are going to the Bicentennial Celebration at Disney World!" But Daddy," Judy interjected, "How can we afford to go? It's expensive!" Liz's eyes met Joe's with the same unspoken request, but after all these years, she knew her husband's exact response to anything that involved how things were to be paid for, "You know I always figure it out." Liz shook her head slowly from side-to-side, smiling softly toward her husband.

It was almost midnight, the Saturday after Joe's "big announcement." All the kids were fast asleep. Liz was not yet home from the restaurant. Joe was not worried, as on many weekend evenings Liz had "late night stragglers." He was a little hungry and toddled over to the fridge to get out some milk to make his favorite late-night snack, a bowl of hot, *Cream of Wheat* cereal. As he opened the refrigerator door, the blaring ring of the kitchen wall phone broke his concentration. "Who in the world would be calling this late?" Irritated by the interruption, Joe yanked the phone off its cradle, speaking rather loudly, he let out an impatient "Hello!"

A frantic voice met his ears, "Joe! Joe! This is Joanie from the restaurant! Liz was carrying a tray out of the kitchen and slipped. I think she hurt her back. I'm calling you from the emergency room at the hospital."

Joe didn't think to wake the kids. His only thought was to reach his Love, his Liz. He did not remember driving to the hospital. As his vehicle careened through the dark streets, his mind reached out to the Great Spirit, "Please, please, don't let her be hurt badly. She doesn't deserve it. She's too sweet and good. She works too hard. I should never have allowed her to work in a restaurant carrying those damn heavy trays!"

Joe and Liz - Florida - Summer of 1976

Liz had a slipped disk injury of the lower spine. Joe listened to the doctor's explanation with paralyzed senses, "A slipped disk is a little like a jelly donut, with a softer center encased within a tougher exterior. It is caused when the softer "jelly" pushes out through a crack in the tougher exterior. It is possible for this to heal with rest and traction. But right now, your wife is having pain and numbness in her lower legs because the disk is irritating nerves in the area." Joe flinched at the doctor's diagnosis. Wanting to give his wife relief from her discomfort, Joe beseeched the doctor, "But what can we do right now to help her with the pain? We are supposed to go on a vacation to Disney World in a couple of weeks. She would be devastated if she could not go! Will it be safe for her to travel? Does she need surgery?" The doctor explained that most times, conservative treatment, avoiding painful positions, and having carefully planned exercises, in combination with pain medications, usually helped most individuals. "If she takes it easy with physical therapy, she could probably get much better in a month or two. Most times the disk just shrinks over time." Joe pondered the doctor's words. "Tell me what I should do when I get her home to keep her safe and comfortable."

The neurologist told Joe he would prescribe a back brace for Liz to wear constantly, unless bathing, and absolutely no working at the restaurant till medically cleared! The doctor instructed Joe in applying alternating heat and ice treatments and prescribed a mild pain prescription.

"Liz, can you hear me?" an emotionally exhausted Joe hovered over his wife's form on the emergency department bed. This was the first time he had seen Liz since his arrival at the hospital. Liz opened her eyes at the sound of her sweetheart's voice, "My Joe, I am sorry. I should have been more careful. I have no idea what I slipped on! It hurt so much!"

With that, Liz broke down, weeping heavily, "I have ruined everything!" Joe leaned over the bed rail, cupping her face with his warm hands, stroking her cheeks with his thumbs. "Don't worry my butterfly, the doctor says you are going to be just fine. You only need to take it easy and not strain yourself. He thinks you'll heal up on your own and won't need surgery. I'll take good care of you. I wish it had been me! *I deserve the pain*. I should not have let you work anymore in that restaurant. It's too hard on your body! It's my fault. I'm always greedy, wanting bigger and better things!"

Joe was now the one crying and Liz the comforter. "My Joe ...do not cry. We both wanted bigger and better things. We chose to do it together, and, for as long as we have each other, I do not care how hard I work. Everything I do is worthwhile because I am doing it for you, for us, because I love you! I will try really hard to get well soon - I promise I will." Joe laid his head on his wife's soft bosom, seeking her warmth, her love and comfort. Liz tenderly stroked his curly, dark tendrils.

"We're going to live in a tree house!" Sonny was ecstatic as he carried his suitcase up the steps of his new home for the next week. Disney World Tree

Houses were fashioned to be reminiscent of the tree house from the "Swiss Family Robinson" film produced by Walt Disney in the 1960's. The homes were built in a densely wooded area a few miles from the main Disney resort. They were two-story creations, with a bottom "stem" or "pedestal" that held up the main structure. The lower half of the building held the washer and dryer, provided a third bedroom, and had extra storage.

Upon this base, a hexagon-shaped structure, featuring window-to-floor sliding glass doors round-a-bout, ensured a panoramic view from any angle. Coming in the front door, the living room area was on the left, with two bedrooms on the right. Straight ahead was a modern kitchen, and in the kitchen, a spiral staircase led to a downstairs bedroom. A column was in the center of the house, simulating a "tree" growing up through the center of the structure. "This is so cool!" exclaimed Judy, not believing how modern, colorful, and roomy the place was - much more home-like and elegant than a stuffy hotel room!

Pilvia and Judy took their bags to the second bedroom. The large windows didn't even require the drapes to be closed due to the massive tropical plants outside the wide expanse of glass. The plant's enormous leaves provided all the privacy they needed, but still allowed plenty of natural light to illuminate the space. A regularly scheduled tram made its way through the Tree House community several times a day providing transportation to the main park.

The lights and sounds of the futuristic community carried one far away from the boring rhythm of everyday life. There were always new rides, foods, and exhibits to explore. A person could spend two weeks in the park and still not experience all the wonders it offered. Each morning the children rode the shuttle tram into the "land of dreams."

The tram ride was far too jarring for Liz because of her back injury; therefore, Joe drove Liz to Disneyworld in their Dodge van, parking at the handicapped entrance. From there, Joe escorted Liz about in her wheelchair to greet the children at their designated meet-up location. Liz's confined condition did not dampen the couple's excitement and exhilaration. Joe propelled Liz around the park in her wheeled conveyance surveying and exploring the fascinating hidden treasures of the gift shops and stunning array of unusual sights and sounds.

Joe had made meticulous arrangements for the family's final night at the resort: a formal dinner at one of Disneyworld's most prestigious and elegant five-star restaurants.

The girls assisted Liz in donning her new, pale yellow, floor-length, organza gown with a low square-cut neckline, gossamer sheer billowing sleeves narrowing at the wrist, and empire waistline, set off by white dress gloves with pearl accents (avoiding any precarious positions for their mother). They dressed their mother's hair and applied her makeup.

Judy's gown was a pale mint green and Kuki's gown a pale sky blue. Both were identical in style, with low-backs and halter necklines. Shiny, silver-toned slippers adorned their feet. Unlike the women, Joe and Sonny had not invaded any stores prior to the trip but were dashing in their best suits and shoes. Joe strutted proudly as he escorted his clan into the Grand Dining Room. "We look like a bunch of movie stars, don't we," bragged Joe as the family approached the polished maître d'.

The room had flauntingly high, multilevel ceilings from which hung dozens of magnificent, sparkling chandeliers. The tables were superbly set with snow-white linen cloths. Elegant dinner plates and shining glasses captured the luminous gleam of the overhead crystal jewels.

The aura and décor of the restaurant screamed out for grandeur and glamour; however, to the family's surprise, most dining room guests were not in formal attire, having come to the establishment immediately after a long, hot day in the parks, still garbed in their shorts, tennis shoes, and sweaty T-shirts, a stark contrast to the stylish tuxes of the all-male wait staff including the garments of Joe's entourage.

Refreshed to see appropriately-dressed folk, the maître d' and servers quickly assisted the family to one of the best tables in the house, allowing a lovely view of an outside garden touting a soaring, colorfully lighted, splashing fountain. The waiters assisted Liz out of her wheelchair into one of the fine dining chairs, fussing over the family's every need, as if they were in the presence of royalty. And, tonight, as far as Joe was concerned, they *were* royalty.

Sitting side by side, Joe tenderly grasped Liz's hand beneath the folds of the fine linen tablecloth. Amongst such pomp and beauty, Joe's mind swirled back twenty years prior, to Hungary in 1956. Back in those terrible revolution days he was a poor, hungry, freedom fighter, a once prominent musician, forced to work in the black pits of the Tatabanya coalmines. He, his baby daughter and wife never had enough to eat. His sweetheart was forced to stand for hours in a food line only to have the food run out by the time she reached the grocer's counter. It was a time when his little girl was too tiny for her years due to the lack of proper nutrition. Visions of his childhood flashed about his head, taking him back to World War II when he had nothing to eat but dandelion soup if he was that fortunate. Liz and her family suffered the same fate, as well as the rest of Hungary in those sad days.

But now, he was here in this *Palace of Dreams*, with his one and only true love, and three children born out of that love, sitting at a table befit for the high monarchs of Europe. Even if the "Blue Fairy" had promised him such things when he was a little boy, he would not have believed such a future could possibly exist, for all the little boy, Jozsef knew in the "war days" was the pain of an empty, rumbling stomach. He and his beautiful wife had endured exorbitant anguish and agony, the likes of which most of the world would never know. But today, as Joe looked across the table upon the faces of his happy children, the realization of the extraordinary accomplishments achieved in America by he and his lovely Erzsebet overwhelmed his senses.

Joe could see his children talking and laughing across the wide expanse of white linen, lost in their own world as they perused the wonder of the sights about them, which was a good thing, for he yearned to speak privately to Liz. He pulled his chair a bit closer to his sweetheart, placing his arm gently about her shoulder. She was as lovely as the first time he gazed upon her, if not more so. "My beautiful *Pillango*, look about us, we've come such a long way since the dreadful days in the old country, haven't we?"

Liz locked eyes with Joe. How she adored him! He was her rock and very foundation for her living. All other men paled compared to *her* Joe. The first time Joe touched her hand, he had stolen her heart. He was virtuous, skillful, talented, and could accomplish anything he set out to do. Joe was her champion!

Liz smiled warmly towards her husband, a loving smile, filling Joe with overpowering feelings of love and pride for the lovely woman who had joined her life with his, the woman who had stayed by his side fighting the battles of life with him to build the wonderful world they now shared. Joe's heart floated into the depths of his Love's glistening, hazel pools expressing his emotions without a word.

After all their years together, it was easy for Liz to read Joe's face and to *feel* his feelings. Liz lifted Joe's hand to her lips, lightly kissing his fingers. "We have come a long way, my *Edes* …but, today, it seems like the terrible things that happened to us was a million years ago. It was a nightmare from which we awoke, at last. But the past does not matter now. You and I, together, have accomplished what most people born in *this* country have not done and will never do. Even with all the pain and suffering we went through, I would not change one thing about our past, because it is due to all the pain and suffering that we found each other! Jozsef, my love, do you not know? Despite all the madness and torment of our early lives together in Hungary …we survived everything because we loved one another - we had *Splendor in Hell!*"

Joe could not hold back tears. Liz stroked his wet cheek, "Oh my *Draga*, my *Edes*, do not cry! Be happy! Did you ever imagine the night our boat sailed out of Bremerhaven Harbor that we would be sitting amidst such luxury! Be proud my Joe, my love, you made all the beauty of this moment happen - everything we have is because of *you*!" Liz kissed Joe solidly on the mouth, with all the ferocity and emotion of one's first kiss, causing Joe's lips to ache with the same passion for his *Edes* as when their lips had touched for the first time.

Excited voices broke the spell, as their children announced, "Look, they are bringing our feast!"

The delectable aroma of the superb cuisine swirled in the air about them. Joe observed the servers as they placed the delightful fare in front of each family member.

Without permission of their owner, Joe's already wet eyes flooded over with tears. *These waiters probably think we're a bunch of rich people who have never known a bad day in all our lives. They cannot possibly imagine our miserable, pitiful beginnings …those days of "hell."*

Joe cleared his throat (and his eyes) as he pushed his chair back from the linen clad circle. Standing tall and proud he surveyed the beaming faces of his loving family. "I wish to propose a toast on this most momentous occasion! Happy Two-Hundred Years America! Thank you, America, for giving us a home when we had nowhere in this world to go, for giving us an opportunity to build the wonderful life we have, for letting us become "Americans," for giving us everything! I toast to all those around the world, to those in Hungary, and to those in America, who fought and gave their lives for freedom!" Glasses were "clicked together" and his loved one's voices echoed his toast.

But there was more Joe wanted to say to his *Edes*, something private, direct from his heart, a heart overflowing with a loving gratitude for all she had withstood by his side over the difficult years. Joe leaned in closer to the softness of his wife, feeling her warmth emanating about him.

Joe lifted his wine glass to honor his wife, the windows of his soul holding back the salty dew once again threatening to escape their bounds, as he softly whispered, so only she could hear, "I offer one more toast, to you my love, my beautiful wife, to my *Erzsebet*, for your goodness and purity, for your sacrifices, for your love, to *Splendor in Hell!* I will love you forever!"

It was late August of 1977 – a very hot Saturday afternoon, with Liz's back injury finally healed, she and Joe had put in a full day of landscaping work about their home. All three kids had helped their parents with a partial portion of that endeavor earlier in the day, but the children were not home this afternoon, for Judy and Pilvia were scheduled to work, and Sonny had a date.

"Liz, I'm heading upstairs for a long soak in the tub to soothe my aching muscles!" announced Joe as he made his way upstairs to the master bedroom landing. "I will take a shower in the kid's bathroom and start something for dinner," chimed Liz, as she headed for the bright yellow bath near Sonny's room. Liz quickly showered and dressed speedily in the clothes she had brought in with her and headed downstairs to prepare a light dinner.

Before placing the final touches on the meal, Liz made her way upstairs to let Joe know it was almost time to eat. Joe was still lying in the tub with his eyes closed. "He fell asleep! He worked too hard outside!" Liz made her way over to Joe and knelt beside the tub. She gently stroked his head, "Joe, my *Draga*, it is time to eat."

Something was not right! Joe's usual rosy cheeks were pale, and his face was ashen in color. "Joe, please wake up! Wake up!" Liz shook Joe's bare, wet shoulders but he remained motionless. "Oh my God, oh God, do not let him be dead!"

Liz screamed in panic. She bolted downstairs, grabbed a gallon jug of ice water from the fridge, ran back up to the bathroom, and poured the frigid contents over her husband's head and chest. Joe gasped, taking in a deep breath, his eyes rolling back in his head, but he did not speak. Liz ran to the bedroom phone and called for an ambulance.

Joe had suffered a severe anterior myocardial infarction. "Your husband must stop smoking cigarettes," instructed the emergency room physician, as he looked deep into Liz's careworn face. "If he stops smoking now, there's a good chance he can avoid bypass surgery and he'll have a long life ahead of him." *Bypass surgery?*

Those words sent shivers of fear through Liz. Was her Joe that sick? *I can fix this,* she reasoned to herself, *I'll cook fat-free meals and make sure he stops smoking.* With those thoughts in mind, she made her way to Joe's bedside where she was greeted with his famous bright smile, the same smile that stole her heart many years ago. "Don't worry Liz, I'm going to be okay, I'll take care of myself." Liz held her husband's cool hand, "That is right my *Draga*," Liz assured him, "You are going to be with me for a long time. I love you! Nothing will take you from me." Joe signaled for Liz to come closer to him. "Pull up a chair beside the bed and rest your head on my lap." It didn't take long for Liz to obey. She placed her tired head on Joe's thigh as he stroked her silken locks. They both fell into a deep, restful sleep.

Joe had only been home from the hospital for two days, but was already up and raring to go, his sense of adventure urging his spirit onward to explore uncharted seas, as he made his announcement one evening after dinner. "I am going to buy a boat!"

"A boat?" queried Liz. "Yes, a boat," repeated Joe. "Liz, my *Edes*, I did a lot of thinking while lying in that hospital bed." I would like to buy a cabin cruiser, with a loft up top where you and I can sit and enjoy the cool sea breezes during the day, and a cabin down below where we can sleep as we "anchor out" for a night on the bay. There is more to life than just working, and if my heart stops suddenly, we are going to "live" before that happens. The cabin cruiser will be our private world, just you and me!"

Joe launched his thirty-two-foot, Bayliner Cruiser from the boat landing of Madeira Beach. The gleaming white siding and gold trim of the "*Elizabeth*" out-shown all the other boats at the dock. Joe and Liz took their place in the "Eagles nest" up top while the kids sat along the bow holding on to the rails. The "*Elizabeth*" chugged out of the harbor on her first adventure toward Egmont Key, a small island off the coast for a day of swimming, snorkeling, and picnicking, but most of all, a *nice afternoon nap* for Joe and his Liz while the kids explored the island. The cabin cruiser carried the family away to new, unseen worlds filled with adventure. Nearly every weekend Joe commandeered his craft through the waves of Egmont Key, the Fort De Soto park waterway and the rippling waves below the Sunshine Skyway.

In April of 1978, in celebration of their twenty-fifth wedding anniversary, Liz and Joe planned their long-awaited return to Hungary. The children were old enough to take care of themselves while they would be away. It had taken nearly twenty-two years, but it was finally safe to make the return trip, even though Hungary remained under the heavy hand of communism. If things worked out well on this visit they would later return to Hungary as a family.

The couple's anticipation built within them as the plane's wheels touched down on Magyar firmament. Would they recognize their relatives waiting for them at the gate? Would their relatives recognize them? People change - they may gain weight or become thin, may lose their hair, or get wrinkly and gray, but one thing remains constant: a person's eyes, the most identifying feature of the human face. As Joe and Liz disembarked the plane, they observed a small mass of people huddled together waving handkerchiefs and little Hungarian flags, and then they saw the eyes - all those beautiful tear-filled Hungarian eyes!

Joe and Liz aboard their boat the "Elizabeth" in 1978

Joe and Liz spent the first few days visiting with relatives and seeking out the streets and places, where, once upon a time, they had lived, played, worked and loved. Many areas remained unchanged, some buildings still bearing scars of bullets from the Revolution! It was a remembrance of bitterness and sweetness, for beneath their feet, in the park where Joe and Liz had spent their wondrous first night together, was an unmarked graveyard. After the revolution, mass graves had been dug to bury the dead. The soil upon which they had surrendered their hearts was now the hallowed, sacred ground of revolutionary heroes, young and old. The vibrations of the past violence that had occurred on the land still hung heavy in the air, as if the souls of all those cut down in their fight for freedom haunted the spaces of the living. And, after all these years, the ugly, revolting Red Star remained atop many buildings- a reminder that the Communist government was still in control.

Ambling down familiar paths, the couple found themselves at the cemetery where both their mothers were buried.

Joe stood at his mother's graveside with feelings of great sadness and confusion. *Mama, my only Mama, did you ever truly love me? Look I am here! Even now I cry the tears for you that you did not shed for me. I loved you. I could not help but love you as you were my only mother. I was just a little boy. Why could you not love me? I needed your love. Do you love me now in your death, in the face of God?*

Liz knelt by her mother's burial place placing a small bouquet of wildflowers against the grave marker. Misty recollections of her mother working hard on the farm, cooking delicious meals in the "good days" and scraping for food in the "bad days," sewing her clothes, and always being loving, kind and gracious despite the hardships she had to suffer flooded her mind.

Mama forgive me for not being here with you as you were dying. I am sorry for not eating the horse food. I know now you were trying to keep me alive, but

I was only a little girl who did not understand what was happening in the world. I did not understand why we had to be hungry and eat things we never would have eaten before the war. I miss you Mama. I am sorry, very sorry I could not see before you died. Please forgive me. I will love you and remember your goodness all the days of my life.

Budapest was a shining star whose beauty had not faded. It was just as they remembered it to be in its "glory days" before the war and revolution devoured her. The Hungarian heart is a strong and determined one, and the Magyar citizens rebuilt and *rebuilt,* until the city was even more magnificent than before. One of the most intense rebuilding operations was that of the Budapest "Chain Bridge," the first permanent stone bridge connecting the two cities of Buda and Pest.

At the end of World War II German troops blew up the bridge on January 18, 1945, but the indomitable, gritty people of Hungary began rebuilding the opulent structure beginning in the spring of 1947 and finished in November of 1949. Miraculously, the two stone lions located at both abutments survived the apocalypse and continued to proudly guard the bridge as the two lovers once again strolled across the mighty landmark spanning the Danube River of their homeland.

At long last, after so many years, Liz journeyed to see her father. He lived in a simple two-room cottage with an outhouse, located just beyond the city limits on a tiny patch of land. Even in his old age he had managed to maintain a small garden and chop wood for a woodstove used for both cooking and heating. His home was a pitiful wooden structure with rickety wooden planks for walls, and a slated wood floor. A small narrow bed and washstand were the only furnishings in the bedroom. The kitchen consisted of a woodstove, a wooden table with two chairs, and a hand pump to bring water into the home. There was no electricity. Joe and Liz had written several times asking Liz's father to come and live with them in the United States, but he adamantly refused their offer. On this day, seeing him face-to-face, Joe and Liz again asked if he would move to America with them, to which he softly replied, "I am too old to start again with new ways. My father's land was here, he and my wife are buried here. Your brother and sister visit me, and I am happy in my simple life. I choose to live here. I have all I need, and today, I am even happier, for I have seen you, my *Edes Erzsebet,* before I go to be with your mother." The old man shuffled his feet over the wooden floor boards and sat on his bed. Waving a shaky arm, he signaled his daughter to sit beside him. He grasped both her hands and rested his nearly-bald head on her shoulder, his eyes silently gushing forth trickles of lamentation for all the years lost between them.

Joe's father lived in a humble dwelling on the second floor of a very old apartment building (without an elevator, only stairs) refurbished from the "war days". It was an outdated, dismal flat. The only redeeming feature of the abode were tall, floor-to-ceiling windows, allowing bright rays of sunlight to enter the tight living space.

Professor Bognar, now nearing his seventh decade of life, was a humble, thin, frail, bent-over man. Joe glanced about the residence. Could it be? On the floor, in front of the furnace, was one of the small rugs he had purchased for his parents when they lived in the apartment in Massachusetts. And on a shelf, was an empty box of Marlboro cigarettes, its colors faded with age. "Father, you still have these items?"

The old man slowly made his way over to the shelf, picking up the cigarette box, stroking it with his right thumb, "Yes, I saved a few things. They are the memory of a happy time, a time when I was with you, my son. I did not want to come back here. It was Hermina's wish. She was not happy in America. She missed her friends and her social life here. She missed her cat. I came back here to make her happy. And she was happy … until. But …she is gone now, and I am here. I am old and have learned an important thing …that a person can make their own happiness, and my happiness is being here in *Magyarország* (Hungarian country) where your mother and I first met, where we both shared happy times. My wonderful memory of the times I had with you and your family in that other far-away world will last me a lifetime."

Joe was overwhelmed. How he loved his father! How much he had missed him! "My *Edes Apukam*" (my dearest father) Joe exclaimed, and his heart ached with the loss of what could have been. He took the small-bony shell of his father into his arms, tenderly hugging his frail figure. "It will be all right father. Please, let me arrange for you to come back and live with us again in America. Florida is a paradise!"

Joe and Liz - Hungary – 1978

"Oh no! No, my son! You have made your place and time and I have made my place and time. I am happy here. I have all I need. I am very proud of you my Jozsef! You made it – you are rich and successful! You have accomplished all I wished I could have. I want you to be happy, for my sake, be happy."

Joe looked searchingly into his father's eyes, "Father, I need to know something. Why have you returned the money I have sent you all this time."

"Jozsef my boy, what more do I need? I have food to eat. I am looked after and checked on frequently. I am comfortable. I want you to have your earnings to build your life for you and your family." Joe was not satisfied, "But Father, what can I do for you?"

Liz and her father in his tiny home - Hungary - 1978

The old man tottered slowly over to a small wooden table residing in front of one of the large windows. "Jozsef, "I want you to have something to give to Judit, something of her grandmother, if you will accept it." Joe could not imagine what his father could be giving to his daughter. He observed his father gingerly pick up an intricately carved wooden box from the table. The old man's shaking hands opened the lid, removing from its confines a gold-plated watch. "This belonged to your mother. I want you to give it to Judit, as a gift from me." Tears flowed from the aged patriarch's eyes as he slowly placed the timepiece into his son's hand.

"Jozsef, I very much regret not making more time with my grandchildren. I do not even know them, not truly. So much time wasted, so much time lost. I wish …"

Joe was determined to wine, dine and entertain all his and Liz's relatives during their visit. Joe rented a van large enough to accommodate the entire family. Nearly every day an excursion was made over the wide Hungarian countryside, including Buda Castle, the Fisherman's Bastion, the medicinal springs of the Gellert Spa and Rudas baths, St. Margaret Island, the Hungarian National Museum, and the place where Joe first entertained heads of state, the Hungarian Parliament House.

The Budapest Hilton was in the heart of the Heritage Site on Castle Hill and offered the most spectacular views of the city. It was where Joe and Liz celebrated their Twenty-Fifth Wedding Anniversary dinner. Joe engaged a Hungarian Gypsy Band with twelve violinists to serenade every female relative at the dinner table. The music of the *Czárdás* and traditional Hungarian favorites echoed through the reception hall of the hotel. While the music played, the wine flowed, and the food was never-ending.

When they had married in a civil ceremony in Hungary, and during the reconfirmation of their wedding vows in America, Liz had worn a simple suit, but on this night of April 10, 1978, twenty-five years later, she was a vision of loveliness in a real wedding gown, complete with a pearl encrusted tiara, and bouquet of live, sweet-smelling, Hungarian, purple lilacs.

Joe escorted his bride to the dance floor, their bodies unconsciously flowing in sync to the centuries-old step of the *Czárdás*. Later, countless toasts to the couple were given by the family as they cut into a delectable three-tiered wedding cake provided by the bakers of the Hilton.

It was two o'clock in the morning. Seven hours of a fantasy-time had passed. Joe asked the twelve violinists, who had made their party a stunning success, to line up, six on each side, in honor formation, to play the *Rákóczi* March, which in many years past, had been the unofficial state anthem of Hungary. The couple and their wedding party made their departure between the stringed instruments. As Joe passed each violinist, he appreciatively placed a one-hundred-dollar bill in the breast pocket of each player. Twenty-two years had passed since the Revolution, but times remained economically difficult for the Hungarian people.

That one-hundred-dollar tip is one-month's wage for them. I know they will never forget this special night. They may believe I am very wealthy, and I will let them believe it. Little do they know how I suffered amongst them, here in poverty, all those years ago. And, I will be paying back credit card debt for years and years, but, at this moment, the amount of money I spend does not matter, not if it brings others happiness.

Joe and Liz dancing together at the Budapest Hilton as they celebrated their 25th Wedding Anniversary - 1978

In July of 1979, determined to take their children "back home to see where they came from," the entire family traveled back to Budapest for a genuine family reunion.

The Lufthansa airliner circled the Magyar soil below. The last time Judy breathed the air of her native land was twenty-three years ago when she was only two-years of age. For all three children, the realization of soon landing in the country of their origins was both exhilarating and daunting. Each felt as though they were free-falling, floating aimlessly on the restless winds of the sky, feeling quietly ungrounded and nervous, not knowing what to expect.

After a smooth landing at the airport the family disembarked the plane via the mobile steps placed firmly against the body of the aircraft. Much to the children's chagrin, soldiers armed with machine guns stood at the bottom of the steps. Judy's reaction to the armed soldiers was one of profound mortification - she had entered a world ruled by a communist government - a world without freedom.

Dozens of relatives excitedly greeted the family. Judy recognized a Hungarian word here and there; however, most words were lost to her. *I wish we had continued to speak Hungarian at home, so I would not feel disconnected with my relatives.*

Everyone had their turn hugging, squeezing, and kissing Judy, Sonny and Kuki. Judy had no recollection of her maternal grandfather, but she had seen photos of him, recognizing him instantly, as he meekly stood in the background of the small airline terminal waiting "his turn" for hugs and kisses, too.

Judy approached him, smiling, and with her best recollection of the Hungarian language, (and having practiced prior to her trip) hugged him announcing, "Hello Nagypapa, én vagyok, Judit. Nagyon örülök, hogy végre találkozunk." (Hello Grandfather, it is me, Judy, I am very happy to see you at last!).

The old man's teary eyes lit up in surprised appreciation, reaching out to his granddaughter for the first time in many years, both kissing each other on the cheek and embracing. Judy's paternal grandfather made his way toward her. His eyes clear and bright. Judy was happy he had come to America and had undergone the cataract removal surgery so he could see how much she had grown up. Her own father looked so much like him! Judy greeted him with an enthusiastic, "Nagyon hiányoztál Nagypapa" (I have missed you very much Grandfather).

Joe had reserved a "two-level "apartment for the family at the Budapest Hilton; the first level consisted of a living room, wet bar, bath, and a staircase with a landing half-way up to the second level where one could sit at a window seat and observe the beautiful views of the city. Upstairs were three bedrooms and two full baths. The suite was impeccably furnished with every amenity one could desire. The hotel offered a magnificent view of the Danube River. Outside its doors, down the wide street, was the famous St. Mathias Church and Fisherman's Bastion. The Grand Palace and several delightful museums were just around the corner. The hotel's restaurant offered delicious hot and cold cuisine, and even prepared "American food" to order. The famous Chain Bridge was not far, and in the cool evenings, the family walked the bridge taking in the spectacular night views of the Danube River.

A few days into their visit, the family visited Joe's godmother in Tatabanya, a town untouched by time, except for the mountain where the coal was mined, which did not seem as tall as Joe had remembered it to be.

The old woman's eyes soaked in the long-awaited sight before her. It was one of the happiest moments of her life: *Her Jozsef* was home with his beautiful wife and children.

The godmother resided in the same wood-framed home, which now, with the passage of decades, had decayed into a state of being unrecognizable from the time Joe and his little family lived there during his coal mining days. It was no more than twenty feet square in either direction with a wood plank floor. The sparse, one-room shack contained a coal stove in the center of the room used for heating, and a small wood-stove was on the opposite wall. The dwelling held a small rectangular table and chair, and against another wall was a thin, narrow, low bed, with a coverlet worn thin from use and age. A wooden cross of Jesus was nailed into the wall above the bed. The domicile held only the barest of essentials for survival. Even so, the godmother scurried about scavenging odd sized teacups and glasses to offer her guests refreshment, all the while signaling for them to sit on the bed. Judy's heart went out to the old woman instantly.

The severe impoverishment of the elderly lady's life was heartbreaking. *I feel undeserving of the wonderful life waiting for me back home. I always appreciated all my parents did for me, but never so much as I do at this moment.* A severe dose of reality struck Judy in that time - that she, also, might have lived in this manner had her parents not made the choice to leave everything behind the fateful night of their escape.

Seeing the severe poverty, and breathing in the thick air of want, coupled with the realization that such a miserable existence might have been hers, caused Judy's stomach to ache, as if she had been gouged with a steel-toed boot. *How can people live like this?* A sudden wave of nausea swept through her, forcing her outside for fresh air.

After visiting his godmother, Joe took the family to Tatabanya's Gerecse Mountain to view the largest bird statue in Central Europe - the magnificent bronze bird wearing a crown: The Turul Bird- perched atop a high stone mound.

The mythological Turul Bird was of paramount significance to the mythical origins of the Magyars (Hungarian people). According to

Hungarian legend, it is a messenger of God. The bird, a massive falcon, representing God, sits on top of the Tree of Life guarding birds (the spirits of unborn children). In his massive talons, the bird holds the Divine Sword of God.

As they viewed the bronze masterpiece, Joe explained to his children, "At one time there were three Turul bird statues in Hungary, before the borders of the country were changed during World War I, during the Treaty of Trianon - that is when Hungary lost a lot of her lands. Did you know this bird's wingspan is almost forty-nine feet across!"

It was a transcendental moment in time for Judy as she stood in the shadow of the Turul bird's great, protective wings, the significance of the bird's meaning to the Hungarian people, to *her* people, engraining itself in her soul. She found herself being pulled by unseen forces to an area away from the others, to a place where the land stopped, a valley dropped below, and the sun-drenched blue sky with its dazzling puffs of white clouds soared overhead. Surveying the panorama before her, Judy inhaled deeply, taking the clean mountain air into the depths of her lungs.

For the first time since arriving in the land of her birth, Judy's eyes reveled in the gorgeously gratifying landscape of the *True Hungary* before her. The voices of her family and relatives drifted away as the welcoming winds from the valley below swept up the mountainside, enveloping their ethereal arms about her. Before her color-drenched eyes spread a vast universe of magnificent mountainous terrain, its layers covered in bluish haze, spreading mile after perpetual mile, across great sweeping plains of greenery, entrenched with numerous types of trees and diverse mounds of color – the expanse of which seemed boundless. The feel of timeworn ages wove its cloak heavily about her shoulders and she welcomed the comforting weight of the ancient mantle.

This view is what the ancient Magyars witnessed as they stood proud on this high terrain.

All the past lives lived in this land and all those whose lives were lost in wars of gain and wars of loss called out to her: *You are home, your blood is our blood!*

Judy stood motionless, facing the invisible breezes carrying the sacred spirits of her kinsman through her being. Unseen messengers from centuries past touched her skin, airing themselves through every breath she breathed, seeding themselves in her soul. The hidden harbingers of eons past filled Judy's spirit with an extraordinary understanding and appreciation of the unfathomable love her parents had for this country - her country. She and her parents, no matter where they lived in this world, would be forever rooted to the rocks, dust, soil, and waters of this primal realm.

I am happy I came back home. I am proud to be Hungarian, to be Magyar, to be part of this hallowed and divine land.

The following week, Joe provided his family and relatives a splendid vacation at the world-famous sparkling Lake Balaton resort. Sun-drenched, lazy days, with nothing to do but play in the shimmering waters, sunbathe on the lake's shore, and consume the finest meals. In the evenings, the men gathered to share stories of the past, and the women to talk women-talk.

Liz and the girls had packed huge suitcases filled with "left-over" elegant suits, gowns, shoes, opera length gloves, hair pieces, and tiaras to dress their female relatives in style for their final extravaganza - an evening dinner at the Hilton. Joe had also packed several "unwanted" suits for his male relatives. The clothes were not old or worn, but simply had become "boring" to the current owners, but to those who had never known the luxury of such fine goods, they were the most beautiful pieces of attire they had ever placed on their person.

Once more, a long table spread with numerous culinary delights highlighted their final evening at the Budapest Hilton. The violinists serenaded the ladies, and again, the strains of the *Czárdás* floated in the air. The food and dancing extended into the early morning hours.

And, as before Joe requested the musicians to line up in honor formation as the family departed the evening's celebrations.

The musicians ecstatically moved their bows to the strains of Joe's favorite, "*Rákóczi* March," as the family's processional exited the Hilton reception room, with Joe pausing at the pocket of each violinist filling the empty void with a more than generous gratuity.

The day to return to the United States came sooner than expected. The Hungarian families escorted the *American* family to the airport. No one could tell if fate would allow them another time together. Joe and Liz had fulfilled their dream of seeing "their Hungary" not only once, but twice. Their trip to Hungary had been a beautiful dream, but all dreamers must eventually awaken, and all enchantment eventually ends, as the reality of everyday living must begin again.

In late August of 1979. Joe and family were driving with Sonny, taking him to a prestigious, military college.

At the college campus, Joe helped Sonny carry a few "allowed" belongings to his assigned barrack. It was a sterile, barren, small room to be shared with another male student. A twin bed clung to each side wall and a locker was placed against the back wall. The room had a simple concrete floor and pale, gray walls. Sonny dropped the bedding given to him by the school officials onto his cot and sat down upon its squeaky frame. Liz and the girls had already said their goodbyes and were waiting in the van, for the all-male school did not allow females in the barracks.

A violin serenade for Liz at the Budapest Hilton - 1979

Joe sat down beside his "little boy." And to Joe, that is who he was, his *little boy*. But in truth, his son was a confident, yet uncertain young man: uncertain if he had made the right choice, yet still wanting to pursue that choice. "Sonny, you don't have to do this. You can come home and go to a local college. I don't even care if you go to college. I just want you to be happy." Joe looked deep into Sonny's face, trying to find answers that eluded him.

Why did his son want to have such a rigid life, not to mention the rigors of a tough, military curriculum? As if he could read his father's thoughts, Sonny responded, "Dad, I really want to be here. It's going to be good for me. You know I'm not too handy around the house, it's even difficult for me to mow grass in a straight line! *I need this!*"

Joe hugged his son firmly to his chest. "I love you Sonny. You can accomplish and do anything about the house, or anywhere you choose, all you need is more experience! Your mother and I love you with all our hearts. We'll support you no matter what happens. If you want to come home, if this place is not for you, please phone us!" A bleary-eyed Sonny placed his hands on his father's shoulders, "I'll be okay Dad. It will be an adventure!" An adventure? Yes, it would be that. Joe knew only too well how much he had always yearned for a good adventure. His son, apparently, was to be no different.

"They called this *Hell Week*, but I thought it was just a metaphor!" thought Sonny, as he endured his first week at college. The college brochures looked exciting and fun, but he had no conception of how physically and mentally demanding his life would be. The day after his arrival, Sonny and dozens of other new recruits received their school uniforms, rifles, had their hair shorn off to the scalp, and went through class orientation and military training exercises. The upper-class cadets instructed the newcomers in the basics of military training and discipline, forcing the new students to do intense physical exercises consisting of push-ups, sit-ups, stomach crunches, and long runs. They were trained to shine shoes, polish brass, make their beds, keep their rooms in order, clean barracks, march, drill, salute and learn rifle basics. Freshman were expected to carry out all orders without questioning.

All this activity made Sonny very hungry by mealtimes, but even then, there was no peace to be found, for even during meals the upper classmen questioned freshman about the college. The topic could be anything, even on the type of flowers planted on the front lawn. If Sonny did not know the answer, he was expected to know the answer by the next mealtime.

Sonny ached to lean back in his chair to relax while he ate, but such luxury was not allowed. All new recruits had to sit stiffly upright, their "behinds" riding only on the first three inches of their chair. They also were expected to serve meals to the upper classmen.

Sonny continued in this manner for the first year of his college life. He had wanted to call home many times and tell his father "Get me out of here! This place is crazy!" But if he went home and just gave up, where would he go? What kind of work would he do? Besides, if thousands of others before him could make it through this "Hell School," so could he.

Sonny concluded the entire thing was just a "game," much like chess. He was the pawn and the upper classmen were the "more important pieces." The whole point of the "game" was not to be kicked off the chess board. Sonny steeled his mind. Every harsh, barked order became a gentle, "please." Every ache in his body became "an imaginary pain." He blocked out the mental and physical discomfort. Sonny's tactics worked to his advantage. The hesitant, uncertain boy was gone forever, for Sonny had placed an impenetrable steel band around his heart and mind that no outsider invader could break.

There was an optical center within the pharmacy where Judy worked. They were looking for an "optical technician trainee." Judy encouraged Pilvia to apply for the position and she was offered the job. Pilvia obtained her optician's license and excelled in filling eyeglass prescriptions, grinding lenses and fitting frames for customers. It was the perfect niche for her! Judy now worked as a medical transcriptionist in a local hospital, blossoming in her chosen field.

In the early spring of 1981, Joe was relaxing on the family room sofa, glancing through the newspaper on a warm and sunlit Sunday morning. An ad caught his eye. "Timeshare suite vacations now available at the Breckenridge Hotel."

"Hmmm, that sounds like a great idea," thought Joe. "It would be great to have a permanent place to stay at the beach!" Liz was in the backyard hanging freshly washed clothes on the clothesline. Joe walked outside to assist her with hanging out the towels. After the last piece was hung, and the two were going back inside, Joe placed his arms around Liz, "My *Edes*, get dressed, we're going for a drive!"

The hotel had an airy, light-filled lobby, with dozens of palms and tropical plants adorning every corner. There was a posh restaurant on its lower level, and an intimate, small bar with live music every evening.

The hotel suite Joe decided upon was a corner room with a full "mini" kitchen, dining table, full bath, sofa bed, and a "Murphy bed" which could be hidden in the wall during the day to provide extra living space. Sliding glass doors led to a large balcony overlooking the pool, and a view of the white sandy beach and turquoise sea. The family decided upon the third week of July to be "their week" at the hotel each year, beginning that very July. Judy inquired, "Daddy, there really isn't enough room for all five of us to sleep in the room. Can we take turns?"

Joe nodded. "Well, I figured that whoever has time off during "our week" can use the room and enjoy the beach. Judy could stay with Pilvia, or Sonny with a friend, or just your mother and I could spend time together. The resort is there for whoever has the time to use it that week!"

The thought of having a *hotel room to themselves* had never occurred to the kids. Judy's mind whirred, "This is even better than I thought it would be!"

July arrived quickly. The question of who would use the timeshare came into discussion. Joe was attending a training school for his company in the Atlanta area that week, Pilvia was going on a cruise with a girlfriend, and Sonny was involved in other pursuits. Judy was working every day at the hospital, but she had a plan. "I'll just move into the hotel for the week, drive to work from there, and drive back to the hotel after work. I'll spend every evening at the beach!"

Judy's anticipation escalated as her timeshare week approached, and then, the day finally arrived. After enjoying a sundrenched day with her mother in the family pool, and still wearing her wet, sky-blue bikini, Judy went to her condo to pack numerous types of clothes suitable for work and beach, as well as foodstuffs, loading them into the back of her Mustang Cobra for the forty-minute drive to the Breckenridge Hotel.

It was nearly 7 p.m. by the time Judy deposited her belongings in her suite. "Oh! I forgot to bring in a bag of clothes from the car!" Still wearing her bikini with its gauzy cover-up, Judy walked to her car, gathered up the forgotten bag, and walked through the hotel lobby toward the elevator. Looking ahead, Judy could see a good-looking man waiting at the elevators. He was tall and lean, yet a strong muscular build was evident beneath the confines of his grass-green polo shirt.

The elevator bell rang signaling its arrival. Judy hurried to catch her conveyance. The man had picked up his bags and was entering the elevator. *I've got to hurry, please don't let me miss that elevator!*

The hotel halls were air-conditioned, and Judy was becoming chilled as the cool air swept against her slightly damp swimwear. She quickened her pace and made it on board the lift just as the doors were closing; however, she and "the man" were the only ones on board.

Something about him made Judy feel uneasy. But it was not fear. It was deep attraction. His hair was light brown, parted down the middle, and rather long, nearly down to his shoulders, but still very neat-looking. *He is so handsome. I've got to say something before we get to my floor!*

Putting on her sweetest smile, she broke the silence. "Do you have a timeshare here?" The man turned his head toward her. "No, I'm here on business," he replied through a broad smile, outlined by a neatly trimmed mustache. His soothing, light Southern accent resonated through her like a gentle breeze. This man looked different than other men. He did not have the appearance of a "tough or macho guy." Like his voice, his countenance was more that of a "Southern Gentleman." His gray-blue eyes were like magnets and Judy could not help being pulled into them. A surge of excitement rushed through Judy's body. *What is it about this man? Why am I drawn to him?* It was one of those moments when a few seconds in time seemed to go on forever. Judy was shaken out of her trance by the opening of the elevator door.

Feeling flustered by her attraction to the handsome stranger, Judy could barely utter, "Well …I hope you have a nice stay …while you are here." She felt silly after saying the remark. Is that the best she could do to discover more about him? The metal doors opened. She stepped across the threshold to her floor, the motorized sound of the door closing echoing behind her. Before the doors sealed shut, she heard his compelling voice call out to her, "I'm in room 412! Call me if you'd like to go to dinner sometime!" His voice faded away and the elevator continued its upward climb. *I should have told him my room number!*

The next day was Monday. Judy drove to the hospital for another exciting day of medical transcription, but her mind was still at the Breckenridge – on him. She was to go on a date with a radiologist from the hospital that evening, but had made up her mind to cancel, determined to find out more about her mysterious "Southern Gentleman."

Judy drove back to the hotel that afternoon. After settling down, her eyes kept drifting to the phone on the nightstand. *Well, it would just be dinner. Nothing else would come of it.*

Her fingers quickly dialed his room number, 4 – 1 – 2. She held her breath. The phone rang five times. *He must not be in his room.* Her disappointed thoughts were interrupted by a hearty, "Hello!"

Suddenly she was lost for words. What does one say when one wants to go out to dinner with a total stranger! Judy felt as if it was taking forever to get her words out, "Umm …is this the gentleman who offered to take me out to dinner? This is the blonde who met you on the elevator." The man's excited voice answered her inquiry, "Yes, yes, it is! But wait… you don't know anything about me. I'll come to your room to introduce myself, and then you can decide if you want to go out with me!" He sounded sincere - and so nice! Judy was thrilled, "Can you come to my room around 6 p.m.?"

A soft knocking sounded upon the door of Judy's suite. Not knowing why, maybe out of nerves, Judy took a quick peep through the door's "spy hole." Yes, it was him!

Judy had groomed herself before his visit: showering, washing her hair, applying her makeup just right, and vigorously brushing her teeth! She had decided upon a pair of tight-fitting, white, hip-hugger pants to accentuate her hips, and a yellow midriff top to show off her trim tummy.

Holding her breath, she slowly opened the door. He leisurely sauntered into the entryway with confidence and assurance. His manly presence was overwhelming. Judy was speechless, but it didn't matter, for he spoke first. "Hi, my name is Charles - Charles Bean!" Judy was captivated by his gleaming blue eyes. "I'm Judy Bognar. I'm so glad you came to introduce yourself." In a relaxed stance, with hands on hips, Charles continued, "Since, you don't know anything about me, I felt you should know who you are going out with!"

Still standing just inside the door's entryway, he proceeded with his introduction, "I'm from North Carolina. I'm here on business to attend classes on repairing dialysis machines. Back home, I'm the supervisor in the dialysis department, doubling as a dialysis technician and dialysis machine repairman in the hospital where I work - I've even got my own office!"

Anything *medical* fascinated Judy and she instantly felt on even ground with him. Charles continued, "I'm here with several other students for a one-week training session on how to repair the latest dialysis machines and then it's back home I go!"

Judy told Charles about living in a condo, her parents and family, where she was born, how she came to be in the United States, about working in a hospital as a medical transcriptionist, and of her timesharing plan at the Breckenridge Hotel for this week.

The rest of the conversation blurred in her mind. The energy of the statuesque man's presence saturated every ion within her body, electrified every cell of her essence, and something about his mannerism infused her mind with memories of a love from long ago thought forever to be lost. Watching his face, his demeanor, his body language, hearing his gentle voice, and feeling as if his eyes could see right through her, as if he could sense her most private thoughts, sent Judy's mind whirling back in time – to a time of that *wonderful feeling*.

Charles' voice snapped her back to the present. His towering 6-feet 2-inch frame made Judy conscious of her delicate vulnerability. He reached out and took one of her hands in his. "You are so beautiful!

Before I leave, may I kiss you on the cheek?" Judy's head swam. Was this man for real? No man had ever *asked* her permission for *anything* ... a feeling suddenly engulfed her, a feeling from many years ago ... on a schoolyard bench.

"Yes ..., yes, you may," she softly replied. His lips were velvety soft and warm, and the tingle of his soft mustache against her face flooded her body with warmth. Her legs were lost beneath her, her head felt light, and her entire being was bathed in memories of a faraway time when love was new, and anything was possible.

I can't believe I feel this way and all he's done is put his lips on my cheek. I wonder how it would be if he ...

Charles made his way out the door, jarring Judy back to the present, "I'll see you soon! I'll be back in fifteen minutes to take you wherever you would like to go!"

They enjoyed dinner and dancing in one of the hotel's more intimate restaurants. Charles was enamored with the girl sitting beside him. *How could a girl of such obvious fine raising be even remotely interested in me?*

Charles did not realize it, but he epitomized all Judy had been seeking in a man: he was handsome (although he did not know it), witty, kind-hearted, charming, self-assured, intelligent, outgoing, was a musician (having played the drums professionally for years during the 1960's), and most important of all– Judy could not help but adore him. The evening flew by with hours of deep thoughtful conversation, laughter, and dancing.

It was nearing time for the restaurant to close, but Judy did not want the evening to end. She dared to be forward, "Charles, would you like to come back to my room with me?" She could not help but ask, for the man with the smiling eyes fascinated her.

Charles' presence had erupted the dormant, hungry ravenousness of the hidden longing and passion locked away in Judy's heart for nearly a decade. And Charles felt the same, for he, also, was awakening from a quiescent sleep into the arms of smoldering ecstasy. On this euphoric, sparkling night, the *Love* Judy believed forever lost to her was at last found, softly entwining about her heart on the arms of softly scented sea breezes swirling through the open balcony doors of her hotel suite, the invisible couriers of love undulating about she and Charles, entangling them in a long-awaited web of longing and desire.

Charles' classes at the hotel were finished each day at 4 p.m. just as Judy arrived back to the Breckenridge Hotel from her workday at the hospital.

The long, lazy days of July provided plenty of hours of sparkling sunshine until nearly 9:30 p.m. Charles obtained the use of a catamaran from his dialysis instructor, a local resident, and he and Judy set sail from the white sandy shore. The billowing sail cut the craft swiftly through the waves as the Gulf's salty spray misted their skin. Charles expertly steered the craft through the blue-green sea; but found it hard to concentrate with Judy sitting only inches from him, noticing her eyes to be the same color as the ocean about her.

Charles was a self-made man, coming from the humble beginnings of a loving, but very poor family, growing up in a dilapidated farmhouse, with a yard consisting of nothing more than a dried-out, powdery turf to play upon. As a young boy, he frequently spoke to the heavens as he walked the dusty, brown backroads of his North Carolina home, with cardboard tucked inside the soles of his worn-out shoes to keep the jagged gravel from stabbing his feet, asking God to help him find a way to rise above the poverty of his current existence. Charles asked God to deliver only four things for his life in exchange for him working hard to achieve those goals: "Let me live long enough to make a better life for myself, to marry a beautiful woman, to have a home on many acres of fine land surrounded by a lush, green lawn, and to know the joys of being a father. After I have those things, you can do as you wish with me."

God had granted Charles a way out of his poverty, and now, God had granted Charles the perfect woman he had always envisioned himself being with, the woman who would be at his side to help him build the life of his dreams. As Charles commandeered the mast of the catamaran, he could not help but wonder, *what in the world does she see in me?* as his eyes followed the silken strands of Judy's long, blonde hair floating on the ocean breeze.

"How many years have you been an expert at sailing a catamaran?" Judy inquired, for she could see how adept Charles was in handling the craft.

"Oh, this is the first time I've ever sailed one of these," replied Charles nonchalantly. Judy noticed they were quite a distance from shore and this new piece of information made her anxious. Seeking an excuse to return to land, Judy suggested, "Well, maybe it's time we head back to grab a bite to eat." In truth, the waves were becoming excessively choppy, inviting the warm sea to spill over her thighs. Judy nervously surveyed her surroundings. *I hope there are no sharks out here*!

As if Charles could read her mind, he assured her, "We'll be back to the beach in no time," and he was good to his word. He swung the sail about and within five minutes they were pulling the "*cat*" onto the sandy beach.

After dinner they held hands while walking along the seashore. Charles' confident presence exuded an aura of strength, making Judy feel safe and secure. He was manly, sexy and sure of himself and she admired his "take charge," attitude, and his sweet boyish charm. Her search was over.

The week passed all too quickly and soon it was time for Charles to return to North Carolina. But, during their final night together, Charles held Judy close, kissing her lips, her neck, her shoulders, sending shudders of rapturous elation through her.

Was it possible to love a stranger, a man she had just met, without knowing "all about him?" Her heart yelled "Yes!" And, her brain agreed, even when common sense should have yelled, "No!" She had loved him the first time his lips brushed her face. He had loved her since the moment in the elevator.

Holding her close in the darkness of his room, Charles could no longer hold back the truth of his emotions, "Judy, I love you. I know you think I'm crazy, but I feel as if we've known each other forever, like we have met before, somewhere in a prior lifetime."

Judy placed her arms about Charles' broad shoulders, "I love you too Charles. I feel the same. I know our feelings are possible, because my parents and their parents felt the same way when they first met. I think it is a sign that we were supposed to meet, that we are supposed to be together. I *do* come from a very long line of *hopeless romantics*! My mother always told me that one simply knows when love enters their heart! I have waited a very long time to find you… far too long of a time to find you, and I don't want to wait for you any longer."

Charles pulled Judy closer to the warmth of his chest, "My life was empty till I saw you. I felt we were meant for each other the moment you looked into my eyes, but I was afraid you would think I was out of my mind if I had told you how I felt in those few seconds of time in the elevator!"

Judy lifted her eyes towards the face of the man holding all her dreams. "I did feel your thoughts, and the very moment I got off the elevator, I regretted not staying on it with you. I should have said something more!"

"Then, you must stay with me, always," begged Charles. Judy's lips flitted over his cheek, "I know I will stay with you forever!"

Judy drove Charles to the Tampa airport. Their departing embrace sought to defy separation. As he boarded his flight, Charles called out to her, I'll be back before you know it and we *will* be married!"

The family flocked to attend Sonny's college graduation in May of 1982. Joe and Liz hearts swelled with elation: their only son had graduated Suma Cum Laude, second in his class.

Liz sat amongst the throngs of happy parents, strikingly lovely in her pale blue suit, edged with a white sweetheart neckline. Pinned to her lapel was a 5 x7 portrait of Sonny in dress uniform so all could see her "pride and joy." Sonny's outstanding academic and military skills had earned him entrance into the military directly from college as a First Lieutenant, and soon, Sonny would go far from home, to Panama, his first assigned post. It was difficult for Joe and Liz to accept the fact that their little boy was now a man, destined to make his own way in the world, but they knew it was the way life was, but that fact did not lessen the pain. The children were leaving the nest.

Judy married Charles in a small, private ceremony in October of 1982 and moved to North Carolina. In Florida, Pilvia's career was thriving in the optical industry, and, after Judy moved to North Carolina, Pilvia moved into Judy's condo. Sonny, stationed in Panama, excelled in his military career.

Liz missed her son and flew to visit Sonny a couple of times while he was in Panama. It was a beautiful place with a climate and ocean-side scenery reminiscent of Florida. Panama - how ironic that Sonny should be there, that she should be on the same island where Jay had spent his time while loving her daughter. Her "other son" had lived here and now her son. What it all meant she did not know, maybe nothing, maybe something, but while there, she envisioned Jay, young and beautiful amongst the tropical flora, alive and happy.

In early March of 1984, Joe searched the classifieds for a new job. He was basically happy with his present position, but he wanted more: he wanted to be "the boss." With the expertise and knowledge gained in the electronics field, Joe knew he was more than capable of achieving far greater things. Every Sunday, Joe sought his next "perfect job."

One ad grabbed his attention: "Seeking manager for large corporate electronics store with opportunity for advancement to general manager within a year. Excellent salary - will pay moving expenses for right candidate."

Joe and Liz had achieved a comfortable lifestyle with their combined work efforts, but the memory of Liz falling at work a few years ago and injuring her back still loomed in the back of his mind. Both were getting older, and he did not want his wife lifting heavy food trays in the "fish house" for many more years.

The only way to keep Liz at home was for him to draw a larger salary, and perhaps, this ad was his way to that goal. It was still early that Sunday morning. Liz was sleeping in as she did not get home till late the night before from work. "Well, it's sure worth a shot, what have I got to lose?" thought Joe. He took out a paper and pen and began composing an extensive resume.

In about an hour he had all the details in place and settled down at his IBM Selectric typewriter to type up the final copy. Joe dropped off the resume and cover letter in a manila envelope at the local post office via certified mail on his way to work the next day.

It was a sun-saturated, Saturday morning near the end of March. Joe and Liz had spent the day planting new marigolds and geraniums in the yard. Joe had forgotten to check the mail until late afternoon having been engrossed in designing new flower beds about the house.

Joe sauntered to the mailbox, and within, found a letter from "the other company." Standing outside in the warm sun, he tightly gripped the bright white envelope in his hands, attempting to soothe feelings of disappointment ahead of time, in case it was "bad news."

"If they rejected me it *is* their loss, who cares…" With that, Joe read the envelope's contents, "We received your resume and are very impressed with your qualifications for the position of manager in one of our corporate stores. We would like to arrange a meeting for an interview on …"

Wedding day for Judy and Charles - October 1982

Liz and Joe in Florida - 1983

Joe clutched the letter to his chest, his mind spinning wildly at a thousand revolutions a second. *They want to interview me?* Joe could barely contain himself as he ran back into the house, shouting, "Liz! Liz! I need to talk with you!"

ATLANTA

The interview was a stunning success. Joe was moving to Atlanta, Georgia, beginning his new career as a manager with a nationally established electronics chain.

Two years earlier, Joe had purchased a motorhome, mainly using it for visits to Judy in North Carolina and overnight trips to the seashore. Joe would use the motor home (with his personal car in tow) as a temporary residence while he looked for a new house. Liz was to stay behind in Florida to help with the sale of the house and direct the organization of packing their belongings.

Liz was elated for Joe's success, happy that soon, she would not have to work late nights carrying heavy food trays; however, she could not help feeling apprehensive about the move.

Florida was lush, tropical and warm nearly all the year. Florida was where their lives had taken hold and blossomed, where their American dream was finally realized, where the brightest and most joyful of times were shared as a family, and where Judy and Jay had shared their love. It would be difficult to leave the home filled with those memories.

Joe's store was grandiose, packed to the brim with every electronic device, gadget and computer system imaginable. And, for the first time in his career, Joe had his own office on the second floor, allowing him a wide, panoramic view of the facility below through its floor to ceiling windows.

Forty employees were under his supervision. During his first two weeks as manager, Joe had one-on-one meetings with each employee. Many confessed to Joe that prior management had been brash and callous. Joe eased their fears, assuring the workers that under his guidance, the employee/management relationship would be far more conducive to a happier work environment. Joe was very business-like and to-the-point, but his genuine, fair, caring attitude towards his team members created a sense of "family." In the following two months, with Joe at the wheel of his store, production, sales, and employee morale soared.

Joe dedicated all his spare time to house-hunting. He came upon a new housing development in the Cherokee County area. Most of the homes were comprised of at least four stories, including the garage level. The house Joe decided upon was nearing completion. Located in a cul-de-sac, the three-thousand square foot home sat on a three-quarter acre wooded lot filled with fragrant Georgia pines, and to his surprise, a small sparkling stream ran through the back yard.

On further exploration of the cedar home, he noted an oversized double-car garage with stairs leading to a second level with entry to an enormous family room, sun room, half-bath, and a room Joe dubbed his "music room and office." Another short flight of steps led Joe to formal living and dining areas, an eat-in kitchen, and beyond sliding glass doors, an enormous deck for entertaining. There were windows galore. Bright sunlight transfused the structure's interior, directing Joe's eyes to a large stone fireplace. And still, another set of stairs led to a hallway with two guest bedrooms, another bath, and a master suite with an adjoining bath.

"There's tons of storage space everywhere and there's plenty of space for all the kids when they come to visit!" rationalized Joe. "Liz deserves to live in such a luxurious and spacious home." He struck a deal that week with the builder, and just in time, for the Florida house had been sold.

The next weekend Joe took a flight to Florida, driving back to Atlanta with Liz in their second car. The moving van was to meet them at their home in two days. The journey went smoothly.

After the moving company deposited the final containers in the garage, Joe and Liz held hands, as they slowly walked up to the top of their long, concrete driveway to take in a bird's-eye view of their property. "It is a pretty place, Joe," sighed Liz, "Thank you for all you have done to make this possible."

Joe pulled Liz closer to him. "Yes, it is beautiful. More than I ever expected to find for us." Liz burrowed closer to Joe, her head coming to rest against his shoulder, "Everything will be all right for us now, right Joe?"

Sensing her fear of being in a new, strange place, Joe wanted to ease her doubts. "My *Pillango*, don't you know that as long as we are together, everything will always be wonderful. Think back about all we have accomplished over the last twenty-eight years? We survived a lot worse than a move to Atlanta!"

Liz turned to Joe, "It is just that everything here is different, but I will learn what I need to learn as I did when I first came to America. As long as I can find the grocery store and get back home, I will be fine!" Joe kissed his wife's forehead. "Yes, everything will be perfect from now on."

Life in Florida had become reliable and predictable. Even the seas Joe had navigated in Florida's sparkling waters had become as easy to chart as a trip to the grocery store, but now, they were standing on alien turf. Not one inch of ground was explored. It was an "unknown land," just as it had been all those years ago when they first arrived in Camp Kilmer.

It was May of 1984. Their old life in Florida, with all its joys, pain, laughter and tears would now become a memory, the same as their lives in Hungary. It was a time to start fresh. Their children were grown and living their own lives, as it should be. It was their time now, a time to learn new things and build from the experiences of each new day.

The couple held hands as the sun's final rays swept across the Atlanta skyline. They were at the threshold of a new adventure. The infinite journey called "life" was marching on.

Liz found the move to Atlanta exceptionally difficult. Joe had not considered the "environmental shock" the move would create upon on his wife. A week after the move, Liz was beyond homesick for the beauty of her Florida home.

Over the past few years, Joe had traveled to the thriving Atlanta metropolis several times on business and was accustomed to its sights and sounds, but everything was "too much concrete and not enough green" for Liz.

For fourteen years Liz had flung wide the doors to her intercoastal waterway home inviting the invisible, refreshing, salty oceanic breezes to swirl through its rooms. How she had enjoyed hanging her freshly washed laundry on the clothesline out by the poolside to be dried by ocean breezes and bright sunshine! The tropical weather had invited her to take year-round "dips" in the backyard pool, as the weightless sensation of floating on liquid arms, was a feeling she never tired of.

Every day, Liz saw Joe off to work, leaving her, alone, to "make them a home" out of the countless boxes placed in each room by the movers. The master bedroom and the kitchen area were the only rooms she and Joe had set up for their immediate needs of living. The house was spacious and elegant; however, Liz did not feel it was "home."

Everything was different: cooking in the new kitchen, sleeping in a new room, having three sets of stairs to negotiate to access different parts of the house. It was like adopting a new child and learning how to create a loving bond with the child.

Why was this loving bond so difficult to come to her? Because of grief. She missed being cocooned in the comforting cradle of her former domain. She mourned for the memories encased within the walls of her old house - memories of a time now lost to her forever. Liz could not be selfish - Joe had finally won the job of his dreams and she did not want to stand in the way of his success. It would be difficult to make this house her home, but she was determined to try.

The idea of making Joe happy pushed Liz into a decorating hysteria. Each day for approximately two months, after Joe left for work, Liz kept her mind and body energized as she delved into the organization of her cache.

Then, one day it happened – all her treasures had been placed into their appropriate spots. There was nothing more to unpack or put away or rearrange. Liz gazed about her surroundings. It *was* a very large home and it *was* very beautiful inside and out, but she still felt "confined." Her "tropical home" had been a mere street away from the intercoastal waterway. Her heart ached to feel and smell the fragrant, fresh, sea breezes!

Despite the austerity of her former occupation, Liz had enjoyed the drive to work over the wide expanses of drawbridges towering the intercoastal waterway. The watery highway was home to hundreds of colorful sailboats and motor boats making their way beneath the bowed expanse of metal as they tooted their melodic horns in greeting to one another as Liz crossed its spans. During those days, the invigorating sounds and scents of the ocean were only minutes away, and now, Liz could only reminisce about the magnificent sunsets on Clearwater Beach, remembering the glorious sight of the bright ball of warmth sliding into the waves as it departed the Florida-side of the world for the evening.

Even going to the grocery store had been a carefree expedition. Liz would simply throw on a beach "cover up" over her swimsuit and jump into her car to join hundreds of other shoppers walking down the aisles wearing the same attire. Here, in this city of concrete, there was no more nearby beach to view the pink and purple evening sunsets, and no more carefree swimsuit jaunts to the store – it was simply *not* done in this corner of the world. She now lived in a cul-de-sac, at the bottom of a hill, in the middle of a housing development, with no ocean breezes, and when wisps of air did sweep in, the choked congestion of the bustling city came with them. Liz felt stagnant, not just from the stale environment, but because she was bored.

Joe had not considered one important fact: that since their beginnings in America, Liz's mind and body had grown accustomed to a challenging schedule and physical work - thriving on meeting the deadlines ahead of her each day. And Liz was lonely. She missed the social interaction with her friends in the restaurant and greeting new and old clients in the same setting. She was a stranger to Atlanta with no one to speak to during the day, except for a few quick exchanges with those she met at the grocery store a few times a week.

Joe left early for work each day and most times came home after 9 p.m., making every day a long day for Joe, and especially long for Liz. Joe phoned Liz during his breaks and at lunch. For those few brief moments during the day, all was well, for Liz was happy and excited to hear about her husband's daily adventures; however, Liz's zest for life fell by the wayside as autumn approached. Darkness came early to the landscape further adding to her depression.

Joe was not blind to the physical and emotional changes in his wife. Her eyes were encased in dark circles and her appetite waned. He was more than aware of her not being happy in Atlanta. He knew she missed her old life. But what was done was done. He could not bring their old way of living back. There was no more Florida job or Florida house. He could have kicked himself for not thinking things through. He should have known Liz was happy *for him*, but not happy for *herself*. Yes, he wanted to kick himself a thousand times for leaving Florida. Liz had been "alive" there and now only "existed" here. In his heart, Joe knew Liz always agreed to do anything he wanted to do, because she wanted *him to be happy*.

"This is my fault," thought Joe, as he drove to work one morning, "If only I had stayed in Florida and gone on the way I was. I could have retired from my Florida job doing what I was doing, and Liz would have been happier. She has never cared about her own needs or wants. She's sacrificing her happiness, so I can have mine."

There were hundreds of "If I had only, and, if I had just" thoughts running through Joe's mind every day. To make things worse, Liz was going through "the change of life," which further exacerbated her depression and moodiness.

Another reason for Liz's sad mood was Sonny. While stationed in Panama, Sonny had met a Panamanian girl, fell in loved and married. Joe and Liz did not know of his marriage until they received the call with the "good news." Why Sonny did not tell them of his upcoming marriage was speculative. He may have feared rejection or disapproval of his choice. He may not have understood that being the "only son," his parents may have had expectations and visions of being present at his marriage. He may not have understood that his parents would have been delighted in being part of such a momentous occasion in the family's history, and that perhaps, his parents felt "left out" in being able to be part of such a monumental moment in time.

Joe and Liz reasoned that maybe their son had become "too caught up in the moment" of his own happiness and excitement about getting married, and simply "did not think" about contacting his family. But, despite their disappointment, knowing their son was happy, made them happy. There was nothing to do now but to accept what had been done. Their son was married to a girl who spoke only Spanish and was of the Mormon faith. Did their son accept that faith also?

Thanksgiving was soon upon them. Judy missed her parents and asked Charles to drive her to Atlanta as she wanted to prepare the holiday dinner for her family. Joe greeted his daughter and son-in-law as they alighted from their car in the driveway, hugging and kissing his *Csimby*, and "bear-hugging" Charles.

Liz had not come out to see them as they arrived. "Daddy, where's Mama?" inquired Judy. The mention of his wife opened a sore wound for Joe. Speaking slowly, staring downward at the concrete driveway beneath his feet, he did his best to explain, "Mama is not well. She hasn't felt well in a while." Joe slowed his pace as he led them into the open garage, for he did not want to go inside to face the gloom residing within. "Daddy, what's wrong?" asked Judy. She knew her father's moods only too well. She could feel the sadness rushing from his being. "Daddy, I've talked to Mama every weekend on the phone and she seemed to be just fine. What happened?" Joe was hesitant to reply, "Your mother has not adjusted well to living here. She misses her old house, her old way of life; she misses *everything* from her old life. I thought she would be happy not worrying about lugging those darn food trays and worrying about falling and hurting her back. I had no idea she would miss her routine so much. I never even thought how being away from the Florida sunshine and ocean would affect her mood. I was only thinking about what I wanted. I thought she would be happy not working, and I hoped she would be happy living in this big beautiful house with no money worries, but I was wrong. On top of all that she is going through menopause and her mind isn't taking it well. I can't make her happy no matter what I do. She is so depressed! If I could dig a hole in the backyard and throw myself in it, I would, and end my misery!"

With that last remark, Joe's broad shoulders heaved, and he let forth a deep, painful moan and tears flowed. He held his hand to his forehead, holding the weight of his head, and staggered slowly toward the family room door. Alarmed, Judy rushed to support her father's sagging form.

"Daddy, you only did what you thought was best! No one could have foreseen how Mama's mind would accept all the changes! She loves you so much! She'll be fine and eventually get used to her new routine!"

Charles helped Joe up the steps to the family room area where Joe "pulled himself together." Joe turned his tired, red eyes toward Charles and Judy, pleading, "*Please* don't tell your mother what just happened. Just act normal." *Normal? How am I supposed to act normal when my father is going insane with worry about my mother's mental and emotional state?* With those thoughts, Judy made her way up to the living room area, quickly taking in the ambiance of her parent's new home. It was gracefully furnished. Hungarian touches were evident about the home including the placement of fine Herend Porcelain in softly lit glass cabinets, Hungarian lace embroidered doilies placed about on tables, as well as framed photographs of the Hungarian countryside adorning the walls. The spacious living room was elaborately outfitted with new furniture. The space touted a stone fireplace and vaulted ceilings. It was a lovely home!

Judy walked on, making her way through the extravagant kitchen, and could not help but stop to appreciate the fashionable, classic, Queen Anne dining room ensemble and sideboard in the large formal dining room.

She slowly made her way up the parquet staircase to the bedroom level toward the master suite. *Act normal. Dad says to act normal. I'll try, but I have no idea how!*

Judy entered the dark master bedroom. The curtains were drawn shut and it took a few moments for her sundrenched eyes to adjust to the dim light. Her mother lay flat on her back on the king-sized bed, her legs propped up on several pillows. Liz saw her daughter in the doorway and reached out both arms, beckoning her little girl to come closer. Judy sat down beside her mother on the bed, leaned over, and pulled her mother deep within her arms. Burying her face in the crook of her mother's neck, Judy breathed in the delicate aroma of lemon verbena lotion, one of her mother's favorite scents since Judy could remember. The sound of Liz's soft weeping echoed in the room.

"Oh Mommy, I know, I know all about it! Just cry a bit, it will help." Judy cradled her mother in her arms, pulling her petite form close to her bosom. "It's okay Mommy, you can cry. You have had a lot of changes to get used to. Daddy loves you so much and I know you love him, that's why you're here in Atlanta! I'll get us both a glass of water and we'll talk it through."

After about an hour, an exhausted Judy made her way down the stairs to the family room, where Joe and Charlie had deposited themselves. "How's your mother doing," queried a teary-eyed Joe. Charlie's face was sad and drawn, exhausted from the long drive, and the melancholy mood striking him upon his arrival.

Judy spoke as gently and sweetly as her depleted emotional strength allowed, "Daddy, I know you wanted Mommy to stay home and not work, but she really needs to get out of the house and do some type of work, even if only for a few hours a day."

Judy took hold of her father's hand, "She was going to tell you, but was afraid. Mom found a job at a small, private dress shop just up the road and wants to work there about five hours a day. The manager said Mama could start next week, but she was afraid to give the manager a definite 'yes' about the job until she spoke with you. Mama said she would place clothes on the racks and help customers coordinate outfits. She feels it would be good for her to get dressed up nicely every day and get out and meet people."

Joe was shocked, but not in a bad way. "Why in the world didn't she tell me? I don't mind if she goes to work in a dress shop. I was only worried about her lugging fifty-pound trays on her shoulders and falling on wet floors in a dingy restaurant kitchen! If your mother wants to get out and mingle with the world to better adjust to this place. then I want her to! All I *ever* wanted for her was to be happy, that's all… that's all!" With that, Joe's voice faded. His breathing became hard as he wept with relief.

"Mama Liz will be fine Joe," Charles assured, as he sympathetically placed his arm around Joe's shoulder, hugging him firmly. Joe walked over to his daughter, tears of happiness streaming down his tired, pale cheeks, as he gave her a strong embrace, "Your mother can do whatever kind of job she wants. I don't care what it is, as long as it makes her happy!"

As the rough edges between Liz and Joe were at last smoothed over, the Thanksgiving meal Charles and Judy prepared went down wonderfully. Joe was grateful to his daughter and her husband for their loving support. The day after Thanksgiving Liz talked to the dress store manager. Liz was to start her new position the following week, leaving the manager relieved, for she *had* been counting on Liz taking the job, feeling she would be "good for her store." Liz's countenance exuded a continental charm, and, with her European accent and aristocratic air, the manager knew she would be the perfect asset to cater toward her upper-crust clientele.

With her new job in place, it appeared Liz would be a success despite of her so-called "odds" in Atlanta. Judy's timing to visit her parents could not have been better. All that happened during Judy's visit was as if it were preordained. Sometimes, even a child can help a parent find their way.

On the Sunday after Thanksgiving, a happy and lighthearted Joe and Liz stood in their driveway waving goodbye to Judy and Charles as their car blurred out of site. When the vehicle's tail lights had disappeared around the corner, Joe protectively placed his arm about his wife as they walked back to the house, their hearts filled with the hopes of future dreams.

On August 27, 1986, Charles stood at a phone fixture on the wall in the waiting room of a local hospital. His fingers shakily dialed Joe's home number in Atlanta. He had forgotten how to say what he was to say, even though he had played out the scenario of his speech several times in his mind, but now, that the time was here, all prior speeches had been forgotten.

Joe answered the phone. "Hello Charlie, what's going on?" With his heart beating rapidly, hardly able to catch his breath to spill out the words, Charles excitedly blurted out, "You have a grandson! He was born at 7:30 this morning and weighs exactly eight pounds!" Judy had taught Charles the words for grandfather and grandmother in Hungarian, and Charles happily announced to Joe, "Papa Joe - you and Mama Liz are now a *Nagypapa* and a *Nagymama*!"

Joe's mind happily swirled with the realization that this baby boy, his grandson, was the first grandchild to be born in America! Timeworn remembrance quickly swept through his mind, peeling back decades as he recalled the dingy, primitive hospital room where his beautiful Elizabeth lay drenched in laboring sweat for countless hours, her thin body wracked in pain as the new life within her demanded to be born. He recalled holding the pink sweetness of his newborn baby girl in his arms. How her tiny presence brought sparkle and sunshine into their drab world! Now "his baby" had given birth to *her baby*. This was a resplendent moment - a celebration of a new soul joining the family.

The thought of being a grandfather was exhilarating and comforting to Joe. He was only fifty-two years old. Nearly thirty years had passed since leaving Hungary, and now, he had a grandson. It was a major milestone in his life. The profundity of that joy was beyond words. In his grandson, the lineage and timeline of his Magyar ancestors would carry on, Joe felt an elated rush of thankfulness consuming his being, thankfulness for being alive in this paradisiacal moment of time.

Charlie's voice broke through Joe's remembrance, "Papa Joe, are you there?" Joe pushed himself to take hold of his emotions, "Charlie, how is Judy doing? Is she in a lot of pain?"

"Well, as you know, Papa Joe, they found the baby was a breech about a month ago during a sonogram, so thankfully, she never had to go into labor, and it was decided she should have a cesarean section. She is doing great…Judy is strong, like you and Mama Liz! She never complains. When she holds her son, all discomfort disappears."

Joe was enormously relieved his daughter did not have to endure endless hours of suffering as her mother had. "The baby … is the baby all right? Tell me about my grandson!" Charlie sighed contentedly, trying his best to reassure his father-in-law, whom he had grown to love and respect as his own father, "Papa Joe, he has a lot of your features, a real Hungarian! He's got your high cheekbones, your chest, but unfortunately - my legs and feet! He has his mother's hands. Judy says he's perfect! I think he's perfect too! I'm going to the hospital gift shop to grab some cigars to hand out to my friends. I'll save the biggest for you!"

Charlie paused a moment, for he had not heard Mama Liz chime into the conversation. "I love you Papa Joe …is Mama Liz there? May I speak with her?" There was a moment of silence from Joe, "I love you too, Charlie. Mama is not here. She did not feel well today and is sleeping. I will tell her as soon as she wakes up."

"Please, Papa Joe," implored Charlie, "I know much Mama Liz *wanted* this grandchild, how much it meant to her. Tell her Judy and I love her! If she feels better later, we can talk then."

After saying their goodbyes Joe hung up the phone. He envisioned Charlie running up and down the hospital halls doing his "cigar run" as he had done many years ago after the birth of his own son, stuffing cigars into both willing and unwilling hands. Joe let out a long breath, "It has all come full circle now. I only wish my Elizabeth was not in the hospital on this fateful day."

The move to Atlanta, going through the change of life, Sonny's unexpected marriage, and knowing she would become a grandmother all within a two-year period was overpowering for Liz, culminating in an "emotional breakdown."

The wars she had survived, the struggles to build a new life in America, and the recent events of the past few years had targeted her already frail emotional state.

Despite her determined demeanor and ferocity in building a new world with her husband all these many years, Liz's mind was a fragile one. Joe had always known of her tender emotional state but had never let his children know the true brittleness of their mother's psyche. The many childhood scars branded into her brain, were kept compartmentalized away from the life she lived daily, but in her later years, when emotionally stressed, her secret traumatized state, would at times, seep through. During those difficult times, Joe would tell his children "Your mother is tired and needs to rest."

A week before her first grandchild was born, Liz "lost touch with reality," her mind slipping away to a place and time where she only spoke Hungarian. Joe was beside himself with fear for her mental and emotional well-being and admitted her to the hospital. Liz thrashed about uncontrollably in her hospital bed, prompting the doctors to tie her down with restraints for her own self-protection.

Despite numerous tests the doctors could not come up with any reason for her "illness." After the "restraint episode" Joe removed Liz from the hospital and brought her home. Determined she would not undergo such degrading humiliation again, Joe decided to shield his wife from the weight of the world.

It was a hard reality to face: his wife could no longer handle the complexity of life stressors. Joe had told none of the children about their mother's worsening condition, especially not Judy, concerned that knowledge of such could cause Judy to have complications with her pregnancy.

After the baby was born, Judy and Charles had implored Joe on several occasions, to permit them to travel to Atlanta so Liz and he could see their new grandson; however, Joe had to deny them the visit, sorrowfully breaking down, telling Judy the truth about her mother's status. It was a crushing blow for Joe each time he thought of being unable to see and hold his little grandson.

Life was very unfair. On the historic occasion of their first grandchild born in America, Joe and Liz *should* have been at the hospital with their daughter, seeing the baby in the nursery, helping to feed him, assisting in the care of the baby when he came home - all the things that "normal" grandparents do.

The news was terribly distressing to Judy. She felt helpless, wanting desperately to help care for her mother; however, it was impossible as she was still healing from the cut in her belly. "We will come to see our grandson, Charlton, soon," Joe assured her. "Your mother will be better …then we will come." And they did.

That Thanksgiving of 1986, Joe and Liz drove their motorhome to North Carolina. The moment Liz held her three-month-old grandson, and his little fist closed about one of her fingers, she fell hopelessly in love with him.

Liz sat on the couch cradling the baby with Joe beside her, and as Judy and Charles looked on, her happy eyes locked onto those of the innocent soul she held tenderly in her arms. Speaking slowly and gently, Elizabeth spoke to the little grandson resting in her lap, oblivious to all those around her:

My sweet grandson, little Charlton Ashley Bean, I am your Nagymama, your grandmother. I am very sorry I was not there on the day you were born. I wanted to be very much, but I was sick. You are the most special baby, with a unique purpose in this world - the first grandchild in our families to be born in America! What a lineage you have! Your roots are from a proud distinguished heritage. I told your mother when she was a little girl about her birthright, and it is now your birthright also. I will tell you now, and your Mama can tell you again when you are older. You are of noble blood. Your great, great, great grandfather Halasz was a devoted subject to the King of Hungary. The king knighted him, and he married into the royal court. The family coat of arms was brandished onto a "dog skin," and my family held the dog skin a long time. When the many wars came to Hungary, the royal titles were no longer valid, and during the last World War, the dog skin was lost, and all proof of our titles, the existence of our lineage, lost along the way. But we need no proof to see you are regal and majestic. One day through your life and deeds your legacy will be noted. Through your mother's Hungarian heritage, and your father's Scottish heritage, you have a history of generations of brave, fighting people and their courage flows through your veins. I wish I could live forever to help you as you make your way in this world, but I know you must make your own way. Remember- trying is not failing. You are the most precious gift God has given to me since the birth of your mother. You are my Drága kincsem (my dearest treasure). I love you with all my heart!

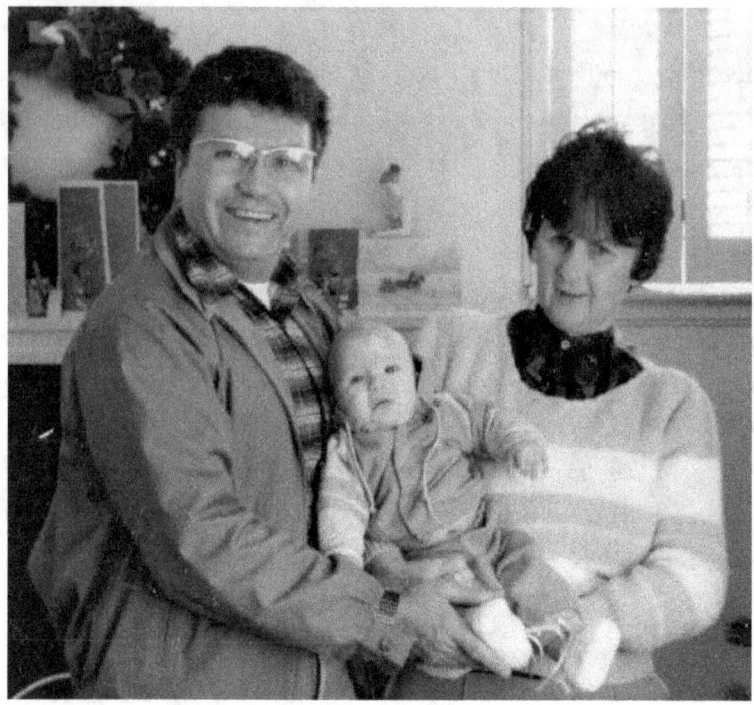

Nagypapa and Nagymama Bognar visit their grandson, Charlton, for the first time - November of 1986

The following May, a daughter was born to Sonny and his wife and the proud grandparents flew out west to visit their new granddaughter.

Since marrying, Sonny was transferred to Salt Lake City, Utah. There, the couple affirmed their "Sealing Ceremony" in the Mormon Temple, but Joe and Liz were not invited. Joe asked a person he worked with (who was Mormon) about Mormon weddings, or "Sealing Ceremonies" at the Temple. He told Joe, that since they were not members of the Church of Latter-Day Saints, they could not have been present at the Temple wedding, anyway, unless they held something called a "Temple Recommend."

As wounded as they were by this knowledge, they held steadfast in their belief that their son's wife most likely wanted to renew her vows in the church (as the couple had a civil ceremony in Panama). Liz understood how important it was for a wife to have a church wedding, remembering how she and Joe had no choice but to marry in the dismal communist magistrate's office in Hungary. "I am sure they just got caught up in the moment about renewing their vows without even thinking that we may have wanted to be there," Liz assured Joe.

Before their move out west, Sonny and his wife visited with Joe and Liz in Atlanta. Even with the Spanish language barrier they formed a good relationship with their new daughter, and she was also making a good effort to learn English. Joe and Liz were frustrated with their son having a post far away in Utah, hoping that one day soon he could be stationed closer to them, because they idolized their only son with all their hearts, and were immensely proud in the knowledge that his children would one day carry on their Hungarian traditions and legacy, and now that legacy had begun with their new granddaughter.

Sonny was always a devoted son to his parents, and Joe and Liz were immensely proud of his tenuous accomplishments. While living at home, Sonny left a note each morning for his mother before departing each day for school on the kitchen table, writing out a simple "I love you, have a good day." He was the most loving and dedicated son a parent could ask for, and upon high school graduation they presented Sonny with a new car: A Pontiac Trans Am.

Charles, Judy and grandson Charlton, had long visits with Nagymama and Nagypapa at least three times a year. During those long, anticipated visits, Joe and Liz doted on their little grandson, cuddling and spoiling him to distraction with lavished attention and countless toys. Sonny visited rarely with his children (he now had two lovely girls), but it could not be helped, for he was constantly on the move with his military career; therefore, Joe and Liz made several visits to wherever he may have been stationed in the states. Their granddaughter's coloring was that of "little gypsies," with dark hair and brown eyes, a mix between their father and mother. Their grandson was quite the opposite: fair-skinned, blonde, hazel eyes, a mix of both his parent's genes. Sometimes, all three children, with their children, came home to visit at one time– those were magical days when the atmosphere of the home crackled with the excitement and laughter of the entire family being together.

Sitting on the upper deck, looking down to the swimming pool below, Joe was immensely pleased with his choice of home, "I knew this big house would come in handy when the kids came to visit! I'm glad I put in the above-ground pool for them to play in!"

Then, out of nowhere, a miracle happened: On October 23, 1989, at the Kossuth Tér, in Budapest, a great proclamation was made - Hungary was free - The *Republic of Hungary* was born, and within its boundaries now stood a land structured within the liberties of all human rights. The monstrous iron chains strangling the lives of millions of Hungarians had, at long last, been severed. The unholy, impious reign of terroristic, oppressive communism had been eradicated. Upon hearing the joyous news, Joe and Liz stood under the shady arms of Georgia pines with tear-filled eyes, their bodies clinging together in mournful gladness, for after decades of grieving the bondage of their country, the reverberating silence of the celebration within their souls was deafening.

Around 1990, a musician friend told Joe about a town called Helen, Georgia, where each year an authentic German Oktoberfest celebration was held, and they were always looking for great musicians! Visitors came to the town for a lighthearted time of drinking traditional Bavarian beers and to tap their feet to the strains of polka music. Joe was never one to turn down an opportunity to play his accordion. He knew hundreds of polka melodies and offered to play his accordion during the festivities.

Joe asked one of the townspeople how all polka and beer business got started and was told about the first Oktoberfest being celebrated in approximately the year 1810 in Munich, Germany, but later, the location was moved to the capital of Bavaria. The roots of this festivity came about to honor a royal wedding. The gala lasted for two weeks and everyone had such a great time that the tradition was carried out every year with beer and large bounties of traditional German culinary delights served, especially bratwursts and schnitzels.

Alpine Helen, Georgia, was the sister city to Bavaria, and the first Oktoberfest was held there in 1970. The town of Helen needed a financial boost; therefore, the local merchants recreated the town to resemble a village in the Bavarian Alps. Every year the banks of the Chattahoochee River were filled with the sounds of "Oom-Pah music." Each October, tourists came from every corner of the United States dressed in full Bavarian costume, coming to eat, drink, and dance to the strains of polka music into the early hours of the morning.

The central grandstand was "Fest Halle" where several bands played uplifting music all day. This is where Joe reveled in his musical glory.

Joe donned authentic German "Lederhosen," (the traditional leather, dark green, knee-length breeches), a white long-sleeved or short-sleeved button-down shirt, and of course, suspenders, matching the green of his breeches, and hunter green or tan-colored hose reaching to the knee. His feet were covered with authentic "Haferischuh" shoes. On his head he wore a hunter green, Alpine felt hat with a band wrapped about the base and a feather attached. Dressed in his Oktoberfest finery, Joe's accordion resounded through the Hall, playing several sets of music during the day.

Being an entrepreneur at heart, Joe recorded dozens of his German Polka music cassettes to sell on-site.

Joe playing his accordion at Oktoberfest - Helen, Georgia, early 1990's

Since the celebration lasted several weeks, Joe lived in the village as a guest of Hofer's Bakery. He was given a tiny upstairs bedroom, more like a storage room, above the bakery during the Festival. Hofer's Bakery was created by a kindly couple, Horst and Gerda Hofer, who migrated from Schwabach, Germany to the United States in the late 1950's. They started their bakery in 1973. After eighteen years of operation they were recognized as one of the best bakeries in the United States, so they opened another bakery in Helen, Georgia, right in the middle of the Alpine Village. It was the perfect place for an authentic German Bakery, its façade blending with the chalets and cobblestone streets. Joe was asked to come back every year.

It was July of 1992. Joe awoke feeling numb and hungry. The anesthesia and pain medications from the surgery were wearing off, and the realization of what he had just lived through came to full light.

"My Joe, are you awake?" Joe heard Liz's worried voice through the dense fog of sedatives clouding his mind. "You are going to be all right now, the doctor told me you would be. You will be coming home soon. I love you so much. Can you hear me my *Edes*?"

Joe had been at work when he suffered another heart attack. Examination at the trauma center revealed blockages of all six arteries necessitating Joe to be transported via ambulance to the hospital for emergency bypass surgery, where Liz was waiting. The children were also on their way - Judy driving from North Carolina, Pilvia flying in from Florida, and Sonny from where he was stationed.

Liz was exhausted and careworn by the time her children arrived. Judy and Charles were first to the hospital, followed by Sonny, and then Pilvia. Joe had come out of surgery by the time his children arrived.

Ten long hours after his hospital admission, Joe's surgeon came out to speak with Liz in the waiting room.

"Your husband's coronary arteries were in bad shape. We grafted healthy blood vessels stripped from your husband's legs to replace his blocked coronary arteries. We had to do all six arteries since all had blockages of a moderate to severe degree. The procedure involved opening his chest and cutting through the sternum to access the heart. He pulled through the procedure very well and is in the recovery room. You'll be able to see him when he awakens." The weight of the surgeon's words, along with her already exhausted state, resulted in Liz crumbling into the arms of her children.

At last, finally able to be at her childhood sweetheart's side, Liz prayed he would be able to recover quickly, and do and be all the things he loved to do and loved to be. Liz squeezed Joe's hand tightly, "Come back to me Joe, come home, I will take care of you till you are strong again. I love you, love you beyond words." Through all the drugs, Joe displayed an encouraging smile for his Beloved. Before falling back into a healing sleep, he managed with shallow breath to speak, "I'll be back home soon, my beautiful butterfly, you can't get rid of me that easy, I love you too much to ever leave you."

It took Joe nearly three months to recover. During that time, he surveyed his chest in the mirror each day reflecting upon the healing, vertical scar. "I feel like a bionic man - held together with stainless steel wires!"

Adding to Joe's heartache was the news from Hungary that his father, and Liz's father had died in August: Joe's father dying, first, of a sudden, massive heart attack in his Budapest apartment, and Liz's father passing, next, quietly, at his home, of "old age."

"We are both orphans now," moaned Liz through rivers of tears. Joe held his mourning wife tightly in his arms, comforting her as best he could. The old legacy of a life filled with both sets of their parents had ended, and now, it was the beginning of a new legacy – the *Legacy of Liz and Joe*. They were now the "*Elder Parents*," the next in line to confront mortality, the next in line to pass into the starlit skies of eternity. Liz allowed herself to be luxuriant in her heartache, able to remember back on the difficult, yet happy times of her childhood, recalling how hard her parents toiled for her and all their children, and how much her parents loved her throughout her life. And Joe, upon hearing of his father's death, went into a solemn shroud of private sorrow, allowing his grief to reign only when alone. Joe's pain was searing and deep, for it was his father who had been his comforter and teacher throughout his life, his father who had taught him to play the music that eased his soul through all the torment, heartache, and agony the world threw at him, and most of all, it was his father who loved him twice over - making up for the love denied him by a selfish mother.

A rumor had been circulating at Joe's work about a large computer and electronics store moving to the area seeking a general manager. Joe researched the company, discovering the salary paid to that company's general manager was *considerably* more than he presently earned. But, the most enticing part for Joe, at least in his eyes, was that being a general manager meant he had reached the pinnacle of his career. "I'll soon be fifty-nine years old," thought Joe, "This may be my last chance to truly reach the very top!"

One week before Christmas Day of 1992, Joe accepted the position of general manager with the new firm, gave his resignation to his current employer, and was scheduled to begin with his new company in January of 1993.

Joe entered the break room for his last day of work with the "old company," on December 31, 1992. As he pushed open the swinging door at his usual time of eight in the morning to grab a cup of coffee, he was met by a chorus of shouts, "Surprise! Good Luck! We'll miss you! Congratulations!" Plates of sausage biscuits, doughnuts and coffee were spread on the main table, amidst colorful streamers and balloons hanging from the ceiling and lighting fixtures. Joe's employees had surprised him with a goodbye party!

A spokesman for the group stepped forward and presented Joe with a plaque engraved with the twenty-one names of the employees who had grown to admire and respect their soon to be former supervisor. Joe's eyes blurred as he read the wording on the award: "Boss of the Year! - From all those in your service. Best wishes."

The director of Joe's new store, a younger man in his mid-thirties, was not at all pleased with the company's decision in choosing Joe for the General Manager in Training (GMIT) program. He made his feelings quite clear to Joe on his first day of employment. "I did not choose you. I wanted a younger person and not someone with an accent!" It was obvious the man had a great distaste for older people *and* those of foreign origins. Joe found it rather odd (when glancing about the store) that every employee appeared to be under the age of forty, except for one other person who appeared to be over the age of fifty, including himself.

What have I gotten into?

One of Joe's responsibilities was to hire employees for open positions; however, each time Joe wanted to hire a person for *any* position, the director had a long list of negative comments regarding Joe's choice of personnel, as well as derogatory comments toward Joe:

"I don't like to hire people who might be a liability to the store because of their age or health problems."

"Didn't I tell you that I wanted young people with whom I would not have any trouble with health expenses? I can't trust you to hire the right employees."

"Hey, you don't look well, are you tired today? Is all this too much for you? Do you need to go home and rest?"

During the weekly office staff meetings, Joe gave several suggestions on ways the store could be run more efficiently. And, somehow, after each suggestion, the director flung belittling remarks in Joe's direction.

"In this store we do things the American way, not the Hungarian way."

"I don't understand what you are saying, say it again."

"I can't understand you because of your heavy Hungarian accent."

Joe did *not* have "an accent" having "lost it" years ago, and if he did, it was almost non-existent.

The callous director's denigrating comments did not go unnoticed by the other employees in attendance, but the man was a tyrant and bully, a domineering despot, who thrived and thirsted on striking fear instead of respect into the hearts of his workers.

Too many employees had lost their jobs at this facility by simply asking the "wrong question at the wrong time." Therefore, the staff, apprehensive of their own job security, chose to "ignore" the director's erratic insults, rather than confront what they dared not fight.

But their personal reasons for silence was no help to Joe. The deluge of tormenting insults and requests from the director increased. One day, he asked Joe to fire an employee who was age sixty-five. Joe was appalled at the thought. "Why, should I fire him, he hasn't done anything wrong?" The director smiled at Joe with a notorious Grinch-like grin, his words chilling Joe to the bone, "He is just too old and slow, and, he *will not* work out."

Joe was kept under constant pressure about only hiring "young people" and to "fire older employees" Despite Joe's protests and to his shock, the other older co-worker was eventually fired when he failed to come into work due to a death in his family.

Being overcome with grief, the employee had not thought to call in immediately about his absence from work until the following day. The director took this opportunity as an excuse to rid himself of the older employee for the reason of "not calling in." Joe always defended older employees emphasizing their worth and experience, which only further aggravated his boss.

The daily insults continued. The director's parrot-like repetitious lines were a daily occurrence, reminding Joe of a certain stanza of propaganda quoted by Vladimir Lenin, a much-despised man in Hungary, the man who founded the Russian Communist party, *"A lie, told often enough, becomes the truth."*

Joe and Liz in 1993 – Atlanta, Georgia, on their 40th Wedding Anniversary

Joe was determined not to allow the director's "lie" to become his "truth."

In September of 1993, the director asked Joe to hire a cleaning crew for the store, but, when he found out the crew spoke little English and mostly Spanish, he ordered Joe to "fire them!" Joe refused, staunchly replying, "They work very hard and do a great job. I will not fire them!"

The director then marched to his office, phoned the company who had dispatched the cleaning crew, giving them strict orders to never send "that bunch out again." He then called another company, choosing a crew of his own liking "without an accent."

Things got worse. Starting in late September of 1993, the director set out to "prove" that Joe was "too old," to physically perform his job description. He intentionally assigned Joe to perform physically onerous tasks, requiring him to work sixteen to eighteen-hour days, and eventually, Joe only had one weekend off in two months!

Joe expressed his complaints about the negativity of his work situation to the regional director, as the ethnic slurs had increased to the point where Joe could no longer "slough" off his feelings of embarrassment and humiliation in front of the other employees, not to mention the unworldly work hours; however, for no explainable reason, nothing was done by Corporate to remedy or investigate Joe's claims of harassment and discrimination in his work environment.

One morning in mid-November of 1993, touting his sardonic, sickening smile, and with absolutely no provocation, the director glaringly spoke into Joe's face, "I told you - if it had been up to me …I would have never hired you. I don't like the way you look or talk, and I don't trust you!"

Joe was desperate for relief and justice! Certainly, there had to be a way to gain the aid of upper management in his discrimination crisis!

He contacted a different person in Corporate, expressing his concerns and requested a transfer to another store. The transfer was denied.

Upon discovering Joe asking for a transfer, the director's verbal attacks intensified, and to spite Joe, he continued arranging "tasks" for Joe to perform, "Now!"

With the intensified demands at work, Joe could find no more than four hours of sleep each night, if he was lucky.

Joe was beyond exhausted in both his mind and body. A few days prior to Thanksgiving in 1993, he wearily stumbled into his office to begin another workday. By now, his exhausted body was nearing its breaking point, easily reflected in his slow, halting gait. He could hardly turn his head for the burning in his neck. As Joe bent down to place his briefcase on the floor by his desk, the tense aching in his back made it nearly impossible for him to raise himself upright. His bloodshot eyes stung from lack of sleep, but on this cool November morning, his eyes ached more than ever before, prompting him to forego the use of the glaring overhead fluorescent lights in his office, resorting to the soft lighting of his desk lamp. Joe looked at his wall calendar, "In one month I'll have been in this hellhole for nearly a year."

The director, upon seeing Joe "trudge in to work," was delighted to see Joe's downtrodden state. Believing he had found the perfect opportunity to push Joe into leaving, he made his way to Joe's office, obviously enjoying the scene of the "beaten man" before him. He quizzed Joe in his now, all too familiar, repetitious, leering, and mocking routine, "Are you sick. Are you tired? Do you need to go home? Is the job too much for you?"

Joe ignored him, not wanting to encourage more insults.

The fear, apprehension and anxiety inflicted upon Joe carried itself home to Liz, who was beside herself with worry for her husband's health.

"Joe, you are not far out from your heart operation! You are not getting any sleep, and you are never home anymore. We never see each other except for a few hours a week! This life is not what we left Florida for!"

Joe knew she was right. It was "hell" to enter "that place" every day, and how he wanted to escape from that bottomless blight of existence! The yearning ache of wanting to go back to the summery paradise he and Liz had shared in Florida settled in the depths of his stomach, becoming an indigestible, toxic bitter pill, spreading its poison throughout his body, to the point, where over the past few months, he had daydreamed about "walking off the job," going home to Liz, packing all their belongings and driving off to "somewhere." But where was a sixty-year-old man going to find a good paying job? He had put in numerous applications every week for employment with other companies but had received no replies or offers. He was trapped in this putrid wretched purgatory! Joe was baffled and bewildered by his current set of circumstances. He never imagined that such hate and bigotry could exist in the workplace! Why was this happening to him? What had he done wrong? It was like the "old days" of persecution in Massachusetts, but this time, he was despised for not only being "a foreigner," but for being older than age forty!

But, unknown to Joe, his salvation was just around the corner, but salvation can come in the most unusual of forms. On Saturday, December 4, 1993, the boss demanded Joe to staff the corporate pick-up section of the store, notwithstanding the fact that Joe's primary responsibility that day was to prepare for the *substantial evening inventory*.

As the director was ordering Joe about in his usual dictatorial fashion, the effects of the eighteen-hour work days coupled with little to no sleep, the daily defiling comments of denigration and humiliation towards Joe's person, as well as the usual discriminatory remarks flung at Joe about being "a stupid Hungarian," and the overall total injustice of his situation, came crashing down on Joe as if he had been crushed by a steamroller.

Joe's chest tightened as his entire body suddenly became stiff, almost paralyzed with anxiety. His head felt detached from his body as everything around him began spinning round-and-round. Joe fought with what little strength he had remaining to keep himself from passing out, and through blurred eyes and a whirring mind, he announced to the corrupt director, "I'm too ill to remain at work and I'm leaving for home."

Even in his addled state, Joe was conscious enough to make sure he followed the company's rules of proper protocol of notifying the employer of not being able to remain on the job due to illness as outlined in the employee handbook. Not even looking back to see the director's "glowing" reaction to his announcement of "finally being sick at work," Joe managed to maneuver his beaten, enfeebled body out of the store.

A foggy bog expanded within Joe's skull as tides of an icy mucilage filled his gut, forcing Joe to summon the last measure of his will, the last waning remains of self-control to help him to the refuge of his car, where at last, he allowed his clammy body, trembling from the cold of his sweat-soaked shirt, to sink gratefully into the driver's seat.

Joe had no recollection of seeking medical treatment at the local hospital, but with the aid of an unseen, guiding force, had made his way to that haven of hope, where after an extensive physical and psychiatric examination, was pronounced by the medical team to have suffered an intense, anxiety-related breakdown resulting from Joe's exceptionally hardened working conditions, uncustomary long hours (which Joe explained to the doctors had never been imposed upon other general managers within the company), malnutrition, and mental anguish, resulting in Joe being emergently hospitalized.

Liz sat by her husband on a cold, hard chair, staring incredulously at what "used to be her Joe." She had switched off the overhead, glaring fluorescent lights as the piercing unnatural light hurt her head. The only light pouring into the room seeped in from the hallway outside the open door of Joe's room. Joe was not sleeping, but would not open his eyes, nor did he talk to her, although he would shake his head slowly from side to side, making a ghastly moaning noise. Liz held her husband's hand, feeling the sparks of her husband's physical and emotional pain emanating through her, sending her to a dark void of hopelessness and despair, her body and senses becoming one with that of her husband. She stood up, leaning over the metal side rails of Joe's bed, feeling the cold of the bars pressing against her stomach as she bent over to kiss her husband's face. Joe made a tiny, whimpering sound when her lips touched his cheek, but he would not, or could not speak to her, but lay motionless. His once beautiful, happy eyes were squeezed shut, blocking out the suffering and torment within his conquered spirit; however, a few pearls of liquid grief managed to snake their way down his cool, gray cheeks. Liz was desperate for Joe to respond to her, "My *Edes* Joe, my love, what have they done to you!" She intentionally squeezed his hand to the point where she caused herself pain in doing so, but even pain could not break the "spell" of Joe's unresponsive state. Liz's mind could not believe this was happening to "her Joe," and the unreal anxiety of her situation was pressing on her own fragile state of body and mind to the verge of collapse.

Just before Liz felt she was about to scream aloud out of desperation and despair for her husband's condition, she heard a light knock on the door as Joe's physician entered the room.

Liz had so many questions to ask of the doctor, but could barely speak, her throat too parched and tight by fear, but managed to implore through grief-stricken tears, "Doctor, please help him! Tell me what is wrong? My husband does not respond to me. Does he even know I am here? Can we get him well?"

The doctor was a man in his early seventies, having worked the rooms of several emergency departments for many decades, very specialized and well-practiced in the areas of physical, emotional and mental trauma, but Joe's condition was beyond all those he had witnessed during his long career.

He pulled up another chair and sat beside Liz. After giving Liz a glass of water, he firmly, but gently said what he had to say, knowing the facts would be devastating not only for Joe, but for Liz, for their entire way of life.

"Mrs. Bognar, I have seen many cases of emotional trauma in my career, mostly in abused women, but in all my years, this is one of the most complex scenarios of physical and mental torment I have seen in a man brought on by overwhelming forces at the workplace. Because of the emotional distress, mental anguish, the extremely long hours of putting in eighteen-hour days with little to no sleep, plus the ethnic humiliation and age discrimination placed upon your husband by his employer, he has suffered a complete physical, emotional, and mental breakdown. He is severely exhausted in his body and mind, having pushed both beyond their capacity. He is no longer a young man, and due to all that has happened, he's "burnt out." His nerves, are, as they say, "shot." From now on your husband must avoid being placed into stressful situations of employment and he must obtain all the sleep and rest he can get - for a very, very long time."

Less than twenty-four hours after being admitted to the hospital, the director utilized Joe's *absence* as an excuse to terminate him from employment, and immediately hired a person under the age of forty to replace Joe's position.

Joe stayed in the hospital for several days. Upon returning home he was greeted by a letter from his employer offering him the job of "team supervisor," to compensate for his job loss. It would mean a twenty thousand dollar a year cut in pay. Joe refused the offer.

It was late September of 1996. Joe had turned age sixty-two in the spring of that year. It was a lovely autumn day. He and Liz were in the car driving home; however, both were too emotionally drained and overwrought to enjoy the beauty of the season.

Joe parked the car in the garage - they had just returned home from the office of his attorney. It had been nearly three years since the day Joe received the letter about losing his job and being offered the lower paying position. During those long, hard years, Joe's attorneys had battled the court system seeking justice for their client – and had won.

Sitting with Liz at their dining room table, Joe's eyes absently stared at the settlement check in his hand. After the attorney's fees, Joe's portion of the lawsuit winnings against his former employer was seventy-six thousand dollars – a mere pittance of what his salary would have been, for Joe could have easily worked ten more years in his former management position. The only thing Joe was happy about, if one could call the emotion "happiness," was as Joe put it, "That I was able to prove the corruptness of the company that allowed this to happen to me."

The attorneys proved Joe's former employer violated Age Discrimination Laws and Title VII of the Civil Rights Act, including wrongful discharge in violation of contractual obligations and by operation of promissory estoppel, as well as wrongful and tortious interference with his employment, his health insurance, and other benefits.

One of the stipulations of the settlement was for Joe's former employer to write a letter of apology to Joe, formally admitting their wrongdoing, which was included in the envelope containing Joe's check. But it was too little, too late. It was a bittersweet victory.

After his hospital discharge three years earlier, due to the psychological and physical torment at the hands of his former employer, Joe had officially been declared "emotionally disabled," unable to return to a gainful means of employment, and now received a monthly disability check.

Joe and Liz had superbly disguised all the major trauma of Joe's "job incident" from their children not wanting to cause any distress that could affect their offspring's personal lives or welfare.

When "it was all over," Joe finally acknowledged his plight to the children, who had a vague idea of their father having a difficult time at work, and being unhappy with his employer, but the news of their father's tragic situation came as a shock, especially upon realizing they had been "kept in the dark about how bad things had become."

Judy and Pilvia, on several occasions, offered their parents assistance in the care and upkeep of their home, not to mention much-needed, in-person, emotional support; however, as much as they would have wanted to see their daughters, Joe and Liz refused all offers, stating they were "Too tired for company and only wanted rest and quiet."

They *were* telling the truth. Joe and Liz were "wrung-out" from all the events that had transpired since moving to Atlanta, and to such an extreme extent, they had become accustomed to their pitiful, miserable routine.

Charlton's tenth birthday came and went in August of 1996. He was excited about traveling to Atlanta for his birthday celebration and was heartbroken when his grandparents stated they were "not well enough for company."

Judy and Charles did their best to explain the extenuating circumstances to their son, but being only ten years old, it was difficult for their little boy to understand the complexities of an adult world.

Charlton's Nagypapa and Nagymama did phone him and sent a loving birthday card on his special day with a monetary gift, for which their grandson was appreciative, but for a young boy who adored his grandparents, it was still not quite the same. Charlton was looking forward to seeing his Nagypapa, wanting to show off his improved chess skills as his Nagypapa had taught him the game.

Joe and Liz had become hollow shells of themselves - beings without longing or aspiration, without future ambitions or expectations, without hope of something better coming along, lamenting what could have been, knowing the life and health they had lost was irredeemable. Nothing had gone as planned upon moving to Atlanta, absolutely nothing. The easy carefree life Joe had imagined for he and his wife had been "washed down the drain." Neither had the willpower, or the strength, to handle the stressors of life. Joe's big dream of financial success and security had evaporated into misery. That failure, coupled with Joe's medical condition, had also taken its toll on Liz, transporting her to a world of melancholy and gloom. The disparity of their situation only serving to further weaken her already fragile mental state.

If ever they needed to have the love and support of family around them – it was now; however, to protect themselves from the invasion of any further stressors from "the outside," Joe and Liz created a cradling bubble about themselves, allowing no one to pierce through their protective armor.

In early Fall of 1996, the children broke through the separation barrier: coming by plane and automobile, descending unannounced upon their parent's abode, where with love, understanding and compassion, they nurtured their parent's grief-stricken bodies and minds, giving them the will and fortitude to transcend the flood of cataclysmic events that had engulfed their lives.

Time pushed onward, and with its passing, the unrelenting pain of defeat reluctantly transitioned into a begrudged acceptance of their circumstances.

But, out of the past crises came unexpected joy: Joe and Liz now had more time to spend with each other than they had in many years.

Since setting foot in America, they had toiled apart from one another, each doing their share to bring their dreams to reality in a world of freedom, not caring how hard they had to work or sacrifice to give their children all the things they, themselves, never had when they were small.

With Joe now at home, only leaving the house for errands, or when, at his leisure, he had the opportunity to earn extra income here and there doing repair jobs for musical instruments in his garage or playing the accordion for anniversary or birthday parties - the couple rediscovered each other, falling more deeply in love than they thought possible after all their years together. Joe and Liz made time to explore the area where they lived: the mountains of Georgia and the many parks and lakes nearby. When not out on an excursion they concentrated on landscaping and painting their home.

Joe and Liz in their backyard hammock in Atlanta 1998

But their favorite time of day was dusk, amongst the glow of flittering lightening bugs, observing the pink glimmer of evening twilight replacing the blue of the daytime sky, as they lay side by side in a swinging hammock under the protective canopy of Georgia pines.

THE BITTER END - Year 2003

A sleek, shiny black limousine with its polished chauffer waited patiently in the driveway as Joe and Liz finished the final touches of their ensembles. Joe was garbed in an impeccably fitted tuxedo touting a rose boutonniere. Liz was beyond beautiful in an elegant creamy-white floor-length gown. The couple stood side-by-side in their bedroom in front of a large floor-to-ceiling mirror.

It was April 10, 2003, their fiftieth wedding anniversary. How had fifty years passed so quickly? When did they get "old?" In their quest for a new life, a new beginning, time had caught up to them. At the ages of sixty-nine and sixty-eight, Joe and Liz stood at the precipice of life where one was no longer young, and yet not aged. "Joe, do you not think we still are beautiful together?" asked Liz of her Beloved as they gazed at their reflections. "Yes, my darling *Pillango*, we are still beautiful, because we have each other." Joe stroked his wife's soft cheek, "My *Edes Erzsebet*, I don't want to get old and leave you one day, alone. The thought of dying frightens me. I worry about my heart. I want to be here to always love you and care for you." Liz gently ran her hand over the softly lined face of her Love, "József, we will have many, many years together. I will never let you ever leave me. I love you too much!" They tenderly embraced, Joe taking care not to crush the bouquet of flowers in his wife's hand.

A sudden rush of emotions overwhelmed Joe, emotions filled with special things he wanted to say to his wife, but also, painfully poignant words he needed to expel, especially on this day of days. "My sweet baby wife, I am very sorry things did not work out in Atlanta as we had hoped – you know …with my last job, with my health. If I could do things all over again, I never would have left Florida."

Liz bit her trembling lower lip, trying hard to be brave, for she could see the shame and pain in her husband's face as he made his confession. Her moist hand clasped that of her lifelong love, "My *Edes*, you did what you felt was best at the time. You have always done *what was best at the time*. And, at the time, it seemed like the best thing to do! I agreed to come to Atlanta, 'member?" Joe led Liz to sit with him on the edge of their bed. "You *do* forgive me, then? You forgive me for all the pain and suffering I put you through?" Liz leaned against Joe, tenderly kissing his cheek, "There is nothing to forgive, you are what you are, and always did what you thought was best. At least you *tried*. Some men never try, they sit back and watch the world go by. You - you my *Edes Draga*, always grabbed the world with both hands to make it into something better than what it was, to make our lives better than what it had been. That is a brave thing to do, year after year, for all these years. You are the solid rock foundation on which our family thrives, you have always been my hero. My greatest happiness was watching you do *all* you loved to do, proud that you wanted to do more and be more. I have been simply content to be your audience standing in the wings off-stage watching you create your special magic. My life has been incredibly happy my *Edes*, just being with you, just being a part of the great adventure of life with you."

Joe swept his petite wife up in his arms, "Oh my *Pillango*, I could not have done any of it without you, you are my inspiration, you give my life meaning, without you I would be nothing, I love you more than ever!" He kissed her, softly, yet passionately, not wanting the moment to end. Liz responded without a word, grasping Joe's hand, kissing the knuckles to each fingertip.

Joe suddenly remembered the limo waiting outside. "Oh, no! We're running late! Let's dry up our old dripping eyes and head off for the *Bitter End*! It's time to celebrate and everyone is waiting for us to arrive!"

The limousine pulled up in front of the *Bitter End Restaurant* in Georgia, the location for their Fiftieth Wedding Anniversary gala. Waiting outside the main entrance were all their children and grandchildren dressed in their grandest finery. The chauffer opened the door of the limo allowing Joe and Liz to be greeted by their family's cheers and applause, accompanied by hugs and kisses from all, including best friends, Tommy and Laura, the sweet young couple who had lived next door to Joe and Liz for nearly twenty years, and were more like family to them than neighbors.

The children requested their parents remain in the main lobby, allowing them time to finalize the opulent scene inside the magnificent private dining space allocated especially for the occasion. The children had arrived early to decorate linen-clad tables, adorned by red and yellow roses floating in shining crystal bowls, amidst the glow of flickering candlelight.

My parents arriving at the Bitter End Restaurant - April 10, 2003 –
For their Fiftieth Wedding Anniversary Celebration

A delectable three-tiered wedding cake, with "golden frosting" crowned with a custom-made, heart-shaped glass cake-topper was placed on its own table, and beside it, elegant cake cutting utensils and wine glasses – all engraved with the couple's name and fiftieth wedding anniversary date.

Judy started the music for the *Rákóczi March*, the same song her father requested the violin players to play for the family as they departed the Budapest Hilton during the great family reunion in Hungary. The strains of the march cued Joe and Liz to make their grand entrance. How beautiful they were – standing regal and proud as a King and Queen on their coronation day! Joyful ovations resounded as the jubilant couple approached their wedding table.

Sonny was present in full-dress military regalia, accompanied by his wife and four daughters, all dressed in flowing, long gowns: the three older girls had grown into exquisitely lovely young women; the youngest, with Down's syndrome, in her picture-perfect party dress and endearing ways, charmed all present. Kuki, with her newfound love, was beautiful in a satin gown of orange and cream, her hair of autumn gold swept up in stunning curls. Judy wore a cream-colored two-piece dress suit, and Charles and Charlton were debonair in their tuxedos.

Music was provided by Joe! Over the years he had recorded countless music CD's of accordion music (now done on a Midi Pier Maria Accordion). At approximately thirty-minute intervals Judy changed music according to the festivities on hand.

After the superb anniversary meal was finished, Joe tapped his dinner knife against his water glass to gain everyone's attention. With his bride seated by his side, Joe slowly pushed his chair back from the table. Joe held up a wine glass in his right hand, and his left hand held that of his lovely wife. Standing tall and stately, he surveyed the glowing, loving faces seated about him on this momentous day.

Joe and Liz making their grand entrance at their Fiftieth Wedding Anniversary Celebration – April 10, 2003

"Two people met and fell in love, and now look, we have three married children and five grandchildren, and have two dear friends who are more like our own children then they are friends. Where did all the time go? It feels like yesterday when I met my beautiful Erzsebet, and just yesterday, when our children were born. It is hard to believe that it has been about forty-seven years since the days of the Hungarian Revolution and when we set foot in America. I remember the hard days of our early married life, especially after Judit was born. How little food we had! One day, I had the good fortune to get an orange, a rare commodity in Hungary during those days. I was very excited to bring it home. I cut it open and watched Judit eagerly suck all the juice out of the orange wedges. As much as me and Mama wanted to eat that orange, we could not eat it, knowing our little girl's growing body needed the vitamins. We sucked what pulp we could off the inner lining of the skin and chewed the skin

of the orange to get what nutrition we could out of it. We felt so very happy just to have that little orange. As I look about me today, I know all my children and grandchildren had good food to eat growing up and did not suffer as we did, having to go to bed at night with growling, empty stomachs. When we burnt our love letters in the old coal stove prior to our escaping Hungary that cold, damp night, a part of your mother and I went up in flames with those letters, but we rather would have the flames take the letters from us, then let strangers read our most private words of love for each other. During our escape we did not know if we would live or die. Other Hungarians were killed or captured as they made the same journey for freedom as we did. After all the suffering and fear, we found ourselves on a ship for America, and eventually in Camp Kilmer. But we had no joy at Kilmer, because our baby girl was dying of pneumonia. Mama and I were slowly dying with her. If Judit died, we wanted to die also. After all the hell we went through to find freedom it was not worth it if she could not share in the new world with us. We had prayed before for help during the war and Revolution, but never prayed as hard as we did during those dreary, dreadful days in Camp Kilmer. When Judit woke up, asking for food, and was well again, I felt as if I could accomplish anything. Despite many obstacles, Mama and I did accomplish a great life for our family in America. But I made some choices in my life that I should not have made. I will tell you all, today, I do deeply regret those choices." Then, Joe remembered the words Liz spoke to him in their bedroom before departing for their anniversary celebration, *"But at the time, they seemed like the best choice to make. That is what we all do. We make the best choice that seems right at that time."* Joe took in a deep breath, *"Sometimes, we reap happiness from our choice, and sometimes we sow sadness from our choice. Well, you kids know we have sowed both the good and bad, but, on the bright side, at least I was in a country where I was free to make those choices, free to say what I wanted, free to be whatever I wanted to be and go wherever I wanted to go and have the freedom to make those mistakes on my own. My only hope is my children and grandchildren will take my mistakes and learn from them to better your own lives. We came to America for a better life, to escape the chains of a Communist government. Through you and your children, our legacy of fighting for freedom will continue. Be proud of your Hungarian Heritage. Never compromise your principles. Never forget the proud and strong people you come from. Your mother and I, your grandmother and I, are truly honored that you have given us this beautiful fiftieth wedding anniversary party, we are honored that you are our children and our grandchildren. We love all of you with all our hearts!"*

With those final words, Joe lifted his glass, "To my beautiful family, to all your hopes and dreams …I am so grateful you are MY family!"

The evening flowed on with the traditional cake cutting ceremony, dancing, the granddaughters singing songs to their grandparents, Judy and Charles reading poems, self-written for the occasion, and many pictures taken by Charles, (who had his own wedding photography business for many years). The couple clung tight to one another during the last song: *The Wind Beneath my Wings.*

The words of the song were true: both had relied on the other's strength over their fifty years of marriage to help the other endure the unendurable, supporting each other through the most difficult and execrable times. Their love had only grown stronger under the arduous circumstances thrown against them – hardships which would have driven many other couples to break apart from one another. At the end of the song, Liz whispered in her sweetheart's ear, "You are my hero."

Joe and Liz dancing at their Fiftieth Wedding Anniversary – April 10, 2003

Joe with grandson, Charlton (age seventeen), April 10, 2003

Joe, with son-in-law Charlie, April 10, 2003

The years pushed forward, and although the couple had tried their best to be accepting of their fateful move to Atlanta, their depleted willpower to fight life's battles, along with Joe's debilitated physical and mental state due to their severed finances, locked the couple into the failures of the past. Haunted by their drained monetary circumstances they saw no future for themselves, no way to advance beyond the hopeless gloom that existed for them at the present.

Sonny had become successful in his career, living well and respected among his peers. He did send "extras" to assist his parents financially. He also tithed a good amount to the Mormon church. Joe was frustrated by this, not understanding why "tithes" were not given to family first. Joe had always felt charity began at home, reasoning that if one was a Christian, why would one not give directly to family where they knew the funds would help their own kin, instead of giving to a large, "business church" where Joe felt there was "no true accounting of who received those funds."

Although Joe lived his life according to "Christian rules," his childhood memories of the physical beatings the priest of his church inflicted upon him as a little boy clouded his mind, sorely affecting his decision about the "business *of* the church." Joe's motto about the art of tithing was, "I'll put my money where I can SEE it do the most good."

Joe brought up the tithing subject with Sonny during one of their weekly phone calls, but apparently the conversation did not fare well on either side. Joe, with all he had gone through since his move to Atlanta, especially having to retire on disability and frustrated with the resultant loss of finances, brought up the subject that tithing should be given to the needs of the family, rather than the church.

However, as reasonable as this may have sounded to Joe, it was not as easy to be accomplished as it sounded for one simple reason: because while family members emanate from the same family pod, they are, however, individuals, living in different realms on the same planet, and although each member of the family grew up under the same roof, with the same teachings, their personal life experiences took them down paths that led to forming views and opinions different from that of the original family unit – some of those views for the better, and, some of those views for the worse.

Sonny and Joe's feelings were misaligned on the tithing topic, leaving Joe feeling helpless, defeated and numb. Immediately after talking with his son about that issue, Joe regretted his words. *People think differently than I do, even my own family - ways of doing things are very different now-days. I had no idea my son was so deeply devoted to the church. But I can't help but feel, that with such a deep devotion for the welfare of humanity, tithing should remain within the boundaries of the home, especially if family members are experiencing desperate times.*

After the "tithing" episode, conversations between parent and son were short and noticeably strained. There had been disagreements with all their children, but none where they ceased speaking to each other, and none where neither had made up before going to sleep at night. But this time it was different.

Talking on the phone, without seeing each other face-to-face, without seeing facial inflections while speaking to each other, allows a person's mind to twist the utterance of the most innocent sounding words into unintended meanings.

Sonny phoned his parents every week, usually on a Sunday, but words between father and son became less and less, due to the feelings of "old hurt," with the father not understanding his son's monetary donations outside the family circle. But in Joe's mind, his reasoning about tithing and helping family was an understandable one. Since his children were born, Joe had aspired to provide each of his offspring a utopian life – a life untouched by the stabs of deprivation known to the parents. But that *is* what frustrated Joe. Had he and his wife not worked themselves "into the ground" since their early days in America to provide all their children a blissful start to their lives? Had he and his wife not suffered physically and emotionally to provide a fairyland existence for their offspring where they grew up in a Shangri-La world filled with milk and honey, never knowing the pangs of hunger or going without the simplest of life's needs, always having a garden of materialistic desires granted them, but most important – did his children not see how much, see how deeply their parents loved them, how *abundantly* their parents loved them, to the point of the parents not caring about their own physical needs if it meant their children's happiness?

Had the "church" done all this for his children?

And that is why Joe's insides were in a turmoil – the "child-part" of his brain remained incensed from the trauma inflicted upon it during his childhood by the "church," rendering him a victim of the painful "sin" inflicted upon his body and mind from that earlier time, leaving Joe's intellect powerless to understand, to fathom, to comprehend why the monetary needs of "the church" came before the everyday needs of the parents: especially such good parents as he and his wife – parents who had sacrificed, sometimes at great physical cost, for their children as they were growing up.

When, in all the past years of he and his wife's toiling labors, had "the church" stepped in and suffered and sacrificed as he and his wife had for his children? It had not.

Joe *did* believe in the higher *power of God*, but *not* in the *coffers* of *religion*.

Much to the distress of both sisters, due to personal financial losses beyond their control, they were not able to offer their parents large sums of monetary support; therefore, they gave of themselves, and of their time, giving their parents emotional support and assisting them in the maintenance of the Atlanta house. Pilvia, (who in the past had amassed a large amount of frequent flyer miles to help pay for her flights from Los Angeles), and Judy, came to Atlanta, frequently, mostly on what they called "cleaning and cooking missions," for the once immaculate Georgia estate was beginning to show the disparaging effects of unintentional neglect. Joe and Liz were "too worn out," to perform any upkeep on their home (inside and out), as well as not having the financial means to do so. But through the diligent efforts of the two sisters, over time, they were able to restore the home back to its former elegance.

Judy had offered to help her parent's sell their home as she had found a reasonably priced living arrangement for them near her house in North Carolina, stating to her father "Come live close to me so I can take care of you and Mama." But Joe's mind and nerves were too "far gone," too deteriorated and frayed, to even think about such a tremendous undertaking, and lovingly refused his daughter's offer.

Joe was grateful to his daughters, and to his son, for all the "extras" each had provide in their own way, but the issue of "charity to the church," remained a sore point in Joe's mind, with him not understanding his son's views on the subject, thus, creating an invisible "wall between them," resulting in increasingly stinted weekly phone conversations, where there were more lapses of "dead air" than dialogue.

The tension between her son and husband, in addition to all their disappointments since moving to Atlanta, and having suffered through too many surreal, tragic events in their early lives, resulted in an already depressed and despondent Liz to spend most of her time in a recliner, leaving Joe to do all the cleaning, cooking and errands, despite the development of severe osteoarthritis in his back and hands.

Joe and Liz were now living on far less than half his original salary. Determined not to lose his home – again, determined not to lose his cars – again, and knowing he and his wife could not "run away,"- again, as neither had the strength to start somewhere new - again – Joe's mind worked on a way to create extra income. Joe found the answer: He created a fresh, contemporary "stage-name" for himself, *The Continental*, landing a job as a roving accordion player in a local Mexican restaurant on the weekends; however, the pain from his arthritis, the deadened zest for living within his heart, the realization that his life had come to this low point after all the great things he had accomplished over the years, only further added to his deeply depressed state of mind. To make things worse, the only way he could manage to carry the weight of his instrument, and to be able to move his once nimble fingertips that now burned with pain along his beloved ivory and ebony keys, was with the use of anti-anxiety and osteoarthritic medications that "barely took the edge off."

The extra pay from that position, and the tips, gave Joe the means to afford several unexpected root canals (dental procedures), as well as other untimely expenses. Joe also sold the motorhome.

Adding to her declining health, Liz was becoming more and more dependent on Joe's anti-anxiety medications, on which she relied to help her sleep, causing Joe to sacrifice his doses and giving them to his wife. But little by little, larger doses were required to aid her in relaxing, and most often, the pills would not take effect until five o'clock in the morning, and because of this, Liz slept most of the day.

It was a ghost-like existence for Joe. He was alone during the daylight hours doing household chores and shopping, and then in the late afternoon when Liz awakened, he assisted her downstairs to the great room area where she immediately went to her recliner waiting for the dinner Joe cooked for her.

After dinner Joe cleaned up the kitchen and then the couple watched television. Neither had much to say to one another - other than complain about their aches and pains. And, as hard as they tried to forget the reason why they were "in this mess," the miserably cruel remembrance of Joe's last employment venture ending in failure continued to cloud their minds, as well worrying over the strained relationship with their son. Most times, both fell asleep in the great room after dinner, eventually forcing Joe to help Liz upstairs, where despite the agony of his crippled arthritic joints, he bathed his wife and put her to bed. Joe would then traverse downstairs to get rest for the same routine the next day, for he had made the "great room" into his own bedroom, sleeping on an air mattress. In this manner he could come and go without disturbing Liz.

After living this way for about a year the couple continued in their physical and emotional decline. Joe had intense chest pain, a form of angina, and the pain in his heart was intensified by his wife's severe depression and physical deterioration.

On the evening of November 16, 2007, Joe sat at his desk in his dimly lighted office. His mind was blank, but his head was full. He glanced at the date on the desk calendar. How ironic! This night marked fifty-one years since their escape from Hungary. Joe found it odd that November sixteenth, seemed to be a pivotal date in his life: it was the day he escaped, the day he was notified of the plans for the destruction of his restaurant business, and again, on this date, Joe was facing a crisis.

Sitting in the quiet, darkened ambiance of his office, Joe's mind faltered backwards through the years of his life - from his childhood to this one moment. He remembered when his children were small, dependent on their parents for all their wants and needs. What wonderful children they had been! But all his children grew up having independent thoughts and ways of living, as do all children. And, as happens between all parents and children, those thoughts and ways of living created circumstances that not only affected the life of the child, but also the lives of the parents. Joe knew that parents and children would always have disagreements and conflicts to be argued and resolved. His daughters had been no exception, especially when they were in their twenties, finding themselves in unhappy life decisions and failed romantic relationships that ended up "going nowhere," leaving him and their mother to "pick up the pieces." Joe and Liz had weathered the storms of their daughter's heartbreaks and their daughter's sorrows and were elated when their daughters at last found happiness. But tonight, Joe had no peace in his mind or heart. He longed to talk with his son, a real talk, filled with mutual understanding for each other.

But where would he begin? When did all this miscommunication start? Was it only about the church tithing? No, there was more - little things that had somehow become big things.

The Atlanta move had been devastating. It was the beginning of the end for Joe and Liz. It nearly cost Joe his mind, if not his life. There was no road back to Florida, and now, with their financial and medical situation, there was no road forward. Every day was the same day – a day trapped in oblivion.

But what happened with the communication between parents and son? Joe knew parenting was not an exact science. *Every* parent makes mistakes in the raising of a child, and *every* child makes mistakes by causing grief for the parents. Every family is different and learns as it grows.

Joe's thoughts went back over the years, recounting what happened between him and his son, asking himself what went wrong: Sonny got married while in Panama. He was their only son, the son they wanted very much to be born. Joe and Liz would have been overjoyed to be present for their son's wedding, albeit, no matter how small a ceremony. Joe deliberated the situation in his mind. Trying to reconcile and rationalize what happened regarding the many "little things that became big things," *Maybe Sonny was just "too much in love," acting impulsively because he wanted to be married quickly and did not stop to think how much his parents might have wanted to be there for that special day? When Sonny and his wife renewed their vows in the Mormon Temple we were not invited. An oversight? Maybe they wanted it to be private? Maybe, because we were not Mormon, we could not be there?* When the last baby with Down's syndrome was born to Sonny and his wife, he and Liz were not told about the child until they discovered it for themselves when first looking upon the baby – a huge emotional shock for both. Joe sought hard to rationalize that moment. *Perhaps, Sonny did not know how to tell us about the medical issues with the child, because it was also painful for him?*

But, as Joe thought back, even on those things, with the passing of years, he and Liz *had recovered* from those disappointments. In hindsight, he now believed that perhaps all the "bad situations" he and Liz thought were so "huge" were simple miscommunications, with his son not realizing how important it would have been to his parents to be informed and notified of all the things he had not made them aware of.

We have no other family in this country. That is why I wanted to stay close to my children. I wanted all of us to be a part of each other's lives in every way –

because "our little family unit was all we had." Mama and I existed only for our children.

Who else did we have here on this earth to give our love to, to live for, to strive for, to dream with? In my trying to "stay close to my son," was I maybe too demanding, or a better word for it, inquisitive of my son's life, or for that matter - of all my children's lives? I know Sonny had a lot of pressure on him with a large family and a responsible career. Did I blow everything out of proportion?

Another factor was the great distance between parents and son - the unforeseen consequences of a military career. Sonny's posts were always far away: Germany, the Middle East, and "out West" in the states, making visitation a challenge. The miles and years of separation had been especially difficult for Liz, as she profoundly missed seeing her son and granddaughters, longing to spend more time with the little ones, but Sonny was always stationed far from Atlanta. Several transfers came and went, and each time, none close to his parents. Joe hoped his son could have had a choice to be posted closer to Atlanta; however, the opportunity for the closer post never materialized. The vast stretch of miles between son, grandchildren, and parents over the years had made it nearly impossible for Joe and Liz to visit with their son and his family. And now, the problem that vanquished Joe and Liz the most, was knowing that with their current circumstances of small financial means and degenerating health, any such trip would be nearly impossible.

Then came the misunderstanding that their son's marriage was not doing well, and when Joe and Liz tried to intervene to "help" his son and wife with their marriage, they were told "nothing was wrong," and the son and his wife politely asked the parents to refrain from any interference. Joe felt terrible about that turn of events, causing him much emotional distress and embarrassment.

Another issue on Joe's mind, was when a few years back, he and Liz had sent Sonny's wife a Herend tea set as a birthday gift; however, according to Joe, "she preferred something different," and returned it. Joe and Liz could not understand what there was "not to like" about the precious porcelain offering. Joe did not understand why she could not have kept it, even if she did not care for the design. The reason Joe and Liz were disappointed about the returned Herend gift was because their son's home had no displays of his Hungarian heritage, but many displays were evident of his wife's Panamanian heritage.

Joe and Liz understood their son's home was not *their* home but had hoped his son's children could have been exposed more to the art, tradition, and culture of the Hungarian side of the family, but their son's home was void of such display.

Judy, from the time she could remember at age three, had seen her parent's struggle for a life in America. She had spent time with Hungarian families and friends in Massachusetts, and even though Judy's knowledge of the Hungarian language was limited, she could speak and remember the Hungarian childhood songs and poems she had learned as a little girl. Thus, having more exposure to "Hungarian ways" from the time she was born. But, Pilvia and Sonny, who were born in the United States, and grew up surrounded by traditional American culture, were not exposed to "all things Hungarian" in their early lives as had their big sister, and, by the time Pilvia and Sonny had formed memories of their childhood, the really "bad days" or struggling to "make it in America days" were over, including the days when Joe and Liz had surrounded themselves with Hungarian acquaintances.

Now, as he neared the final juncture of his life, Joe regretted his decision to stop speaking Hungarian at home, a decision made under duress due to the ethnic discrimination tormenting them in Massachusetts.

Joe had "thought about" teaching the children more of their language in later years, but soon, even in Florida, everyday living and survival got in the way, and the time to teach their children "more of who they were" was lost in the hustle and bustle of scraping out an existence in a new place.

The more Joe thought about this issue, the more Joe reasoned this was the only possible explanation of why his son's home was void of anything from the "Hungarian side of the family."

But even this explanation did not ease the ache of wishing his granddaughters knew more about the "other side" of who they were. Joe would have been glad to teach them about *Magyar* ways and traditions, but he saw them so rarely, and when they were together, it never seemed to be the right time to take on the subject.

Distressed about the strained relationship with his son and having regrets of not teaching his children and grandchildren more about their ethnic roots, Joe called his oldest, expressing to her, "I should have taught all my children more about their heritage, especially since I yearned for them to know more about it, but your mother and I were too busy making money for you kids, to give you all the wonderful things you had. Even after our trip to Hungary, your brother and sister did not express further interest in their culture. But neither did your mother and me. After we got home from Hungary, all of us got caught up in our daily routines and we never discussed it further. Maybe I said too much to Sonny about that subject, and many other things I regret. The strange thing is I can't remember much of what I was upset with him about before, or what I may have said. One thing for sure, I did not intend for him to feel guilty over something that was not his fault, and it seems that, somehow, that is what has happened. I should have kept my mouth shut. Too many things have happened to me and your mother over the past few years, so many things that I most likely don't even realize, or remember, what I said to anyone - my head feels tight and heavy, nothing makes sense anymore, most days I don't even know who I am, or what I want out of life anymore. It's a wonder your mother and I haven't already had a total collapse after all the hell the world has thrown our way since we were kids."

Her father stated to Judy, that many times, when he and Sonny were speaking on the phone, he sensed Sonny, as well as himself, holding back on saying the things they really wanted to say to each other, fearing one of them would interpret the other's words as a reprisal or a consternation, fearing someone would "say the wrong thing," causing an unintended "hurtful emotion."

The anxiety of wanting to say something positive but not knowing where to begin that positivity, the aura of trepidation between parents and son in knowing something had gone wrong in their relationship, but no one knowing where to start to make things right, eventually culminated into the "quiet time."

By April of 2008, the phone calls between parents and son became less and less. Joe wanted to say things - things to make the silence disappear. He and Liz loved their son and knew he loved them.

Joe tended to become withdrawn and quiet during the trying times of his life. With his son now a grown man, with a very responsible job and family to take care of, Joe concluded that his son's withdrawal from frequent contact with his parents could likely be due to trying times in his own life, things his son did not want to discuss with his parents, wanting to take care of things on his own.

Remembering this, Joe hoped that whatever was going on would heal with understanding and time. But as the days, months and years had passed them by, the foundation to whatever issues causing the silent time between parents and son had become more disjointed, to where Joe could not even remember exactly where it all went awry.

Joe's head was in a constant blur, too overwhelmingly tired due to his ailing health issues, as well as his wife's. This, compounded by all the disastrous consequences of moving to Atlanta, left Joe in a state of utter exhaustion, too worn out to think about how to "fix things."

During a phone conversation with Judy, the first week of July in 2008, her father related, "This whole situation with Sonny is a big misunderstanding. I can't help but regret the whole "church thing." I regret a lot of things. I know that one day soon I will find a way to let Sonny know he did nothing wrong, how everything was a misunderstanding on all sides. We'll find each other again. I will resolve it somehow. I am the parent. I am the one who must make amends, to break through to him. Your mother and I love Sonny, and we love you and Pilvia with all our hearts."

Then, Joe's exhausted, frail voice broke into a hoarse confession, "My *Csimby*, I am so very sorry that your mother and I are in this sad condition. We are falling apart in both our bodies and our minds. We wanted to do so much more with you, with our grandson, but your mother and I are at our breaking point. There is only so much a person can go through in their lifetime. Your mother and I have gone through *too much of a living hell* since we were children, too much more of that same living hell in the past few years. I wish I had done many things differently, if I had, your mother and I would not be in this condition, our world would not be falling apart, and all of us would be much happier. *Csimby*, my little girl, my beautiful baby, we are at the end of our rope. The world has taken our last ounce of strength from us. We are simply worn out from fighting *everything*."

The once brave and mighty man whose noble actions had rallied a nation towards the Flames of Freedom, whose courageous deeds had saved countless lives, whose thirst for righteousness had sent the *Carriers of Evil to Hell*, who had given his family every ounce of all he had to give, whose gentleness and strength had carried his little girl to freedom, and whose musical genius had once graced the world with his rhapsodies, then proceeded to lacerate the heart of his *Csimby* with words so sharp, so icy, so forlorn, that she clutched her chest in agony, as the utterance of her father's pathetic devastation stabbed at her senses, "Mama and I will die soon my *Csimby* baby, we are at the edge of extinction!"

It would never be known if Joe had found the emotional strength to begin the healing process with his son, for two weeks after speaking with his *Csimby*, the courageous, indomitable, invulnerable, 1956 Freedom Fighter, Jozsef Frank Bognar, exhaled the last of his life's essence, taking the answer with him.

THE DAYS OF MAMA AND ME

It was late January of 2009. Mama's early weeks in the nursing home had been a wearisome, arduous adjustment for both of us. I did not want my mother to be in a rehabilitation facility. But I was selfish. I wanted my mother to be well physically and emotionally. I was determined to ignite what few embers of life remained deep within her. I *could* bring her back with love - lots of love. I knew I could!

My lovely mother what happened to you! Once, my mother had been a beautiful woman with shining eyes and silky dark hair who ran, laughed and played with her children. Once my mother was strong and fearless. Once my mother was a lovely young girl whose beauty drew my father to her side at a school dance. And now - my mother – was a shell of who she once was: white hair, sunken hollow eyes, parched loose skin, a crumpled, worn-out "thing."

Mama's gait consisted of shuffling her feet in tiny baby steps, losing balance frequently, unable to perform the simplest task of self-care. Adding to my despair was the fact that when she looked at me - she was not looking *at* me, but through me, past me, as if I was not even there. Her face conveyed no expression, her mind somewhere else, far, far away. And she was sad, despondent and so very frail! No matter how much love I had for my mother, I understood my love was not enough. She was empty inside - *incomplete*.

My parents had not left each other's side since the first time they met. For many decades, they had been faithful to one another, shared days filled with happiness and adversity, and no matter what challenges life placed in front of them, their deep abiding love gave each a purpose for living and surviving.

But, for Mama, all those years, days, and moments of loving her husband were pulled out from under her overnight. My mother was now in a foreign world with an unfamiliar landscape. All the things my parents had endured together and dreamed together had disappeared in an instant: the shared emotional scars of a hellish world war, fighting a revolution together, surviving against the worst of odds in escaping Hungary to make a new life in America, fighting the ugly enemy of ignorant prejudice as they struggled to make a life in the early days in Massachusetts, and later combating the same repugnant prejudice that led to the downfall of their life in Atlanta.

Despite every unfathomable obstacle life threw their way, they marched on, shouldering the challenges of life, grappling countless battles and celebrating innumerable victories – always together.

But, now, the predictable rhythm and pattern of "life with Papa" had disappeared. The world Mama loved had drifted away. How she adored devoting herself to her husband, dedicating every inch of her being, all her love into cooking his favorite meals, maintaining their home in perfect order and cleanliness, pressing his clothes, cutting his hair, and holding him close! But I believe it was the everyday things she missed the most: straightening his tie, talking together, celebrating special days, and writing their love notes to one another. They had complemented one another.

One evening as I was helping Mama with her grooming she asked, "Who am I now? What am I going to do without Papa?"

What *was* she going to do? I was not sure of the answer; however, I was determined to succor my mother out of her dark abyss into a new world filled with the light of happiness.

I was my mother's only grasp on the outside world. My presence grounded her to reality, assuring her that beyond the confining walls of the lackluster nursing home there was a wonderful new life waiting for her "on the outside."

Breakfast at the facility was the only meal Mama enjoyed; otherwise, the bland fare was not to her liking. Every day at noontime and dinner I brought her piping hot, freshly made meals. For the first few weeks of her confinement in the nursing center I hand fed those meals to her for she had no strength to feed herself. With the home-cooked food Mama regained her strength and her appetite!

At each visit, I assisted my mother with all personal hygienic needs, and once a week, arranged for the on-site hairdresser and pedicurist to attend to Mama, hoping that these tiny "human touches" would help Mama regain her self-confidence. Not wanting her clothes washed in the same washing machine as the other nursing home residents, I gathered all Mama's laundry at each visit to wash and dry at home, bringing the clean clothes back the next day. When the weather was nice and sunny, I placed Mama in a wheelchair and pushed her around the facilities nicely kept grounds to allow the revitalizing rays of the sun to revive her spirit.

I counted my blessings for having flexible at-home work hours permitting me to visit with my mother at the nursing facility, twice a day, every day; however, with the physical and emotional demands of my day job, the everyday chores for my own home, and caring for Mama, my energy reserves were becoming depleted.

My husband now worked in law enforcement, and my son was in college, each with their own personal set of demands to deal with every day. They helped whenever they could, but due to the way circumstances were presented, mostly all of Mama's needs fell to me.

I lost track of time. Each week, each month, was one, long continuous day. There was an incredible amount of work to be accomplished by 11 a.m. each day including weekends! Monday through Friday, I had to be at the nursing home by 11:30 a.m. to see Mama, as I started work at 2 p.m. We had our supper as a family at 5:30 p.m. and by 6:30 p.m. I was at

Mama's bedside feeding her dinner. I came home by 8:30 p.m. and continued my transcription work until midnight.

As soon as I went to bed at night, it was time to wake up to another day of the same. When my husband's work schedule permitted, he would take over for me, giving me a brief respite. He visited with Mama assisting her with feeding, her nightly tooth-brushing, and her facial and hand wash routine. We visited Mama as a family on Saturday or Sunday, bringing photo albums of our early days in America and photographs of my own little family that Mama had not yet seen.

Charles also brought my father's "old-time movie reel" to Mama's room and played movies taken by my father in the 1960's.

As much as Mama enjoyed having all my little family visit with her, our happiest times were when it was just the two of us, for Mama and I had a special bond knitting our hearts together. We had come from the same place and shared the same memories of the early days and years. We always could "feel" each other's thoughts and emotions.

The unsaid said everything between us.

Mama enjoyed her physical therapy classes where she rode a reclining bike and worked out with light weights. The glow on Mama's face as she conquered the limitations of her once frail body sent waves of euphoria through me. With each rotation of the bike's pedals I cheered Mama on, inspiring her to try even harder. Mama's spark *had* been lit and she desperately wanted to regain her strength to be able come home.

Mama's medical insurance only paid for the first thirty days in the nursing facility, but after that timeframe, she was still not strong enough to come home. Mama had shared a room with another woman at the facility. It was not the most tolerable situation for Mama, for the other person had no control over her bodily functions, and often Mama was awakened during the night with caregivers coming to change the other resident's soiled garments and bed.

During a dinner visit with Mama, she looked up at me from her hospital bed with tear-filled eyes, pleading with me, "I *know* I need to stay here longer, but please transfer me to my own private room. I can no longer endure the smell and noises of the other person. I need my own private room, please! I have the money so please get me away from this mess!"

This request was a blessing: Mama was fighting to get well, and wanting to fight was a good thing, for it meant she was getting stronger emotionally.

In early March of 2009, Mama decided the house in Atlanta was to be sold. In her room at the nursing center, I sat beside my mother on her bed. Mama reached out to me, taking my hand in her own, her eyes filled with tears as she explained her decision. "The house in Atlanta is no good without your father. When I get well, I do not want to go back there even to visit. It is too heartbreaking for me. It was only beautiful when Papa and I were there together. Now, it does not matter. Hopefully, someone else can find happiness there once more. I leave it up to you to sell it, to sell most of what is there. Here, take this."

Mama handed me a paper. "This is the list of everything that is to be kept, the most important, sentimental things. The rest you are to sell." The shock of being the person responsible for selling my parent's home was overwhelmingly sad, stinging tears poured over my cheek. Mama grasped by hand tightly, "Do not cry my baby, your father will understand." We hugged cheek-to-cheek, our rivulets of tears cascading into a single stream.

On March 21, 2009, ironically on what would have been my father's seventy-fifth birthday, my husband, sister, and I held a heavily advertised estate sale where "everything had to go." We arrived a few days earlier to separate items to be kept according to Mama's wishes. A good friend of my husband came along to assist us.

The morning of the estate sale promised to be a clear day with plenty of sun and clear, blue skies. Beginning at 5 a.m., we had the grueling, painful task of placing rows of tables upon the long expanse of concrete drive leading to my parent's home. On these, we placed their lifetime accumulation of household goods. The larger furnishings were kept inside. "Buyers" were escorted through the home on a "tour" for the highest bidder to take their prize home. Items to be saved for Mama (as she had instructed) were set aside in a locked room away from the viewing public).

People came in droves with their trucks and trailers! Never had I seen so many people turn out for a yard sale or estate sale! By 7 p.m. the house was empty and Mama's cash box was full.

My father had a "built-in" office: his desk and cabinets literally attached to the walls wrapping about the room, and therefore, had to be sold with the house. It was the only room in the house partially intact. I felt compelled to separate myself from all the outside commotion in the driveway, including my family, as I yearned to be "alone with my father" in his special space.

I sat crouched in an empty corner, hands wrapped about both knees, my back supported by the precious walls that had once reverberated the extraordinary music my father performed within the solitude of this room. The misery and bitterness of the day had branded its pain into my heart. I stared at the center of the room, envisioning my father sitting before me playing his accordion, with tears flowing down his face.

My father had often sat in this manner with closed eyes and tear-stained cheeks, as he played his beloved Hungarian number by *Liszt*, "Hungarian Fantasy." It was not unusual for my father to display such emotion while playing his instrument.

When I was a little girl, I asked my father as he was making his music, "Daddy why do you cry when you play your songs?" Folding the bellows of his accordion shut, he took a deep breath, shrugging his shoulders as if the weight of the world was upon them. "I cry for all the pain and suffering of the war and revolution, for all the ugly things your Mama and I had to see and endure. We were only little children, but we had no childhood. The war took it all away. We had to grow up too fast. We were hungry more than fed in those days. In the cold, snowy winter we had no shoes. We had to wrap cardboard or rags around our feet to go outside. Our feet froze. It was a bad time. I cry for having to leave my beautiful country because of communism. I also cry for happiness that my children will never know the pain your mother and I had."

I remember my father petting my head, stroking my hair, as he broke down, crying heavily after his confession. I was very young and could not comprehend the depth of all he said to me, but I remember holding my father's arm and placing my head against it, my child's heart trying its best to comfort him.

Now, at this moment, it was my time to cry, for in my older years *I understood everything* my father was trying to tell me in those days, and I gave myself permission to shed long overdue tears.

It was hot in the room and I was sticky with sweat, not just from the unexpected high temperatures on this date, but my body was under severe stress, for the realization of what I had done on this infamous day made me sick to my stomach: I had "sold my parent's lives."

My father died in the family room adjoining his office/music room. He died as he sat on the couch that no longer occupied its prior space. Was his spirit still floating nearby? Did my father see me in my misery and sadness? Did he understand why I had to do what could now not be undone?

The atmosphere was thick with my father's aura. I looked about me, screaming into the air, "Daddy, oh, Daddy! I am so very sorry! I didn't want to do this! I didn't want to sell your dreams!" The loathing of what I had done that day was more than I could bear. The full force of my fury focused at the walls about me, "Why did it have to be me! I hate doing this! I despise it!" I pounded both hands on the heavily carpeted floor. "Why did you have to die! Oh Daddy - why did you leave us?"

My parent's essence was in this home. Each inch of this house had been lovingly crafted over the years they spent in it, together. The very walls emanated the laughter, the loving, and the heartaches of those who once dwelled within. The memories within the walls of this home were immortal. Even after the structure would disintegrate with passing time, the vibrations of the life that happened here would always remain.

Standing by my father's desk, my attention was drawn to a shimmering streak crossing the floor – the last rays of the day's golden sunlight slipping through the window blinds. I found my senses overrun with memories of each house we had lived in as a family. My body felt as if I were spinning uncontrollably in space, tumbling over and over, as each home's image added more weight to my head in my struggle to "crawl" towards them.

Then an important thought struck me: This house and all our homes, were the vessels that held our family memories, and now, those vessels were empty. The only place they would now exist was in my brain, but where would they exist after I was gone? Maybe somewhere out in the infinite?

The next day, after loading the remaining items onto a large rental truck to take home and place in storage for Mama, we made ready to pull out of my parent's driveway back to North Carolina. A limo took my sister to the airport.

This was it. The devastating finality of knowing I would never walk these hallowed grounds again numbed my body. My poor Mama! Never again would her bare feet walk upon her cool, lush green lawn, nor would she smell the spring flowers she had planted about her yard or take in the scent of this plot of earth as she dug into the soil about her home. How Mama adored her plants! I scouted the property, digging up as many plants as possible to replant in my yard. I also collected several large rocks and seashells my parents had placed about their estate.

I was glad, yes ...and relieved, that my mother was not here for the sale and packing of her belongings. The unfathomable pain of her heartstrings being severed once more would have been too much for her. The ache in my own heart was terrifying and heavy. I don't think I could have been as brave as I had been throughout the "selling ordeal," had I seen the sadness in my mother's eyes as her precious "life" was being toted off by strangers.

Before closing the home for the final time, we scrubbed each nook and cranny to immaculate brilliance, and then photographed the inside and outside of the home for my mother - if she could tolerate the pain of seeing them. Using my legal power-of-attorney status set up by Mama, the house was placed on the market to be sold.

Upon our return home, we placed Mama's belongings in climate-controlled storage (including my father's accordion). I visited Mama the next day at the facility. My insides felt uneasy, for I did not know the state of mind Mama would be in, knowing the home she had shared with her husband, and nearly everything contained within its walls, was gone, except for the things we had placed in storage.

I was taken aback when I walked into my mother's room at the rehab center, for she was dressed, sitting up in bed, resting against several pillows. Her hair was combed, and she had applied a little makeup to prepare for my arrival. She looked pretty. Making my way to her, I enveloped her slight frame in my arms. Mama softly whispered, "It is all done?" I hesitated to reply, taking in a deep breath, "Yes," and also whispered, "Everything was done as you requested. I have the money with me if you want to see it."

Mama leaned back and opened the cashbox I placed on her lap. She gazed, for what seemed to be forever at the stacks of money bundled within. "So …this is the result of a lifetime of love and sacrifice." She closed her eyes and handed the box to me, her face contorted for a moment, as if she was going to burst into tears. Before I could reach out to comfort her, she rallied herself, and spoke kindly, yet with authority, "Keep it for me. Put it in the bank. You will need it." Why would I need it, I wondered? Mama continued on, making her wishes known in a voice that would not take "no" for an answer, "There is no room for me in your house. I need my own place to live."

This thought had occurred to me hundreds of times. The plan *was* to give Mama our master bedroom with adjoining bath. Unfortunately, this plan retired my husband and me to sleep on the pullout couch in the living room. But he did not mind, nor did I, if it meant Mama could come home.

I had explained this plan to Mama, but she would not think of it. "Please build me a little house on your land. That way I can be private, and you can be private, but we will still be together. We will use the rest of the money Papa left me in the bank, of course you must leave enough money in the bank for this nursing home, and if we need to, we can use the money from selling the house and what is in this box. Any leftover money I will save and use for things I will need later."

We researched compact home plans and found the perfect house for Mama. After looking at all the technicalities ranging from plumbing, electricity and sewer lines, and easy accessibility to reach Mama in an emergency, it was decided the best option would be to attach the small home directly to our main home via an enclosed breezeway.

Perhaps it was the thought of having her *own home* that gave Mama renewed strength to get better and stronger, but Mama was discharged from the nursing home in late April of 2009.

Mama moved slowly, but was ambulatory, and thankfully, stronger in body and mind. Mama was glowingly beautiful ...at last. My Mama was ready to come home. But Mama's house was not ready. Our home was small; however, we had three acres of land, and a very large, wide driveway, large enough to accommodate a full-size motorhome rented to be Mama's temporary housing until her "real home" was completed. Mama stayed inside our house during the day, where I assisted with her meals, bathing and personal care. In the evening, she retired to the motorhome for bedtime. We arranged for an intercom system between the motor home and our house enabling Mama to contact us by pushing a button.

Mama had not been inside her new dwelling during the construction phase, being content to passively stand by watching the construction of her "mini-Atlanta" house: a tiny recreation of the home she left behind, complete with cedar siding and Parquet floors.

On a glowingly brilliant, sunny morning in mid-June of 2009, almost eleven months after Daddy died, Mama stepped over the threshold of her new lodging. The few key pieces of furniture from her Atlanta home fit well in the 750 square-foot floor space consisting of a living room/dining area, kitchen, bathroom, and bedroom, touting extra space beyond those dimensions in the basement and attic.

Mama's lighted walnut and glass curio cabinet holding all her collection of precious Herend porcelain, fit perfectly in the living room as well as my father's computer, desk and chair, and large screen television. A newly purchased loveseat and her former recliner were placed in the living room accompanied by the glass tables and oriental rugs and lamps that once dwelled within her Atlanta home. Her French provincial canopy bed and dresser fit well in her bedroom. We stocked the kitchen with Mama's own pots, pans, dishes, glasses and silverware. The bathroom held all her personal towels and toiletries.

Mama stood frozen at the entryway taking in the scene before her. Her shoulders heaved as she let out an audible sigh. She did not say a word but made her way towards the new couch. Although surrounded by many familiar objects, she stood silent, not saying a word about her new home. The look on her face said it all - sad and lost. For nearly a year Mama had gone through countless emotions of loss: denial, anger, resentment, yearning, suffering, sadness, and now, she had come to this phase of her loss - acceptance.

Since July of 2008, Mama had been shuffled from her Atlanta home to Virginia to live with my brother, was treated in a hospital in North Carolina for a month, had therapy in a nursing home for several months, and then lived in a motorhome.

Mama's mouth trembled amidst this new reality. She sought my eyes seeking reassurance for her new fear, "I have slept in too many beds for too long. I don't know how long *this new bed* will last!" I embraced my mother, supporting her weight against me, "Oh my *Edes* Mama, everything will be all right now! I am here for you and will always take care of you!"

To distract Mama from her despair I gently took her by the arm, "Come Mama, come and see how beautiful everything is for you!" With my assistance we slowly looked at the other rooms. As we walked along, I drew Mama's attention to her personal objects here and there. Her mood especially brightened upon entering her bedroom and laying eyes on her "old bedroom furniture."

On her dresser was the piano wood vessel holding her Beloved's ashes. Mama ran her hand reverently across the smooth container, leaned over and kissed it. On the wall, across from the bed, was a portrait of her sweetheart. Mama made her way over to the bed, sitting on the edge, contemplating her departed husband's image. Her face twisted in harsh lines, reflecting the deep-rooted pain wracking her soul, as she cried out, "I miss Papa!"

It was a time of adjustment for all of us. Since the days when we children left home to begin our own life journeys, my mother and father had learned to adapt to a life without children, and again, my parents had become who they were in the beginning: lovers and partners in life. Now, my mother was "the child," her daily sustenance dependent on the love and care of my little family.

After Mama moved in with us, our daily routine seemed foreign, on an uneven keel, as if we had all moved to a new country and had to adjust to the ways and customs of that strange land. It is hard to say exactly when, or how long it took, but eventually we all found the rhythm of our days, melding our schedules around each other's wants and needs.

Mama had regained at least ninety percent of her mobility and got around her little house by "touching walls" and the assisted aid of a walker when she felt it was warranted. We had intentionally designed the home to be "handicapped friendly" with extra wide doors to accommodate a walker or wheelchair, as well as "grab bars" in the shower and on the bathroom walls.

Mama slept late each morning, usually awakening around 10 a.m., and always awoke very hungry! She adored my culinary creation of scrambled egg sandwiches made with toasted English muffins (usually eating two), with a cup of hot tea. I would assist her with showering, washing and styling her hair, and selecting an outfit to wear for the day.

My favorite time was sitting together before I began work. Mama told me several "stories" of her and my father, but her favorite was the "meadow story" to which I always listened attentively.

"Your father and I had a special meadow where we would go to be alone. We were so much in love, your father and me. Before we were married, it was difficult to wait to "be together" so we "were together" whenever we had a chance to be alone. But after we were married, our most precious meadow day was in the very early July of 1953. The sun was high in the sky. The meadow was tall with flowers of every color, but I especially liked the yellow ones. Your father and I lay down in the middle of the tall meadow grasses invisible from the world. We remained hidden away there for a long time, loving each other. I know it was then we conceived you as you were born nearly nine months later! How happy your father and I were to have you for our baby!"

Mama's eyes drifted far back in memory, "Our best times were Sundays when we took you to Szilas Patak (Silas Creek). Your father would swing you about and dangle your tiny feet in the water! I would sit there on the grass listening to the sounds of the water swirling by as I breastfed you and watched you sleep in my arms. We were very poor in money, but very rich in love, the three of us: Papa, me, and you."

While I worked in my home office from 1 p.m. to 6 p.m., Mama was content to sit on her private porch in the "glider chair" we had brought back from Atlanta, where she rocked back and forth, lost in private thoughts, comforted by cheerful chirping birds, enjoying the backyard garden filled with exotic trees, shrubs, and flowers. The summer flew by filled with the everyday things of living. Mama and I walked about the acreage of our home together, planted flowers, and we took extra special care with the pruning and fertilizing of her large pink rose bush that had been transported from her Atlanta home onto our own deck. Mama went with us everywhere: out to eat at her favorite restaurant, shopping for clothes, window shopping, outings to parks, the hairdresser, the manicurist, and the grocery store. She was incredibly proud of her physical progress. However, the extent of her emotional progress was not clear to me until the day she announced, out of the blue, "Judy, I want to make a new Will. I have to make some changes, because my entire life has changed."

My mother holding me, little baby Judit - Hungary - 1954 - Szilas Patek

In early September of 2009, dressed impeccably in a navy-blue pants suit, her hair freshly styled from her visit to the hairdresser the prior day, Mama sat with her lawyer in his office. My husband and I sat in silence as Mama explicitly detailed her wants and desires to the attorney. She assigned me to be her executer. Everything was arranged as she wished, and for the first time, in a long time, true peace came over my mother's face, as if a tremendous burden had been lifted from her heart.

The author, her mother, and husband, Charles – 2009

Last photo taken of Mama when she was still able to walk – late 2009

With my mother's improved condition, she encouraged my husband, son and me to take a few hours on Saturday mornings for ourselves, to get away from the house to run errands and shopping without having to bring her along.

It may have been selfish of me, but I needed some alone time to do things with my husband and son. Through all the long nights and days of the past year's ordeal they both had been strongly supportive of my helping Mama, but we had little time to attend to one another.

We would leave home most Saturday mornings around 8 a.m. and return home around noon. It was only four hours a week, but my mind and body needed that time to recharge. I was beyond exhausted, not only from the long ordeal of caregiving for my mother, but also suffering unrequited grief for my father. With all my care and time pouring into Mama, I never had closure with my father's passing.

In early November of 2009 my family and I were out for our usual Saturday morning "errand run." We stopped at a restaurant for a quick lunch. I phoned Mama to see what she would like us to bring her home to eat.

We had installed a landline phone for my mother and provided her with a cell phone with "unlimited calling overseas." At least twice a month Mama phoned her sister in Hungary and my father's cousins to whom she was very close. Sometimes they talked for hours in her native Hungarian. Speaking with her family across the ocean was excellent therapy for Mama's mind and soul.

I attempted several calls to Mama but was unable to reach her on either phone. First, I thought she might have been on a call to one of her overseas relatives and did not want to interrupt that call by picking up the second phone. Then, I thought the worst. My husband couldn't drive home fast enough.

I burst into Mama's side of the house finding her on the cold kitchen floor clad only in her underwear, "Oh, my *Csimby*!" she painfully cried out, "I fell! I fell! My legs got weak and I fell!"

I quickly summoned an ambulance to take Mama to the hospital as she was complaining of back pain. On evaluation, she was found to have a collapsed vertebra and was taken to surgery where a kyphoplasty was performed. I spent that evening in the hospital with Mama and she was discharged home the next day. Mama had no ill effects or repercussions from the kyphoplasty and went about her life as if nothing had happened.

About two days after Thanksgiving of 2009, Mama had several episodes of unsteadiness, dizziness and low blood pressure. Her extremities had progressively become less flexible and were becoming "rigid." Her gait had become wide-based and she had difficulty holding her bladder. Due to the severity of her symptoms I installed a camera/monitor in Mama's bedroom to allow me to observe her while working in my home office. I also provided Mama with an alarm to wear around her neck to signal me should she need assistance. As I could no longer leave Mama alone, I made sure someone was at home with Mama when I ran my errands.

Years back, in the 1990's, a very kind, but very poor family lived behind us "through the woods." They had a beautiful eight-year-old daughter by the name of Elizabeth Mae. Elizabeth Mae became a "regular" at my household. She was always hungry and predictably showed up most evenings in time for supper. And for many years, until she grew up and had children of her own, lived with me more "on" than "off." We became very close in our relationship, more like a mother and daughter, and I grew to love her as my own little girl. Elizabeth Mae was kind and compassionate, and during my son's younger years, when he was on summer break from school, she stayed at my home caring for him while I worked at the hospital during the day. We had kept in touch through the years, and to my surprise, she had recently obtained her CNA certification, and I asked Elizabeth Mae to care for Mama on an as-needed basis.

In the interim, I had made Mama an appointment with a well-known, much loved, and respected neurologist, who had seen both my husband and me for various past issues. Unfortunately, being very popular, it was two weeks before we could get in to see him.

After a physical examination of my mother, a thorough history of Mama's signs and symptoms (and being informed of all Mama had gone through in the past year), including nerve conduction studies and a brain MRI, he arranged a private conference for us to discuss the findings.

Behind the closed doors of his private office the neurologist directed me to a comfortable, padded leather chair; however, instead of sitting down behind his desk, he pulled up his own large chair beside mine. His expression and the sadness in his eyes instantly put me on edge: *there was something wrong.* The same sick feeling of when Daddy died scraped at my heart. I knew before he said anything that my Mama would not get better. The doctor gently placed a steadying hand on my wrist. With a grave tone, he explained, "Your mother has a condition called multisystem atrophy. It's in the same family as Parkinson's disease, but much more aggressive. She has all the tell-tale signs and symptoms that you brought her in with including the "masked" appearance of her face, inability to sleep, severe weakness, loss of sweating, dizziness, no bladder control, her gait problems, hypotension, and a soft, low voice. And, of course, she is very depressed, still grieving the loss of her husband."

I sat motionless, unable to speak, as he patiently explained, "The etiology of the disease is undetermined. But one thing for sure, it is a rapidly progressive, multisystem, neurodegenerative fatal disease."

The doctor saw the unspoken question in my eyes, the question of how much time my mother had left. He continued, slowly, "Given the extremely rapid progression to date, if she is fortunate, she may have another year of time, but again …she has had such swift progression in such a short time …it is more likely to be less than one year. I am truly very, very sorry for all of you. She is such a sweet lady. I will take steps to have Hospice assist you in the home."

Sweet, yes, Mama was sweet, loving, adorable and perfectly wonderful. And now, *just* now, when she was "coming alive again," *just* when we were so very happy as a family and looking forward to years of laughter and love, *just* when she was healing from all the terrible things she had gone through - she was leaving me - she was slowly dying, and I could do nothing.

By mid-December 2009, Mama's condition had her bedbound, her French provincial bed replaced by a motorized hospital bed with a grab/trapeze bar overhead. Hospice was a tremendous help, coming every other day during the week to bathe Mama.

Hospice washed my mother's hair in a "bed sink," bathed her, changed her bed sheets, and administered medications. Eventually, a Foley catheter had to be inserted into Mama's urethra to drain her urine for she had lost all bladder control. I emptied her Foley catheter bag at least four times a day and kept a close watch on the drainage tube for signs of bacterial growth. My only dilemma with Mama's personal care was helping her with constipation caused by her inactivity. Three times a day, I would manually pump Mama's legs (in a bicycle riding motion) to help with blood flow to her extremities. I then would bend each leg to her chest to stimulate her organs and stretch her back muscles. Lying flat on her back made "evacuation" nearly impossible. I finally worked out a system of elevating both legs, pushing them toward her chest, to assist her with that issue, but not always with perfect results. This, according to Mama, made her "humiliation complete."

Each time I helped Mama in this manner her eyes filled with tears. Her disease had now taken another fragile piece of her dignity away. During those times she whispered softly to me, for the illness was causing her voice to change, and it no longer had the volume it once did, "I am sorry, I am so sorry, it is too much for you my baby." Her pitiful apologies for a condition she had no control over broke my heart. When "it was all over," I would lie beside Mama in her bed, holding and reassuring her. "Mama, remember all the years you took care of me? It is now my turn to take care of you. I love you more than anything, and I will do everything I can to help you feel better."

A registered nurse came once a week to take vital signs and to assess Mama's overall condition. Mama began to experience a lot of restlessness and agitation due her bed-bound condition, as well as a profound insomnia (up all night and sleeping during the day). Mama's mental clarity was sharp, but her body was ravaged. This made her inactivity even more intolerable. At times, I wished Mama had dementia, wishing she was not lucid, wishing her mind could take her "someplace far away to a beautiful place" where there was no sickness or pain.

Medications were given by Hospice to help Mama cope. Her muscles were severely weakened to where she could no longer roll over from one side to the other without assistance. Every hour, on the hour, I rolled Mama over and wedged pillows behind her back to support her new position. I placed pillows between her thighs to support her legs and lower back.

Due to having to roll and turn Mama frequently, dealing with the ureteral tube for her urine, and her bowel issues, Mama declared she did not want to wear any clothing, as it "Only got in the way." I made sure she was warm enough with sufficient sheets and blankets. I placed a television in Mama's bedroom to help distract her from her situation.

During the day, I pulled Mama's hospital bed beside the bedroom window to give Mama a better view of the green Juniper bushes, the Holly tree with its red berries, as well as the "winter birds" gathering to eat the seeds in their birdfeeder on her window sill. On pretty days, I bundled Mama up with lots of blankets and opened all the windows in her house, allowing the various scents and sounds of nature into her closed-off world.

Christmas came. Mama slept through it. I slept too.

Mama's seventy-fifth birthday, January 11, 2010, was a happy one, because my sister, Pilvia, came to visit me. She offered to stay with Mama in her little home for a while, giving me a much-needed respite.

Our family celebrated a beautiful birthday dinner served in Mama's room, complete with a luscious birthday cake ablaze with candles.

After a week of caring for our mother, my sister was already exhausted. And no wonder. I had months of easing into this rigorous schedule, and time to get used to seeing Mama in her present condition; however, my sister had not seen our mother in a long time, and the shock of seeing her in such a debilitated state was very overwhelming. But, before I knew it, Pilvia was on her way back to California. I missed her presence, just knowing my sister was here with me, that "we children" were caring for our mother together, made me feel less isolated and alone in my caretaker role. When she left life seemed emptier and sadder than before she had arrived.

We ordered a stretcher (the kind used by ambulance services) on which to transfer Mama from her hospital bed to wheel her outside to get fresh air on the deck when weather permitted. Even though it was technically winter, there were a few days here and there with above-normal temperatures.

The thought of Mama never being outside to enjoy the beauty of the world and to breathe in fresh air greatly troubled me. I wanted her to feel the warm embrace of the sun, to feel the gentle kiss of snowflakes against her cheeks, to see the glistening morning dew settled on the blades of bright green grass, and most important of all, to see the beauty of the spring.

The spring seemed so far away - an eternity away. My eyes filled with tears wondering if she would live that long.

The second week of March 2010 brought beautifully warm temperatures resulting in a fiery frenzy of color amidst the yellow daffodils, pink Camellias and red azaleas about our property. At last, we could "air Mama out" often about the yard allowing her eyes to feast on nature's colorful spectacle after the long, dreary winter.

A week before what would have been my father's seventy-sixth birthday, Mama would not wake up. I shook her shoulders and spoke loudly, but she did not respond. She was breathing very deeply. No type of stimulation would arouse her. I panicked! I did not understand what was happening. I did not know if she was in pain and the idea of her being in a "coma" terrified me. I immediately called Hospice and they arranged for their ambulance service to take Mama to the Hospice Center for "watching."

Mama had created a Living Will stating that if she could not speak for herself, was unconscious, that she wanted no fluids, no food, and no life-giving medicines administered. She only wanted to be kept comfortable and out of pain.

For three days Mama remained "comatose." For three days, I slept in a window-bench bed in her Hospice room, listening to her horrifying, rattled breathing. Her extremities were mottled, and her urine output was tea-colored and barely existent. A very kind nurse assigned to Mama explained these symptoms were very common for those experiencing end of life.

But it was "not common" for me! My precious Mama who had suffered so much in this life, who had sacrificed all her life for me, for her children, my sweet Mama was dying in front of me. I wanted to scream orders at the nursing staff, "Give her everything so she will have a chance to live!"

But I could not scream it. I dared not ask it, for the memory of one very special evening when Mama and I were alone in her room rushed through my brain.

That evening started out as any other ordinary evening talking about little things: what Mama would like for breakfast, or Mama watching me as I refilled her pill containers for the next day. Even though I was in deep despair knowing that my mother could pass away at any moment, I was always upbeat and positive in spirit when around her - a difficult act to carry on when my heart was breaking. However, Mama was my mother, and just as she had done for decades, Mama could always "read me." It was almost impossible to hide anything from her. From out of nowhere, she asked me the "dreaded question" as I was brushing her hair during our nightly bedtime routine, "Am I dying?" She "knew." I couldn't lie to my mother. She would know I was not telling the truth. I positioned myself on the bed beside her, placing her cool hand in my own. My body was trembling from the thought of what I was going to say. My voice weakly acknowledged, "Yes, Mama, yes, you are." I began crying, a hard cry, with retching sobs, the exhaustion of everything finally exacting its toll upon my mind and body.

Through convulsive gasps, I laid my head on my mother's chest as a child seeking comfort. Mama petted my head, stroking my hair ever so slightly for she had little strength. She was not crying. She was not upset. She spoke softly and gently as if I was a little girl again.

"It is all right my *Csimby*. It *is* all right. I have known I would die for a long time. I did not talk about it. I did not want to upset you. Just do not let me suffer. Give me something, a drug, so I do not know what is going on if I cannot speak for myself. Remember the Living Will made in the lawyer office? Promise me, please?"

How could Mama be so calm? Wasn't she afraid of dying? I was terrified to think about a life without my mother *and* father. Mama's words broke my train of thought, her words coming in a soft, yet determined tone, "I am *ready* to be with your Papa. I miss him very much. It is no life without him. I am ready when it will be the time."

I could not hold back my tears. I was facing this all alone. No brother. No sister. No husband. No son. I was alone with Mama in her room as she poured out her last wishes. My heart was on the verge of exploding from the pain of her words.

"Please do not cry my little *Csimby*. I have a lot on my mind, with so much to say, and I must confess something to you now." Lying beside Mama on the bed, she continued her thoughts, "I know it is wrong to have a favorite child, but I cannot help feeling the way I do. You were always special to me. The first moment I held you in my arms I gave you my entire heart and soul. My baby, you were the most beautiful thing Papa and I had in the ugly world we inherited after "The War." Mama took in a deep breath, "The three of us have gone through everything together since that day in the meadow. I love your brother and sister with all my heart, and would do anything for them, but you…" Mama weakly pulled her hand out of mine, clenched her frail fists, and slowly placed them over her heart as beads of tears swam down her pale cheeks, "But for you …it hurts right here!"

I was overwhelmed, I didn't know what to say, except, "Oh Mama!" as I crumpled inward upon her bosom once more. We both cried tears mixed with relief and exhaustion. I cried myself to sleep on Mama's chest. I slept there for about an hour.

Upon awakening, I gazed down at Mama's sweet face, at last free of the contortions of grief and pain. I kissed her forehead lightly. My legs were shaky from emotion, barely supporting me as I exited Mama's bedroom toward my side of the house, my mind reeling from the shock of our revelations to one another.

Now she knew. Now I knew.

Out of fear of "being haunted" by Mama should I not go by her wishes, I was determined to do as she requested.

I remembered an article I had read in years past that a person's hearing is believed to be the last sense to go in the dying process. Therefore, I decided to "talk" to Mama. I sat beside Mama on her Hospice bed, telling her how much I loved her, how much I wanted her to live so we could be happy for many years to come, how much her grandson loved her and needed her, how much we all loved and needed her. My husband worked only half-days during those days and spent several hours a day sitting at Mama's bedside reading a book of beautiful poetry dedicated to mothers, constantly talking to her, reading to her, hoping to stimulate Mama's brain to help her awaken.

I called my sister in California to tell her our Mama was leaving us, was dying. She got on the first plane and was by my side within twelve hours.

The day before my father's birthday, March 20, 2010 with all of us present, Mama woke up with no recollection of "being asleep" for all those days. She refused to accept that the hospital staff and I believed her to be dying. But Mama knew it had to be true, for she could see my sister was here, in North Carolina, at Hospice, with a puffy face and eyes swollen from crying.

My mother awoke with a voracious appetite, eating and drinking everything the superb chef at the Hospice facility prepared for her. She looked radiant.

The next day, by Mama's "royal decree," at her Hospice bedside, we celebrated my father's seventy-sixth birthday, with a candlelit birthday cake. Mama asked we plant a "tulip tree" (a magnolia species) in honor of her husband's birthday. The same afternoon, my husband scoured nurseries, purchasing a pink flowering variety, and that very evening, my husband and I finished planting the sacred tree in our front yard, just as the pale, purple streaks of dusk melted into the approaching night sky.

My sister flew back home to Los Angeles and Mama came home two days later. Although, still bed-bound, she looked rested, her face beaming with a healthy glow. It had been years since I had seen my mother look so stunningly beautiful.

But I was frightened. I had heard "stories" of how many people with terminal illnesses had a sudden surge of energy and a glow of vitality about them just before they died. *And ...Mama was glowing –glowing with the excitement of "true love" as a woman glows when her beloved one is near.*

Mama became more alert and remarkably more lucid. Her mind was clear, and she talked to me about endearing memories. "I remember when you and your sister would go out to play, how I would put your hair in a ponytail and placed a huge, thick, white ribbon about your hair, and how your dresses would billow in the wind as you jumped rope and rode bikes. You were the only children who went outside to play in dresses on any day of the week other than Sunday, but you girls looked very pretty, and I saw no need for you to wear anything else. You were my princesses!"

Two days after Mama came home, we placed her on the hospital stretcher allowing her a first-hand view of the intense stain of color about the yard. Every plant and flower on our property had come to life: daffodils, camellias, azaleas, and the pink rose bush from Mama's house in Atlanta. By some miracle, nature must have known it would be my mother's last spring, and by intentional plan or not, everything had bloomed much earlier than normal for this time of year. But my Mama had blossomed into the most beautiful flower of all.

Mama's respite was short-lived. By the second week of April 2010 the glorious glow of health vanished. I spent every moment I could with Mama, talking with her, massaging her, moving her legs, just being with her. Each morning, I treaded softly into her bedroom to check on her, my heart full of dread that I may find her lifeless, but each morning, in the dim light of her room, I found reassurance in the rhythmic rise and fall of her chest.

Through all her emotional and physical pain, Mama had not once brought up the subject of her estranged son - until one evening. Mama weakly grasped my hand in mid-air as I was about to apply another stroke of the brush to her silver strands, "*Csimby* ... I miss my son." Since coming to live with me, for whatever reason, there had been no communication between Mama and her son. "I suppose I no longer have a son. I do not know why he does not call me. I suppose he must have his reasons for not contacting me. I think it is because of all the "old pain" that never got resolved with Papa and me. But I have been grieving deeply for Papa and have been too tired and too sick to call him to ask why he does not call me. My energy in my heart, body and mind for such things is gone. I am emotionally depleted. Now, I am dying. He does not even know I am sick! But ...I do not want him to know I am very sick. I do not want him to worry about me or Papa anymore. *Nothing* is his fault. It is no one's fault. It is all right, though. He has his own life, a good life. I wanted him to have a good life. It seems like a once-upon-a-time dream when I had a little boy. How I loved that beautiful little boy. Do not tell him when I die!"

Mama's blunt declaration was unexpected, but even more unexpected, was the tone of her voice. Mama's inflection was flat - not upset, not angry, but rather "that's the way it is" in tone. A voice of acceptance.

At that moment Charles walked in with a surprise for Mama: a freshly brewed cup of Chamomile tea and an English muffin - Mama's favorite meal or snack any time of the day. "Here you are Mama, I made this with extra loving care for you." Mama smiled appreciatively at my husband as she sipped her tea and took bites from her muffin. Charles made himself comfortable in a chair at the foot of the bed. "Mama, did you know there's a half-moon out tonight? You can see it from your bedroom window!"

Charles helped me pull Mama's bed to the window to see the shining orb. Although only at half phase, it was already bright enough to cast light on the yard outside. Mama was quiet for a moment, transfixed by the heavenly shower of light on the grounds outside her window. Mama's eyes locked on the luminous mass, "How pretty it looks up there! Sonny was born when the moon was full. I remember Papa carrying me to the car to take me to the hospital for Sonny to be born. I remember looking up and seeing the big moon up in the sky. I felt it was a good sign that the light of God was shining down upon me that night. But now it seems like a dream. My son ...he ..."

Mama stared steadily and intently at Charles with a crestfallen, woebegone expression, the edges of her mouth turning downwards as she cried out to my husband, "You are my son now, my *only* son!" Mama could no longer hold in her brittle emotions, and at long last, her tormented soul spewed out the last dregs of mournful misery and anguish festering in her heart, over the "loss of her son," as an explosion of hot, bitter tears rushed down her pale cheeks. Mama reached out to Charles for comfort; however, her arms were too weak to hold out, except for a few seconds, and her limp limbs fell onto the bed.

Charles rushed to Mama's side embracing her waiflike form to his broad chest. He rocked Mama back and forth, stroking her hair and running his hands over her back to soothe her. "Yes, Mama, I'm proud to be your son." Charles' voice cracked, his voice choking through sobs, "Oh Mama,

I truly am very proud and honored to be your son! I love you…I *do* love you Mama!"

April 24, 2010 was like any other evening Mama and I spent together except it was a Saturday night and I looked forward to a quiet Sunday with my family.

The weather forecast for Sunday was unseasonably warm and beautiful, calling for bright blue cloudless skies and lots of yellow sunshine. "Mama, tomorrow I'm going to "roll you" outside to soak up some sun!" Mama weakly grasped my hand appreciatively, "It will be wonderful. Maybe I can eat on the deck outside?" I squeezed Mama's hand, "Oh, that would be very nice. Maybe all of us can – we're all home together at last!"

Mama looked at the ceiling, her eyes fluttering as if she would fall asleep at any moment. But, suddenly, they burst wide with recollection.

And then, Mama spoke more openly to me than she ever had, spilling her heart, uncloaking her inner-most secret thoughts, "Remember the other night when we looked at the moon? There was a full moon the night I met your father. A full moon and a sky full of stars. I could not help myself to love him as soon as I saw him. He was so handsome, so beautiful. The moment we saw each other we felt as if we had always known each other, had always been together, would always be together. That May night under the stars, under the Acacia tree, was a night of splendor. We had both gone through so much hell with the War, but under the full moon we found in each other peace, hope and deep love. That night we could not let go of each other. We promised we would hold strong and tight to each other forever."

The Moon of Mama's Life

Mama's eyes darted about her bedroom, her weary eyes going from the ceiling, to my father's portrait, to my face. "The night before Papa died, he complained of being extremely tired, but the next day was *garbage day*. Papa complained of not feeling well, a feeling of utter exhaustion, but he forced himself to haul the trash cans up the steep driveway to the top of the road. The next morning, he made his rounds to get his coffee at his favorite place and to pick up his medicines. It was unusual for me to already be awake, but I was waiting for him when he got back home. It was as if something cried out to me to "wake up!" Papa got home around eleven o'clock in the morning. Papa complained about everything in our yard being so "dry." We had not had a good rain in weeks and the lawn was turning brown. He had worked hard for us to have nice green grass and was upset there was no rain! He said he was terribly tired but was hungry." Mama took a deep, shuddering breath as she continued with her memories, "Papa sat down on the couch in the family room to rest. I went to the kitchen to get him a bowl of cereal. Papa always waited on me, but he looked worn out, and somehow, I found the strength to wait on him this time. I sat beside Papa on the couch as he held the cereal bowl. He tilted his head backwards to rest it on the pillow behind his head and fell asleep. He almost dropped the bowl and I caught it before it spilled. I rested my head on your father's shoulder and fell asleep with him. When I woke up it was one o'clock in the afternoon. Papa was still sleeping. But …he was not sleeping."

Mama's attention returned to her husband's portrait, her eyes unblinking, as if she had transported herself back to that very moment. "His face was a gray color and he was not breathing. I shouted to him Papa! Papa wake up! I shook his shoulders, but he did not move. The end came too suddenly. It was not fair! We did not even have a chance to say goodbye or tell each other one more time how much we loved one another. I did not have a chance to feel his strong arms about me one last time. Our world, our life, all we had struggled for was over …our time of loving was over. I once wrote in a birthday card to your father: *Our love is not measured by time …time is measured by our love.* But at that moment, we were out of time – our time was gone. My beautiful love, my *Edes* Papa, was dead. I wanted to keep him there with me. I did not want him to be taken away. I wanted to freeze time and hold him there until I died in his arms. I flung myself across his chest holding him as strong as I could, feeling his still warm body against me. I kissed his hands, his neck, his eyes and cheeks until his face was wet from my tears. I found strength I did not know I had and pulled him onto my body, on top of me, and we lay on the couch together. I remembered our entire life together. I could see us as being young again at the dance, making love under our tree, running from the Russians, coming to America, working very hard to make a new life, loving each other with a pure sweet love every day, and struggling with happy hearts every day to give you children all we never had, seeing my

Papa smile, seeing him play his accordion music." I held firmly to my mother's hand, as she stared intently into my eyes, a smile of sadness upon her gentle face, "It is strange when you think about where you might be when you die. We do not know – how can we? To die so far from where you were born? I think about it – the joy and happiness, the pain and heartache of Papa's life, of my life, beginning in Hungary and ending in America, in Atlanta, on a couch together, at a moment in time chosen by destiny. Now, when I die, I will die in North Carolina, so very far away from where I was born, but close to you my *Csimby*. Did you know your father wrote me a love letter every day since we came to America? Papa promised he would write me a love letter every day on the night we escaped from Hungary after we had to burn our original love letters in the coal stove. After Papa died, I placed all the notes and letters he wrote me in the red, white and blue *Bicentennial Trunk* from Disneyworld, the one that is in my attic right now. The key to it is in my jewelry box. Promise me, after I die, that you will go outside onto your wide-open land, and then I want you to burn them all, so the smoke of the letters containing our love will go up to heaven. Promise to cremate me after I die and keep your father's ashes and my ashes with you all the time. Promise me you will never forget what your Papa and I accomplished on this earth, and how very much we loved you, loved all our children."

My eyes were full of heavy tears. I squeezed my mother close to my heart, trying hard to speak through an engorged throat, but managed to reply to her request in a hoarse whisper, "I promise Mama to do everything you ask. I promise to always remember everything. I promise to keep you and Daddy with me all the days of my life, to love you forever."

For some reason, Mama's mind was filled with many thoughts on this exceptional evening, and she continued her recitations, telling me things she had never mentioned before in a tight voice, choked with painful emotion.

"All the years Papa and I had together, everything we had gone through, ended in that room in Atlanta. I was not afraid to be alone with Papa when he died. I was grateful even in my grief that God allowed me to be with my husband, my love, at the very end. I kissed his lips, very gently, several times, hoping my love would wake him up, but nothing I did woke him up." Tears trickled down Mama's face and mine. I lay down beside Mama in her bed, holding her close, feeling her agony in my heart and in my mind, as I envisioned her alone with my father at his death. Mama's warm hand enfolded in mine, as she relayed tiny details of the day my father died, of which I was never aware.

"I cannot remember how I got up from holding your father, but somehow I called Tommy and Laura next door to help me. The police came. The police called you. The ambulance came. They took my Papa away."

Mama yawned, her eyes quivered, fighting the exhaustion of her memories, fighting the exhaustion wanting to take over her thoughts. "*Csimby* ... 'member the meadow I told you about, where we conceived you?" I nodded my head in remembrance. "It was a most splendid day. If it was possible for me to wish for the perfect day to live over, it would be that day. The air was washed fresh by a previous gentle rain the night before. The birds were singing love songs to us from the trees. That day, we confirmed our vows of love, each of us swearing to the other that we would belong only to each other from that day for eternity. If only Papa and I could have once again found that meadow where he held me in his arms, so tenderly, and we loved each other as no one has ever loved before."

My eyes were drowning in tears, my mind envisioning the innocent beauty of that day. Suddenly, my reverie was broken by Mama firmly squeezing my hand, and I was shaken by her sudden surge of strength.

At that moment, her eyes were looking past me, to a place I had never seen, a place only known to her and my father. "The first time I gave your father all my heart, all my body and soul, was that special night under the full moon, under the Acacia tree with the beautiful white flowers." Mama's smile was joyful and jubilant, her glistening hazel orbs sparkling with the memory of two sweethearts giving the essence of their love to one another under a shining sea of stars. Mama yawned, and I pulled her closer to me. Her voice was tired, raspy, soft, but filled with happiness, "*Csimby Edes*, loving your father under the full moon, under our tree, and in the meadow …were the most beautiful times he and I ever had together." I felt Mama's grip loosen from my hand as, at long last, the tide of a restful sleep carried her away to a time of splendor, a time when she and my father were young and beautiful, and dreamt of all the wonderful things they wanted to do and wanted to be.

The sounds of Mama's soft breathing filled the room. I quietly slipped out of her bed and tiptoed out of the bedroom. As I entered the breezeway toward my part of the house, I remembered what Mama said about my father complaining of "No rain for a long time" prior to his death.

On the evening of my father's cremation, the moisture-laden heaven's burst forth a cannonade of wet arrows upon the landscape of my parent's home.

ELEGY FOR MY MAMA

I tossed and turned, unable to sleep the night of April 24, 2010, my emotions raw, and my head achy and cloudy, as my brain could not "shut off" Mama's summary of her final wishes and her last memories of being with my father. My restless legs carried me back to Mama's side of the house. I went to her bedroom. The soft glow of a small nightlight made it difficult to see her clearly, however, I immediately noticed Mama's breathing sounding exceptionally raspy and labored. I called out to Mama but there was no answer. I turned on the kitchen light, its yellow incandescence spreading onto Mama in her bed. I was mortified by a green foamy slime oozing from the corner of Mama's mouth down her chin. I shook Mama gently several times to wake her up, but she was unresponsive to my touch or voice. I immediately phoned Hospice for their ambulance. The ambulance staff examined Mama. She was breathing. She was not moaning to indicate pain. She simply would not wake up. They prepared Mama for transport to Hospice. Mama had no clothes on. I assisted in covering her with a blanket to preserve her dignity. By now, my husband was there beside me, helping the emergency response team take Mama on her stretcher down the stairs of our deck. I followed behind as Mama was lifted into the back of the ambulance. I jumped in to be beside Mama. I hugged her, kissed her, and held her hand.

My body was stiff, nearly paralyzed, as was my mind. I thought I heard the ambulance driver ask if I wanted to ride with them, but I was not able to respond. The next thing I remember was standing in the driveway as my mother was taken away. I felt numb, nauseated, as if I was not in my body, feeling as if I were suspended in the air as a feather floating on a breeze. I found myself sitting on my couch in the living room having no memory of how I got there.

I was frightened, fearful that Mama would be in another coma, petrified of watching her "die again" for another three days at Hospice. My body and brain could not cope with the trauma of seeing her waste away as she had done only a month earlier. I was cold. My body was shaking, and my teeth were chattering as if I was outside in the middle of a winter snow storm without a coat or shoes. I was obtunded to everything about me.

My eyes opened at 8:30 a.m. on April 25, 2010. I was in my own bed. I had no recollection of my husband placing me there. The trauma of seeing my mother's face with green drool oozing from her mouth had caused my body and mind to shut down in utter unacceptance of her illness.

A tremendous wave of guilt washed over me. I should be at Hospice with my mother! With my husband's assistance I forced my reluctant body out of bed to get dressed. The phone rang at 9:10 a.m. I answered the call. "Is this Judith?" asked the kind voice. I hesitantly replied, "Yes …it is." I had seen the phone number display on the caller I.D. I *knew* it was Hospice. "Judith, your mother passed at 9 a.m. She did not suffer. She never woke up. I am so sorry for your loss."

I had prepared myself hundreds of times for this scenario, but how can anyone be ready for a call declaring the death of your parent. I felt as if I had been punched in the stomach, but with a spinning head and a dry throat, managed to quietly respond, "Please do not move my mother from her room. I will be there very soon."

By 10 a.m. I was at Hospice with my husband and son. I asked them to please remain in the waiting area to allow me time alone with my mother.

The room at Hospice where I had spent my three nights and days with Mama the prior month had been filled with an oppressive air, the atmosphere thick and heavy, but today, upon entering my mother's private sanctuary, the air was light, and a feeling of pure love resounded about me. Mama was lying on her bed. The nurses had prepared her for my arrival: her hair combed, a fresh gown on her person, and clean bedding. A stream of yellow morning sunshine cascaded between the closed draperies casting a shining ray of light upon Mama's face. I was taken aback by my mother's beauty. Her face was soft, relaxed, with almost a hint of a smile upon her lips, as if she had seen something wonderfully beautiful just prior to her passing, something that gave her hope, gave her peace. I had prepared myself for the worst, but Mama, even in death, had made sure I would see her at her best.

My legs were giving way. I lay down on the bed beside my mother and pulled her close to me. Her body was warm, especially behind her head where she had rested it against her pillow. I had not yet cried at all, …not until I felt the warmth of her next to me. Tears burst forth from deep within, for once I left this place of grief today, I would never again feel the soft warmth of my mother against me. Only too soon, would the last glowing embers of her life's warming essence dissolve into infinity.

A shower of teary stars swept over my mother as I cradled her lifeless form against my shuddering body, "Mama, I am so sorry you suffered! I am so sorry I was not here with you when you died! Please, forgive me!" Guilt licked at my emotional wounds. How could I have not been here for my mother at the last?

The nurses told me that my mother had never awakened. She had never known she was at Hospice. Mama never knew I was not there with her. Or did Mama know?

Then, as if a window had been opened to the outside world, the sweet smell of lemon verbena rushed past me, its memorable scent entering my heart, causing my body to feel light and hopeful, as a flickering light of peaceful redemption inundated every fiber of my being. I sensed Mama's soul, sensed Mama's spirit with me, comforting me, loving me.

Could it be that my Mama wanted it to end this way? Could it be that my Mama did not want me to sit by her side for hours, or days, watching her suffer knowing how it tormented me? My lapse of memory, my paralysis, my not being able to think or move after Mama was taken to Hospice …there had to be a reason for it - Mama wanted to be alone, alone with my father when it was time for her to go with him. I could not help but believe, with all my heart, that Mama dying alone was the way she wanted it to be. I lay there with my mother for what seemed to be hours, stroking her hair, feeling the smoothness of her lovely face, as I held her hand in mine, whispering in her ear, "My *Edes Anukam* (my darling mother), I will love you forever. I am an orphan now Mama!"

I kissed her still rosy cheeks. *Oh, my Mama! How will I live without you! How can I accept that you are gone!* Mama carried me in her body till the beckoning to be born brought me into the world. In her death, my body sensed her physical loss, as if I could feel the "other part of me" severed away.

As I lay next to my mother clasping her snug against my body, the full meaning of why Mama had been compelled to spill her memories, her deepest thoughts with me, the prior night, was now evident.

Somehow, someway, her soul was already in the process of slowly evaporating from her body, urging her subconscious mind to confess her most treasured thoughts to me prior to her passing - her soul "knew" that it would be our final time of "being alive" together, and her last surviving life's essence understood I would never hear her beautiful words of love for me again, never again hear her sweet laughter once more, and never again feel the warmth of her protective, loving arms enveloping me.

There would never be another "anything" for Mama. Anything that was something for my Mama was now gone forever. The life she lived was now a stolen moment in the annals of time.

I would miss Mama's touch, her lemon verbena scent, her tender words of love and reassurance, her strength and courage, everything that had made my mother – my Mama, and I would miss the glow of her presence in this world. A soft knock at the door sought my attention. It was my husband and son asking if they could say goodbye to Mama.

I called my sister from Hospice, but I could barely get the words out, but *my Pilvia* knew why I was calling, for my anguished cries of heartbreak said all.

As my sister was in the recovery stages from a recent surgery, we both felt the stress of flying out to North Carolina, once more, and the strain of going to Mama's cremation, would be detrimental to her recovery. I told my sister I would take care of everything for our Mama. We cried together on the phone. I comforted her, and she comforted me. Mama had asked me not to tell my brother when she died. I promised my mother I would not tell, but my sister felt he should know and phoned him about our mother's passing. I knew nothing more of my sister's call to my brother, all I did know was that I had kept *my* promise to Mama.

The cremation arrangements were made for the next day. My husband purchased a lovely remembrance box, identical to my father's, made of the finest piano wood in which to place Mama's ashes.

I had known for a long time that my mother was dying. For all the months prior to her death I experienced countless days of grief, sadness, anger, depression and feelings of isolation.

I suffered extreme caregiver exhaustion. I dreaded each day thinking "today could be the day." I, too, died slowly every day, as I watched my mother lose her ability to take care of herself, lose her independence, lose hope, lose dreams for any future. I watched the cruel illness rob her dignity.

Yes, in every way possible, my body and mind "died" with Mama during the culmination of countless days and nights, as I helplessly watched the once lovely, vivacious woman, my mother, disintegrate before my eyes.

That evening, the day of leaving Mama at Hospice, I lay in bed thinking about my precious Mama's body far away from me, lying in an icy morgue, waiting for transport to the facility where she would be cremated the following day. And, I could not help but to think about the last minutes I had spent with my father, remembering the feel of his chest against me as I embraced his lifeless form on the gurney at the funeral home.

When I was a child my parents were full of love and life, serious and funny, rebels for a cause, devoutly devoted to one another, and fervently patriotic in their love for America, the country that gave them a home when they had nowhere else to go. My parent's strength to carry on against all odds, in Hungary, and in America, taught me to never give up; however, in the past few years, I had seen my parents travel down a road of deep depression, fragility, anxiousness and susceptibility. And, in my sorrow, I followed them down the same dark path. Deep within my being, I knew my parents did not want me to sink into the same bed of tortuous pain they had shared, and I was determined to salvage myself from that pain, determined to harness the unfathomable inner strength and courageous fortitude to endure the unendurable that once embodied the spirit of my parents – determined to be strong and resilient, and determined, if world events deemed it necessary in future years, to be a "Freedom Fighter" like my father.

The following afternoon my husband, son and I traveled to say our goodbyes to Mama at the funeral home where her cremation was to be held. The lady director led me to the viewing room to see my mother. Mama was laid out on a platform, atop, graceful, white Grecian columns. Soft torch lights spread their golden radiance about the room.

The staff at the funeral home had prepared Mama beautifully. Her hair was perfectly arranged, and they had applied a small amount of makeup. Mama's cream-colored gown, the dress she wore to dance with my father on their Fiftieth Wedding Anniversary, now served as her burial shroud, as were her wishes. I carried a bouquet of flowers in my hands.

Mama appeared to be as if asleep. Her hands and feet were not cyanotic. I draped myself over her, gathering her cool torso to mine. I was surprised! Unlike my father who had been rigid to the touch, Mama was soft and delicate, as when she was alive. And, Mama looked years younger, even her hair seemed darker. She reminded me of "The Sleeping Beauty," waiting for the kiss of true love to awaken her.

I kissed Mama's face, her eyes, her hands, holding her close to me for a long time, for after I left this house of mourning, everything that was once my mother would turn to ashes. This would be the last time I would ever kiss, touch, hug or look upon my Mama. I soaked up every sensation of touching her, of holding her, of looking upon her beautiful face, wanting the memory to remain always, to smolder into my mind, the feel of her to burn into my hands, wanting the memory of our last time together to leave its imprint upon my soul forever.

Carriers of grief relentlessly trickled down my cheeks. Holding my Mama close, I spoke softly in her ear, making a vow, "Mama, I promise you I will never forget anything, never forget all you taught me, all you told me about Hungary, about where I came from, my *Magyar* roots. I will never forget all the love you and Daddy gave me, how you sacrificed to bring me to a world of freedom. I will remember everything about your lives, all that happened. I promise I will keep you and Daddy in my heart forever.

I promise Mama! I promise I will never forget! Thank you, Mama for everything you did for me all my life."

Mama's hands rested upon her bosom. I placed my bouquet of carnations (Mama's favorite flower) inside her palms, clenching her slender fingers around the stems. In my possession was a Hungarian Flag. I remembered how much Mama had wanted to bring a Hungarian flag to drape over my father at his funeral, but in her grief, had forgotten to do so.

Determined to make amends for my father, I draped a Hungarian flag over my mother, the length of it covering her from the mid-chest down over her toes.

On July 24, 1998, almost ten years to the day when my father died on July 25, 2008, he wrote a letter to my mother to be opened only upon his death. Mama had read the letter after her husband's passing, and on this day, I carried the original letter with me, intending to place it between the carnation petals, its ashes to be mingled with those of my mother.

Fearing he could die at any time due to his heart condition, my father had written the letter to my mother, expressing his deep love for her...

I want you to know my sweet love, that you have given me everything in life that most men are only dreaming of: Love, compassion, selfless sacrifice, faithfulness, adoration and many more things that are impossible to describe.

Please forgive me for any wrongs I may have caused you. I hope this fear of mine is unfounded, but if I should leave you unexpectedly, I want you to know that without you my life would have been as empty as a dried-out lake bed, but with you, my life had meaning, beauty, and a richness beyond expression. So, my love, please do not despair, because life was worth living because of you. No matter what happens, I will be happy, for I have been truly loved, and what more can anyone ask from this life? I love you with all my heart, I always have, and always will, alive or dead, and nothing will change this. Goodbye, my Love, see you somewhere in the Great Plains Out There!

I will love you forever, always, and unconditionally, my sweet Pillangó, my butterfly. You were my entire life and I will always cherish the times we spent together. I love you with all my being and soul. Your József.

I read the letter once more before placing my father's words of love for his *Edes* wife in their final resting place, and in that moment, I at last understood where my parent's souls would meet again - *The Great Plains Out There*!

The original Hungarian flag draped over Mama at her funeral

It was in Hungary - the Great Pannonian Plains of Hungary – a fertile, wonderous place filled with bountiful, colorful expanses of flowering meadows, tundra, steppes and grasslands, crisscrossed with cool winding rivers, an area lush with fragrant flowers, wheat fields, wide open spaces, and wildlife.

My father had sent Mama a message where she was to find him: their secret *Garden of Paradise*! The vision of my parents residing in that infinite, majestic, and immortal world caused my heart to burst its banks with resplendent tranquility and peace, for a deep, eternal, ageless love such as theirs, was, without a doubt, *a deathless love*, predestined and foreordained to extend beyond the dimensions of this earthly realm.

My Mother and Father: Prelude to True Love's Kiss - Circa 2000

Soon, the time would come for Mama to let go of her human form, for in a few minutes the funerary staff would come to take her away. I sought my husband and son to allow them time to see Mama before she journeyed onward to meet my father.

The following day, we returned to gather my *"Anukam Edes"* - her featherlight ashes resting in a piano wood cremation box lovingly placed upon my lap by my husband, my tears christening the vessel during the car ride home, where I would keep my promise to Mama, and place her beautiful ashes beside that of my father in a setting of loving honor.

My mind was blank, my overwhelming grief for everything that was once my parents, and no longer my parents, blotting out all thought, and then, out of nowhere, my father's term of endearment for his *Draga Erzsebet* flickered in my mind: *Pillangó* - butterfly.

I suddenly felt at peace, as the gentle fluttering of velvety-soft, luminously delicate wings, quivered against the ruins of my broken heart, comforting me, consoling me. It was Mama and Papa telling me they will be with me – always.

"Pillangó" of my Parent's Love

MY PRIVATE THOUGHTS

I will never know the complete factuality of the many events leading to my parent's morbid depth of despair. Too many things had happened to them over the course of their lives to pin down their depression to any one incident or to any one moment.

Both parents deeply regretted the error of moving to Atlanta, and until the day they died, paid a high penance for attempting to build a new life in that city in their later years. There was no way for my father to foresee the evil web of altercation waiting to ensnare him within the walls of his new employment. How could my parents possibly envision the modern metropolis of Atlanta, that sparkling icon of the South holding all their future dreams, would also be the place where a foreboding impetus waited in the shadows, waiting silently to lead my father on a disastrous journey, onto a path where he would lose his health, his very life essence, disseminating the robust, formidable man he once was, into a pitiful semblance of the original, destroying all his hopes and ambitions for a meaningful future.

The grief and shock of her husband's plight was a crushing blow to my mother's mind and physical well-being, and further compounding her sorrow, was the realization that they could never go back to the utopia of Florida, for the employment and home they had once held dear, were no more.

The numerous tragic stressors my parents suffered in their early childhood during World War II, and then a few years later by the Hungarian Revolution of 1956, combined with those of building new lives in Massachusetts, Florida, and finally, in Atlanta, coupled with them not knowing how to reconcile with their son, became a cankerous wound continually nourished by an ongoing, unfortunate sequence of circumstances, trapping the family in an unfathomable state of unforgiveness for scores of slight transgressions. There had been too many misunderstood words and missed signals - the epiphany of which created a self-imposed asylum for my parents, and within the walls of that asylum, their daily sustenance consisted of the bitter brine of resentment mixed with tears of hopelessness.

Many parents would like their children to be as they are, to think as they do, to believe in what they believe; however, every child is born different. None is the mirror image of either parent. Children are born with their own persona, born with their own mind, and born with their own ways of viewing the world, of doing things their own way. This is *not* to say that the child's views and opinions are superior to that of their parents – sometimes they are better, but sometimes, they can be worse.

And …All children grow up. When the son's belief system did not mesh with the parent's belief system, and when the son's viewpoints and way of living collided with the parent's viewpoints and way of living - the parents could not understand how all the differences between parents and son had come about, causing their world to become one of confusion.

Since their childhood, my parents had gone through too much agony and suffering, had been too emotionally torn apart by the atrocious things they had witnessed, too devastated by the many harbingers of defeat that had flown into their lives over the span of several decades, too overstrained from the countless shadows of strife that had impinged upon their world, too worn down – worn down to the point in their existence where my mother and father no longer had the remaining emotional strength necessary to begin the healing process within themselves or their son. Feeling trapped and frustrated amongst all the losses thrown against them, and no longer having the will and stamina to fight back against those losses, my parent's lives imploded.

My parents encased themselves in their solitude, nourishing their festering feelings of bitterness toward the world that had destroyed their dreams, and in the midst of that bitterness, languished amongst old misinterpreted rancor and dispute with their son – the roots of which towered back for so many years, for so far back in time, that the very reason for my parents being unable to reconcile their differences with their boy became a blur. But their Sonny was never lost to them – even if he was not physically present, he was always with them, loving them, as did all their children.

Like conjoined twins, my parents clung close to each other's crushing agony; so accustomed to their circumstantial, self-imposed emotional pain, they knew no other way of living, no other way of thinking, eventually not being able to reason their way out of their dark gloom, as they cloaked themselves in a bitter shroud of destructive despair.

Alas, what could have been said to resolve the hurt on all sides was never said. Parents and son, sisters and brother, were caught in the spiny thorns of bitterness spreading throughout our family, each too "hurt" to say what could have *possibly* freed us all from our tangled trap: the courage and the strength to speak out and proclaim, "Forget the past! We will make this day the first new day of our lives together!" But the severe emotional exhaustion of fighting the world, mixed with deep past hurts of family misunderstanding, held those words in a deadlocked quagmire of silence.

At last, the chasms created by such bitterness boiled over to a point where the only outcome possible for my family was utter devastation, a jagged knife laced with venom, cutting deep into the hearts of parents and children.

We were all lost at sea, floundering to stay aboard a doomed ship with nowhere to go, except down to the murky depths of despair at the last heartbeat of the parents.

All the love and joy that was once our family, all the blood, sweat and tears our parents sacrificed to build a new world in America, was drowned in a stifling storm of bitter despair created by a raging turmoil of unfortunate events.

My parents rode a stormy sea on the ship bringing them to America, and the stormy waters of that sea, carried out of this world, the two people they once were: a beautiful boy and beautiful girl who came to love one another during one of the most horrific times in the history of humankind, but with the strength of their magnificent love for each other, rose above all the inequity, savagery, and turmoil of their early lives to build an opulent way of life in their beloved America, a life filled with the hopes and dreams that only those who had once lived in an oppressed world without freedom, could hope and dream.

The same tumultuous storm of life caught our family's "ship" in the suction of a mighty whirlpool, forcing the vessel of our lives to spiral deep into the darkest oblivion as the waves of a bittersweet tempest washed over us, erasing all evidence of the glory of what dreams my parents had dreamed, obliterating the beauty of the "Camelot" that was once our family, forever drowning the memory of the brave people they once were.

There was once a time when my parents lived, loved, and walked upon this earth, once a time when they were beautiful, young and filled with a million hopes for a million beautiful tomorrows, and, at the end of their last tomorrow, all they had accomplished, all they had loved for, all they had fought for, all that *could have been*, and now, all they had died for, was a Story for the Ages, a story I promised my parents I would never forget - A Story of *Bittersweet Freedom*.

Judith Bognar Bean

Everything can be replaced by Love, but
Love cannot be replaced by anything

— Sándor Petőfi

www.ingramcontent.com/pod-product-compliance
Lightning Source LLC
Chambersburg PA
CBHW052006070526
44584CB00016B/1638